EPISCOPACY IN SCOTLAND:

to Arlene and Joel

EPISCOPACY
IN SCOTLAND:
The History of an Idea, 1560-1638

DAVID GEORGE MULLAN
BA BD ThM PhD

JOHN DONALD PUBLISHERS LTD
EDINBURGH

ISBN 0 85976 150 9

Exclusive distribution in the United States of
America and Canada by Humanities Press Inc.,
Atlantic Highlands, NJ 07716, USA.

The publisher acknowledges the financial assistance
of the Scottish Arts Council in the publication of
this volume.

Photo typesetting by Print Origination, Formby.
Printed in Great Britain by Bell & Bain Ltd.,
Glasgow.

Preface

The study which follows is based on the Ph.D. thesis I submitted to the University of Guelph in 1984. During a happy and stimulating period of almost four years there I was the beneficiary of many pleasant relationships in the academic world. The staff of the McLaughlin Library were never failing in their courtesy and helpfulness, not least of all in handling a constant stream of requests for inter-library loans. The library also supported my research by bearing the cost of photocopies and micro-reproductions of manuscripts and old printed works found in various British repositories. I must likewise express my appreciation to the staff of the following institutions: the National Library of Scotland, Edinburgh; the Scottish Record Office, Edinburgh; Edinburgh University Library; New College Library, Edinburgh; Glasgow University Library; the Library, King's College, Aberdeen; St. Andrews University Library; Birmingham University Library; the Bodleian Library, Oxford; and the British Library, London.

Faculty members of the department of history were a constant source of friendly encouragement and constructive suggestion. Foremost among them is Professor E. J. Cowan who supervised the research and interested himself in its progress from the first day. I benefited from conversations with a number of Scottish historians who were most accommodating toward a visiting student. Dr. G. I. R. McMahon, now of Homerton College, Cambridge, kindly granted permission to the University of Birmingham to supply me with a photocopy of his Ph.D. thesis.

The department of history and faculty of arts contributed immensely to my years of study through the provision of teaching assistantships and also the privilege of two sessional lectureships. I was fortunate to receive an Ontario Graduate Scholarship for 1981-1982, and from 1982 until 1984 a doctoral fellowship from the Social Sciences and Humanities Research Council of Canada. This award also covered the costs of travel for a six-week research trip to the United Kingdom. Further assistance was obtained from the Alexander H. Brodie Memorial Award, administered by the Interdepartmental Committee on Scottish Studies, University of Guelph.

A number of readers have commented on the study both before and after its acceptance as a thesis, and I wish to record my thanks to all who have done so. Some of their suggestions have been incorporated, to the improvement of the final draft. Perhaps it might have been better to act upon more of the comments, but of course the decision *pro* or *con* is the point at which an author owns his work and with trepidation presents it to the wider world as that which best serves his purpose. I believe that what follows accomplishes this — but having said so, I must therefore also lay claim to all the shortcomings and errors within the work.

An author ought not to take his publisher for granted, and I am glad to acknowledge the helpfulness and co-operation of Mr. John Tuckwell. The typescript presented to him was the work of Mrs. Barbara Hall, to whom I am indebted for her understanding of that technological marvel, the word processor.

This book, like the thesis behind it, is dedicated to those two persons who have borne with a sometimes distracted and irritable husband and father.

Belleville, Ontario

A note on dates and spellings: Scotland adopted the Gregorian Calendar in 1600; earlier dates are also given as New Style. Original grammatical forms and spellings have been retained in quoted material, with the exceptions of contractions which have been expanded and of the obsolete use of certain letters, hence, *e.g.*, u has commonly been changed to w, i to j, etc. Scripture references are to the Geneva Bible.

Contents

CHAPTER 1

An Episcopate Assailed

This is the story of an idea, an idea about how the church of Scotland should be structured and governed. Throughout much of the often turbulent period 1560-1638, the Reformation to the Revolution, the eye of the storm in both kirk and state was episcopacy. For this idea was intended not to be discussed in ivory towers but reified as one of the central social institutions of Scotland. In a time when governments believed their divinely given role was to control their subjects and protect hierarchical society from a return to primeval chaos, the episcopate formed an integral aspect of the mechanism of power and order.

This entailed possible conflict between the lords of the church and the lords of the old feudal political order as they competed for the same financial resources and as the new monarchy used the bishops as a political counterweight against its mighty subjects. Further trouble arose from the fact that episcopacy was erected upon a theological foundation of more than a millennium's duration. It was presumed to bear apostolic and divine warrant, and without its enabling presence there could not be a church, or at least a healthy church. But as part of the welter of theological ideas emerging from Reformation Europe this ecclesiological axiom was called into question. Was episcopacy even the *bene esse* of the church, let alone its *esse?* Was it demonstrably biblical? Scotland proved fertile ground for these ideas and the result was decades of stormy seas for the kirk as the crown insisted on bishops, whether or not for genuine theological reasons, while many of the ablest and most vociferous ministers opposed the entire institution as popish and Antichristian. Eventually these presbyterians gained a powerful ally in the nobility and secured more effective opposition to the crown's ecclesiastical policies.

In order to study this theme several approaches are indicated. At the heart of it is an investigation of theological documents and treatises which articulated the nature of episcopacy as an ecclesiastical entity along with works which negated it, sometimes with remarkable asperity. However, it is also necessary to look at the institution in its working form, not to attempt a full portrait of its daily operation, but to understand the persons, pressures, and events which deeply affected the way in which contemporaries viewed the idea itself and which also provided the ammunition for emerging historiographical battles about the nature of Scotland's reformed past. So as to demonstrate both development and continuity the various chapters follow an essentially chronological pattern, although this is, in the later stages, somewhat subordinated to thematic concerns which dominate the research after the full re-establishment of episcopacy under James VI. It is hoped that this study will elucidate some major consistent themes that animated a lengthy and formative period of Scottish history, not least of all the long roots of the covenanting ideology which emerged in full flower in 1638.

1

In sixteenth-century Scotland ecclesiastical government was distributed among thirteen dioceses.[1] Since 1472 the primacy had belonged to the archbishop of St. Andrews, though considerable lustre was lost in 1492 with the designation of Glasgow as another archdiocese.[2] As elsewhere in western Europe the Scottish episcopate was deeply embedded in not only the ecclesiastical order, but also in the social, political, and juridical structures of the state, and to provide a full portrait of the bishops would therefore entail a study of the entire fabric of society. The historian meets representatives of the episcopate at every turn, for the manner in which society had evolved up to the sixteenth century entailed a deep-rooted dependency upon these men.

The church was a hierarchy, a structure that was not regarded as accidental, relative, or mutable. The monarchical episcopate, preserving the historic connection with Peter who held, from Christ, the keys of the kingdom, was the *esse* of the church. In its absence the work of the church must necessarily cease, for without bishops there could be no ordination of the lower clergy, no consecration of other members of their superior order, no confirmation of new communicants, no excommunication or release through absolution.[3] To these 'successouris of the Apostils' pertained the 'power of jurisdictioun [*potestas jurisdictionis*, the power to administer discipline] in preeminence and dignitie above ane simpil preist'[4] who possessed only the *potestas ordinis*, the right to preach and administer five of the seven sacraments. The episcopate was the source of spiritual power and ecclesiastical jurisdiction on earth.

With such considerable authority bishops could pose an at least theoretical challenge to the crowned heads of Europe. An excommunicated ruler might stand on shaky ground, even though Pius V's bull which excommunicated and deposed Elizabeth proved to be nothing more than an impotent and embarrassing squib.[5] But bishops had other powers within social institutions. Episcopal courts handled a wide range of cases from matrimony to legitimations of natural children to testamentary processes. The education and wealth of bishops meant that secular powers came to rely heavily upon these ostensibly spiritual figures for counsel and for revenue; thus the two spheres of jurisdiction were closely connected through the episcopate.

Because of this close relationship it was natural for a king to seek to place his own men in the bishoprics. At the same time, the princely office in the church was commonly aspired to by members of the upper echelons of society who saw it as an appropriate career and style of life;[6] thus the church reflected the interests and needs of the monarchy and high-ranking nobles. As Mahoney has demonstrated, during the half-century from Flodden to the death of Mary of Guise, episcopal nominations reflected the diplomatic, financial, and dynastic interests of the controlling faction in the state.[7] It was, by way of illustration, no accident that the Arran government nominated two natural brothers of the governor to the two archdioceses in 1546-1547.[8]

The problem of royal control over the appointment of bishops was in great part resolved in Scotland in 1487 through the grant of a papal indult whereby the pope withheld for eight months appointments to Scottish benefices in cathedrals and monasteries worth more than a specified sum. The delay permitted the king to submit his own nominations to Rome, bypassing chapter elections altogether. Royal candidates were generally accepted by Rome, and the crown received the added benefit of drawing episcopal temporalities during vacancies. Pope Paul III confirmed and extended the arrangement in 1535 by his recognition that the *jus nominandi* pertained to the crown, granting a stay of twelve months during which royal nominations might be forwarded to Rome.[9]

It has been remarked that, 'if the machinery of appointment worked reasonably well, the quality of bishops that it produced was not impressive'.[10] Under James IV the king's eighteen-year-old brother was nominated to St. Andrews, followed by James's natural son, aged eleven years, prompting Nicholson's description of the late medieval Scottish church as an 'employment bureau for the illegitimate sons of the crown and nobility'.[11] His successor James V wrote a famous letter to Clement VII asking that his numerous bastard sons be legitimated and exempted from the minimum age requirement for admission to orders, and be granted permission to hold any number of benefices. Such modesty as James possessed led him to concede at the same time that his sons would not be elevated to the episcopate until their twentieth year.[12] Thomson's observation is justified, that, although popes might properly be blamed for permitting some of the abuses, it was the secular powers that demanded the lowering of standards — hence they were equally to blame.[13]

Along with the other prelates the bishops constituted one of the three estates in the parliaments and conventions of the realm,[14] while high ecclesiastical office might also entail prominence elsewhere in the state. Precedent was not lacking when the youthful Alexander Stewart, archbishop of St. Andrews, was appointed chancellor in 1511.[15] He was followed by James Beaton (I) of Glasgow from 1513 to 1526,[16] Gavin Dunbar of Glasgow from 1528 to 1543,[17] and David Beaton of St. Andrews from 1543 to 1546 (with interruption).[18] By a reversal of this procedure it was not uncommon for royal servants to be rewarded by nominations to bishoprics. In the early years of the sixteenth century Andrew Forman, a diplomat, and George Hepburn, treasurer, were both promoted to bishoprics, and the aforementioned archbishop and chancellor James Beaton (I) had also been treasurer before he received preferment to the episcopate.[19]

Once a man was elevated, it was commonplace for his relatives to make headway up the ladder of success in the church. James Beaton (II) and David Beaton, respectively archbishops of Glasgow and St. Andrews, were both nephews of James Beaton (I). In the see of Dunblane, held by a succession of Chisholms from 1487 to the Reformation, the archdeaconry, deanery, chancellery, subdeanery, and three prebends were at one time all filled by Chisholms.[20] Thus the church suffered from inbreeding and ambition in its highest quarters. Such abuse set in motion by the crown and those near to it led inevitably to a real degradation of the pre-Reformation episcopate. Because the bishops owed their place to court favours, or perhaps because of their own cynical negligence, they submitted to the impoverishment of their dioceses through reservations of pensions to laymen. The outcome was that some dioceses lost the large part of their revenues, contributing to an impecunious parochial clergy and ruinous churches and cathedrals. Both by paucity of funds and want of spiritual inclination, combined with the depredations of the laity, the late medieval episcopate witnessed the growth of a situation whereby a marked deterioration or even complete cessation of ecclesiastical functions might eventuate. In the see of Argyll there was no consecrated bishop after 1465 except for a few years in the 1530s, and the same lack plagued the Isles after its last consecrated ordinary fell at Flodden.[21]

Naturally, the morality of the episcopate, based upon celibacy, suffered greatly, for these appointees were not committed to upholding the ethic of an institution which was for the most part a refuge or a reward. David Hay Fleming recorded that David Beaton, archbishop of St. Andrews, had at least five sons and three daughters, and the numbers may have been as high as eleven and four.[22] His successor, John Hamilton, likewise fathered a bevy of natural children,[23] as did William Gordon of Aberdeen who was petitioned in 1559 by his dean and chapter to set a better example for the rest of the clergy: 'in speciale in removing and dischargeing him selff of cumpany of the gentill woman be quhom he is gretlie sclanderit'.[24] When the bishop of Dunblane died in 1564 his successor was 'lyke hym in conditions, savinge thys man hathe but ii childrene, whear thother had x or xii, bysydes that which he begotte upon his owne dawghter — but in papystrie all one, or worce yf yt maye be,' wrote Randolph to Cecil.[25]

There was in fact from the first quarter of the century a growing clamour for reform of the church, hence of the episcopate from which the church flowed. The call for renewal came from all sides — clergy and laity, orthodox and heretical.

With the advent of Christian Humanism in Scotland came 'not merely a revival of learning, but also a revival of moral concern: for what really interested men like [Hector] Boece, Archibald Hay, [Florence] Wilson and Bishop [Robert] Reid was reform, and reform from within the household of faith'.[26] In 1522 Boece published a work on the lives of earlier bishops for Gavin Dunbar, bishop of Aberdeen, and by reviewing the diocesan past he upheld the ideal bishop as one who was of devout life and committed to careful administration of his see. Preaching, clerical education, and conscientious use of revenue figured largely in Boece's portrait of the exemplary bishop.[27] Alexander Myln, later abbot of Cambuskenneth, had in about 1516 written *Lives of the Bishops of Dunkeld* for the new bishop of that see, Gavin Douglas. Good diocesan administration and provision of preachers were regarded by the writer as praiseworthy episcopal qualities.[28] Upon David Beaton's elevation to St. Andrews, Archibald Hay, later principal of St. Mary's College, composed the *Panegyricus* in which he called upon the new primate to reform a corrupt church wherein careless bishops had ordained degenerate men to the priesthood:[29] 'Ignorance on the part of priests is a very muddy spring, from which flow the most of the calamities of the Church. Bishops blame the examiners of candidates for the priesthood, but the bishop is responsible for the examiner, the archdeacon'.[30] John Major, the great Scholastic theologian who taught in France and Scotland, complained of the abuse of ecclesiastical finances, and in a dedicatory letter to archbishop James Beaton (I) he made clear the prelate's primary evangelical responsibility.[31]

The gulf between ideal and real bishops was widely recognised in Scotland, and this led to the calling of the 'Provincial Council holden by the Prelates and Clergy of the realm of Scotland at Edinburgh, A.D. 1549'.[32] Bishops were not excepted from its summons to the clergy 'to reform their life and morals to better purpose, in accordance with the statutes and regulations of the present council, that by this means all occasions of heresy in this realm may be more easily obviated'. The council recognised the hypocrisy of immoral prelates attempting to correct the impieties of others, 'since from this cause arises the greatest scandal to the laity, and the largest proportion of the heresy',[33] the extirpation of which was the reason for calling the council.[34] Having appealed for reformation of moral life, the council went on to call for preaching throughout the dioceses of the kingdom, and to place responsibility for oversight of these evangelical duties upon the ordinaries who would examine all their curates and force the unfit to demit office.[35] Even the bishops themselves were to preach to their flocks at least four times each year.[36]

At about this time there was issued archbishop Hamilton's *Catechism*, written by an English Dominican, Richard Marshall, who had taken refuge in Scotland rather than submit to Henry VIII's supremacy in the church.[37] Produced in recognition of the growing heresy in Scotland, it admitted that there were very real problems among the clergy. Augustine was cited to the effect that despite the easy and pleasant appearance of 'the office of ane bischop, preist or dekin', if not done with due care and attention, 'thair is na thing afore God mair miserabil, mair hevy & mair damnabil'.[38] In the section on the eighth commandment ('thou shalt not steal') the writer made application of the command to contemporary life: rulers demanding exhorbitant taxes and those selling justice were in breach thereof, just as were all, including bishops, who presented unfit ministers to livings with a view to personal advantage, presumably through the reservation of pensions. 'Quhy sulde nocht that be callit theift, quhilk is gevin for lufe of geir, that suld be geffin frelie for the lufe of God and in respect of leirnyng and vertew?'[39]

But this reforming impulse flowing from the Council of Trent[40] was more easily reduced to statutory form than implemented, hence the recognition of failure at another provincial council held in 1552.[41] Consequently it ratified the decisions of 1549, above all 'that formerly published statute anent the exposition of God's word to be held by rectors and bishops four times a year', with fines appointed to those offending against the article.[42]

Still, it would seem, nothing was done to ameliorate the low state of the episcopate. Before the sitting of the 1559 council 'sum temporall Lordis and Barronis' had memorialised the queen regent concerning the moral standards of the bishops and the other prelates constituting the spiritual estate. The presentation recalled the act of parliament passed in March 1541, 'For reforming of kirks and kirkmen'.[43] This legislation stated that it was because of 'the unhonestie and misreule of kirkmen baith in witt, knawlege And maneris' that both church and clerics were held in derision and condemnation. Therefore, 'The kingis grace exhortis and prayis oppinly all archibischopis Ordinaris and uthir prelatis . . . To reforme thare selfis . . . In habit and maneris to god and man'. Should anyone choose to exempt himself from the law the king would seek remedy 'at the papis haylynes And siclik aganis the saidis prelatis giff thai be negligent'. Next, recalling the provincial councils of 1549 and 1552, the lords and barons stated the obvious, that despite the various reforming statutes, 'thar hes folowit nan or litill fruict as yett, bot rathare the said Estate is deteriorate'. The reform of the prelates was so necessary since the ecclesiastical estate was a 'mirror and lantern to the rest'.[44]

Subsequently the final Roman Catholic council to be held in Scotland acted against concubinage, including in its scope 'the archbishops and the bishops thair suffragans as upon the other prelates and the lower clergy of this realm'.[45] However, Robert Lindesay of Pitscottie wrote that the bishop of Moray opposed any interference in such matters. The Protestant historian described him as

> ane hure maister all his dayis and committit huredome and adulterie baitht witht meadins and mens wyffis, saying he wald nocht put away his hure noe mor nor the bischope of Sanctandrois wald put his away ffor it was as lesum to him to have ane hure as hie; and farder he wald preif it lesum to him, to call the popis bowis [bulls] that is written in the degreis, that he might have ane hure in absence of his wyffe.[46]

If his own child were to remain in the archbishop's household for more than four days in a three-month period a fine of £200 should be levied for the first offence, to be quadrupled for a third,[47] a contingency which suggests little confidence in the powers of the synodal decrees. Nor were prelates to collate their sons to any of their own churches — presumably they might find employment in another diocese — and the pope was to be petitioned by the queen to grant no further dispensations from this statute. The former preaching article was enhanced, the required four annual sermons to be added to if possible, and preaching was also to accompany biennial diocesan visitations.[48] Clearly the belief was that the church was in need of reform, if only to live up to the canon law laid down over the preceding centuries, whether at Trent or even at the Fourth Lateran Council of 1215.[49] And if reform were to be accomplished it must begin with the episcopate, for only from there might flow a pure stream. The widespread opinion was that, at mid-century, the fountain was polluted.

Awareness of decay in the church was a common theme for writers of the time. In 1550 an anonymous Scot,[50] pro-Catholic and anti-English, published *The complaynt of Scotland*. He encouraged his country to defend itself against the encroachments of its southern neighbour, expressing his sentiments through the mouth of 'the affligit lady dame Scotia'. The spiritual estate was warned that because of its privileged receipt of knowledge and authority from God it would merit the more severe punishment for its 'malversatione'. To that segment of Scottish society and its abuse of office the writer attributed 'the special cause of the scisma and of divers sectis that trublis al cristianite'.[51] Persecution was a worthless remedy for heresy since it served only to breed three more where one heretic had stood before. Instead, kirkmen ought to be as ready to correct their own dissolute lives as to reprove their critics, with whom the author agreed, at least in terms of morals if not doctrine.[52]

William Lauder, probably a priest until joining the Protestants at the Reformation,[53] wrote in 1556 his *Ane compendious and breve tractate* where, during the course of providing admonition of a highly moralistic sort to kings (or queens, one must assume), he commented upon the sort of men whom the king should appoint to spiritual office. Not on account of blood or wealth ought they to be chosen, nor should he incline to drunkards or to the irascible. Instead let him favour those who were 'prudent, wyse, and vigelant':

> All sic ye suld, frome yow depesche
> None covatus, of wardly glore
> None to heape, ryches upe in store
> None hasardours, at cards, nor dyce
> None gevin to foule, nor fylthie vyce.

The ideal was the pastor capable of instructing his flock and of leading by an exemplary life, 'To edefye, Man, Maid, and wyffe', preaching the word

> As Peter did, thare predecessour
> Geve thay wald be, his trew successour.[54]

The evil memory continued after 1560. Alexander Scott's 'Ane New Yere Gift' to the young queen summoned 'perversit prelattis' and 'wickit pastouris' to reform their lives,[55] while Richard Maitland's poem entitled 'On the Miseries of the Tyme' condemned priests for 'lychorie gluttunrie vane gloir and avarice', and persecution. On account of these sins God had punished them, though had they abjured 'thair auld abusioun' and preached God's word faithfully,

> Thai had nocht cumit to sic confusioun
> Nor tholit had as yit sic miserie.[56]

But of all contemporary critics sir David Lindsay was and remains the most renowned,[57] especially on account of the dramatic piece, *Ane satyre of the thrie estates*. This was first performed before James V and Mary of Guise at Linlithgow in 1540, and either reflected or promoted the desire for episcopal reform that was articulated in the act of parliament of 1541. Later versions were performed in 1552 and in 1554.[58] The *Satyre* took the form of parliamentary proceedings, during which the prelates were severely castigated for their wrongdoing. Echoing what was a commonplace sentiment, heresy was attributed to the waywardness of high churchmen:

> Quhat bene the caus of all the heresies,
> Bot the abusion of the prelacies? (3039-3040)

Most prominent among Lindsay's catalogue of abuses were those of a sexual nature:

> For all the Prelats of this natioun,
>   For the maist part,
> Thay think na schame to have ane huir,
> And sum hes thrie under their cuir. (253-256)

A pauper complained that while he was bound in marriage, there was no such constraint upon the lusty appetites of the prelates:

> Bot thay lyke rams rudlie in thair rage,
> Unpysalt rinnis amang the sillie yowis,
> Sa lang as kynde of nature in them growis. (2764-2766)

And while guilty of sins of commission the bishops were also guilty of omission, particularly the failure to preach:

> Ane Bischops office is for to be ane preichour,
> And of the law of God ane publick teachour. (2899-2900)

But clearly the bishops were inexpert in their proper vocation, unlike 'sowtars and tailyeours' (3147-3152). To achieve an amelioration of the kirk the imaginary parliament passed a series of acts, among them this, the twelfth:

> It is decreit that in this Parliament
> Ilk Bischop, Minister, Priour and Persoun,
> To the effect thay may tak better tent
> To saulis under thair dominioun,
> Efter the forme of thair fundation,
> Ilk Bischop in his Diosie sall remaine,
> And everilk Persone in his parachoun,
> Teaching thair folk from vices to refraine. (3905-3912)

Lindsay expressed the ideal of a resident, moral, pastoral, teaching clergy, led by their bishops.

Sir David Lindsay's critique of the kirk was not confined to the *Satyre*. He added to it in his *The Tragedie of the Umquhyle Maist Reverend Father David, be the Mercy of God, Cardinale and Archibyschope of Sanctandrous* [*The Tragedy of the Late Cardinal Beaton*].[59] This poetic work, presented as a visitation by the departed prelate who was murdered in May 1546 in revenge for his prosecution and execution of the heretic George Wishart, was both an attack on the policy and life of the primate and a plea for reform.

Beaton was vilified for his repression of all advocates of Bible reading and study who did not conform to permitted usage:

> And purposit tyll put to gret Torment
> All favoraris of the auld and new Testament. (216-217)

Speaking from the hindsight of death, Beaton gave sombre warning to his successors and living peers:

> Ye knaw quhow Iesu his Disciplis sent,
> Ambassaldouris, tyll every Natioun,
> To schaw his law and his commandiment

To all peple, by Predycatioun:
Tharefor I mak to you Narratioun,
Sen ye to thame ar verray Successouris,
ye aucht tyll do as did your Predicessouris. (281-287)

How could they fulfil their calling, 'beand dum . . . Lyke Menstralis that can
nocht play nor sing' (291-292)? Lindsay then diagnosed the seat of the malady, the
princes of the realm who granted spiritual office 'to blynd Pastouris' (350).

Mak hym Byschope that prudentlie can preche,
As dois pertene tyll his vocatioun;
Ane Persone quhilk his Parisone can teche. (365-367)

Finally he appealed to the only authority that could effectively reform the church:

Quharefor I counsayle everyilk christinit kyng
With in his realme mak Reformatioun,
And suffer no mo Rebaldis for to ryng
Abuse Christis trew Congregatioun. (421-424)

However, as Ian Cowan has observed, the crown had too great a stake in the status
quo, being a prime beneficiary of the right to install its own candidates and thereby
to extract considerable financial concessions from a defenceless church.[60]

It is difficult to discern exactly where Lindsay stood in the theological spectrum
of his day, though there are hints in his defence of Bible reading and study of some
sympathy toward Protestantism. One writer has suggested that Lindsay 'would
seem to shade off from a reforming Catholic into a Catholic-minded Reformer'.[61]
But whatever the uncertainty about this major literary figure, there can be no
doubt about the orthodoxy of other writers. Quintin Kennedy, the abbot of
Crossraguel, hence himself a prelate, published in 1558 *Ane compendius tractive*.
Therein he complained about the ignorance of many clergy and the dilapidation of
benefices by 'the gret men of the realme' who went so far as to grant them to an
ignorant and immoral kinsman of whom it might be questioned 'quhether he or his
mule knawis best to do his office'. He added bitterly that it was they, 'quha ar the
procuraris, disponaris, and upsteraris of such monsterus farssis to be in the Kirk of
God, [who] ar the maist principalis cryaris out on the vices of Kirk-men'. The
solution he proposed to these evils, a solution which would end heresy and mass
ignorance, was a return to the 'auld ancient libertie' of the kirk, whereby 'ane
bischop were frelie chosin by his chapitre'.[62] One may compare this programme of
free election with the later demands of Protestants for greater self-rule by the kirk,
however much the dimensions and content of that liberty may have differed.

In his *Certane tractatis for reformatioun of doctryne and maneris in Scotland*,
published after the erection of a Protestant kirk, Ninian Winzet, priest and
schoolmaster at Linlithgow, recorded some of the bitterest invective and sarcasm
to be found on either side of the Reformation religious debate. Winzet was actually
a thoroughly orthodox Roman Catholic, and the great portion of his work was a
challenge to John Knox and Protestant reform in general. He described his
criticism of Knox, who had repudiated his episcopal ordination,[63] and his co-

B

religionists in the metaphor of a storm-tossed vessel caught between a sandy shoal on the right and rocks on the left. The Knoxians had grasped the rudder away from 'sleuthfull Marinaris, and sleipand sterismen (we mein of the Pastores of the kirk, and in that part of thair promoveris)',[64] and in fleeing one danger were now in peril of another. Though he had no sympathy for what the Protestants were doing to the church, Winzet was too candid a man with too much love for it to pretend that there was no danger while the ship was washed toward the sand under the governance of inattentive sailors. Thus he launched against the prelates and princes a stream of abuse that is nothing short of breathtaking. Writing to the 'Fatheris Bischoipis and utheris Pastores', he mocked their sincerity of purpose and devotion: 'And albeit the time be schort, sumthing of your prais man we speik. Bot quhidder sal we begin your commendation and living at your haly lyfes, or at youre helthful doctrine, we are doutsum'. Reiterating sentiments already heard, he attacked the grant of benefices to the unfit: 'Your godly and circumspect distribution of benefices, to your babeis ignorantis and filthy anis, al Ethnik, Turk, and Jow may lauch at it, that being the special ground of al impietie and division this day within the O Scotland'. Through prelatical inactivity, 'keiping in silence the trew word of god', many had remained ignorant of their Christian duty, and the sacraments had been prophaned by the unwholesome lives of ignorant and wicked clerics.[65] Resounding with prophetic ardour,[66] he demanded, 'War ye commandit in vaine of God be the mouthis off his Prophetis and Apostolis to walke attentilie and continualie upon your flok, and know diligentlie the samyn be fact?' But instead of being resident preachers the prelates were immoral men spending their ecclesiastical revenues upon their paramours and bastard off-spring. He concluded with near-apocalyptic fervour: 'Awalke, awalk we say, and put to your hande stoutlie to saif Peteris schip: For he nother slepis nor slumeris, quha beholdis al your doingis, and seis youre thochtis: bot sall require the blude oute of your handis, of the smallaste ane that sall perise throw your negligence'.[67]

Leaving the prelates aside, he then railed against the avaricious nobles to whom he attributed the presence of 'unqualifeit bischopis and utheris pastores in Scotland'.[68] It was they who had substituted in place of 'godly Ministeris, and trew successouris of the Apostolis' a different sort of man whom Winzet, like many Protestants, termed 'dum doggis'.[69]

With or without Protestantism there was a clamour for reform within the kirk. Non-residency, simony, nepotism, ignorance, immorality, non-performance of duties, dilapidation of benefices — all these and more episcopal vices were noted by Catholic writers up to the early 1560s. They were unanimous also concerning the root cause of the deterioration in the quality of the bishops — the avarice of the nobles who placed their own favourites or kin who could be relied upon not to resist their pillage of diocesan revenues. Obviously the critique of the episcopate was not a purely or even originally Protestant pastime. Protestants simply piled heresy on top of criticism.

In John Knox's *History* the bishops took on a far more menacing visage, and from the execution of the Bohemian Paul Craw in c.1433 they were portrayed as the minions of Antichrist, their hands stained with the blood of true believers. In committing Craw to the secular arm for burning, the bishops, wrote Knox, were followers of Pilate 'who both did condemn and also wash his hands'.[70] In the articles against the so-called Lollards of Kyle (1494), Knox recorded that they were accused of saying the pope and the bishops were deceivers of the people through the issuance of pardons (article xv), and 'that the blessings of the bishops (of dumb dogs they should have been styled) are of no value'.[71] One of the accused called the archbishop of Glasgow a churl and attacked him for failing to preach and for playing the proud prelate, 'as all the rabble of you do this day'.[72] Knox then continued to the next archbishop, James Beaton (I), 'who was more careful for the world than he was to preach Christ'. He scorned this prelate's accumulation of honours, holding simultaneously the primacy of the kirk (he was translated from Glasgow to St. Andrews in 1523), the abbacies of Dunfermline, Arbroath, and Kilwinning, and the chancellorship of the realm.[73]

Friar Alexander Seton was arraigned before the archbishop of St. Andrews where he denounced the non-preaching bishops as 'belly-gods'.[74] As a result he was obliged to flee to the haven of Berwick whence he wrote a letter to James V complaining that the king was so under the influence of bishops and other kirkmen 'that apparently they were rather King, and thou the subject (which unjust regiment is of the self false, and contrary to holy Scripture and law of God), than thou their King and master, and they thy subjects'. Thus controlling the king's ear the prelates were able to keep Seton from expressing his mind before James. Seton proceeded to berate them for evangelical negligence, choosing instead to contend 'who may be most high, most rich, and nearest thy Grace, to put the temporal Lords and lieges out of thy council and favour, who should be, and are, most tender servants to thy Grace in all time of need, to the defence of thee and thy crown'.[75] Knox blamed the bishops for overruling James's inclination to grant clemency to David Stratoun who was executed in 1534,[76] and like sir David Lindsay, he held David Beaton responsible for the disastrous campaign at Solway Moss[77] and further discountenanced him for his opposition to the projected marriage of young Mary Stewart to Edward Tudor.[78] Thus Knox portrayed the bishops not only as 'bloody beasts'[79] but also as worthless meddlers in affairs of state.

Knox was filled with sarcasm toward the bishops. After describing a case of sexual immorality he noted caustically, 'Such is the example of holiness that the flock may receive of the Papistical Bishops'.[80] Scornful mention of the archbishop of Glasgow's attempt at preaching was made,[81] and Knox seemed to take great delight in relating the story of the visit of cardinal David Beaton, archbishop of St. Andrews, to Glasgow where he and Gavin Dunbar, archbishop of Glasgow and chancellor of Scotland, feuded over who should have pre-eminence in procession. 'And then began no little fray, but yet a merry game; for rochets were rent, tippets were torn, crowns were knapped, and side gowns might have been seen wantonly wag from the one wall to the other'.[82] Instead of writing of John Hamilton's *consecration* as archbishop, Knox substituted *execration*,[83] and he mentioned — surely in jest — the stranding of the French vessel *Cardinal* on a fair and calm day, the lesson being that 'god would show that the country of Scotland can bear no Cardinals'.[84] When narrating the deaths of the bishops of Ross and Orkney he described their dissolution, Orkney supposedly saying on his deathbed, 'I am well where I am . . . for I am near unto my friends', which, Knox interpolated, were 'his coffers and the gold therein'.[85]

Those bishops presently in the kirk Knox called 'that adulterous and pestilent generation of Antichrists servants',[86] accusing them 'of idolatrie, of murther and of blasphemie against God committed'.[87] Such offenders had been condemned by the Old Testament to die, and after Christ's coming were all the more worthy of the capital sentence.[88] Knox himself was accused of maintaining that 'there are no bishops, except they preach even by themselves, without any substitute'.[89] Adam Wallace, martyr, called upon bishops 'to preach the Evangel of Jesus Christ, and to feed the flock, which he hath redeemed by his own blood, and has commanded the same to the care of all true pastors'. He went on to denounce them as 'dumb dogs, and unsavoury salt, that has altogether lost the season'.[90]

Two seventeenth-century historians recorded the trial of an 'old decrepit Priest',[91] Walter Mill, who was proceeded against and burned in 1558 at the instigation of John Hamilton. When accused of denying the office of bishop he declared: 'I affirm they whom you call Bishops, do not Bishop's works, nor use the Offices of Bishops, but live after their own sensual plesures, taking no care for the flock, nor yet regarding the word of God'.[92]

Protestants regarded preaching as the *sine qua non* of the true church and authentic ministry. George Wishart stated at his 1546 heresy trial that 'through the preaching of the word of God his glory is made manifest'.[93] The Catholic episcopate was, commensurately, discredited by its kerygmatic failure. The people were starved of pure spiritual food, and in place of genuine ministers 'the generation of Antichrist'[94] had intruded. The 'evil trees' which had brought forth 'these pestilent and wicked fruits' were the idle, immoral, avaricious, and persecuting bishops.[95]

The collection known as *Gude and Godlie Ballatis* included such comment as:

> The blind Bischop, he culd not preiche,
> For playing with the lassis.[96]

Personal reform was still possible, but one of the conditions was to 'leirne to preiche'.[97] However, Protestants were in no patient mood. Unlike reforming Catholics who sought correction of the existing episcopate, Protestants wanted to throw overboard the whole institution as it then stood in Scotland. Not that they denied the term or even the office of bishop. But the medieval episcopate of the James Beatons, David Beaton, and John Hamilton had forfeited all claim to authentic ministry, thus a new beginning would have to be made.

Roman Catholic and Protestant did not differ in their respective analyses of the problem. Their solutions were, however, at variance, the one seeing renewal in terms of tradition and canon law and councils, while the other claimed to return all the way to Paul the apostle and the primitive church without the intermediate hermeneutical authority of Rome which claimed an apostolic succession of unbroken historical continuity through the laying-on of hands at consecration, a succession rite without which there could be no authentic episcopate, and consequently, no genuine Christian church.

As John Knox told the story in book two of his *History,* the barons came to resent the tyrannical power wielded by the bishops who were in league with the rejected Mary of Guise, the queen regent.[98] Tension grew so great that 'the Congregation of Jesus Christ' in Scotland, angered and frustrated by the hostility and opposition fostered by the prelates, actually threatened violence:

> To the end that ye ['the generation of Antichrist, the pestilent prelates and their shavelings'] shall not be abused, thinking to escape just punishment, after that ye in your blind fury have caused the blood of many to be shed, this we notify and declare unto you, that if ye proceed in this your malicious cruelty, ye shall be entreated, wheresoever ye shall be apprehended, as murderers and open enemies to God and unto mankind.

Thus they were warned to desist tyrannising over body and soul lest 'we shall begin that same war which God commanded Israel against the Canaanites'.[99] That is, the bishops, maintainers of the idolatrous mass, were under judgement for idolatry just as the inhabitants of Canaan had been long ago, a judgement which Protestants would execute in a holy war.

By October 1559 the lords of the congregation and their backers felt strong enough to pronounce the deposition of the regent and to constitute out of their own number a 'great council of the realm'.[100] Mary's death in mid-June and the English-French pacification of 6 July granted a new political slate, and with the permission of queen Mary and her husband Francis a parliament was called, convening on 1 August 1560. Among those in attendance were a number of bishops: John Hamilton of St. Andrews, Robert Crichton of Dunkeld, William Chisholm of Dunblane, James Hamilton of Argyll, Alexander Gordon of Gallo-way, and John Campbell of the Isles,[101] designated by Knox as 'the chief pillars of the Papistical Kirk',[102] though according to Gordon Donaldson the latter three were actually 'committed Protestants'.[103] Despite the royal prohibition against meddling with religious affairs[104] parliament 'ratifeit and apprevit' a Confession of faith presented by the Protestants, solemnly pronouncing it to be 'hailsome and sound doctrine groundit upoun the infallibill trewth of gods word'.[105] Knox wrote that the bishops remained silent during the presentation and approval, and to this behaviour he attributed the decision of many to affirm the Confession.[106] It was reported that St. Andrews, Dunkeld, and Dunblane wanted time to consider it further, professing this much, 'that they wold aggre to all thing myght stand with Godes Word, and consent to abolish all abuses crept in in the Churche not agreable with the Scriptures'.[107]

The Confession sounded an undisguised anti-Roman note. In the preface apology was made for the Confession's late appearance, the explanation being that the 'Rage of Sathan' had been too great to allow such an enterprise.[108] There can be no doubt as to the meaning of the allusion to 'the stubburne, inobedient, cruell oppressours, filthie personis, idolaters', all of whom would be 'cast in the dungeon of utter darknesse'.[109] It was part of the task of the Confession to distinguish the 'true Kirk' from the synagogues of Satan, a common reference to the unreformed church, which identification would be done through the three marks of true preaching of God's word, the proper administration of the sacraments, and finally church discipline for repressing vice and nurturing virtue.[110] The basis of the Confession was the Old and New Testaments, 'in those buikis we meane quhilk of the ancient have been reputed canonicall',[111] a clear repudiation of the Apocrypha. Furthermore the confessors exempted themselves from any obsequious adherence to the councils of the church should these prove to have made erroneous pronouncements.[112] Touching the sacraments, of so great importance in the Scottish experience of the Reformation, transubstantiation was execrated[113] while a doctrine of spiritual presence was articulated which clearly avoided the Zwinglian view of 'naked and bair Signes'.[114] The Confession spoke of fleeing 'the doctrine of the Papistical Kirk, in participatioun of their sacraments' because of the failure of celebrant priests to preach the word and because the ceremonies had been so adulterated with 'their awin inventions'.[115] The mass was thus utterly invalidated. Knox, who claimed to have been one of the six authors of the Confession,[116] also turned his back as has been seen, on Catholic ordination, but there was no denial of baptism's validity even under the corrupt administration, the Confession demanding only the removal of 'oyle, salt, spittill, and sik lyke'.[117] Certainly the Confession of 1560 contained no olive branch of reconciliation. It was instead a challenge to combat.

The parliament passed acts abrogating all previous legislation 'not aggreing with goddis word and now contrair to the confessioun of oure fayth according to the said word publist in this parliament', and banning the sacramental usages of the 'papis kirk'. This legislation also prohibited administration of sacraments by any 'bot thai that ar admittit and havand power to that effect'. Thus the Protestant parliament theoretically terminated the religious function of the Roman Catholic priesthood, and simultaneously ensured an ongoing battle with a Catholic queen whose as yet unforeseen return was but one year distant.

The other legislative action had to do with the termination of papal authority in Scotland which was described as 'verray hurtfull and prejudiciall to our soveranis autoritie and comone weill of this realme'. Also, no Scot might seek title or right from the pope, under pain of banishment. The act concluded with a statement bound to generate confusion: 'that no bischop nor uther prelat of this realme use ony Jurisdictioun in tymes to cum be the said bischop of Romeis autoritie'.[118]

About the only thing settled hereby was that the act effectively finished the potential for strife between crown and papacy over episcopal appointments. Henceforth the crown could, if it chose, do altogether as it pleased, its power augmented from that of nomination to that of appointment.[119] In fact, Mary gave Ross to her husband Henry Darnley in 1565.[120] Of course, Rome would not have recognised there titular creations, and as it turned out, neither would the reformed kirk.

The question over continued episcopal authority remained — did the act inhibiting papal power intend to terminate the bishops' jurisdiction by virtue of their relationship to the pope, or did it simply prohibit appeals to Rome and abrogate legatine status that clearly originated abroad? Gordon Donaldson, arguing for both the moderation and inconclusiveness of the early Reformation years, has claimed that of the bishops in 1560 only two were 'conscientious papalists'[121] inclined to continue the exercise of papally derived authority —

James Beaton (II) of Glasgow who fled to France in 1560 where he died in 1603, and William Chisholm of Dunblane who died in 1564. Of the others, including the primate John Hamilton, Donaldson has shown a sometimes less than enthusiastic attachment to Catholicism and even the occasional benevolent gesture toward the reformed kirk. Beside the three or four positively reforming bishops he writes, 'It seems very likely that several bishops could have been won over,'[122] the failure being attributed to deep hostility on the part of reformers like Knox towards old foes like Hamilton.

But there was more to the problem. In August 1560 Dunkeld called Knox 'an olde condemned hereticke',[123] language untouched by notions of reconciliation. St. Andrews was thought to have repudiated the mass near that time but Randolph dismissed the rumour. He wrote that the primate was ensconced at Paisley with 'the ladie his love the lord Symple dawghter'.[124] Although one of the archbishop's mistresses by whom he had five or six children repented her moral laxity,[125] there is no sign that he was prepared to make a similar gesture. It is difficult to conclude otherwise than that most of the bishops entertained little thought of becoming Protestants. If they hesitated in the face of a Protestant Confession, it may well be that in August 1560 many of them were confronted for the first time in their lives with a serious and inescapable theological problem. The fact that Arran (Hamilton) and Argyll (Campbell) supported the Protestants would also have given their episcopal kinsmen cause for reflection lest by outright opposition they repudiate the bond of kinship.

Whatever the reforming party thought of it, appointment of 'old guard' bishops continued. William Chisholm (III), nephew of his predecessor of the same name, succeeded to Dunblane in 1564, John Sinclair was provided to Brechin in 1565, and John Lesley to Ross in 1566.[126] Though he would soon show himself a Protestant, young Alexander Campbell was appointed to succeed Sinclair in the see of Brechin in 1566. Mary petitioned Pius V on the youth's behalf, basing her request upon 'his purity of blood, and singular learning, joined to his integrity of lyfe'.[127] Evidently the Catholic episcopate was neither extinguished nor even set upon the path toward extinction in 1560. There was simply no way the weak reformed kirk could get rid of the bishops, so rooted were their functions and their persons in the social, economic, and political life of the nation, and thus it was that archbishop Hamilton, and not John Knox, baptised the infant prince James on 17 December 1566.[128] The new kirk could not even enforce its financial programme delineated in the first Book of Discipline whereby episcopal temporalities were to be appropriated to support the work of the reformed kirk.[129] Some bishops may be found attending parliament,[130] continuing to perform their duties as members of the ecclesiastical estate. Futhermore there is evidence of an at least intermittent exercise of the old consistorial powers dealing with questions of marriage and divorce, of deeds and testaments. Attempting to clear the confusion, though more likely adding to it, archbishop Hamilton's powers were formally confirmed on 23 December 1566. But as Gordon Donaldson has commented, 'It is really not all clear that the judicial powers of the bishops had ever wholly lapsed'.[131] What is clear is that the general assembly, meeting two days later, shot back to 'the nobilitie of this realme that professes the Lord Jesus with them, and hes renounceit that Roman antichryst' an angry, fearful, and defensive supplication. It described the restoration of Hamilton's archbishopric, his judicatories and his right of admission to benefices as the curing of 'the head of that venemous beast' formerly broken down by God's power.[132] Great dissatisfaction was recorded concerning the archbishop's former treatment of so-called heresy. Earlier, perhaps as a show of defiant strength, the general assembly of June 1563 had reversed a decision made in 1534 by the bishop of Ross in his role as commissioner for the then archbishop of St. Andrews, when a certain James Hamilton was condemned for some heretical articles such as were commonly alleged against Protestants. The assembly decreed that he 'be restored in integrum to his honour, fame, and dignitie'.[133]

As far as the Catholics were concerned all was not lost in 1560, nor could the Protestants celebrate complete victory at that time. A Catholic sovereign in conjunction with an avaricious Protestant nobility put firm restraints upon reforming ambitions, and therefore little could be done by way of overthrowing the old episcopate or setting up a new one. Still, some new structure had to be created, in part to fill the void left by an inefficient and, more recently, discredited ecclesiastical hierarchy. To that programme of rebuilding the following chapter is devoted.

CHAPTER 2

The Superintendency

The first steps toward a reconstitution of the kirk at a national level had actually been taken as early as 29 April 1560 when a group of men was commissioned by the 'Great Councell of Scotland'[1] to frame a new polity. The work was completed by 20 May, as indicated by the conclusion to the document which came eventually to be known as the first Book of Discipline.[2] But nothing was done that year by way of official ratification,[3] and it was at the August parliament, wrote Knox, that the 'six Johns', Winram, Spottiswood, Willock, Douglas, Row and Knox, were charged 'to draw in a volume the Policy and Discipline of the Kirk, as well as they had done the Doctrine [Confession]'.[4] It was this document, embodying at least some aspects of the earlier one, which was given qualified approval by the nobility on 27 January 1561.[5]

The discipline is not a literary unity.[6] It is divided into 'heads', but between the fifth and sixth heads three additional heads have been intruded presumably at some time subsequent to the draft which provided the basic structure.

The first of the interpolations is entitled 'Of the Superintendents',[7] and the debate over the meaning of the section and the office it describes has been a commonplace for more than three centuries. Put briefly, are the superintendents to be regarded as new bishops?

Certainly there was concern lest they become like the pre-Reformation episcopate: 'Those men must not be suffered to live as your idle Bishops have done heretofore; neither must they remain where gladly they would, but they must be preachers themselves'. These sentiments comprehend much of the attack on the old order: they must not be holders of sinecures, caring only for their own leisure, and that probably of an immoral kind; they must be resident officers; and above all they must be evangelists, *i.e.* preachers of the word, and concomitantly, planters of churches. Their responsibilities meant that they must not stay put for more than twenty days until the whole area under their charge had been visited, and optimistically, each parish provided with a minister or at least a reader. Where the reforming councils had called for the bishops to preach at least four times each year, the superintendents were to do so at least three times each week while visiting, 'and when they returne to their principall Towne and Residence, they must be likewise exercised in preaching and edification of the Kirk'.[8] After three or four months at home, they must go off again, not only preaching but also examining 'the life, diligence and behaviour of the Ministers, as also the order of the kirkes, the manners of the people'. It was likewise within their duties to see that the poor were properly cared for and the young adequately educated, two items of profound importance and interest to the reformers. There was to be no tolerance of shortcoming:

> If the Superintendent be found negligent in any of the chiefe points of his office, and
> especially if he be noted negligent in preaching of the word, and visitation of the
> Kirkes, or if he be convict of such crimes, which in common Ministers are damned,
> he must be deposed, without respect of his person, or office.[9]

His work would be subject to review and censure by ministers and elders of his
province and by the general assembly.[10]

The superintendents bore, consequently, responsibility for oversight of clergy
and parishes in their 'dioceses'.[11] These were preachers, evangelists, with special
duties arising from their divine endowment with 'singular graces'.[12]

James Kirk writes that the superintendency did not belong to the 'reformers'
original strategy'; rather its presentation by way of an interpolation suggests that it
was an 'afterthought' based upon the situation defined by a shortage of suitable
ministers.[13] He goes on to state that if church government under Elizabeth was
episcopal, then in Scotland it was conciliar.[14] Superintendency was thus a
temporary measure, and so long as it continued it was most certainly not an
episcopate whereby it ruled the church. This view of the early period of Protestant
reform originated with certain seventeenth-century presbyterian writers and has
subsequently been accepted by McCrie, Mathieson, Fleming, Brown, Ainslie, W.
S. Reid, and most recently Kirk.[15] The significance of this interpretation of
superintendency is to deny the fundamentally episcopalian intentions of the first
Book of Discipline and to see that document as continuous with the second Book
of Discipline (1581), stating thereby that the reformed kirk was from its earliest
days grounded in a presbyterian, or at least proto-presbyterian, polity.

However, a strong case has also been made for the episcopal nature of
superintendency, an interpretation which also originated among the debaters of
the first half of the seventeenth century. More recently, F. W. Maitland wrote that
Knox's version of the kirk was 'prelatic', and he discounted suggestions that 'its
prelatic constitution' was of a temporary sort. Parity was an illusion: 'the
[superintendent] may command, the [minister] must obey'.[16] James Cooper
argued that superintendency was temporary insofar as it was a makeshift until the
old episcopal sees became vacant,[17] but this suggestion is not without difficulties.
Vacant sees continued to be filled with Catholics, though probably this was
unforeseen in 1560; but as Kirk notes, no superintendent other than John Carswell
was ever appointed to a bishopric, even after 1572.[18] Of course, this argument loses
itself in the uncertainties of Scottish politics of the civil war and regencies. It is also
to be considered that the first Book of Discipline disendowed the bishoprics,
though the temporalities were in part destined to support the superintendents,[19]
and that the bishops described in 1572 were defined more or less as superintendents.

Gordon Donaldson, in his commanding *Scottish Reformation*, has provided the
fullest argument for the view of the superintendency as a reformed episcopate on a
more or less permanent footing,[20] stating that the superintendents assumed many
of the old episcopal functions including examination of clergy, oversight of
discipline, and certain judicial functions through diocesan courts.

The first Book of Discipline did in fact tender some apologetic words about superintendents — not, however, for instituting them, but for not being able to clear their way immediately. Actually the discipline suggests that the office was not an 'afterthought' in the sense of an undesirable concession to be amended at the earliest practicable moment; rather, the reformers decided that despite the practical difficulties of establishing the office it could not be postponed until more favourable circumstances allowed. The section 'Of the Superintendents' begins:

> Because we have appointed a larger stipend to them that shall be Superintendents than to the rest of the Ministers, we have thought good to signifie to your Honours such reasons as moved us to make difference betwixt Preachers at this time, as also how many Superintendents we thinke necessarie, with their bounds, office, election and causes that may deserve deposition from the charge.
> . . . And therefore we have thought it a thing most expedient at this time [to appoint ten superintendents, etc.] . . . .[21]

There was indeed some murmuring against taking ministers away from churches at a time of extreme shortage. A John Douglas, representing John Spottiswood's church at Calder, complained 'that they are defrauded divers times of the preaching of the word, since their minister was elected superintendent of Lothian', and requested Spottiswood's return or replacement. 'It was answered, the profit of many kirks was to be preferred to the profit of one particular.' Given 'this rarity of the ministry', Douglas was told in effect to do the job himself and that he ought to have complained before the superintendent's admission.[22] A second complaint followed since by reason of holding the superintendency Spottiswood was 'abstracted from his cure at the said kirk the most part of the yeere'. It was further suggested that this situation approximated the plurality of benefices so common in the former 'popish kirk'. Though it might have been replied that the office of superintendent was in reality far more likely to become a financial liability than a gold mine, no other response was given than that offered earlier.[23]

Perhaps in anticipation of the second complaint Spottiswood had asked the general assembly for 'libertie to returne to his former cure, becaus he was not able to discharge so great a burthen as he was burthened with'.[24] But as it turned out, once a superintendent was inaugurated he was never permitted to resign his diocesan responsibilities, although numerous plaintive requests for relief from office were submitted to general assemblies.[25]

There is further evidence in the first Book of Discipline that the superintendent was to be a continuous fixture in the kirk. Certain regulations point in this direction, such as that which called upon the superintendent to nominate ministers if kirks failed to do so within forty days of a vacancy.[26] This intrusive, almost punitive, act had no real relevance at the inception of the reformed kirk because ministers were simply not available. Such policy was designed to deal with incompetent, lackadaisical, or divided kirks in a more settled post-Reformation time.

When the polity was functioning properly the provision of superintendents was to follow the usual pattern for other ministers — nomination, examination, and election. Nomination lay in the hands of the ministers, elders, deacons, magistracy, and council of the 'cheefe Towne', *i.e.* the superintendent's town or home base, though any kirk in the diocese might make a nomination. On an announced day the nominees were to be publicly examined in life and doctrine by diocesan ministers and three or four neighbouring superintendents, with the intention of presenting the best-suited candidate for election by the people of the diocese. Failure of the chief town to act accordingly entailed the intervention of 'three of the next adjacent Provinces with consent of their Superintendents, Ministers and Elders' to act in its place.

This, the regular procedure for election, was to take effect 'after three yeares',[27] a phrase which has nothing to do with describing the length of term for a superintendent. But until then a different procedure must necessarily be followed: 'In this present necessity, the nomination, examination and admission of the Superintendent cannot be so straight as we require and as afterwards must be'. Because so few kirks were properly reformed, the desired pattern was unattainable; therefore 'your Honours' were called upon to nominate and appoint superintendents, though in conjuction with the gentlemen and burgesses of each diocese 'to bring the kirk in some practise of her liberty', *i.e.* to sustain a pretence of free election which really had no hope of attainment. The lords were counselled not to choose unfit persons simply to fill the offices; it would be better to wait for the emergence of more suitable persons, 'for experience hath teached us what pestilence hath been ingendered in the Kirk by men unable to discharge their offices [*i.e.* the old bishops]'.[28] A further requirement of office would come into force in three years to the effect that henceforth any candidate for superintendent must have ministered in the reformed kirk for a minimum of two years. Finally the reformers commended the lords not to 'disappoint . . . your chief towns . . . of such ministers as more may profit by residence in one place than by countinuall travell from place to place'. Greater benefit would be had from their faithful education of the young by which means 'the Commonwealth shall shortly feast of their fruit, to the comfort of the godly'.[29] The implication — in this section, at least — is that although superintendents are vital to the kirk's health, better to temper present fulfilment so as to plan for the future. However different statements might describe the urgency or the judicious postponement of appointments to the superintendency, there is not one shred of evidence in the Book of Discipline that this office would at some unforeseen date prove redundant and therefore wither away. The discipline outlined a polity for the kirk in which superintendents were an integral aspect.

Neither the term nor the concept of superintendency was a Scottish innovation. Various sources have been proposed: Denmark, Cologne (archbishop Hermann von Wied), Hesse (François Lambert), Lutheran Germany (Melanchthon), the strangers' congregation in London (John à Lasco), and the reformed church in France.[30] Of course precise identification of the provenance is not only impossible in the welter of reforming ideas then in circulation, but it is also unnecessary in view of the commonplace character of the office. To have questioned its propriety 'would have been contrary to almost all contemporary thought'.[31]

Indeed the continental reformers did attack the medieval bishops, but the condemnations originated not in hostility to a position of oversight and responsibility above the level of the parish minister but in the sins, both of commission and omission, of the Catholic bishops.[32] On the one hand their lives contradicted the precepts of Christian morality while on the other they had failed to fulfil the apostolic tasks pertinent to the episcopate — preaching, administration of the sacraments (without idolatrous accretions), and church discipline (reformers generally complained that the bishops took cognisance of vices which, though petty, produced revenue through fines easily levied while they ignored greater sins in the church). Even Calvin did not execrate the office of bishop *per se*. Genevan visitors were, of course, not solitary judges nor were they permanent,[33] but one must look beyond the narrow confines of Geneva to determine the true dimensions of Calvin's view on ecclesiastical government. As was normal among the Protestant reformers, Calvin's 'bishop' referred to any minister, and the essential mark of the minister was preaching.[34] However, he recognised that during the post-apostolic period the presbyters of each city chose one of their body to be a bishop, one somehow distinct from the others, 'in order that dissensions might not arise . . . from equality of rank. Still the bishop was not so much higher in honor and dignity as to have lordship over his colleagues'. Thus the episcopal function was to report, admonish, preside, counsel, all the while fulfilling the responsibility to minister the word and the sacraments. Calvin's concern was evident in his insistence that even 'the ancients' admitted that this benign episcopacy 'was introduced by human agreement to meet the need of the times' and that the bishops themselves recognised the human rather than the dominical origins of episcopal superiority, and also that their authority was to be exercised co-operatively with the presbyters.[35] Calvin's bishop was therefore an acceptable innovation so long as he remained an authentic minister by biblical criteria and performed his particular duties in consultation with those who had chosen him from their own ranks.[36]

Another reformer, Martin Bucer, active both in Strasbourg and in Edwardian England, described a reformed episcopate for the young king. Bucer claimed biblical sanction for a bishop of 'singular care for the churches and [who] in that care and solicitude presides over all the others [elders]'. The bishop was the 'chief administrator of the churches', performing his functions in consultation with the other presbyters, 'who are also called bishops in the Scriptures because of this common ministry'. Bucer's bishops took precedence over 'all the rest of the order of the sacred ministry'.[37] They would indeed still be teachers and pastors, but would also watch over the other ministers and make yearly visitations to their diocesan churches.[38] Bucer reflected none of Calvin's reserve:

One who is but little acquainted with the Holy Scriptures, the writings of the ancient churchmen, and the laws of pious emperors knows that this [episcopal precedence in the church] has been amply sanctioned and handed down *and is also strictly required by divine laws*, the holy canons of the early churches, the writings of all the holy fathers, and finally also by many sanctions of pious princes.[39]

On this foundation one might predict that in Scotland the reformers would call for a reformed episcopate (though perhaps known by another term), grounded in a preaching ministry, but also directed to rule in conciliar fashion over the other clergy and churches in the dioceses. It would in fact be altogether remarkable if such an institution had not appeared in a sprawling and sparsely populated country lacking experienced ministers where Calvin's visitation teams would have been terribly inefficient.

Nearly twenty years have passed since Maurice Lee, Jr. wrote, 'We also need to know more about the careers and the thought of the reformers other than Knox'.[40] The need generally remains, but what little we do know suggests two things: first, that appointments to the superintendency followed, at least in part, the pattern of preferment at work in the medieval episcopate; and second, that the organisers of the reformed kirk, including both the authors of the first Book of Discipline and the superintendents, had no deepseated hostility to the concept of a reformed episcopate.

Of the superintendents probably all but John Erskine had taken Catholic orders. John Winram (1492?-1582), superintendent of Fife, was subprior of the Augustinian priory of St.Andrews and dean of the University's divinity faculty. A Doctor of Theology, he was present at the 1549 provincial council,[41] and in Knox's *History* he appears as a less than ardent defender of orthodoxy.[42]

John Willock (c.1516-1585),[43] superintendent of Glasgow, had been a Franciscan friar and had earned the STB (Bachelor of Sacred Theology), probably in Cologne. He appears to have contacted Lutheran ideas in the 1530s, and in 1541 he fled to the more congenial atmosphere of England. Licensed there as a preacher, he was nonetheless imprisoned for a time in the Fleet. With his close friend John Knox he was subsequently granted freedom to preach anywhere in England, and was presented to a Leicestershire benefice which he held for life, though for many years as an absentee. Upon Mary Tudor's accession he removed to Emden in Friesland, an enclave of Zwinglian theology. He returned to Scotland in 1558 where he preached in Dundee and in Edinburgh. Shaw claims that he had 'first hand knowledge of superintendents' and that similar officers 'were known in Leicestershire after [his] return there in 1568'.[44]

John Spottiswood (1510-1585), superintendent of Lothian, graduated MA from Glasgow in 1536, proceeding to London where he imbibed Protestant doctrines from archbishop Cranmer. He returned to Scotland in 1543 and in 1548 was presented to the living at Calder by the laird of Calder, sir James Sandilands, a Protestant sympathiser. He was in the favour of Glencairn and Lennox and also accompanied lord James Stewart, later the earl of Moray, on his embassy to France in 1550.[45] If indeed a sincere Protestant before 1560, he must have kept his counsel for there is no indication of an earlier outspoken commitment to the cause.

John Erskine (1509-1589?),[46] superintendent of Angus and the Mearns, was the laird of Dun. His education included King's College, Aberdeen, and possibly some continental school.[47] His wealth and status were considerable, and so his adherence to the Protestant side from an early date was of real importance.[48] Among Erskine's holdings was an interest in the temporality of the see of Brechin, leading Gordon Donaldson to query whether this led him to expect eventual elevation to the bishopric since it lay within his superintending bounds.[49]

John Carswell (1520-1572), superintendent of Argyll,[50] graduated MA from St. Andrews in 1544, and from the records of the University it would appear that his family was not a wealthy one. However, kinship ties connected the Carswells with the powerful Campbells (earls of Argyll), and to this may be credited his upward movement.[51] Carswell was appointed treasurer of Lismore in 1550 (diocese of Argyll) and in 1553 he became parson at Kilmartin. On his way up the ladder, he was in 1559 collated chancellor of the Chapel Royal[52] and had ample opportunity to acquire a reputation as a grasping cleric, being both a pluralist and a dilapidator. He took a wife from the Campbells and in 1559 received custody of Carnassery Castle which might have been a reward for his adherence to reform and a means of assuring his continued allegiance.[53] By March 1560 he had acquired three more tracts of heritable land, and further grants were received in subsequent years.

However base his origins might have been, by the advent of the Reformation he was no 'humble parish minister',[54] but rather a laird of substance. 'No other parson in the district received a comparable amount of land, and, indeed, his appointment as superintendent of Argyll after 1560 could scarcely have come as a surprise to his contemporaries.'[55] Nor would there have been amazement at the future course of his career.

Several factors seem to have been at work in the selection of the superintendents. Winram and Carswell held prominent officers in the old kirk; Carswell, Erskine, and Spottiswood were well connected with leading political and social figures; Willock was a well known Protestant preacher, long an associate of Knox and knowledgeable concerning the workings of kirk polity.

Winram, Willock, and Spottiswood were also employed in drafting the discipline, assisted by John Douglas, John Row, and John Knox. Douglas was an academic, a graduate of the University of Paris, and during the early Reformation period rector of the University of St. Andrews.[56] In later years he accepted an archbishopric. Row followed a university education at St. Andrews with an ecclesiastical legal career which took him to Rome where he gained the favour of the pope. He was subsequently forced to return home for the sake of his health, whereupon he converted to Protestantism in the course of theological disputation with Knox and others.[57]

There is nothing in the foregoing lives to suggest any real hostility to a form of episcopacy in the reformed kirk. Nor is John Knox an exception.[58] His rejection in 1552 of the see of Rochester under Edward VI and Thomas Cranmer is not to be attributed to inveterate opposition to episcopacy, even if he did dislike some features of the church of England. Probably he preferred to remain in the north so as to be closer to events in Scotland, and he may also have foreseen the coming of tribulation under Mary.[59] His later refusal of a superintendency in Scotland was due to his satisfaction with the place of minister of St. Giles in Edinburgh which certainly did nothing to lower his profile at court.[60]

Far from repudiating episcopacy, Knox sent a letter of advice on the subject to England in 1559. There he contrasted the types of bishops and also expressed his more positive view on the role of reformed bishops:

Thirdly let no man be charged in preaching of Christ Jesus above that, which one man may do, I meane, that your Bishoprikes be so devided, that of every one, as they be nowe (for the most part) be made ten, and so in every Citie and great towne there may be placed a godly learned man with so many joyned with him for preaching and instruction, as shalbe thoght sufficient for the bondes committed to their charge. The utilitie wherof you shal understand, within few yeares greatly to redounde to the profit of the simple flocke. For your prowde prelates great dominion & charge (impossible by one man to be discharged) are no parte of christs ministerie, but are the maintenance of the tyrannie first invented & yet reteyned by the Romane Antichrist.[61]

These are scarcely the words of a man disposed to renounce all forms of episcopacy.

According to Knox five superintendents were nominated in July 1560.[62] It is not possible to substantiate this report; in fact, that thesis which would remove superintendents from the earliest draft of the first Book of Discipline renders it highly suspect, as does the absence of superintendents from the register of the December 1560 assembly.[63] It is, however, sufficiently clear that the process of nomination, election, and inauguration (*not* consecration) had begun by March 1561, but the matter of Willock's appointment to the West, or Glasgow, remains problematic. A dispatch to England stated that his admission had been on 14 September 1561,[64] while a letter to the former archbishop indicated some sort of high function in Glasgow for Willock in August 1560.[65] One is tempted to propose the emendation of either date, probably rendering the second one August 1561. But another, simpler, explanation may prove satisfactory. It was reported on 25 August 1560 that Knox was to preach at Edinburgh, Christopher Goodman at St. Andrews, and Willock at Glasgow,[66] adding nothing about superintendents as Knox had (erroneously) done. Thus the letter to the exiled archbishop may have reflected nothing more than Willock's appointment to the cathedral pulpit — apparently he collected diocesan revenues and dwelt in the dean's house[67] — and thus with Willock the highest, if not the only, Protestant minister in the burgh or even the diocese, the reporter may have drawn a conclusion based upon his own no longer relevant perception of ecclesiastical business.

Two prominent considerations emerge from an examination of the role of the superintendents up to the mid-1570s. First, the general assembly sought to foster a truly reformed episcopal or superintending polity by emphasising preaching, visitation, and exercise of authority in consultation with diocesan ministers within a context of parity. Second, that there was no effort to diminish the importance of the superintendents is evident in the affirmation of their role in the examination and admission of ministers, and in the appointment of commissioners to fill the gaps due to only a one-half complement of superintendents.

The December 1566 general assembly noted its almost unconditional approval of the Second Helvetic Confession. Among the significant features was the statement, 'superioritie of ministers above ministers is called ane humane appointment'.[68] Indeed, the Confession does claim to 'return to the old appointment of God', *i.e.* parity of all ministers, 'and rather receive that than the custom devised by men'. But a careful reading of the text does not deny a distinction among the clergy 'for order's sake'. Peter himself provided a biblical precedent of one who was obviously an outstanding figure, although the authors of the document could still say he 'neither was above the rest, nor had greater authority than the rest'. Even in the earliest days one specified minister summoned the assembly, moderated its proceedings, and generally assured good order in place of confusion.[69] Potential for superiority in a negatively construed sense was limited by a conciliar form of government in which human authority resided, only delegating certain responsibilities to particular individuals for specified terms of office or with strict limitations of jurisdiction. However, lest it be thought this approbation of the Swiss Confession by the kirk entailed an abrupt about-face in polity, it should be noted that the superintendents were among the correspondents who wrote back to those who had sent a copy of the Confession, 'that they agreed in all points with those Churches, and differed in nothing from them' except for the observance of certain holy days.[70] Thus no contradiction was seen between the reformed episcopacy of the superintendents and a forthright affirmation of parity — whatever that term signified. Certainly it implied that all clergy had the same responsibility to preach, and this function demonstrated their capacity as ministers to officiate at sacramental celebrations. Indeed an episcopal superintendency was not grounded in an order of sacramentally superior prelates. But by no means was the kirk blind to differences in ability, going so far as to consider adjusting stipends in accordance with it.[71] And in considering the constitution of the general assembly in 1568 it was concluded: 'That none have place nor power to vote, except superintendents, commissioners appointit for visiteing kirks, ministers brocht with them presentit as persons abill to reason, and having knowledge to judge'.[72] Parity did not entail equal democratic rights in directing the affairs of the kirk. It referred predominantly to the evangelical tasks of ministry but was not intended to pose a direct threat to hierarchical and aristocratic patterns of authority in Scottish society.

The election of John Spottiswood on 9 March 1561 studiously avoided any suggestion of continuity with the old hierarchy. Perhaps the most significant aspect of the service was the rubric, 'The Forme and Order of the Election of the Superintendent, which may serve in election of all other Ministers'.[73] Provision was made in the service for an appropriate sermon, formal confirmation of the election, questions directed to the one elected and to the people, prayers for the occasion, and finally, 'The last exhortation, to the elected'. This charged the superintendent to 'usurp not dominion nor tyrannicall authoritie over thy brethren'. Devoid of references to succession and the sacramental imposition of hands by other members of an elevated episcopal order, this was clearly no consecration of an Elizabethan bishop. The only ceremony was the invitation to other ministers and elders to 'take the elected by the hand'.[74]

Although the Register of St.Andrews referred to superintendents as 'cheef ministeris',[75] the general assembly intended that there should not be uncontrolled growth of power and prominence in the office. As a result the assembly meeting in June 1562 appointed that superintendents should be tried at the beginning of proceedings.[76] Further action was taken in support of this practice one year later when it was declared 'that every superintendent convein the first day appointit for the Assemblie, under the paine of fourtie shillings, to be distribute to the poor without remissioun therof'.[77] During these trials complaints were received concerning the conduct and activity of superintendents, commonly their failure to visit regularly and to preach.[78] In March 1573 it was enacted that all ministers should have full information about the office of superintendent so that trials might be conducted.[79]

Unlike the English bishop, the superintendent was not a sovereign power. On the one hand, as has been seen, he was required to answer to the general assembly for his actions, while on the other hand he was to be assisted in his labours. Superintendents were to call twice-yearly synods to which ministers, elders, and deacons would come 'to consult upon the comon affaires of these diocies'.[80] The Register of St. Andrews, the most complete extant record of a superintendent's diocesan activities, shows John Winram being assisted by a variety of people including John Douglas, Christopher Goodman, 'and hol ministerie'.[81] Emphasis was placed upon the derivative and shared aspects of superintending authority, including the exercise of discipline. The assembly thought the superintendents should act with some elders 'for avoiding all corruption and partiality'.[82] Decisions of superintendents and their synods could be appealed to the general assembly, the fountain of ecclesiastical jurisdiction and the final juridical authority in the kirk.[83]

This does not, however, mean that the Book of the Universal Kirk and other documents do not chronicle the strengthening and solidification of the office of superintendent. Certainly the kirk at St. Andrews had no qualms about inaugurating its overseer, John Winram. The Register reads:

> Wythout the cayr [of] superintendentis neyther can the kyrk be suddenlie erected, neyther can th[ei] be retened in disciplin and unite of doctrin; and farther seing that [of] Crist Jesus and of his apostolis we have command and exempill to appoynt me[n] to sic chargis . . . .[84]

Fourteen years later a letter from Dumfries was presented to the general assembly reflecting the same view of the necessity of oversight. The letter 'lamented, that these three years bygane, their bounds, for laike of Superintendents and visiters, had become altogether forgettful of their duty toward God, and altogether before this time had shaken off obedience' had Peter Watson not taken it upon himself to pick up some of the necessary work.[85] It was thus recognised that the wellbeing of the kirk demanded more than a settled pastoral ministry.

Had the superintendent's role been based solely upon the establishment of new kirks, the office would eventually have become redundant as the Reformation spread throughout the country. But other tasks of a more permanent nature were added.[86] The superintendent was charged with communicating the decrees of general assemblies to the ministers of his diocese and to announce to them future convocations.[87] Ministers and others were not to petition the general assembly 'with sick things as superintendents may and aught decyde in their synodall conventiouns'.[88] He was to attend to the repair of churches and to act as a censor of books 'tuiching religioun or doctrine' before their publication.[89] Oversight of education was also included in the burden of responsibility.[90] Care for church finances through the supervision of the collectors of thirds of benefices[91] and the modification of ministerial stipends[92] likewise pertained to the superintendent.

The superintendents' oversight of other ministers was clarified in June 1562. 'It is concludit be the haill ministers assemblit, that all ministers salbe subject to ther superintendents in all lawfull admonitiouns, as is prescryvit alsweill in the Booke of Discipline as in the electioun of superintendents'.[93] At the same time the superintendents of Lothian and Glasgow were authorised to take trial of and to impose sanctions upon erring ministers, and to pronounce sentence of excommunication upon recalcitrant elders in diocesan kirks.[94] The assembly held in December of that year declared that only those ministers — including the old bishops — examined and appointed by a superintendent were authorised to serve in the kirk,[95] though of course it could do nothing to inhibit a bishop. Furthermore it was added in June 1564 that no minister could move to another charge 'without knowledge of the floke, his superintendent or haill kirk',[96] while the assembly held one year later added the threat of deposition to any offender against the clause.[97] Obedience was expected and enforced. As early as May 1561 a submission to the lords of secret council had been made asking 'for punishing of the contemners of the said superintendents and dissobeyars of them'.[98] Similar requests were made at other times,[99] indicating a conviction that the furtherance of true religion depended upon obedience to the rightful directives of the superintendents who bore the delegated authority of the general assembly.

The authentic church was predicated upon not only preaching and correct administration of the sacraments but also upon the maintenance of discipline. Nobles and superintendents were to collaborate in the enforcement of laws against 'violators of the Sabboth day, committers of adulterie and fornicatioun'.[100] Though the superintendent did not hold sole responsibility in the maintenance of discipline, he was to ensure its right operation even to the extent of calling upon the 'supreme magistrate, requyring him to minister justice and punisch sick haynous offences according to the law of God'.[101] However, aid from the secular arm was not always forthcoming.[102]

Marital issues figured largely in the disciplinary work of the early superintendency. By act of the general assembly in December 1562 it was ordained 'that no minister nor others bearing office within the Kirk, take in hand to cognosce and decide in the actiouns of divorcement, except the superintendents, and they to whom they sall give speciall commissioun, and betwixt speciall persons'.[103] Thus for a time it appeared that the superintendents would assume the functions of the old diocesan courts.[104] Actually the kirk had already expressed unease at its role in this arena, and sought relief from the privy council:

> Anent the actiouns for divorcements, to make supplicatioun to the secreit counsell, that either they give up universallie the judgement of divorce to the kirk and their sessiouns, or else to establish men of good lyves, knowledge and judgement, to take the order thereof; provyding alwayes that the saids Lords make provisioun and ordinance how the guiltie persons divorced salbe punished.[105]

In response, on 28 December 1563 the privy council acted to erect commissary courts to deal with marriage, teinds, deeds, testaments, and defamations, 'the caussis quhilkis the prelattis of this realme had decidit in the consistoriis of befoir'.[106]

The original intention of the first Book of Discipline had been the erection of ten superintending dioceses on a redrawn ecclesiastical map, each with about one hundred parishes.[107] But only the five men already mentioned were ever appointed. Certainly the general assembly sought to add to their number. In May 1561 it petitioned the lords of secret council 'for the erecting and establishing of moe [superintendents] in places convenient'.[108] Nominations were made for three additional dioceses in December 1562 (Jedburgh, Dumfries, Aberdeen and Banff),[109] and further suit was made to the queen in December 1564.[110] Naturally, there lay a major hindrance — a Roman Catholic queen being called upon to provide superintendents in a Protestant kirk. Also, given that the superintendents were to be paid — at a rate much greater than that assigned to other ministers — out of episcopal temporalities which were often in lay hands, there was a financial problem. Archbishop Spottiswood the historian remarked that once nobles and others got 'into their hands the possessions of the Church, [they] could never be induced to part therewith, and turned greater enemies in that point of Church Patrimony, then were the Papists or any other whatsoever'.[111] In fact financial hardship for superintendents was chronic. Winram used the 'evill payment of his stipend' as a justification for his 'slackness in visitation of his kirks'.[112] But the coming of a Protestant regime under a succession of regents from 1567 did not alleviate the difficulty or lead to the appointment[113] of more superintendents at the continued requests of the general assembly, lending credence to Spottiswood's accusation. His father, the superintendent of Lothian, could neither quit on account of age and infirmity (and perhaps frustration!) nor could he get payment of his stipend, although the assembly excused his failure to visit 'the whole kirks' because he was paying his own way.[114] In August 1574 it was recorded that 'the Assembly shall procure at my Lord Regents Grace provision to be made to him, and others of like vocation and charge within the Kirk, for their stipend'.[115] As late as August 1575 the assembly was still petitioning the regent Morton for superintendents to fill gaps in the new episcopal structure and for 'payment to them that hes travellit befor as Commissioners in the yeirs of God 1573,1574, and so foorth in time coming, without the quhilk the travells of sick men will cease'.[116]

One man reached the end of his tether and abandoned his superintendency. In January 1568 the general assembly wrote to John Willock, who had resorted to his Loughborough charge in Leicestershire, to return to his superintendency, assuring him that there were 'throughout the realme commissioners and superintendents placed'.[117] Willock did in fact return[118] and was moderator of assembly in July,[119] but his view of the situation was less sanguine than the invitation implied in its introductory inscription, 'Videbam Satanam sicut fulgum de coelo cadentem'.[120] In a letter to Cecil he commented that men attended church complete with armour and weaponry, and even in the assembly complaint was made of 'the sturdines of the poeplle'. Thus even at the time of the July assembly he had determined to return to England after less than two months, having obtained the licence to do so, 'wherof I praise God'.[121]

Given that the office of superintendent was regarded as necessary to the good health of the kirk, some means of circumventing the reluctance of the state had to be found. This was accomplished by two interrelated means. First, Gordon Donaldson has noted that none of the original five superintendencies 'conflicted with the jurisdiction of the three bishops engaged on behalf of the reformed church'.[122] They were Adam Bothwell, bishop of Orkney, Alexander Gordon, bishop of Galloway, and Robert Stewart, unconsecrated administrator of Caithness.

Bothwell was born c.1530, and it was possibly through his step-father Oliver Sinclair, a favourite of James V and a crown officer in Orkney, that he acquired nomination to the northernmost diocese,[123] where he was known to be promoting reform by March 1561.[124] Against considerable opposition he laboured sedulously to organise a reformed church in his diocese, making great strides toward providing sufficient clergy despite a badly dilapidated revenue.

Gordon was grandson of James IV through a natural daughter married to lord Gordon, hence he was brother to the fourth earl of Huntly and cousin to queen Mary. Born in 1516, his early adult years saw him striving to gain a foothold in the ecclesiastical hierarchy.[125] Unsuccessful in his quests for Caithness and then Glasgow, he was consoled with the titular archbishopric of Athens and the commendatorship of Inchaffray. Later he was made bishop-elect of the Isles and commendator of Iona, though he never gained a full title to these benefices as his family was on the wrong side of political contests. Finally he acquired the see of Galloway in 1559, though still not its full title. It may have been self-interest which drew him toward the Protestant party in hope of securing his somewhat tenuous position.[126] Apparently he was successful. Though listed at the August 1560 parliament as 'Archibischop off Athenis elect off Galloway',[127] Randolph wrote that he had been 'confirmed at this parliament [*i.e.* August 1560] bishop of Galloway'.[128] He was one of the signatories of the first Book of Discipline,[129] and from at least 1562 his work gained the recognition of the reforming party. In the early years it was queen Mary who discountenanced Gordon, while Knox defended him: 'But if he fear not God now, he deceives many more than me'.[130] Knox later complained about the bishop's ambition,[131] though he also recorded his service to the kirk in making representations to the queen.[132] Incidentally, he shared with his peers not only the status of a pluralist but also that of a celibate father, though his children were all borne by one woman, for all intents and purposes his wife. Eventually his sons came into possession of the see's temporalities.[133]

Robert Stewart of Caithness was the brother of Lennox, hence he was an uncle of Henry lord Darnley, husband of queen Mary. There is no evidence that he ever received consecration after his appointment as diocesan administrator of Caithness in 1542 when he was only nineteen. He went into exile in England with others of his politically active family 'where he clearly conformed to Henrician and Edwardian Anglicanism, and he was appointed to a prebend of Canterbury'.[134] He emerged on the reforming side in 1561.

However, if a formerly Catholic bishop were to be recognised by the reformed

kirk he would sooner or later have to be properly appointed or elected, thereby
subjecting himself to the assembly.[135] This recognition occurred in the office of
the commissioner:

> Commisssions war given to the bishops of Galloway, Orknay and Catness, for the
> space of a yeere, to plant kirks, etc. within their owne bounds, and that the bishop of
> Galloway haunt asweill the shirefdome of Wigton as the stewartie or Kirkcudbrigh,
> reckoned to be within his owne bounds.[136]

Granted the apparent impossibility or at least indefinite delay of further appointments of superintendents, the general assembly named commissioners or visitors,
aptly described by Calderwood as 'temporarie superintendents'.[137] These men,
either parochial ministers or superintendents, were granted temporary authority
to plant kirks, to suspend or depose unfit ministers, and generally act as
superintendents,[138] but without the need for state authorisation and apparently
without the larger stipend proposed for superintendents. The appointments, to
specific geographical areas, were generally for one year and renewable thereafter;
in George Hay's case, 'till a Superintendent be admitted in the North, or at least
till nixt Generall Assemblie'.[139] Renewal was so common — Hay was still
commissioner ten years later[140] — that in 1575 action was taken to move
commissioners to new areas annually, lest their 'lang continuance' in office 'should
induce some ambition and inconvenience in the Kirk'.[141] The net effect was a
continuation, under an alternate name, of superintendency. Donaldson writes that
the commissioners differed from actual superintendents only in that the former
held parochial charges while the latter did not.[142] Even here the distinction is
blurred by the superintendent of Lothian's pastoral charge at Calder,[143] and the
fact that Robert Pont, visitor for Moray, had no congregation.[144] Also, it is
doubtful whether the reforming bishops functioned as pastors of particular
congregations.

Caithness, once described as 'honeste inoughe',[145] seems to have got along
without notable difficulty or rebuke,[146] although the general assembly accused
him in 1595, after his death, of dilapidating the see,[147] but the other two ran into
stormy weather. In Galloway and Orkney one observes the collision of two
approaches to an ecclesiastical career, the conflict of the old and the new, medieval
and reformed. Of course they were accused of failing to visit, but so were all those
unfortunate enough to have been designated superintendents or commissioners.
But it was their behaviour after the pattern of the old episcopate that created their
greatest problems. Both became judges in the court of session; Galloway was also
appointed to the privy council, 'quhich cannot agree with the office of a pastor or a
bishop', and it was further alleged that he had granted the benefice of Inchaffray to
a child and had 'set diverse lands in feu, in prejudice of the kirk'.[148] Orkney had
given benefices to a papist. Upon confession of his faults Galloway was continued
but Orkney was deprived from any ministerial function due to his performance of
the marriage of Mary and the earl of Bothwell:[149] in so doing 'he transgrest the act
of the Kirk in marrying the divorcit adulterer [Bothwell]'.[150] Upon his confession[151] he was readmitted at the next assembly (July 1568), but his troubles began

again that year when he was forced, partly by ill health, to transfer his diocesan temporalities to the vicious lord Robert Stewart in exchange for Holyrood Abbey. For this and numerous other shortcomings in his work as diocesan he was delated before the March 1570 assembly.[152] He provided a spirited defence, and as to his exercising the office of a lord of session he said he had accepted it from Mary, 'with the advice of godly and learned men, compting it not repugnant or contrariouse to any good order as yet established in the Kirke; and alledged that diverse others having benefices, have done the like, and are not condemned for so doing'.[153] He may be excused for wondering why he was singled out, and the mystery grows in that in January 1572 the assembly granted the request of Robert Pont to join the college of justice, '*provydeing always that he leave not the office of the ministrie*'.[154] Pont, however, had the good sense to seek permission first,[155] thereby gaining a dispensation from the judgement that the confusion of the two jurisdictions was 'neither aggrieable to the word of God nor to the practise of the primitive Kirk'.[156] In any event Adam Bothwell thereafter all but faded from view, except that in January 1572 he was one of the regent's commissioners to treat with kirk representatives at the Leith convention,[157] and in October 1582 he was told to take upon himself a congregational ministry, which he declined because of sickness.[158] In 1590 he attended Anne's coronation,[159] and then finally, a few months before his death in 1593 he was under suspicion of having demolished the kirk at Birsay. If found responsible he was either to repair it or else to be proceeded against.[160]

Gordon of Galloway's troubles, though briefly resolved, actually grew worse with the passage of time. Apparently the assembly was still not satisfied 'whether he will awaite on court and counsell, or upon preaching the word and planting kirks',[161] and it would appear by the appointment of a commissioner for Galloway that he was deposed at that time (July 1568).[162] Another sentence of deposition was recorded in March 1573,[163] marking the commencement of a protracted battle. Gordon had allied himself with the Marian party in the recent civil war and stood accused of 'persuading, entysing and exhorting to rebell against our Soveraign Lord, and to join with manifest rebells and conjured enemies'. He also went counter — and this is perhaps the essence of the matter — to an assembly order 'for the prayer for our Soveraign Lord'.[164] Gordon's fault was fundamentally political in a church which was to show an increasing predilection for interfering in the political life of the nation. Therefore as part of his defence he appealed to the act of pacification in order to plead his innocence before the kirk.[165] He was very nearly excommunicated[166] but finally satisfied the church court in August 1575. He was at that time exhorted to assist John Duncanson, commissioner for Galloway,[167] but in response to a query it was clarified that he was as yet suspended from his own work as a commissioner; he might, however, preach and assist Duncanson 'for keeping good order and discipline within these bounds'.[168] The unhappy story ended with his death on 11 November following,[169] though in 1610 he was remembered only to be blamed by the incumbent for severely impairing the see's revenues.[170]

The old bishops belonged to a different era in terms of kirk polity and the realm's political life. Even their title was a source of irritation for at least some in the reformed kirk, and thus we read of 'Adam called Bishop of Orkney, Commissioner for Orkney'.[171] The old associations were too strong, and even the rather less troublesome Robert Stewart never achieved great standing in the new church. The medieval episcopate was anathema, and the curse clung to its members even when they did their best to become good servants of the Reformation.

CHAPTER 3

A Decade of New Beginnings

The common member of the kirk could be excused for failing to observe any significant difference between old bishop and new superintendent. Great honour accompanied the reformed visitor, and his diocesan synods may have been viewed as continuations of their medieval counterparts, which in part they were. The aforementioned letter to the exiled archbishop Beaton of Glasgow stated that 'Johne Willockis is maid Bischop of Glasquo, now in your Lordschipis absens, and placit in your place of Glasquo'.[1] If Thomas Archibald thus identified Willock with the old order, John Winram did so for himself, simply adding his newest office, superintendent of Strathearn (a variant nomenclature which appeared in the 1570s[2] following the resuscitation of the archbishopric of St. Andrews as a Protestant see), to his other titles — prior of Portmoak, subprior of St. Andrews, and parson of Kirkness.[3] Indeed, some of the complaints levelled against him had a familiar ring. He was accused of neglect of visitation and preaching, 'he wes too much gevin to wordlie affairis', too hasty to excommunicate, and 'sharper nor became him in making acts for payment of small tithes'.[4] When he died in 1582 he was buried in St. Leonard's College where his tombstone described him as *Fifanorum episcopo*.[5]

One superintendent went much further than these somewhat casual approximations to episcopacy. John Carswell was, as noted earlier, advanced in ecclesiastical preferments due to the patronage of Argyll. There remain few traces of his work as a superintendent, in part because of his absence from the general assemblies. But in a letter dated 29 May 1564 he countered charges that he was a turncoat and a too rigorous collector of teinds. He went on to declare his constancy and to describe his need of money to undertake the travels required by his office. He appealed to a letter from 'my brether the minister of Edinburgh and Superintendent of Glasgo . . . that thai will excuse me at the Generall Assemblie, and thinkis that my travell now in the Ilis may do mair gude to the Kirk nor my presens at the Assemblie'.[6]

A new but not remarkable direction was taken in 1565 when queen Mary appointed Carswell bishop of the Isles. The elevation was confirmed in 1567[7] but it should be noted that insofar as the kirk was concerned Carswell's jursidiction was unaltered. His new office was predicated upon the withdrawal of the bishop-elect Patrick Maclean[8] and 'should perhaps be seen against a background of strained relations between the Campbells and the Macleans'.[9] Like Alexander Gordon, Carswell supported Mary, but in spite of his episcopal see and his political leanings the general assembly in July 1569 had no more to say than that he should be 'reproved for accepting the Bishoprick of the Isles, without making the Assembly foreseen; and for riding at, and assisting of the Parliament holden by the Queen, after the murther of the King'.[10] Perhaps it could say little more to a man who had translated the Book of Common Order into Gaelic, despite his inclusion of several revisions which might have nettled contemporaries, especially his limitation of the laity's role in local church government and his inclination toward what would later be known as 'Erastianism'.[11] This latter point will receive greater attention in the following chapter.

By the time Carswell died in summer 1572 more Protestants were being presented to episcopal sees. This turn of events offered to the kirk an alleviation of the considerable financial difficulty experienced since 1560. The first Book of Discipline sought to reverse the alienations of kirk revenues and thereby provide for parish ministers, the poor, and the education of the young.[12] Undoubtedly the discipline's financial innovations such as that which prohibited setting teinds in tack were ample grounds to ensure its rejection by those nobles whose wealth was clearly threatened. The crown, too, was in straitened circumstances, and thus in December 1561 it was determined that benefice holders would disburse one-third of their income to the crown, from which the kirk would then receive its operating funds, particularly ministerial stipends.[13] Knox described the arrangement in these terms: 'I see two parts freely given to the Devil, and the third must be divided betwix God and the Devil'.[14] He fully expected that soon enough the devil would possess the entirety. In fact, the arrangement, designed only as 'a temporary expedient',[15] proved unsatisfactory and the kirk began to petition for the right to control presentations to benefices. This meant in effect a plan to take over the old ecclesiastical machinery, substituting reformed benefice holders for papists and laymen. The general assembly stipulated in June 1563 'that when anie benefice sall vaike, qualified persons may be presented to the Superintendent of the province, where the benefice vaiketh, that they may be admitted in the places destitute'.[16] But without the state's countenance of this programme of presentation a patron might continue to present his own men to benefices without regard for their ecclesiastical aptitudes or the approval of the kirk and its authorised officers. Thus were remained a deep rift between possession of kirk revenue and the exercise of spiritual responsibility.[17] However, by act of parliament in December 1567 it was made law that superintendents and commissioners only were to admit to benefices, while presentation was left with the patrons[18] — perhaps the best compromise the kirk could hope for given the unsettled conditions.

In all these transactions there was no hint of any suppression of the old bishoprics, and the general assembly reacted strongly against the secularisation of Orkney when Adam Bothwell exchanged its revenues for those of Holyrood Abbey.[19]

We must now attempt to account for the state's desire to have bishops. First, with the abolition of papal jurisdiction in 1560 the state's right of patronage was given free rein; thus it could appoint whomever it wished to benefices. This expanded the power of patrons by which they controlled the hierarchical social structure of Scotland. The magnate was able to reward his faithful servants and ensure future loyalty by securing prelacies which would henceforth be occupied by the compliant who would in turn grant lesser benefices to the patron's candidates. Second, a revivified episcopate would ensure the continued viability of the ecclesiastical estate in parliament where once again compliant men would be good servants of their secular lords. Third, it might be expected that bishops and other prelates would reward their patrons with generous pensions and tacks. This would have merely followed pre-Reformation precedent. Gordon Donaldson has resisted a too ready condemnation of the Protestant bishops of the 1570s on this ground, claiming that they were lesser villains than their Catholic predecessors.[20] James Kirk argues, however, that the whole episcopal programme arose from the financial exigencies of the anti-Marians during the years of civil strife. Thus the appointments of Douglas and Porterfield, adherents of Morton and Glencairn, to the archbishoprics, fit in well with the pattern of financial advantage.[21] Fourth, the polity of crown-appointed bishops offered a state-directed kirk that might well prove to be thoroughly obsequious.[22] Magnates generally had no love for outspoken preachers. Finally, episcopacy according to the English pattern was attractive to the Anglophile party led by the earl of Morton who sought for Scotland that ecclesiastical government by magistrate and bishop then established in England.[23]

There were signs of increasing tension in church-state relations during summer 1571, reflecting perhaps some premonition of the government's plans. Bannatyne recorded a letter sent by a wide group of Protestants to the regent in which they complained about the financial distress of the kirk. Not only the Marians were denounced as 'enemies to Christ Jesus', but also those who 'deface the ministrie of his blissed evangle' by pressing the admission of 'dumb dogis to the office, dignitie, and rentis appointed for sustentatioune of preiching pastoris, and for uther godly uses'. Genuine ministers had been reduced by these alienations to a status lower than that of beggars and must see their families 'sterve for hunger'. The thirds had been wrongfully seized, and warning was given to the guilty 'that God can nocht lang delay to powre furth his just venegeance for this proud contempt of his servantis'.[24] Not only were God's true ministers subverted through poverty, they were being supplanted by earls and lords who received bishoprics and abbacies while 'gentlmen, courteouris, babes, and persons unable to guyde thaim selves, ar promoted by you to sic benefices as requyre learned preicheris'. Final caution was given that failure to rectify the tragic circumstances of the kirk would lead to a weakening 'of the mutuall contract that God hes placed betwixt the supreme power and the subjectis'.[25]

The ultimate possibility of a Protestant primate emerged in April 1571 when John Hamilton was hanged on account of his political misdeeds.[26] On 6 August the rector of the University of St. Andrews, John Douglas, one of the authors of the first Book of Discipline, was appointed to the see of St. Andrews[27] by Morton who held the archbishopric in repayment of his ambassadorial expenses.[28] The bruit of this anticipated event may have provided the impetus to cause Knox to write to the general assembly a stern letter of warning; 'Unfaithfull and traitours to the flock sall ye be before the Lord Jesus, if that, with your consent, directilie or indirectlie, ye suffer unworthie men to be thrust into the ministrie of the Kirk, under quhat pretence that ever it be'. He called also for vigilance against 'the mercilesse devorers of the patrimonie of the Kirk'.[29] The assembly read the letter with approbation and cautioned superintendents and commissioners to take care when they admitted to benefices since they would be accountable for their choices to God and the kirk.

The assembly commissioned a group to seek redress from the regent concerning abuses such as the improper disposition of benefices and misappropriation of the kirk's properties.[30] But it would appear that, despite Lennox's acquiescence, the subsequent parliament repudiated the petitions and subjected the ministers to abuse. Worst of all, wrote Bannatyne, was Morton, 'who rewled all, [and] said he sould lay thair pryde, and put order to thame, with mony other injurious wordis'.[31] Thus, when youthful John Davidson criticised Morton's policy in his 'Ane Dialog or Mutuall talking betuix a Clerk and ane Courteour concerning foure Parische Kirks till ane Minister',[32] he was brought to book and eventually entered exile in England and then on the Continent.[33] There is also a story to the effect that Morton tortured and executed a minister who denounced him.[34]

Archbishop Douglas found himself between two millstones. As archbishop he was a voting member of the ecclesiastical estate in parliament, but John Winram commanded him not to vote with the kirk's voice 'till he sould be admitted be the kirke, undir the paine of excommunicatioune. Mortoun commandit him to voit (as bischope of Sanct Androis), undir the paine of treasone'.[35] Thus far there was no complaint about the appointment of an archbishop, but until he was subjected to the Kirk's examination he must not arrogate to himself any ecclesiastical function, including a vote in parliament. This was particularly significant, for it suggested that some elements within the kirk were prepared to claim the entire pre-Reformation ecclesiastical constitution — unencumbered by secular controls — and to restore to itself the full spectrum of right and jurisdiction.

Douglas ran into more heavy weather in November. He had attempted to lift some of the revenue pertaining to the archbishopric but had been inhibited by the kirk-appointed collector of thirds, the reason being, on Bannatyne's account, that Douglas held office only through the auspices of Morton, 'without ony consent, assent, or admissione of the kirke'[36] — *i.e.*, he was a mere titular. Again the unfortunate Douglas was caught in a church-state battle, this time concerning the jurisdiction over ecclesiastical revenue. Morton, probably the real power in Scotland though not yet regent, reacted by discharging the collectors, claiming they had failed to pay poor ministers their allotted stipends and to provide the royal household with its portion of the thirds.

The unilateral appointment of archbishops precipitated the writing of a famous letter on 10 November 1571 by John Erskine, superintendent of Angus and the Mearns and laird of Dun. Respectful but undaunted, he addressed himself to the regent Mar, delineating his position upon the whole matter of polity and patrimony.

Erskine stated the principle that teinds were joined to the spiritual office of word and sacraments, *ergo* benefices established upon teinds were ecclesiastical offices. He grounded his second principle in the pastoral epistles of the New Testament wherein the bishop and superintendent must examine and admit men to 'benefices and offices of spirituall cuire, whatsoever benefice it be, alsweill bischoprikis, abbacies, and priories, as uther inferiour benefices'.[37] The contemporary overseer of ministers, known by whatever name, succeeded to Timothy and Titus who were enjoined to examine the fitness of men before admitting them to office. Erskine then enunciated what amounted to a statement of divine right episcopacy:

> To take this power fra the bischope or superintendent, is to take away the office of ane bischope, that no bischope be in the kirke; whilk wer to alter and abolishe the ordore that God has appointed in his kirke. [38]

This order was distorted when magisterial power, ordained of God to operate in its own proper sphere, intruded into the spiritual affairs of the realm, just as Jeroboam of old did when he made priests, 'whereupon followed destructioune of that king and his seid' — a thinly veiled threat directed toward Morton and other secular lords who sought to impose their own will upon the kirk.

Erskine declared the kirk's responsibility to withstand the heinous wrong perpetrated against it: 'Ane gritter offence or contempt of God and his kirke can no prince do, then to set up be his authoritie men in spirituall offices, as to creat bischopis and pastoris of the kirke'. [39] For to deny the kirk its liberty to govern its own offices was to negate the *esse* of the church. Apparently the reformed kirk was no more willing to sanction secular appointment of spiritual officers than was the Roman. By his protest Erskine was not seeking to terminate patronage whereby secular lords might present candidates for benefices. What he sought to safeguard was the kirk's jurisdiction in the examination and subsequent admission of candidates. Furthermore, perhaps by way of allaying aristocratic fears, Erskine wrote that the kirk was not unwilling to contribute financially toward the upkeep of the realm, but first the ministry must be paid.

With the return of kirk-approved bishops another problem was seen to arise. What would happen if a bishop were erected where a superintendent had previously been inaugurated? As far as Erskine was concerned the kirk was already episcopal: 'I understand ane bischop or superintendent to be but ane office; and whair the one is the uther is'. However, in the present circumstances the bishops had no ecclesiastical right, and thus it was the superintendents who continued to bear the kirk's authority, 'and the uther bischopis, so called, hes no office nor jurisdictione in the kirk of God, for thai enter not be the doure, but be ane uther way, and thairfoir ar not pastoris, as sayis Christ, but theivis and rubbaris'. [40] Erskine's comments did not contradict his earlier approbation of episcopacy. His concern was jurisdictional — bishops must submit themselves to the kirk's procedures for admission whereby the kirk was sustained in its divinely given freedom. State admission of a bishop to an authentic function in the kirk was an impossibility.

The preceding parliament had, in giving votes to bishops (St. Andrews and Orkney were noted as present[41]), acted against the kirk and in contempt of God. [42] Thus the kirk would complain to God, its own members, 'and to all reformed kirkis within Europe'. As for those avaricious persons who would bring down outspoken ministers, 'lat sic men understand, of whatsoever estait thei be, that the ministeris of Godis kirke has receavit ane office of God above thaim, whairunto thai aucht to be subject and obedient'. [43] Erskine concluded with 'Ane admonitione of David to Kingis and Magistratis', culled from Psalm 2:10-12:

> Be wyse, O ye kyngis; be warned, ye that are judges of the earthe. Serve the Lord with feir, and rejoyse befoir him with reverence. Kis the Sonne, least the Lord be angrie, and so ye pereis from the rycht way; ffor his wraith salbe shortly kendled. [44]

Despite Erskine's pessimistic rejection of an offer from the regent to meet on 16 November, some gathering did take place. Alexander Hay, writing on 14 December to John Knox, indicated that a conference had been held between representatives of kirk and state 'for agriement in materis twiching the policie of the kirke and dispositioun of benefices. The matter is differit till the viii of Januar'. [45] Erskine seems to have been eventually won over, and at the regent's request he wrote letters to the superintendents and other representatives of the kirk to deal with the question of money for the royal household taken from the thirds, 'and for creating of the said Mr Johne Douglas to be bischope of Sanct Androis'. [46]

The meeting, later accounted a genuine assembly of the kirk, [47] though never accorded the parliamentary ratification it was intended to receive, [48] commenced at Leith on 16 January 1572. Morton and Erskine were among those commissioned on either side to deal 'anent all matters tending to the ordering and establishing of the policy of the Kirk' [49] — with a view toward conformity with England. [50] The various articles of agreement concerned the disposition of prelacies, particularly the bishoprics. It was stipulated, for the foreseeable future at least, that the titles of archbishop and bishop would remain, similarly the traditional diocesan boundaries instead of the revamped superintending dioceses. Candidates were to fulfil 'the qualiteis specifeit in the Epistlis of Paule to Timothe and Tytus,' [51] presumably the character definitions in I Timothy 3:1-7 and Titus 1:7-9; they must also be at least thirty years of age. Their spiritual jurisdiction was not to exceed that of the superintendents, and the conciliar nature of their work was safeguarded, or so it was hoped, by provision for chapters of 'lernit ministers', at least six in number, to assist them while they were to be subject to the general assembly 'in spiritualibus'. In recognition of the fact that the bishops were also temporal officers, it was established that 'in temporalibus' they were beholden to the crown. This was straightforward, but it left unresolved the matter of the parliamentary vote [52] — whether the bishops must consult the assembly before exercising this right. Obviously the kirk thought that those voting in the ecclesiastical estate were not private individuals but servants of the general assemblies. Thus in August 1573 the bishop of Dunkeld was delated for voting 'anent the Act of Divorcement made in prejudice of the Assembly who had suspended their judgement in this matter till farther advisement'. [53]

The concordat of Leith provided various forms for making bishops and even refusing unacceptable candidates. Provision was made for royal presentations, [54] and one wonders whether the regent Mar and his associates seriously anticipated use of the form, 'In cais the Persoun nominat be not found qualifiet'[55] or of the 'Licence to Cheis',[56] whereby chapters might proceed to free elections.

It remains a confusing episode. Clearly the kirk achieved a written recognition of some of its concerns, particularly the right to examine candidates for the episcopate and to take account of the work of bishops before the superior court of the general assembly. This and the provision for chapters upheld the conciliar intentions of a reformed episcopate in continuity with the superintendency of the preceding decade. Unlike the superintendents, though, the bishops held the traditional endowments including the temporalities[57] which the kirk assumed would be used for its own work. However, the state made certain inroads as may be seen in the oath: 'Efter the Consecratioun, the new maid bischop sall compeir befoir the Kingis Majestie or his Regent, and mak his ayth, as follows'.[58] The oath of episcopal office recognised the crown's superiority not only in temporal affairs but also 'in the conservatioun and purgatioun of the religioun'. The bishop promised to remain loyal and obedient to the crown, and more, he also acknowledged 'to have and hald the said bischoprik and possessionis of the same, under God, only of youre Majestie and croun Royale of this youre realme'.

This obviously political concordat contained something for everyone and permitted the state to believe it had confirmed its power over the kirk, while the kirk could congratulate itself upon having safeguarded its liberty and independence. Of course, this possibility of divergent interpretations implied not only some degree of immediate peace but also future conflict. For the moment, however, the kirk was by no means fundamentally dissatisfied with a renewed and reformed episcopate.

Pursuant to the terms of the concordat of Leith, Morton proceeded to St. Andrews 'for the chousing of ane new archbischope'.[59] John Douglas, still the earl's nominee, gave proof of his preaching and was then elected by the archdiocesan chapter, 'notwithstanding that mony of the godly ministeris wer against it; and George Scot, minister of Kirkaldie, tuike ane instrument that he condescendit not, etc.'.[60] John Knox refused to share in the inauguration, perhaps because of his fear of the influence of the universities in the kirk,[61] and also because the aged Douglas was incapable of handling responsibility 'quhilk twentie [men] of the best gifts could nocht bear', but not because Knox opposed bishops in general, despite James Melville's assertion that he 'opponit him selff directlie and zealuslie'.[62] In fact Knox called for all the sees to be filled with qualified men,[63] and he complained when the revenues for the diocese of Ross were granted to lord Methven during a vacancy.[64] Nevertheless, in place of Knox John Winram performed the inauguration following the order for making a superintendent, conceivably an unpleasant duty as Douglas's office had in some degree supplanted that of the superintendent of Fife. Then Robert Stewart, bishop of Caithness, John Spottiswood, superintendent of Lothian, and David Lindsay, minister of Leith and commissioner for Kyle, 'laid thair hands and embraced the said rector, Mr Johne Douglas, in taiken of admissione to the bischopricke'.[65] As in the case of the superintendents appointed ten years earlier, this was no traditional episcopal consecration grounded in the belief that only bishops can make bishops.[66] The kirk

saw no need to assure itself of an Anglican-style apostolic succession in the
episcopate.

From the beginning there was a jurisdictional assimiliation of 'lauchfull
Archebischoppis Bischoppis Superintendentis and Commissionairis'[67] in the eyes
of both kirk and state. But the elevation of bishops with ecclesiastical powers led to
an overlapping of geographical areas as had been foreseen in Erskine's correspondence — who would have priority? The problem arose immediately because St.
Andrews was a sprawling diocese that included at least portions of the superintending dioceses of Lothian, Fife, and Angus and the Mearns, thereby calling into
doubt the status of John Spottiswood, John Winram, and John Erskine. At the
March 1572 assembly they were continued in office 'as of befoir in the provinces
not yet subject to the Archbischoprick of Sanct Androes' and directed to help as
called upon.[68] At the subsequent assembly in August the priority of the archbishop was upheld though Douglas would have responded negatively to the question
set before that assembly, 'Whether shall the Superintendents Jurisdiction expire
or not'.[69] Recognising the great dimensions of his diocese, he requested the
assistance of superintendents,[70] and in 1574 the archbishop of Glasgow was
granted the assistance of two commissioners in view of the vast expanse of that
diocese.[71] On the other hand the superintendents, who had long sought relief from
their duties, asked to be excused from visitation in those areas pertaining to the
bishoprics.[72] This reasoning could also operate in reverse order. When in August
1573 James Paton of Dunkeld was accused of failing to perform the work of a
bishop, he argued that he was innocent of any wrong because of the presence of a
superintendent in the diocese, and thus there was no necessity for him to
undertake any episcopal duties.[73]

Despite the fact that the assembly upheld the rights of bishops, this did not
mean that the superintendents were utterly disregarded. When Douglas admitted
to the ministry a papist whom he believed had recanted, the assembly sent the
priest back to Spottiswood who had previously inhibited him from entering the
ministry of the reformed kirk.[74] The superintendent of Lothian must be the one to
re-examine the man. As superintendent of Angus John Erskine was engaged by
the general assembly as a tutor for the young bishop of Brechin who was enjoined
to accompany Erskine on visitation, 'that he may see the order and proceeding
used by the Superintendent in his office'.[75]

The bishops were tried just like superintendents and commissioners. Not only
were they admonished to be present at assemblies lest they appear unfit for
office,[76] but an act of assembly was passed identifying the place of the bishops:

> The Kirk presentlie assemblit hes concludit, That the same sall not exceid the
> jursidictioun of Superintendentis, quhilk heirtofoir they have had and presentlie hes;
> and that they salbe subject to the discipline of the Generall Assemblie as members
> therof, as the Superintendents hes bein heirtofor in all sorts.[77]

At the same time, the conciliar nature of the office was strengthened by the proviso
that admissions to the ministry should take place only with the help of three other
ministers, while at the next assembly bishops, superintendents, and commission-

ers were cautioned that negligence whether in 'visitation, doctrine or life' could lead ultimately to permanent deprivation.[78]

At the beginning of the Leith episcopate the kirk pressed for fulfilment of the terms of the concordat. In August 1573 Morton was petitioned to fill vacant sees, though it was allowed that the problem was the residue from an earlier regime when livings had been given into the hands of noblemen. Where bishops were not yet elected, commissioners should be erected as an interim measure.[79] One year later the petition was renewed: 'Because there are sundry Bischopricks vacand, such as Dumblaine, Rosse and others, That his grace wald take order that some qualified persons be provided thereto with diligence'.[80]

Thus it may be seen that the kirk accepted the settlement and tried to make it work, perhaps with an eye toward the reforming bishops of the 1560s but with greater subjection to kirk discipline and more ample attention to the authentic ecclesiastical nature of episcopacy. There were problems, as will be seen in greater detail below, but there is also evidence of some success in the presence of as many as six bishops at the general assembly[81] and in the appearance of the archbishop of Glasgow as moderator of the March 1575 assembly.[82]

The bishops appointed in the 1570s came to be known by contemporaries as 'tulchans', a derogatory term meaning 'calfis' skinnes stuffed with stra, to cause the cow giff milk; for everie lord gat a bischoprie, and sought and presented to the kirk sic a man as wald be content with least, and sett them maist of fewes, takes, and pensiones'.[83] Donaldson's defence of these bishops compares them favourably to pre-Reformation and Elizabethan episcopates. He admits that they were dilapidators, but doubts whether there were genuine 'simoniacal' pactions' or substantial reservations made at the time of appointment.[84] But certainly the kirk was worried about this issue. Already there had been the transfer of the episcopal lands and revenues of Orkney to lord Robert Stewart, and Alexander Gordon of Galloway had conveyed his see's temporalities to his son John in 1568.[85] It comes as no surprise, then, to read that John Douglas was asked at his consecration whether he had impaired the revenues of his see through an unlawful arrangement. He responded, 'That none was nor suld be made'.[86] The kirk's fear, nonetheless, seemed to find justification in the rumours and suspicions surrounding James Paton who became bishop of Dunkeld in 1572.[87] At the August 1573 assembly it was recorded, 'That he was suspect of Simonie committed betwixt him and the Earle of Argill, anent the profite of the Bishopricke; and suspected of perjury in receiving of the said Bishoprik, because he giveth acquittances, and the Earle receiveth the Silver of the said Bishoprick'.[88] One year following he admitted he had been forced to grant Argyll 'certain pensions forth of the Bishoprick' but maintained he had since repudiated them,[89] and in March 1575 stated that he had refused to make a paction when asked for one.[90] This led bishop Alexander Campbell of Brechin, not without his own reputation as a dilapidator,[91] to enter the fray, complaining that Paton had slandered the now departed Argyll, his kinsman. Paton retorted that he could make good his accusation.

The tangled affair arose again in August 1575 when Paton confessed to the assembly that he had set some victual in tack to Argyll, and it was demanded why he ought not to be deprived for dilapidating his benefice.[92] Denied a delay in the case, Paton said that he had not dealt voluntarily with Argyll 'and that divers tymes it repented him therof.'[93] He had asked the regent to sort out the affair for him, and upon the regent's request the assembly then agreed to defer the case until the next assembly. Finally in April 1576 the dénouement came. Paton defended himself by saying that the act against feuing passed in 1569[94] was directed toward ministers not bishops, and, perhaps with more hope of success, that what he had done was motivated by 'a most just fear, which might fall on a most constant man, his house being beseiged, and his son taken away'.[95] But the assembly was less impressed by the defence than by the alienation for nineteen years of thirty-six chalders of victual and proceeded to deprive him, though apparently not by a unanimous vote. Dunkeld appealed to Morton, but without avail; he found no fault with the process, noting only that a set procedure should be laid down.[96] The bishop had still not remedied the dilapidation in 1580,[97] but he was presumably set free from his yoke when in 1584 he was removed to make way for the restoration of the see's revenues to the former Catholic bishop, Robert Crichton.[98]

An even more convoluted history is that of George Douglas, bishop of Moray. Elected at the end of 1573,[99] he was accused at the March 1574 assembly of fornication.[100] But not only was *he* under suspicion, the chapter which elected him also came under review for its apparent failure to assess his fitness with proper diligence. It was even objected that he could not be tried as a bishop because it was unclear whether 'he be Bishop lawfully chosen or not'.[101] Moray did not deny his sin and even agreed to confess it again,[102] but the case dragged on, compounded by another complaint that he lacked a congregation of his own, and at one point he was at the horn for some undefined offence.[103] As late as October 1576 neither bishop nor chapter had cleared their names before the assembly[104] but the bishop seems to have survived this confusion and suspicion, for he appeared in the minutes of assembly in July 1579, if only to be delated for his absence.[105]

Moray's lack of a particular parochial charge was not unique. Boyd of Glasgow, admitting the fact, defended himself by declaring he had been given none at the time when he entered office.[106] Dunkeld was accused, perhaps unjustly in view of the intimidation to which he was subjected, of non-residence,[107] while charges of failure to visit and preach sufficiently were, as with the superintendents, commonplace.[108] The archbishop of Glasgow excused his failure to perform his ecclesiastical duties on account of the 'temporall affairs of the Bishoprick'.[109] He may have taken his life in his hands when he protested that his lack of preaching reflected his want of divinely given ability, for preaching 'is the good gift of God, which is not equally bestowed on all'.[110]

Dunkeld found that the assembly's bite was as severe as its bark not only in affairs of revenue but also when its disciplinary directives met with non-compliance. He had been ordered to excommunicate the earl of Atholl and his wife, and when he failed to act the assembly of March 1574 ordered him to preach a sermon confessing his fault in his cathedral.[111] In August he was again commanded to proceed, on pain of suspension.[112] Finally, after some delay in order to grant Atholl a conference with the godly to resolve his doubts about the reformed faith[113] Dunkeld was suspended at the August 1575 assembly for his failure,[114] even before his deprivation for dilapidation. He may have had an excuse, that of fear, as in the other affair, for those delegated to pronounce the sentence in the bishop's place were told to do so in Dunkeld, 'and if they be stopped, or troubled there, that they may not pronounce the same, to execute and pronounce the samen in Sanct Johnstoun'.[115]

It appears that the episcopal settlement of 1572 was subject not only to the same terminology and geography as the pre-Reformation episcopate, but also to similar problems — non-residency, dilapidation, failure to supervise the diocese properly, scandal, intimidation, and even where the spirit was willing the body was too weak to fulfil the onerous duties pertaining to diocesan care. And a brief survey of appointments following the concordat of Leith indicates continuity with pre-1572 appointments, *i.e.*, bishops were advanced on the basis of kinship with the magnatial families of Scotland. Observing episcopal sees in the 1570s (including titulars),[116] one finds Campbells in Argyll (1580), Brechin (1566), and the Isles (1572); Galloway witnessed a succession of Gordons, including two sons of Alexander; St. Andrews (1572) and Moray (1573) were occupied by Douglases; Glasgow went briefly to John Porterfield (1571)[117] and then to James Boyd (1573), both of them clients of Glencairn whose family name was Cunningham, while David Cunningham was elevated to the see of Aberdeen (1577). Dunblane went to a Graham (1575) and Ross to a Hepburn (1576). Besides Alexander Campbell of Brechin, carryovers from earlier decades included, at one time or another, a Hamilton in Argyll and a Stewart in Caithness, while another Stewart received the revenue of Orkney though the title belonged to Adam Bothwell. James Boyd of Glasgow, David Cunningham of Aberdeen,[118] Alexander Campbell of Brechin, and John Campbell of the Isles seem to have been of lairdly descent; in all likelihood Andrew Graham of Dunblane was the son of the laird of Morphie.[119] George Douglas of Moray was a natural son of Angus. He played a prominent role in the murder of David Riccio, and took the regent Moray's side against Mary at the York conference in 1568.[120] John Douglas was principal of St. Mary's College and rector of the University of St. Andrews. James Paton was presented to Dunkeld by gift,[121] and despite the lack of any obvious ties to an aristocratic family this pathetic and beleaguered man proved easy game for the pressure tactics of Argyll and Atholl. Though several of these men had some pastoral experience, they attained their offices not by aptitude but by attachment. None were the free choices of chapters, and none were prominent pastors in the kirk.

These observations are not intended to imply that a man of high birth could not serve the kirk well. One need only look to superintendent John Erskine, the laird of Dun, or to James Boyd of Trochrig, archbishop of Glasgow, to find examples of those who devoted themselves to the good cause. But it remains the case that the episcopate predicated upon the concordat of Leith continued to reflect the structure and interests of the magnatial families of the realm. And therein lay a great part of the cause of episcopal collapse in the later 1570s. Those who controlled the election of bishops made no consistent effort to ensure that their candidates were the sort of men who would nurture the kirk. Other interests were foremost, and so usually the bishops of the 1570s met at best a minimum standard of acceptability, hence the continued wrangling over qualifications throughout the decade. The fact is that if the kirk had depended upon its bishops to shepherd and feed it through the 1570s it would have wandered aimlessly before finally starving to death. The basis for an anti-episcopal reaction in the later years of the decade is not shrouded in mystery. Episcopacy could never function properly under the existing conditions because there was no means of divorcing it from the ambitions of the magnates. So long as they controlled the bishoprics, the kirk could not be its own master. Thus even apart from the developing ideological concerns, kirkmen, who may actually have favoured episcopal polity, had ample reason to give up hope that the kirk could be well managed by bishops. Its only future was with another polity.

Clearly then, the Leith settlement was a failure. It need not have been so, but the self-interest of Morton and his cronies, compounded by the growth of a new anti-episcopal ideology in the kirk, spelled doom. As early as August 1572 the general assembly had expressed its dissatisfaction with certain titles such as archbishop, dean, archdean, chancellor, and chapter, 'quhilks names were found slanderous and offensive to the ears of many of the brethren, appeirand to sound to papistrie'.[122] A disclaimer followed to the effect that their acceptance for the present implied no consent to anything papistical or superstitious, and the assembly suggested some substitutions: archbishop to become simply bishop, chapter to become the bishop's assembly, and dean the moderator thereof. Furthermore, the whole arrangement, it was protested, was received only 'as ane interim, untill farder and more perfyte ordeur be obtainit at the hands of the Kings Majesties Regent and Nobilitie'.[123] Nor was the regent Morton wholly satisfied. Writing to Robert Campbell in January 1574, he expressed his wish that 'in this tyme of repose quhilk God hes grantit us, efter our lang troubles, we be cairfull for the gude ordour and provisioun of the Policie of the Kirk in thingis ambiguouss and irresolute, or not heirtofore weill observit and execute'.[124] To that end there should be called, before the next general assembly scheduled for March, a gathering of the nobles, estates, and barons to settle 'the Policie of the trew Reformit Kirk, to the lesting repose thairof, and commoun weill of the realme'.[125] Though one year late, a convention in March 1575 with Glasgow, Caithness, Moray, Orkney, Galloway, Dunkeld, and Brechin in attendance, declared that 'thair is not to this day ony perfyte policie' in the kirk, and this had resulted in a variety of problems with the promise of more to come 'gif tymous remeid be not providit'. Thus a committee was appointed to frame a polity 'maist aggreabill to the trewth of goddis word and maist convenient for the estate and people of this realm',[126] to be reported to the next convention and eventually made law.

Apparently nothing came of this directive, but clearly, changes were called for, and in the absence of conclusive state action the kirk began to create its own new order by tightening the procedure for episcopal elections, by establishing a new form of oversight, and finally by calling into question the entire concept of episcopacy.

The process used to appoint bishops had, in harmony with the articles of 1572, permitted crown or other nomination to be followed by examination by the appropriate chapter, issuing either in election or rejection. This process had been circumvented in the case of James Paton, and in George Douglas's instance the chapter of the see of Moray had permitted an incompetent to slip through the net. Therefore in the case of Andrew Graham, elect of Dunblane, it was decided at the assembly in March 1575 to examine this non-preacher then and there. [127] Indeed the chapter members who were able to be present were invited to hear his handling of a biblical text, but he would also be heard by bishops, superintendents, and ministers, particularly those of Edinburgh. [128] It may be that the kirk was still undecided whether a bishop must first be a preacher, but what else could he be in a reformed kirk, and how else could he fulfil the biblical qualifications imposed by the concordat of 1572, especially that of the teaching bishop depicted in the pastoral epistles? [129] Graham must have proved himself to his listeners' satisfaction for he thereafter appeared among the bishops without any protest. Alexander Hepburn of Ross had to undergo the like process following which 'the brethren with one consent approved the said exercise and doctrine, and praised God for the same'. [130] However, some question must have remained, as John Spottiswood was later in trouble for inaugurating Hepburn despite advice from other ministers to refrain from so doing, possibly because of shortcomings in Ross's visitations. [131] The upshot of these unprecedented intrusions upon the jurisdiction of the chapters was a proposal in March 1575 to unilaterally amend procedures so that no chapter was to elect a bishop 'before he give proof of his doctrine before the Generall Assembly, and triall be taken be them of his doctrine, life and conversation'. [132]

Although the concordat of Leith was intended primarily as an interim solution to the problem of ecclesiastical endowment, the bishops produced by the articles were designed to be ecclesiastical personages — they were to share in the administration of the kirk, hence the considerable attention devoted to their character by the general assemblies. But they were too often negligent in their visitation, the essential aspect of the reformed episcopate whereby churches would be planted and nurtured through word, sacraments, and discipline. Whatever the personal shortcomings of the bishops, the office had proved to be excessively burdensome, not only for them but also for superintendents and commissioners. Under any title of visiting officer, visitation had never since the Reformation been established on a manageable and practicable basis. Therefore in April 1576 the general assembly divided up the land among 'Visitors of Countries', [133] without regard for the claims of existing bishops or superintendents upon specific geographical areas. The description of the visitor's office recalled the work of the superintendents [134] — in fact nothing new was proposed, only an attempt to recapture something that seemed in danger of vanishing. The visitor, appointed only until the next assembly, was 'to call the rest of the Ministers together within the bounds of his vistation, as also to hold Synodall Assemblies, to be Moderator there, to try the Ministers, and have the oversight of the schools; and he to be tried be this Assemblie', whence authority was derived. [135] Simply, this meant that the kirk had given up on the Leith episcopate, and that it regarded the agreement as a dead letter.

Parallel to the patent disenchantment with the outcome of the new episcopate were the murmurings of dissatisfaction with 'the said office and name of a Bischop' expressed in August 1575 by John Dury of Edinburgh. [136] Before then there had been expressions of concern *vis-à-vis* the problem of parity and superiority among the ministers, and episcopal figures had consistently been subjected to review and correction by the rest of the ministry. But from this point forward the concept of a more or less distinct episcopal order, even though mitigated in the Scottish context, was scrutinised and criticised with increasing clamour.

In response to Dury's concern the assembly appointed two teams to consider 'Whither if the Bischops, as they are now in the Kirk of Scotland, hes thair function of the word of God or not, or if the Chapiter appointit for creating them aucht to be tolleratéd in this reformed Kirk'.[137] On one side were John Craig of Aberdeen, James Lawson of Edinburgh, and Andrew Melville, principal of the University of Glasgow. On the other side were George Hay, commissioner of Caithness, David Lindsay of Leith, and John Row of Perth. Their report skirted the question whether or not Scottish episcopacy was derived from the Bible, though it did demand that bishops should at least bear 'sick qualities as the Word of God requyres',[138] otherwise to be tried again and deposed. A joint statement of clarification was issued under the heading, 'The poyntis quherin they aggrie concerning the office of ane Bischop or ane Superintendent', suggesting a contemporary readiness to join Erskine in an identification of the two offices. It was laid down that all pastors were bishops; beyond this it was permissible for some pastors/bishops to be granted 'power to oversie and visite sick reasonable bounds, besydes his awin flocke, as the Generall Kirk sall appoint',[139] an allowance that was then amplified in accordance with the superintendency.

Although the committee avoided direct confrontation, it was evident that there could be no accommodation between this ideal and the episcopate revived (in practice if not in theory) by the concordat of Leith with its non-preaching, dilapidating, and unfit bishops. The only means of preserving the office of oversight was the creation of commissioners for visitation.

At the next assembly held in April 1576, when the commissioners were erected, the paper on bishops was 'resolutelie approvit and affirmit', and supplemented with the demand that all bishops inform the assembly which individual cures they would accept as their own, an attempt to ensure, through coercion if necessary, that bishops would be pastors.[140]

The question arises here concerning the origins of anti-episcopal sentiment, or put positively, presbyterian theory. Necessarily one confronts the figure of Andrew Melville whom Gordon Donaldson has described as 'the presbyterian missionary to Scotland',[141] an assertion that has been resisted by James Kirk who has laboured to broaden the basis of early presbyterian sentiment and to present Melville as just one of the brethren.[142] This debate is not an integral aspect of the present theme, but what is important for this study is to look beyond the older Melville to Geneva whence he returned in mid-1574 after sitting for several years at the feet of Theodore Beza, Calvin's successor in Geneva and the informal head of international Calvinism.

Two years earlier (12 April 1572) Beza had been in correspondence with Knox and had counselled him against the re-introduction of bishops into the kirk:

But of this also, my Knox, which is now almost patent to our very eyes, I would remind yourself and the other brethren, that as Bishops brought forth the Papacy, so will false Bishops (the relicts of Popery) shall bring in Epicurism into the world. Let those who devise the safety of the Church avoid this pestilence, and when in process of time you shall have subdued that plague in Scotland, do not, I pray you, ever admit it again, however it may flatter by the pretence of preserving unity, which deceived even many of the best of those of former times. [143]

Then, at approximately the same time as the assembly's affirmation of the report on bishops, Glamis, lord chancellor of Scotland and a highly respected member of the kirk, wrote to Beza for advice on kirk polity. [144] He presented six queries relating to the perpetuation of the general assembly and limits of that body's jurisdiction, the nature of appropriate punishment for papists, the proper bases for excommunication, the disposition of ecclesiastical patrimony, and first and foremost, concerning the office of bishop.

In his reply Beza first offered some general observations on episcopacy before considering in more specific terms the questions proposed by Glamis. Beza's judgement was that there were three kinds of bishops — of God, of man, and of the devil. God's bishop was identical with the pastor, called to feed the church, and who helped to exercise authority in the church by meeting with the other ministers and elders or governors (as distinct from the pastors) in a body known as the eldership or seignory. Perhaps remarkably, in view of Beza's radical political theory which included the possibility of tyrannicide, he counselled that the bishop of God was to be subject even to a profane magistrate. [145]

The bishop of man was he who held greater powers than the rest of the ministers, but who was 'limited with certain orders or rules provided against tyranny'. [146] However, this enhancement of jurisdiction was not to be found in the New Testament where the only superiority was one of order, the president of the church assembly.

The devil's bishop was the second stage of deterioration from the original 'ordained of God'. [147] These bishops had exceeded the bounds and entered upon a tyrannical regime, arrogating to themselves power to elect, depose, and excommunicate. Against New Testament injunctions 'they have invaded uppon temporall dominions', [148] and usurped ecclesiastical revenues for the sake of ostentation. [149] Because these bishops had assumed the political pattern of the Roman Empire they now bore the image of the apocalyptic beast of Revelation 13. [150]

Glamis's question about bishops was a clear reflection of the political controversy then gathering steam in the kirk. He remarked that the question had been raised, in view of ministerial parity, whether bishops were truly required in order to maintain order in the kirk, or were the ministers able to perform this work among themselves without calling upon a superior kirkman? Nonetheless,

Two considerations can move us to the retention of bishops: one is the character and unruliness of the people, who can only with difficulty, if indeed at all, be retained in their duty unless constrained by the authority of bishops, who visit and inspect all the churches

— an argument also employed to request the appointment of a superintendent. The second consideration was the constitutional one of whether the bishops, as 'one of the three orders and estates of the realm', should be present in parliaments and conventions.[151]

Beza, in accord with his preliminary remarks on the three kinds of bishops, called for the abolition of episcopacy by godly princes who 'mind the reformation of the church and their own safety'.[152] It would not do to keep even the bishop of man because the lesson of history was that of his decline into the third type, the devil's bishop. Superiority of bishops was directly proportional to ecclesiastical decay. Beza's only concession was that the present bishops might be allowed by the sovereign to retain their revenues 'to keep the common peace',[153] but he would have nothing to do with Glamis's two considerations in favour of episcopacy. Order in the church would be better preserved by preaching, by discipline shared by church and state, and by visitation conducted under the auspices of the eldership. As for the parliamentary concern, the civil function of bishops was 'contrary to the Word, and therefore in our mind is to be utterly abolished; for the bishop hath nothing to do in ordering of mere civil affairs'. Of course the seignories might send advisers especially when church affairs were — legitimately, Beza granted — being discussed by godly magistrates following Old Testament precedents, but these were to act only 'as their elderships have given them in charge'.[154] In place of bishops Beza formulated what might be termed a consistorial or presbyterian polity for the church, predicated upon the parity of ministers and a graduated series of church courts, including 'a general council of the land', though for 'great causes' rather than on a regular basis as the kirk practised.[155] Whether Andrew Melville imported and helped to impose this polity on the kirk, or else Beza's vision simply confirmed a tendency inherent in the kirk from the earliest days of the Reformation, it was in great part the shape of things to come.

The regent Morton was not unaware of the rumblings over polity emanating from the general assemblies, and in October 1576 a list of forty-two questions sent by him was presented.[156] The queries, dealing with polity, kirk finance, and the like, had at times a decidedly testy and even sarcastic tone, evincing a delight in certain inconsistencies in the direction the kirk had chosen for itself.[157] The assembly was asked about the lawfulness of various titles, including archbishop, bishop, superintendent, commissioner, and visitor, and the differences between these offices (no. 6). Glamis's constitutional concern reappeared: 'Who sall occupie the place of the Ecclesiastical Estate in the Kings Parliaments, Conventions and Counsels, and how mony' (no. 11), the implication being a dearth of bishops in time to come if the presbyterian juggernaut continued on its appointed course. The debate over confused jurisdictions emerged again when it was asked, 'Whether may a man be both a Bishop, and a Lord of the Seat' (no. 23). The crux of the matter, though, concerned the concordat of Leith: should it be continued, 'or altogether presently to be casten off and rejected' (no. 39)?

The insistence of the general assembly that bishops have charge of a particular flock and that in effect they surrender charge of their dioceses with the possible grant of a temporary visitation commission created some puzzlement and opposition. Graham of Dunblane and Hepburn of Ross accepted.[158] Boyd of Glasgow, however, asked the April 1576 assembly to leave him, for the present, without a charge, and, demonstrating the tension caused by the archbishop's two masters, he also requested that he should not be 'precluded of his office accustomed in the rest of the parts of his Diocie, and service of the King, conform to the first admission'.[159] At the next assembly Boyd, who generally was beyond reproach unlike some of his fellows, made what must be accounted a courageous response to the prevailing sentiments in the kirk. He reminded the assembly that 'the name, style, power and jurisdictioun of the Bischops' was to continue during the royal minority or until an act of parliament effected a legal amendment of the polity.[160] It was on these indubitably constitutional terms that the archbishop had entered his office, and were he to tamper with 'any thing pertaining to the ordour, manner, or priviledges, or power of the samein, I should be afrayit to incurre perjurie, and might be callit befor the Kings Majestie, for changing ane Member of his Estate'.[161] However, so far as he did not come into conflict with the original terms of his office, he would obey the assembly's wishes. For the moment this proved acceptable,[162] but his troubles were not over.

The year 1578 marked a watershed in that the kirk abandoned any episcopal element in its polity, apart from the office of temporary visitors,[163] presenting in that year its second Book of Discipline.[164] At the April assembly the title of bishop was more or less abolished, and henceforth all ministers were to be called by their names or else simply 'Brethren'.[165] Further steps were taken at the same assembly by which one is reminded of Beza's warning of the deterioration of the bishop of man into the bishop of the devil:

Forsameikle as ther is great corruption in the estate of Bischops, as they are presentlie made in this realme, quherunto the Kirk wold provyde some stay in tyme comeing, so farre as they may, *to the effect further corruption may be brydlit,*

no further bishops were to be elected before the subsequent assembly, and anyone participating in such an election did so 'under the paine of perpetuall deprivatioun from thair offices'.[166] Further discussion would follow at the next assembly. Two months later this act was 'extendit for all tymes to come, ay and quhill the corruptioun of the Estate of Bischops be alluterlie tane away'.[167] As for those bishops then in the kirk, it was prescribed that they submit to the assembly 'concernin the reformation of the corruption of that Estate of Bischops', with excommunication provided for the obdurate.[168] Andrew Graham made an immediate submission,[169] but once again James Boyd was not easily overawed by these peremptory ecclesiastical pronouncements. When summoned in October 1578 to submit 'for the reformation of the corruption of the state of a Bishop in his person', he replied that he did not know what the phrase meant.[170] He defended the 'name, office, and modest reverence borne to a Bischop, to be borne to a Bischop, to be lawful and allowable be the Scriptures of God', and declared that his twofold election by kirk and king rendered his 'calling and office lawful'. Not that he was unwilling to receive the assembly's reproof of his faults, but he recalled that the criterion for his judgement should be I Timothy 3, 'seing that place was appointit to me at my receipt, to understand therefra the dueties of a Bischop', a passage, it might be noted, that does not refer to oversight of a particular pastoral charge. This awkward bishop even defended his role in the estates as permissible and beneficial since he did his duty in accordance with biblical directives and the requirements of 'a weill reformit country'.[171] It is hardly necessary to add that these rationalisations were not accepted by the assembly which by then was long past any retraction or mollification of its anti-episcopal doctrines.

The episcopal corruptions in need of reform were summed up in eight articles.[172] Bishops must have charge of one flock; they must not augment their livings at the expense of other ministers, the schools, or the poor; they must not attempt to dominate the church courts; nor might they visit without commission. With respect to the civil sphere bishops were prohibited from accepting 'criminal jurisdictioun'; they might vote in parliament in the kirk's name only with its specific instruction; they must accept no lordly titles or temporal jurisdictions. This condition may have been directed specifically against Robert Stewart, bishop of Caithness, who in 1578 succeeded to the title earl of Lennox.[173] The articles accepted the presence of bishops in Scottish society, but if the Kirk could not utterly depose them and abolish their office, it would put rigid constraints upon their place in the kirk.

The condemnation of episcopacy was summed up in the second Book of Discipline which, though ready as early as 1577 in preliminary form,[174] was finally entered in the acts of assembly in April 1581.[175] Its advancement was in spite of a 1579 royal decree to cease meddling with the polity.[176] Thus the discipline's final approval was a unilateral act taken at a time when Scotland was ruled by the Lennox regime which was hardly amenable to a stridently reformed Protestantism despite the pretended conversion[177] of the new bearer of that title, Esmé Stewart. But the administration was not unwilling to temporise and did offer some assistance toward the creation of presbyteries.[178] Like its predecessor, however, the second Book of Discipline never acquired legal stature, and consequently James VI could write in June 1584 of the lack of 'a solide and stablished order of policie'.[179] All told, these events served only to muddy the waters for decades to come.

Even if one were to view the second Book of Discipline as the culmination of a process of radicalisation along the lines of Beza's model, it is still the case that there was a great deal of continuity between the new polity and the preceding two decades of the reformed experience in Scotland. James Kirk has shown that, of twenty-two committee members appointed to begin work on a new polity, only archbishop James Boyd, James Lawson, and Andrew Melville were not part of the class of 1560. All the rest had been engaged in the kirk's life from the earliest days of the Reformation.[180] However, Gordon Donaldson writes that apart from Robert Pont the presbyterian *leaders* were of a new generation, 'their dates of birth separated by almost two decades from those of most of the reformers'.[181] Several years later three stalwarts of the early reformed kirk would be blamed for encouraging ministers to abandon the discipline and accept the king's (episcopal) programme for the kirk. But at 1581 acquiescence in the presbyterian polity may be attributed to the failure of the 1572 concordat to resolve financial problems — in fact, it accomplished little more than a debasement of episcopacy — and to the sedulous efforts of a few outspoken presbyterians. Despite the loss of bishops, the second Book of Discipline could hardly be described as a thoroughgoing innovation in two of its three major thrusts — church-state relations, the patrimony of the kirk, and the internal government of the kirk.

The kirk claimed full spiritual jurisdiction for itself distinct from the power of the sword, although the two, when working properly, would find themselves in perfect harmony. 'For this power ecclesiasticall flowis immediatlic frome God and the Mediatour Chryst Jesus, and is spirituall, not having ane temporall heid in eirth bot onlie Chryst, the onlie spirituall king and governour of his kirk'.[182] This independence and distinctiveness entailed several corollaries: the secular power was, in ecclesiastical and spiritual concerns, subject to the direction and discipline of the kirk;[183] the two jurisdictions or kingdoms must not be united, *i.e.* confused, in one person;[184] the kirk was free to order its own affairs, to establish its own polity, and to convene when and where it wished.[185]

Second, the kirk after years of negotiation and denunciation was still plagued by financial problems. Thus the patrimony was claimed anew, to be restored in its entirety to its rightful ecclesiastical usages, its diversion being designated 'ane detestable sacralege befor God'.[186] The ends to which the kirk revenues should be appointed were four — the support of the ministry; other church officers including the doctors; the poor; and 'for reparatioun of the kirkis and utheris extraordinar chargis as ar profitable for the kirk and also for the commoun welth, gif neid require'.[187]

Certainly the discipline's financial ambitions were not new, and examples of similar opinion about the rights of the kirk over against the state can be found as far back as the Reformation,[188] though in the reformed kirk's infancy there was recognition of the need for assistance from the magistrate, for example in the appointment of superintendents. And even in the third major aspect of the new polity, that of the kirk's constitutional form, there were ample reminders of the past. A preaching and resident ministry and graduated church courts were familiar requirements of the kirk. The first discipline was insistent that even superintendents preach regularly, and from the beginning the kirk sought to settle ministers in every parish where they would feed the flock and administer discipline. Kirk sessions, provincial synods, and a national or general assembly were integral components of the reformed kirk. Thus there were few noteworthy features even here. The court of presbytery, which might obviate kirk sessions in areas of low population, appeared under the name of the eldership,[189] consisting in part of lay elders, also known as 'presendentis or governouris'.[190] Deacons appeared not as the first rung on the ladder of ministry but as lay officers charged with 'the collection and distributioun of the almous of the faithfull'.[191] Doctors were to teach but not to discipline or to administer the sacraments.[192] Most striking, however, though in step with opinions voiced by some during the 1570s, was the repudiation of hierarchy as expressed in the traditional role of the bishop. In the second Book of Discipline the bishop was identified with the pastor or minister[193] in a system of church government where, by divine appointment, there was equality of power among the ministers. Given that there were only four offices of service in the kirk (ministers, doctors, elders, deacons), 'all the ambitious titles inventid in the kingdome of antichryst and in his usurpit hierarchie . . . in ane word aucht to be rejectid'.[194] The authentic bishop cared for a particular flock,[195] in no way attempted to usurp authority over his peers, and submitted himself to correction by others.[196] The term might not even be reserved for visitors since visitation was not an 'ordinar office ecclesiasticall in the persone of ane man'.[197] Visitors were to be chosen by the presbyteries and would bear only a temporary commission.[198] Recognising that there were still some so-called bishops in Scotland having a tenuous relationship with the kirk, the general assembly therefore stated through its discipline that

> we desyr the bischoppis that now ar ather to aggrie with that ordour that Goddis word requiris thame and as the generall kirk will prescryve unto thame not passing that boundis nather in ecclesiasticall nor civile effairis or ellis to be deposit frome all functioun in the kirk.[199]

Thus at 1581 the kirk had determined that it would rid itself of the episcopal millstone. There was no refuge left, not even for titulars since feuars of church lands were subject to excommunication, those holding benefices must be qualified for church office, and no one might vote in parliament as a member of the ecclesiastical estate without special commission from the general assembly. The ecclesiastical estate, nevertheless, was not repudiated. As for superintendents, they simply vanished from the second Book of Discipline.

But the discipline was to prove unacceptable on all accounts — revenue, jurisdiction, and polity. Writing to Beza in 1579, Andrew Melville attributed opposition to nearly the whole of the nobility:

> They complain that, if the pseudo-episcopacy be abolished, the state of the kingdom will be overturned; if presbyteries be established, the royal authority will be diminished; if the ecclesiastical goods are restored to their legitimate use, the royal treasury will be exhausted. They plead that bishops, with abbots and priors, form the third estate in parliament; that all jurisdiction, ecclesiastical as well as civil, pertains solely to the king and his council, and that the whole of the ecclesiastical property should go into the exchequer.[200]

The battle lines were drawn, and it was not long before shows of strength began.

Two problems were apparent at the October 1581 general assembly. The one was the constitutional question posed by the kirk's anathematisation of episcopacy,

> quherunto is annexit also ane temporall jurisdictioun, quherin the Kirk is servit be voting in Parliament, assisting in his Hienes Counsell, contributioun in taxatiouns and sick lyke, What overture they wald shew, quherby the King be not prejudgit be the taking away of that Estate.[201]

It was evident, and would become more so, that no facile separation of church and state, of the two jurisdictions, could be made without a great upheaval in the structure of the realm. For too long the two kingdoms had been entwined, and no unilateral action on the part of the kirk would suddenly overthrow a status quo of such lengthy establishment.

The second area of difficulty was that of appointments to vacant sees, a right which the crown had by no means relinquished; in fact, on 28 October 1581 the king and the council declared their opinion that the terms of the concordat of 1572 'be continewit and followit out in tyme cuming', as per the original agreement.[202] Upon the death of archbishop James Boyd in 1581 the crown presented Robert Montgomery, minister of Stirling,[203] a nomination unpopular with all but the 'King, counsell and court'.[204] There were many complaints against this man, including personal faults[205] and doctrinal deviations.[206] Not only had he expressed indifference toward questions of polity, he took steps toward justifying episcopacy and denying the New Testament foundations of presbytery. The October 1581 assembly refrained, upon royal request, from proceeding further at that time in the matter of Montgomery's acceptance of the see,[207] but the kirk did admonish him 'not to middle with any uther office or functioun in the Kirk, namely, in aspyring to the Bischoprick of Glasgow, aganis the Word of God and actis of the Kirk, or vexe any of his brether to admitt him thereto', under threat of excommunication. Montgomery did not, however, cease and desist from his pursuit of the archbishopric,[208] and in spite of James's threat of horning the April 1582 assembly took all but the final step of pronouncement of his excommunication, grounded upon his doctrinal and behavioural faults along with 'manifest contempt of the ordinance of the Kirk, and stirring up of ane feareful schisme betwixt certaine of the Nobilitie and the Kirk'.[209] This reference to the nobility alluded to the bargain Montgomery had made with his benefactor Lennox whereby the former got the title and 800 merks while the latter took the remaining, larger, share.[210] The kirk could not abide any such pact, and thus it blamed the archbishop for creating trouble by putting it in an untenable position.

At the same time the privy council dealt with the Glasgow affair. Since the chapter had refused to follow the election procedure detailed at Leith and which was 'to stand and continew to his Hienes majoritie or consent of Parliament',[211] disposition of the see had reverted to the crown which might appoint any candidate it chose. Again, Montgomery was sheltered from any kirk process launched against his presentation to the archbishopric.[212] But on 10 June 1582 Montgomery was formally excommunicated by John Davidson who 'cut him of as a corrupt and rottin member'.[213] There were subsequent complaints about those persons continuing to associate with him,[214] to which Lennox replied, 'Whether the King or the Kirk were superiours?'[215] Lennox answered his own question in a proclamation issued on 13 July setting aside the kirk's sentence.[216] This only added to the kirk's concerns over state intrusions into the ecclesiastical jurisdiction.[217]

Whether it was this confrontation alone making the kirk increasingly obstreperous or the more congenial climes of a sympathetic administration following the Ruthven raid in August 1582, at the assembly held the following October a further attack was made upon bishops accusing them of neglect of word and sacrament, dilapidation of benefices, and arrogation to themselves of the collation to benefices.[218] Montgomery was even charged with having purchased the Stirling kirk's pastoral stipend for his young son.[219]

But in reality, Montgomery was only small game and a minor actor. In Patrick Adamson, though, the presbyterians found a wily, treacherous, and capable opponent.

CHAPTER 4

Patrick Adamson

In Patrick Adamson the crown had an ally, even though this archbishop of Saint Andrews (1576-1592) left an impression of vacillation and opportunism. His presbyterian contemporary James Melville wrote, after recording Adamson's death:

> Thus God delyverit his Kirk of a maist dangerus enemie, wha, if he haid bein endowit bot withe a comoun civill piece of honestie in his delling and conversation, he haid ma meanes to haiff wrought mischeiff in a kirk or countrey nor anie I haiff knawin or hard of in our yland.[1]

Adamson, also known as Coustane, Constance, etc.,[2] was born in Perth in 1527, the son of a baker.[3] He obtained his M.A. at St. Andrews and at the first general assembly (December 1560) was recognised as a man fit to minister.[4] Subsequently he assumed the charge of Ceres and was also commissioned 'to plant kirks from Dee to Aithan'.[5] In June 1564 he requested the kirk's leave to travel abroad 'for augmenting of his knowledge'.[6] The assembly unanimously refused its consent. But whether or not permission was finally granted, Adamson did in fact go abroad as tutor to a nobleman's son.

In France Adamson's literary predilections got him in trouble. In 1566 he published at Paris his *Genethliacum*,[7] congratulatory verses upon the birth of prince James of Scotland, wherein he made the Scottish sovereign ruler of France and England also. He spent six months in a French jail for his patriotic zeal,[8] and in that one mighty stroke he also aroused a furor in London. Elizabeth sought to move Mary to punish the offender and prohibit circulation of the book.[9] A correspondent of the English queen termed the *Genethliacum* 'this lewde and evill writing of Adamson the Scot',[10] who had, if nothing else, demonstrated the courtly mind of an ambitious ecclesiastic. In 1573 he wrote of his intention to court Elizabeth's goodwill, and in a brief poem published that year he referred to her as queen of England, France, and Ireland.[11] Bancroft advised him in 1591 to praise the queen more gaudily, though by then he was assured of good treatment in the event of travelling to England.[12]

Back in Scotland by 1570, Adamson began to practise law[13] and also acted as a chaplain to the regent.[14] In March he was presented to succeed George Buchanan as principal of St. Leonard's College but upon his failure to fulfil certain conditions the office reverted to Buchanan.[15] He was pressed by the assembly 'to enter again in the ministry, in respect of the good gifts that God had given him, and scarceness of ministers in diverse countries'.[16] He responded that he would give final answer to the next assembly on whether he would accede to the request or else leave the ministry altogether. In fact he did re-enter,[17] taking up the charge at Paisley,[18] but showing a concern for his financial affairs that might have raised a few eyebrows.[19]

Already disappointed ambition was disturbing Adamson's equilibrium. He had hoped, said Melville, to gain the archbishopric of St. Andrews from Morton at the time John Douglas was nominated.[20] Then, in a moment of frustration, he attacked episcopacy in a sermon wherein he described the papist 'My Lord Bishop', the tulchan 'My Lord's Bishop', and 'The Lord's Bishop' who was 'the trew Minister of the Gospell'. Apparently this pastoral zeal was short-lived as he was named at the August 1575 assembly as one of a number of non-residents.[21] He was by then Morton's chaplain[22] and he soon aroused Andrew Melville's suspicions as he was 'sa courtlie'.[23]

The archiepiscopal plum finally fell into Adamson's lap in 1576, after it had been refused by Andrew Melville, according to one presbyterian,[24] but with it came immediate conflict with the assembly because he refused to subject himself to trial by the kirk. Morton told him not to acquiesce in the matter because 'the said act and ordinance of the Kirk is not accordit on'.[25] Thus in April 1577 Adamson, 'callit Bischop of Sanct Androes', was charged with entering his episcopal see contrary to the acts of assembly and having 'usurpit the office of Visitatioun within the bounds of Fyfe unauthorized be the commission or power of the Kirk, and left his ordinar office of Ministrie'.[26]

More charges were laid against him in 1579. He was accused of voting in parliament without the kirk's sanction, of admitting the unqualified, of usurping authority beyond the limits of his area for visitation, and of failing to concur with certain aspects of the polity then gaining acceptance in the kirk.[27] Nevertheless, he seems to have survived these suspicions and charges so that in 1581 he was called upon to assist with the formation of a presbytery — alongside Andrew Melville![28] Indeed James Melville and other presbyterians claimed that Adamson 'aggreit to all the poincts of the Buik of Polecie, and concerning the office of Bischope'.[29] Calderwood recorded three documents, subscribed by Adamson with some others including Andrew Melville, in which the archbishop affirmed the equality of all ministers:

> The name BISHOP is relative to the flocke, and not to the eldership; for he is bishop of his flocke, and not of other pastors or fellow-elders. For the pre-eminence that one beares over the rest, it is the inventioun of man, and not the institutioun of the holie writt.[30]

The concentration of power in the hands of one bishop was a sign of corruption in the church, the foundation of the 'Papisticall supremacie'.[31] Even the office of visitor had no permanent place in kirk polity, and the ecclesiastical vote in parliament should endure only in time of disorder. In the present state of incomplete reform, parliamentary voting (in the ecclesiastical estate) by those lacking kirk office and commission was 'a profane and ungodlie thing'.[32]

But there can be little doubt that Patrick Adamson was even then a favourer — whether from conviction or courtly ambition — of a hostile polity. He opined that the king ought to be 'the chief governour' in the kirk, ruling it by bishops, 'conform to antiquite and maist flurissing esteat of the Christian Kirk under the best Emperour, Constantine'. When the archbishop declared 'that the discipline of the Kirk of Scotland could nocht stand with a frie kingdome and monarchie', James Melville compared him to 'Bischope Caiaphas' and king Herod who feared Jesus's threat to the state.[33]

Adamson spent the winter of 1583-1584 in England. The pretext for his journey southward had been to travel abroad for the sake of his health,[34] but suspicions were raised that negotiation in England was the genuine purpose, and to that end Adamson bore with him a certificate from king James to queen Elizabeth that he would, on his way to the Continent, bring messages to her.[35] Melville wrote that in England, Adamson 'practised with the Bischopes for Conformitie',[36] which he did, stated one contemporary chronicler, with royal blessing.[37] His desire was to obtain their sanction for a royal head of the kirk who would be keeper of both tables,[38] and approbation for the apostolic and primitive episcopal polity whereby bishops ordained, disciplined, visited, and moderated, while lay elders and presbyteries were deprived of any role in governing the church. Adamson's bishops would also take their rightful places in parliament and council.

If Adamson valued the seeming importance and stature of his embassy many detractors thought otherwise. Sir James Melville of Halhill, royal servant and diplomat, reminisced that the archbishop 'dishonored his contre be borowing of gold and pretioux fourringis fra the bischop of Londoun and dyvers uthers, quhilk was never restored nor payed again'.[39] The balladeer Robert Sempill wrote in 'The Legend of the Lymmar's Life':[40]

> Amongis the Bischopis of the towne,
> He played the beggar up and downe,
> Without respect of honestie,
> Or office of embassadrie. (900-903)

At home his unpopularity was so great that he was manhandled and otherwise abused. In April 1586 he was struck by several lairds 'for his undecent lyfe, and excommunicat be the ministrie'.[41] Some listeners walked out when he began to preach,[42] while others voiced their displeasure.[43] On at least one occasion he required a guard to protect him when preaching at St. Giles,[44] and when he and other bishops did preach the result was a somewhat less than edifying raillery against the opposition.[45] The impression was that the archbishop cared little for the welfare of the kirk.[46]

With the ascendancy of another anti-presbyterian regime in 1583 under Arran's leadership, the state took action against the kirk. In the so-called Black Acts of May 1584 the crown claimed authority 'over all statis alsweill spirituall as temporall within this realme'.[47] Parliament made accusation of treason against those persons seeking to alter the constitutional structure of the three estates, a transparent reference to the kirk's repudiation of episcopal representation in the ecclesiastical estate, while bishops, who had never been suppressed by the civil power, were confirmed in their rights of visitation and presentation.[48] Legislation subjected the summoning of all convocations, including those of the kirk, to royal licence.[49]

The reassertion of state hegemony over the kirk was further articulated in an act which nullified the 'pretendit excommunicatioun' of Robert Montgomery. It was alleged that the sentence had been implemented without due order, and declaration was made that

> seing the sentence of excommunicatioun is maist feirfull and terrible and be his hienes lawis men thairby debarrit from all civill societie and benefitc of his hienes lawis It appertenis cheiflie to his princelie cair to sie that the same be not abusit . . . .[50]

Thereafter the crown might 'stay and suspend' ecclesiastical judgements.

The parliament held the following August gave proof of the royal intention to rule the kirk through bishops. Pensions given out of the episcopal revenues of St. Andrews and Aberdeen were, with exceptions, revoked since the sees were so impoverished that the ordinaries were unable 'to sustcne the charge of the owirsicht of thair dioceises and to assist his hienes with thair advise and counsall quhen the necessitie of the commoun effairis sall require'.[51]

In all likelihood it was shortly after the promulgation of the Black Acts that king James issued a bull[52] authorising Patrick Adamson to exercise his archiepiscopal powers; as Calderwood suggested, the document constituted 'a commentaire to the late acts of parliament'.[53] Adamson was thereby restored to full powers of summoning synods, admitting ministers to benefices, deposing the unfit, and visiting kirks, colleges, and other institutions. Furthermore, his primatial status among the other bishops was recognised.[54]

Scotland did not enter quietly into a new episcopal era. Both archbishops were subjected to abuse,[55] while presbyterians loosed their tongues and sharpened their pens for counter-attack on 'the most cursed laws that ever were made into our countrie'.[56] Writing from his haven in Newcastle in August 1584, James Melville expressed his horror that the king would take himself 'to be the onlie Head and Monarche in the Kirk' as he was in the state.[57] From this distemper arose another, that the bishops should, as in Adamson's bull (and in the oath laid down at Leith in 1572), derive their office from him, 'quhilk is pleane Popish Hierarchie, and so mikle wars, as the Pope is a Bischope, an ecclesiastik persone and office-bearer, provyding he and his Kirk was trew'.[58]

Others joined the fray from the presbyterian side. A letter to the king, subscribed by John Craig, Robert Pont, and Patrick Simson *inter alios,* rejected the titles of archbishop and ordinary as unscriptural and reminiscent of popery, the stuff of which had long since been abrogated by parliament. But worse than the names was the dreaded superiority entailed by hierarchical titles. The bishop in the New Testament was identical with the elder, and any breach of ministerial equality was contrary to the biblical constitution of the kirk.[59] Bishops were disturbing the tranquillity of the kirk and should be suppressed by James who had been 'brought up in the feare of God, even from your infancie'.[60] Even apart from all these considerations submission to Adamson was an ecclesiastical impossibility since the assembly had suspended him from all his functions.[61]

But this intransigence was not shared by all. Melville blamed in particular John Craig who had originally refused obedience. A royal chaplain, he acquiesced at the end of 1584 'be weaknes and a sort of sophistication', drawing with him 'the graittest part of the Ministerie of Scotland'.[62] He rationalised his submission as only 'a testimonie of our obedience to his Majestie'[63] — a response accepted by Adamson as sufficient for the king[64] — and denied that it implied approval of the Black Acts or of bishops. One wonders whether Craig knew exactly where he wanted to be. He had in fact been one of bishop David Cunningham's collators in 1577.[65]

Others blamed John Erskine. 'What the North hath done we hear not; but I look for little good at their hands, for the Laird of Dun is a pest to them'.[66] In a similar vein, 'As to the North, I cannot tell anything, but I fear that Dun hath corrupted all'.[67] Another old reformer, David Lindsay, also subscribed,[68] while in January 1585 Erskine was among those who received royal appointments to act as ecclesiastical commissioners in lieu of bishops.[69]

Subscription meant an acknowledgement of royal authority in the kirk and a promise of obedience to bishops and commissioners.[70] Apparently ministers were required to resign their benefices into the exchequer and to receive them back if they subscribed,[71] otherwise to be deprived and to lose their legal benefits.

Melville was beside himself when he heard of events back in Scotland and was moved to letter writing:

> To the breithring of the Ministerie of Scotland, Wha hes latlie subscryvit to the Popish Supremacie of the King, and ambitius tyrannie of the Bischops over thair Brithring, JM wissethe unfeinyit repentance.[72]

Bishops, he protested, brought tyranny and overthrew the dominical institution of parity.[73] At their feet lay all manner of vice and corruption — offences against the second table, division in the church, heresy, pride.[74] Like Beza, to whose *De triplici episcopatu* Melville attributed 'mikle guid',[75] he held bishops responsible for the entrance of all manner of abomination along with 'Heresie, Atheisme, and Papistrie'[76] into the kirk. Unlike Adamson he took a rather negative view of the early Christian emperors of Rome. The 'warldlie ritches and honour'[77] acquired by bishops under imperial protection enticed them to usurp

> lordlie authoritie and preheminence over thair breithring. Fra that tyme, as never of befor, miserablie hes the Kirk been cut and devydit be controversies, schismes, and heresies; sa pernitius hes it bein to ley asyde the Word of God, and right rewlles of governing of his Kirk be aequalitie amangs the Pastors.[78]

Such bishops scarcely deserved to be known as Christians: their confused exercise of civil and criminal jurisdiction 'loudlie cryes that they war never of Chryst'.

In presbyterian eyes traditional episcopacy was one of the distinguishing marks of popery, hence of Antichrist. The survival of true religion was in doubt should such false bishops continue in the kirk.

An official statement on the Black Acts was published in 1585 (in January, according to Calderwood[79]) under the title *A declaration of the kings majesties intention and meaning toward the lait actis of parliament*. Written by archbishop Patrick Adamson at the behest of chancellor Arran and secretary John Maitland,[80] it was an amplification of the views which Melville claimed Adamson had expressed several years earlier.

The *Declaration* falls into two major sections. The first, by far the longer, discussed the course of events that had led the state to act as it did in 1584. The abbreviated second section provided, in fourteen points, a brief summation of the conditions under which the kirk must thenceforth operate.

There is a loud note of apologetic in the *Declaration,* designed to defend James both at home and abroad from those slanderous reports to the effect that he 'had declynit to Papistrie, and had, made many actis, to derogate the frie passage of the gospell, gude ordour and discipline in the kirk'.[81] Of course the presbyterians thought that was what had occured but the *Declaration* explained the rebellious character of Andrew Melville's conduct and the disruptive nature of presbyteries, which were now prohibited. In addition, the general assembly, in its accustomed form, was also terminated due to its seditious tendencies demonstrated in its support for the Ruthven Raid. The choice was clear: 'it behovit his Hienes, ether to discharge him self of the Crowne, or the ministrie of that forme of the assemblie'.[82]

In place of presbyterian independence the crown's rights were asserted. Young James was extolled as a divine, his heart 'replenishit with the knawlege of the heavenly Philosophie'.[83] It was indeed recognised that the king could not be the head of the kirk, for only Christ might bear that title. But although a member of the kirk, James was not just any member; he was 'the cheife and principall member, appointed be the lawe of God'[84] to ensure proper worship and to uphold virtue. Citing the examples of Old Testament kings and the ancient emperors, the author of the *Declaration* granted James full sovereignty over the kirk. Those denying his authority in the kirk were guilty of 'a great error' common to papists which contradicted ancient precedent in which it was the Roman emperors who deposed or otherwise censured bishops and who were the ultimate authorities in ecclesiastical disputes.[85] Just as the emperors must call a general council of the church, so James reserved for himself the calling of the kirk's general assemblies.[86]

Naturally, the king could not rule over the kirk by himself. Bishops were therefore to be the means whereby he would govern. Divine right episcopacy was not expressed for, although the antiquity of bishops was acknowledged,[87] the point at stake was the royal supremacy and its preference for a particular polity rather than the autonomous jurisdiction of the episcopate. The king was the 'Bishop of Bishops, and universall Bishop within his Realm',[88] to whom the episcopate would be responsible for its care of diocesan kirks.

Within the kirk bishops would not be completely independent. They must hold twice-yearly synods[89] and generally govern with a council of clergy, 'that baith tyrannie and confusion may be evitit in the kirk'.[90] Representation of the ministry would pertain to them since they would be seated in parliament and on the council.[91] Their conduct would be tried by the assembly when necessary, though the assembly might be called only with royal approval[92] and it would no longer consist of a 'confusit multitude' as before.[93] With an episcopal structure in place the expectation was one of 'godlie harmony, unitie, concord, and peax in the estate, and ane solide ordour in the kirk'.[94]

The *Declaration* was quickly answered by 'An answere to the declaration of certan intentions sett out in the kings name',[95] dated 7 February 1585, and written, according to McCrie,[96] by Andrew Melville. It added little that was new: bishops were one with elders, ministers, and pastors. The assertion was backed up with appropriate patristic proofs.[97] Whereas the *Declaration* identified the presbyterian claim of the kirk's independence as popery, the 'Answere' retorted that 'these Tulchan and bastard bishops' were but a means of uniting the two jurisdictions, aiming 'to re-establishe a new Popedome in the person of the king'.[98] Antichrist was poised to reappear in Scotland.[99]

Melville's treatise concluded with a plea to God, remarkable for its pathos:

> Therefore, lett all the godlie in Scotland crie, 'Arise, O Lord, and let thy enemeis be confounded; lett them flee farre from thy presence that hate thy godlie name: lett the sighes and sobs of thy owne childrein, banished, imprisouned, and distressed, enter in before thee! Lett not thy enemeis thus triumphe to the end, but lett them understand it is against thee that they fight: lett thy strenth and power be reveeled in the weaknesse of thy owne deare servants! Deliver thy owne distressed Church of Scotland; and make thy blessed vine, planted there with thy owne hand, enjoy the libertie of thy everlasting truthe and Evangell, as it did before, through Jesus Christ thy Sonne; to whom, with the Father and Holie Ghost, be all praise for ever and ever.'[100]

James Melville also wrote a treatise at the same time from his exile home in Newcastle.[101] Cast in the form of a conversation, 'Zelator, Temporizar, Palemon' discussed the *Declaration,* particularly from the perspective of the two kingdoms and the wrong done by those who would blur the distinctions. Of relevance to bishops, he provided an assessment of the episcopate as it was at the time. Several sees were so financially destitute that ministers were refusing to accept appointments to them even for provision of a pastoral stipend. 'Dunkelden, an old dotted Papist; Brechin, Dumblane, Glasgow, Orkney, Cathnesse, and the rest, als meet for that purpose as I am for singing of a solemne masse'. Melville granted that Adamson, 'the father of all this course', was not an ignorant man but one grotesquely misguided, 'a renegat apostat' moving from side to side.[102]

One need not fear overstatement when describing the outright hatred with which Adamson was regarded. 'A jugler, a Holliglasse, a drunkard, a vile Epicurean!' declaimed James Melville.[103] The wives of the two Edinburgh ministers who fled the country wrote Adamson a letter in which they spewed out some startling invective that serves to remind the modern reader of the deep passions aroused by what was far more than a small-scale brush fire in the kirk:

> O flattering panche-god! that would bring out of the envennomed treasure of thy invyous heart, discord betwixt God's servants and their naturall and loving prince. Envennomed vespe! sucker of poysoun out of wholesome and comfortable flowers![104]

Melville agreed that Adamson was the truly guilty party, and forecast that when James made a careful examination of the *Declaration* 'that blasphemous villain' would find his end upon a gibbet.[105] Time would prove that Melville had yet to learn some unhappy truths about his godly prince.

King James responded to further criticisms of the Black Acts in a handwritten document of 7 December 1585,[106] a conciliatory statement issued in the eclipse of the deposed Arran. James denied any intention of diminishing the freedom of the kirk, including its right to discipline faulty bishops, and stated that the annulment of Montgomery's excommunication was based upon the faultiness of the pronouncement, not on the actual content of the process and decision. As for bishops in general, James wrote, 'I allow na Bischopes according to the traditions of men, or inventionnes of the Pape, but onlie according to God's Word', which would, apparently, entail the performance of their duties only with the advice of a diocesan council. James did insist, though, that they would have 'sum prelation and dignitie' above other ministers, as in the early church according to his own reading of the matter. Needless to say, these bishops would sit in parliament.[107]

The development of rhetoric about kirk polity was dominated by a fundamental hermeneutical disagreement. The crown and its supporters, eminently Patrick Adamson, not only discovered episcopacy in the apostolic and succeeding ages of the church, but also derived their view of the godly monarch as earthly head of the kirk from the precedent of Old Testament kings who were characterised in Isaiah 49:23 as 'nourcing fathers' to the people of God, an example followed by the Christian emperors. Thus interpreted, the king bore a divine commission to rule the kirk.

Such were also the sentiments of the Swiss-born Thomas Erastus (1524-1583), physician and theologian at Heidelberg, whose political ideas concerning the jurisdictional problem of excommunication gained widespread circulation. He concluded his treatise by affirming magisterial power in the church: 'I see no reason why the Christian magistrate at the present day should not possess the same power, which God commanded the magistrate to exercise in the Jewish commonwealth'.[108] Wherever there existed a Christian ruler, the linchpin of this 'Erastian' polity, there was no requirement of another disciplinary jurisdiction, *i.e.* the church, in the body politic.[109] Erastus also rejected the reduction of the prince 'to the rank of a subject of other men'.[110]

Scottish Protestants also loved the godly prince, but instead of developing under a Protestant elector, their political theory had germinated during a time of tribulation under hostile Catholic sovereigns. Thus John Knox expressed his view of the matter in an appeal to the estates of Scotland to protect him from his tormentors and to bring them to trial instead. He therefore rejected the contentions of those who denied that ecclesiastical jurisdiction pertained to the magistrate: 'who dar esteme that the civile power is now becomed so prophane in Gods eyes, that it is sequestred from all intromission with the matters of religion'.[111]

Knox did not, however, grant unlimited power to the magistrate. Indeed, he and his colleagues, with minds steeped in Old Testament patterns of thinking, read how good and godly kings reformed the Israelite cult. As the English-born

Scottish reformer Christopher Goodman wrote to Cecil, the old persecuting bishops ought to be killed. God had already sentenced them to death, and to that purpose 'he hath committed the sword in your hands, who are now placed in authority'.[112] But Knox, and undoubtedly Goodman, also read how idolatrous and tyrannical kings were removed. It was God's ordinance for a king to abolish idolatry — but not to restore it. Thus, writing to England just after the death of Mary Tudor and before firm assurance of a Protestant future, he demanded that magistrates who 'go aboute to destroy Gods true religion once established, and to erect Idolatrie, which God detesteth, *be adjudged to death* according to Gods commaundement'.[113] The godly ruler reformed the church but subsequently handed control to the proper, ecclesiastical, authorities and submitted himself humbly and obediently to its discipline. Otherwise, the church should resist him to the uttermost.[114]

Similarly in another Reformation document addressed to the regent Mary by 'the professouris of Christis evangell' warning was given that she ought not to transgress her bounds because Christ alone was head of the kirk, in which she was 'ane servand and na quein'.[115] She was reminded of the violent ends met by usurpers, an end to which some were quite prepared to deliver her. On the other hand, those who disobeyed godless magistrates were securely within the will of God. The address to the regent may have been written by John Erskine, but Knox would have been well satisfied with the warning issued to Mary:

> Madame, be not dissavit be that leand sprit in the mowthe of thair falss prophetis, nor corrupt in your judgement to usurp in you forthir power na God hes gevin, nor persecuyt the sanctis, bot be your authorite set fordwardis the glorie of God, menten his kyrk in the awin libertye, and donthring all abhominatioun and papistrie . . . .[116]

Magisterial power in the kirk did, nonetheless, receive favourable comment as well. In the 1560 Confession 'the conservation and purgation' of religion were functions committed to the magistrate, recognising a responsibility established upon Old Testament example.[117] Eight years later the kirk's letter to John Willock exclaimed the presence at last of a godly ruler, the earl of Moray, 'whom God of his eternall and heavenly Providence hath reserved to this age, to put in execution whatsoever he by his law commandeth'.[118]

John Carswell, superintendent and bishop, concurred with this high opinion of the princely role in the church. In dedicating his Gaelic liturgy to Argyll he appealed both to the Old Testament and 'the history of traditions of the gentile people'[119] to demonstrate that Christian magistrates must enforce divine law, including religious observances, or else become 'enemies to divine nature'.[120] And in the liturgy itself Carswell's translation showed a tendency toward moderation absent from some of his contemporaries:

> The church ought to have a lord or secular noble over it, called in Latin, *magistratus civilis*, and that magistrate ought to deal fairly with all men, in such matters as giving honour and protection to the good and in punishing the bad; and the church ought to render obedience and honour to those nobles in anything that does not conflict with the will or command of God.[121]

But how far did the express will of God extend? Did it include matters of polity and ceremony? And who would be the final hermeneutical authority?

Ultimately it was the narrower and more rigid view that prevailed in the kirk, and as a result the presbyterian rhetoric of the 1570s and 1580s could readily sound like a continuation of early Reformation language even including the Confession of 1560 where it asserted that Christ was the sole head of the kirk. Should any magistrate intrude into this sacred ground he would be abhorred as a blasphemer.[122] The effect, therefore, was the statement of a limited monarchy, one sequestered from ecclesiastical jurisdiction.[123] Even in 1568 the general assembly had complained of a book entitled *Fall of the Romane kirk* wherein the king was named 'supreame head of the primitive kirk'.[124] In presbyterian thought the sovereign had to find a more subdued place. Andrew Melville wrote that in the kirk's synods a king sat there 'to receave the lawes from God to obey'.[125] This subordinate ecclesiastical function was elucidated in a letter which the general assembly prefaced to the 1579 Edinburgh edition of the Geneva Bible. James was addressed as one called by God to maintain the truth. As 'a singulare instrument' to safeguard the kirk's freedom, purity, and (presbyterian) polity, he was implored to 'imitate the fervent faith of Jehoshaphat, putting his hail trust in the Lord, *and believing his prophets*'[126] — an allusion to those ministers importuning him for the establishment of the second Book of Discipline.

According to James Melville the Christian magistrate might review appeals in ecclesiastical cases, but only insofar as he studied the rectitude of a decision, not the validity of the underlying constitutional basis upon which the kirk had originally pronounced sentence. Ideally magistrate and kirk ought to co-operate 'as two loving and most inteere sisters' and as Hippocrates' twins.[127] But when conflict arose — as it happened, the two siblings seemed nearly always to be temperamentally unsuited to one another — the ardent presbyterian would think it treason to Christ to submit to a wayward king. John Howeson made clear the kirk's position in case of an irreconcilable difference of opinion. Preaching on 8 July 1584, he declared, 'We will acknawlage na Prince, na magistrat in teaching of the Word, nor be bund to na injunctionis, nor obey na Actes of Parliament, nor na uyer thing that is repugnant to the Word of God'.[128] Ecclesiastical power flowed from Christ, the only king of the church, an authority which might not be abrogated by any earthly sovereign.[129]

The presbyterian path proved to be a constricted one for the young king James, and the Melvilles and their friends were quick to see evidence of a resuscitated Catholic tyranny, albeit with a secular head, whenever he diverged from the appointed ways.[130] To the presbyterians the danger to their religion in 1584 was equal to that which threatened before 1560. For them it was not enough to be Protestant. Only presbytery was sound and biblical. Anything less was apostasy.

The presbyterians wanted a godly prince in the kirk — in special circumstances, even over the kirk — as in 1592 when they called on James to act as *custos utriusque tabulae* and take strong action against 'poperie and sin of all sorts'.[131] Thus their political theory suffered considerably from ambiguity. But this should not hastily be blamed on the ministers themselves, for this ambiguity inhered in their book, the Bible, from which more than one approach to the magistracy and its relationship to the people of God could be extracted. The Bible's portrayal of the matter was relative — situational, to borrow from modern ethical terminology — to changing circumstances and needs. The presbyterians availed themselves of this variable approach. In rare moments they might rejoice in their godly ruler, but more often they set themselves up as prophets to oppose a king whose policies ran against the presbyterian current.

The effect of Knoxian thought in later minds was to convey to presbyterians a profoundly unrealistic view of political life in Scotland. There was no possibility that a sovereign power would institute reformed worship and polity only to surrender all further ecclesiastical jurisdiction into the hands of subjects who might then use their pulpits to preach the virtues of disobedience and even rebellion. The stalwart presbyterian was at his or her best a courageous person, but the political views associated with that faction were exceedingly naive in the later decades of the sixteenth century. Presbyterian political theory was out of phase with the real world of centralising monarchy. King James, however, would soon subject his unwilling students to some lessons in political realism.

There could be little hope of reconciliation between such patently contradictory views, but nonetheless a conference was held at Holyroodhouse on 17 February 1586 between representatives of the council and the ministry.[132] A number of articles were agreed upon, most significantly concerning episcopacy. It was decided that bishops were ministers of the word and must be resident pastors of particular congregations. They would be presented by the king, then elected and admitted by the general assembly, which would also select a council to be associated with each bishop. Without his senate or presbytery the bishop might do nothing beyond his normal pastoral duties, and for usurpation of power or fault 'in his life or doctrine' he was liable to deprivation. Bishops would visit but only in those areas appointed to them, with commissioners to share the burden where necessary. In exchange, the meetings of church courts including the presbytery were upheld, though the king was to be involved in the determination of time and place for the general assembly, while the kirk's jurisdiction in 'doctrine, ministratioun of the Sacraments, exercise of discipline, and correction of maners, by excommunication' was recognised.

The question of episcopacy was raised at the May 1586 assembly where, in response to a question about episcopal pre-eminence a despondent kirk replied: 'It could not stand with the Word of God, only they must tolerate it, in case it be forced upon them be the civil power'.[133] Furthermore, it was reaffirmed that the office of bishop belonged to all pastors, but by now the kirk recognised defeat. The royal commissioners declared that the entire proceedings of the February conference must be approved, 'or else that all things must remain as they were; for except the estate of Bishops were received as was agreed in that conference, the King would grant nothing'.[134] The kirk would get bishops, but through compliance it could cut its losses and safeguard some of its sacred cows.

Thus the kirk assented but only with the reluctant condition 'that be the name of a Bischop, they only meane such a Bischop as is descryvit be Paul'.[135] One alteration was attempted, that of subjecting bishops to censure by the lower courts of the kirk, but the royal commissioners protested against this amendment of the Holyroodhouse agreement. [136] The king also rejected the proposal. At the same assembly it was accepted that bishops and commissioners would moderate the presbyteries in which they resided. [137]

The settlement looked back to the visitors of 1576 whereby the assembly retained control of visitation, but it also recalled the concordat of Leith in that the bishops were not temporary but permanent unless deprived and they should vote as members of the third estate. This article was not raised in 1586. Presumably James did not regard it as open to any form of alteration, hence discussion was superfluous. Royal control was strengthened by the crown's reservation of the right of nomination, though this was what had happened after 1572 despite provision for chapters to nominate as well as to elect. [138]

But from the crown's perspective, all was for nought. The Black Acts had been passed during Arran's ascendancy but he had been overthrown in December 1585, and under the Maitland administration presbytery was, for the sake of greater national stability, permitted to flourish [139] so that by 1592 there 'was a presbyterian system operating over the greater part of the country'. [140] The bishops described in 1584 and 1586 never gained control of the kirk, while the duties intended for them increasingly devolved upon the presbyteries. [141] Some bishops, for example David Cunningham of Aberdeen, functioned within the kirk as parochial ministers, [142] and the crown made no discernible effort to appoint bishops capable of ecclesiastical function. Peter Rollock was presented to Dunkeld in 1585, but he was not a minister. His future lay in the court of session and as comptroller for the royal household 1603-1605. [143] George Gordon, presented to Galloway in 1586, was also a titular. [144] And when William Erskine, who was a minister, was appointed to the archbishopric of Glasgow in 1585 (until Beaton should be rehabilitated by parliament [145]), the 1587 general assembly rejected him. It refused to admit a bishop only to the temporality, 'the ecclesiastical jurisdiction being devolved by him in the Kirks hands'. [146] The archbishop had been admitted by 'the brethren of the West' — a procedure which sounds more like 1572 than 1586 — against their better judgement, but they believed the admission to be a lesser evil than what might have transpired in case of intransigence. The assembly voted to annul the admission, terming it a 'slander'. Perhaps feeling stronger in its opposition to episcopacy, the kirk inhibited the worthy Robert Pont from accepting the see of Caithness which was to be given to him as a financial settlement. [147] Just one year after its surrender to episcopacy the assembly wrote to the king that Pont was already a bishop:

But as to that corrupt estate or office of them quho hes bein termed Bischops heirtofoir, we find it not agreeable to the Word of God, and it hes bein damnit in diverse uther our Assemblies; neither is the said Mr Robert willing to attempt the samein in that manner. [148]

The kirk would not accept the unworthy and it would not permit the qualified.

The act of annexation in 1587 [149] was a financial move by the crown to enhance its resources by laying claim to the temporalities of benefices. By its provisions episcopacy received a setback, though there was nothing in the act about ecclesiastical jurisdiction to make the presbyterians rejoice. In fact James Melville complained that the kirk was thereby 'spuilyet be a plane law of the ane halff of her patrimonie'.[150] He wrote also that promises were made concerning the abolition of bishoprics and prelacies and the kirk's full possession of the teinds: 'Bot of God's just judgment, that annexation of the temporalitie hes done the King alsmikle guid as sic promises of the Kirk's Spiritualitie'.

Disciplinary problems with some of the bishops remained. Once again James requested Montgomery's full reception back into 'the fellowschip and favour of the Kirk',[151] which the kirk was willing to do with dispensation from some of the usual procedures for repentance 'in case they find his Majestie willing to remitt somequhat of the rigour of his Majesties satisfactioun cravit of the twa [presbyterian] brethren [James Gibson and John Cowper], be quhom he finds his Hienes offendit'.[152] Though no longer archbishop, he was to be restored to the work of ministry, a compromise solution.[153] David Cunningham of Aberdeen was under suspicion for adultery, and preparation for his trial was made,[154] but once again the crown intervened on the side of its servant. Whereas the assembly stated there had not been 'any clear purgatione as yet', James replied that the alleged fault 'is sufficiently tryit and removeit'.[155] This appears to have concluded the case, though the assembly cannot have been pleased at Cunningham's letters from the king prohibiting Peter Blackburn and George Hay from visiting in the diocese.[156] Nor can there have been anything but horror at the possible restoration of Catholic bishops to their temporalities[157] and the return of William Chisholm to Dunblane in the company of a stranger 'supposed be many probable appearances, by men of great judgment, to be imployed here in some strange turne'.[158] It was feared that the aged bishop's return would foster papistry.[159]

The complex and contradictory character of Patrick Adamson posed the most trying episcopal issue following the passage of the Black Acts. Although the mutilation of the register of the general assemblies leaves a gap from October 1583 to May 1586,[160] it would appear that the archbishop had been suspended from the ministry in October 1583.[161] Despite this fact he continued to exercise his office in St. Andrews. This irregularity, along with 'his imperious behaviour and contempt' of the synod,[162] plus suspicions of 'antichristian Poprie and blasphemous heresie',[163] led to his excommunication by the synod of Fife in April 1586.[164] The kirk had no room for a man who called hierarchical, diocesan episcopacy a scriptural office.[165] Adamson reacted to his sentence by excommunicating the Melvilles and some others — an abjectly futile measure. But as it turned out, the next assembly restored Adamson as a gesture of goodwill toward the king, justifying its decision by appealing to some impropriety in the process.[166] Adamson actually submitted but this did not suffice to quell the anger so that finally the assembly felt obliged to enact a ban on public discussion of its handling of the matter.[167] It did, however, exclude the archbishop from the act which installed bishops as moderators of presbyteries.[168]

Adamson's troubles persisted in one way or another. He was at the horn in 1586 for some legal fault[169] and again in 1587 for non-payment of stipends (had his revenues been restored in accordance with the act of August 1584?) and for his failure to supply two gallons of communion wine.[170] In 1588 he was summoned before the assembly for having collated without the consent of presbytery,[171] to which he replied that incumbents in his see, by reason of 'an old indenture', were compelled to make the grant in favour of the earl of Rothes.[172] This led directly to deprivation from his commission to visit.[173] Next he incurred further displeasure by performing a marriage for the earl of Huntly who was under the kirk's eye for his papistry.[174] For not appearing to answer this charge he was, in June 1589, deposed from all function in the kirk.[175]

And then there was the Bancroft affair. Richard Bancroft, a bright and steadily rising star in the English ecclesiastical firmament, preached a sermon at Paul's Cross on 9 February 1589. Delivered at the beginning of parliament, it was a harsh but well considered attack upon the presbyterian faction in the church of England, and directed especially against Thomas Cartwright and the scurrilous pamphleteer jocularly named Martin Marprelate.

Bancroft, who would later be elevated to the sees of London and then Canterbury, was convinced of the superiority of episcopacy, though it would be excessive to claim, as does William Lamont,[176] that the Paul's Cross sermon advocated *jure divino* episcopacy. Nonetheless, anyone standing on Bancroft's ground would not have far to shift to arrive at the divine right of bishops, whither he himself moved within a few years.[177] But in 1589 Bancroft went only so far as to say that bishops had governed the church since the time of Mark,[178] and even if presbytery had once been known, it had disappeared in the early part of the fourth century. He berated the presbyterians for their rigid insistence upon their chosen polity without which 'we can never attaine to a right and true feeling of Christian Religion, but are to be reckoned amongst those who are accounted to say of Christ as it is in Luke, We will not have this man to raigne over us'.[179] Bancroft protested that presbyterian exegesis perverted Christ's teaching and murdered the Scriptures. As to the motivation of such men, whom he regarded as schismatics and false prophets,[180] he attributed it to four factors: contempt for bishops, ambition, self-love, and covetousness.[181] He regarded episcopacy as 'lawfull and godlie',[182] a prophylactic against schism,[183] while the identification of bishop and priest was 'full of follie', the fruit of disappointed ambition when Aerius of old failed to obtain a desired bishopric.[184] The presbyterian limitation of magisterial power in the church was also criticised by Bancroft. He alleged that Cartwright agreed with papists in the contention that to the magistrate belonged only '*Potestatem facti non juris*',[185] thus he — or she, since Cartwright was concerned with queen Elizabeth — might only execute decisions established by the church's ministers.

Seeking to bar the door to any presbyterian-inspired amendment of the church of England, Bancroft was able to point to the dreaded effects of presbyterian polity in a neighbouring realm, namely Scotland. He later expressed his judgement of the kirk in its presbyterian form as 'a meere humane device devised by shifteinge and sleight, attayned by tiranny and bloud, and mainteyned with untollerable pride and with most straunge boldnes in expoundinge the scriptures and falsify-inge of all antiquitye'.[186] For his sermon Bancroft drew from two sources to describe the baneful effects of Scottish presbytery. The first was a letter by the father of English separatism, Robert Browne. Written to Browne's uncle and only published in 1904 as *A New Years Guift,* the manuscript came into Bancroft's possession and he quoted portions of the material relevant to Scotland. In order to provide a fuller background to Bancroft's negative view of the kirk, Browne's entire assessment is included here. Portions which Bancroft quoted in the sermon are identified**:

This therefore is my Judgement, good Unckle, that though the names of pastors, doctors, & presbyters be lawful, being found in the scriptures, yet that a pope or proud popelinge may ly hyd under the names. yea and further **I Judge, that if the Parliament should establish such names, & those the officers according to those names, which seeke their owne discipline that then in stead of one Pope we should have a thousand & of some Lord byshops in name, a thousand Lordly Tyrants in deed, which now do disdaine the names. This have I found by experience to be trewe,** both in forreine contries and in myne owne Contrie. **I can testifie by trial of Scotland, which have traveled it over in their best reformed places, as in Donde, Sct. Andrewes, Edenborowe & sundrie other Townes And have knowne the king in great daunger & feare of his lyfe by their Lordlie Discipline,** the nobles & people at great discord and much distracted, & yet all men made slaves to the preachers & their fellowe elders. So that myne owne ears have hard the king by name to be verie spitefully abused by their preachers in pulpitt, his doings & commaundements called in, revoked, or repealed, or els established & performed as he durst or could do for feare or daunger of them. Also in everie Towne I found the cheife Magistrates in awe of them, much murmuring grudging & whispering conspiracies to be made on all hands, some tymes them on the kings syde to be put out of office, & their adversaries put in & some tymes them on the preachers syde put downe, & others sett up. Further **I have sene all manner of wickednes to abound much more in their best places in Scotland, then in our worser places here in England.** And to conclude when I came away, all the whole land was in a manner wholie divided into parts, much people in armes, & redie to join battel, some with the king, & some against him, & all about the preachers discipline. In England also I have found much more wronge done me by the preachers of discipline, then by anie the Byshops & more Lordly usurping by them, then by the other, so that as in Scotland, the preachers having no names of byshops did imprison me more wrongfully then anie Bishop would have done, so theis having nether the name, nor the power, have yet usurped more then the Byshops which have power. For before my first voiag beyond sea, & sence my last retourne, I have bene in more then twentie prisons And for once imprisonment by the byshops, I have bene more then thrise imprisoned by the preachers or their procuring.[187]

The other document used by Bancroft — it was first in order in the sermon — was of far greater significance to Scotland. It was none other than Patrick Adamson's work published as the *Declaration of the kings majesties intention,*[188] a publication which received more than passing attention in England. It was reissued in London in 1585 as *Treason pretended against the king of Scots* with a prefatory letter concerning 'secret practising against the kinges Majestie of Scotland'[189] which served to set the complaints of the *Declaration* even more firmly in a context of sedition. Two years later it was inserted in the 1587 edition of Holinshed's *Chronicles*.[190] Having reviewed James's actions against the presbyterians and directed readers to the *Declaration,* Bancroft asserted: 'For the king, he is not altered'.[191] This statement would have further ramifications, for it cast James in the shape of a dissembler since he had recently dealt more generously with the presbyterians.

Responses to Bancroft's 'schismaticall libell'[192] were not long in appearing. The first came from the pen of the fugitive John Penry, then in Edinburgh with his equally notorious printer Robert Waldegrave. In the tract, *A briefe discovery,*[193] issued anonymously, Penry affirmed the divine origin and intended perpetuity of presbyterian polity, including ministerial parity. When writing to Timothy, the apostle Paul made the retention of 'Pastors, Doctors, Elders, &c.' no matter of indifference to be settled according to the exigencies of time and place, 'but a commaundement which is to bee kept inviolable, untill the appearing of the Lord Jesus'.[194] According to Penry, bishop was simply another term for the teaching elder, no superiority among ministers being permissible.[195] As for the presumed necessity of bishops for the sake of a well-ordered government, Penry allowed only that they were essential to the 'kingdome of Antichrist'.[196]

A published reply from the Scottish presbyterians came from John Davidson, already known in England as a 'thunderer'.[197] He was no less scathing than Penry in his assault on 'that heavie bondage of Antichristian government by loftie Lordes, wrongfully called Bishops (an hurtfull relicke of Romish confusion)', which the English brethren sought to replace with that (presbyterian) polity found in the Bible and designed to endure until the parousia.[198] When he came to Adamson, the supplier of false testimony to Bancroft, Davidson's presbyterian venom overflowed:

> For as touching the former of them, corruptlie and falslie called Bishop of S. Androis, it is much better that the legend of his leud life bee buried in eternall oblivion, then that Christian eares should bee polluted with the unsavorie mention thereof . . . . For what will that man be ashamed to doe, that durst father his owne forgerie uppon the Lords lieuetenant the K. Majestie himselfe, and that in a matter of no lesse importance, then the declaration of the meaning of some acts of Parliament, which howbeit it was but his own declaration, (as his Majestie hath plainely witnessed by his own hand writ yet extant to be seene) and not the Kings. Yet durst he bee bolde to give it out in the Kinges name, as though, hee had beene the verie undouted author therof: If this be not to play the falsarie forger, & that in the hiest degree, let the Chaplain [Bancroft] himself be judge.[199]

There are two letters extant from the presbyterian ministers addressed to queen Elizabeth calling upon her to discipline Bancroft.[200] Neither epistle was ever sent[201] but they do reveal the depth of feeling aroused in Scotland. The letters complained about the publication of the *Declaration* in London[202] and called for its deletion from Holinshed because it was the work not of king James but of 'the apostat Bishop of Sanctandrois', which the utterly rejected Adamson could not deny.[203] One of the letters concluded by appealing for a cessation of English calumnies against the kirk 'untill it may please God to move your wisdoms to a farther consideratioun of reforming the great present abuses of your church government, according to the Word of God'.[204]

Of course there was little hope for presbyterian reform in England, particularly since the movement led by Cartwright and Travers had shot its bolt by then. In 1590 Elizabeth wrote a letter of her own to James, warning him of that perilous sect which threatened to usurp royal power and condemned every variant religious judgement. 'I pray you stop the mouthes, or make shortar the toungz, of suche ministars as dare presume to make oraison in ther pulpitz for the persecuted in Ingland for gospel'.[205] She made perfectly clear that she could not tolerate attacks on her own government, however much James might have been disposed to bear the proud behaviour of presbyterians, and that he should return fugitives (presumably Penry and Waldegrave) to their own country, or at least banish them, undoubtedly as a demonstration of loyalty to a throne he wished ultimately to sit upon.

It was claimed that James 'bursted foorth into great choler' against Bancroft, and he would have answered the sermon had he not been absent from Scotland,[206] though a member of the English embassy in Edinburgh suggested that James had every interest in preserving the peace and goodwill between Scotland and England.[207]

This same writer communicated that the presbyterian outburst against Bancroft came about only because the king was in Norway, the ministers availing themselves of the opportunity 'to make their market in England'.[208] Thus one is left with ambivalence — where did the king stand? On the one hand the presbyterians could note that James had promised to the assembly to support the kirk polity 'as presentlie it is taught and professed in Scotland'.[209] Davidson had defended the king, and while noting that the youthful monarch had been led astray 'by crafty men', observed that James had in his maturity given his support to the true, biblical polity.[210] The presbyterian champion even quoted James's marginal note in the king's own copy of Bancroft's sermon: 'My speaking, writing, and actions, were and are ever one, without dissembling, or bearing up at any time, whatever I thought'.[211] On the other side, though, there was a report sent to Burghley that James had sought to suppress Davidson's tract and had taken action against the printer;[212] and as Bancroft had pointed out, the *Declaration* had been published *cum privilegio regali* and its author had never been rebuked by the king for issuing it.

In the light of future developments it may not be possible to shield James from accusations of deceitfulness. His anger toward Bancroft was due not to any inaccuracy in the sermon but to his embarrassment arising from implications of insincerity. The future English king was irate at his future archbishop of Canterbury because the preacher had spoken presumptuously in letting the royal cat out of the bag.

Patrick Adamson had a curious relationship with the Melvilles. When Andrew and James took up new responsibilities at the University of St. Andrews in 1580, he welcomed them warmly and promised his support,[213] though debate would soon follow.[214] Also the strains of the 1580s brought both Melvilles to turn on him in vicious speeches.[215] Then at the assembly in August 1590 James Melville warned the brethren of

> a poisonable and vennemus Psyllus, a warlow, . . . sa empoisoned be the vennome of that auld serpent, and sa altered in his substance and naturall, that the deadlie poisone of the vipere is his familiar fuid and nuriture, to wit, lies, falshode, malice, and knaverie . . . .[216]

Adamson's excommunication was demanded, and by this time there was no one left to defend him. He had alienated royal favour by making an insincere gesture toward the presbyterians when James was abroad,[217] and the king, thoroughly disgusted and disillusioned with the archbishop's cowardice and all the complaints alleged against him, finally repudiated his primate.[218] His income was diverted to Lennox so that he was forced to turn to Andrew Melville who supported the forlorn prelate for several months.

During the winter of 1590-1591 Adamson sought absolution and his request was granted, though the air was clouded with suspicions about his motives.[219] To clear himself he presented to the April 1591 synod of St. Andrews four terse Latin articles of confession — *me pecasse agnosco* — in which he disowned his former views which favoured a monarchical episcopate and denigrated presbytery (*delirium humanum*); he similarly abandoned co-mingling of the two kingdoms and the grant of royal authority in ecclesiastical affairs.[220] This was a passable beginning but the synod wanted further satisfaction, 'a mair cleir and ample Recantation, and that in the vulgare langage, that all might understand the sam'.[221] Full penance would have to be performed.

Adamson's *Recantation* was eventually published in 1598 at Middelburg, and when it reached Scotland James burned all but two books of the shipment in his own fireplace.[222] Presumably it was as great an embarrassment to him as the Bancroft sermon and its Scottish sequels. But for the presbyterians the archbishops's confession was a coup — as the printer stated in his letter to the reader, it was the work of 'a chiefe Ringleader'.[223] The work reads like a sickbed conversion to the tenets of a man's now irresistible opponents. The beleagured Adamson attributed his episcopal yearnings to ambition, vainglory, and covetousness,[224] and admitted that episcopacy 'hath no warrand of the word of God, but is grunded upon the policie of the invention of man, quhairupon the primacie of the Pope or antichrist is risen, quhilk is worthie to be disallowed & forbidden'. Presbyteries, he now saw, would better serve the church because a bishop's attention was frequently distracted by worldly affairs.[225] It may be that the archbishop wrote this 'without compulsion or persuasion of any man',[226] but he certainly knew what his presbyterian audience desired to hear. Either that, or else archbishop Spottiswood's accusations of fraud were true.[227]

Patrick Adamson did not lack for intelligence. He has been described as 'a man of rare learnying'[228] and 'an able and accomplished scholar, and a Latin poet scarcely inferior to Buchanan and Melville'.[229] Indeed poetry formed a large proportion of his published works beginning with *De papistarum superstitiosus ineptiis,* published in 1564.

Adamson may have been the translator of the Confession of 1560 which was issued in a Latin version in 1572.[230] There is no mention of Adamson in the preface, but following the final page of the Confession itself there stands a new heading:

Caput Jobi quartum quia ad pietatem & probitatem adhortatur subjunxi, a Patricio Adamsono eleganter redditum latino carmine ut reliquum totum opus.

This inclusion of an advertisement for Adamson's work does not give certain proof of his responsibility for the *Confessio,* but the possibility gains credence from its place among a collection of his other works published in 1619 where its title page included the phrase, 'Per Patricium Adamsonum descripta'.[231]

Whatever the case with the Confession, Adamson did turn the book of Job into Latin verse as the above note promised, complete with a two-page sampler. Its publication, however, had to wait. In August 1574 a four-man committee was appointed 'for reviewing and sighting of the history of Job compiled be Mr Patrick Adamsone in Latine verse'. George Buchanan, Peter Young, Andrew Melville, and James Lawson were to pass judgement on it, presumably with a view to its publication.[232] For some reason it, like his Latin renderings of Revelation and Lamentations, remained, and to some extent circulated,[233] in manuscript until 1619 when Adamson's son-in-law Thomas Wilson (Volusenus) published an Adamson miscellany as *Poemata sacra.* A better reception was accorded his *Catechismus latino carmine redditus.*[234] James Melville commented that on its account 'the author was mikle estimed of'.[235]

During the episode of recantation Adamson wrote of his various works, mainly by way of contrition, even to the extent of saying that 'if it pleased God I were restored to my health, I wald change my style'[236] — providing a hint as to the apparent rejection of his paraphrase of Job. He had written a commentary upon part of I Timothy wherein he allowed bishops.[237] This work, of which he himself had not kept a copy, may have been that which was printed in 1619 as *De sacro pastoris munere tractatus* in which bishops appeared as central to the process of excommunication and Andrew Melville's name was introduced in the author's denial of ministerial parity.[238]

Regret was also expressed for offensive material in the preface to his work on Revelation. Written less than one year before his recantation, if it was known to others it could only have served to generate real anxiety about the intentions of this sly fox. In the prefatory letter to the king he depicted himself as one 'who groaned over the miseries of the realm inspired by' his presbyterian foes, 'those impious and execrable men'. He complained that they had accused him of heresy for defending propositions on episcopal and Erastian authority.[239] Adamson also remarked upon his composition of 'Psyllus' (*i.e.* snake charmer) in which he described the presbyterian plague and offered a warning to England. Certainly this work was no secret — James Melville referred to it in 'Zelator, Temporizar, Palemon'[240] and in his 1590 diatribe. But it would never see the light of day. 'God would not suffer me to finishe' it, wrote the archbishop, adding that what he had written he had subsequently destroyed.[241] That is a pity. Undoubtedly it would have given a far more accurate picture of his thought than one finds in his *Recantation*.

Archbishop Adamson had committed just about every sin in the presbyterian book, his acceptance of such an office perhaps the greatest of all. He had been suspected of consulting witches and submitting to their cure,[242] used the English marriage ceremony,[243] performed the Huntly wedding against the kirk's will, written the *Declaration* and other wrong-headed works, insulted presbytery,[244] defamed the kirk abroad,[245] conspired with English bishops, inhibited the stipends of ministers not subscribing the Black Acts,[246] assisted in the mutilation of the register of the general assembly,[247] rebuked the Edinburgh ministers for fleeing during the aftermath of the Black Acts,[248] and written to archbishop John Whitgift not to harbour the Scottish fugitives.[249] Less than a year after his recantation, feigned or otherwise, Patrick Adamson was dead, perhaps to the relief of many and not least of all, himself.

It is perhaps ironical that Adamson's elevation to the archbishopric in 1576 coincided with the translation of Edmund Grindal from York to Canterbury. One cannot resist pondering the impact had Adamson the vacillating and ambitious courtier possessed the same irenic spirit as his English counterpart known for his deep piety and gentle pastoral quality. And yet, Grindal was no fawning flatterer or yes-man bent on peace — or advancement — at any cost. His career was more or less terminated not long after his appointment to Canterbury due to his refusal to prostrate the church before Elizabeth's demand that he suppress the exercise (prophesying). Patrick Collinson has demonstrated how Grindal drew inspiration from Ambrose of Milan, the fourth-century bishop who championed the rights of the church against the emperors of Rome. Thus the archbishop wrote to Elizabeth that the exercise was a good and edifying thing which he could suppress only at the price of affronting God. 'Bear with me, I beseech you, Madam, if I choose rather to offend your earthly Majesty than to offend the heavenly majesty of God'.[250]
But instead of a Grindal, it was an Adamson who appeared in Scotland, despised by nearly everyone, admired for little else than his poetical skills. The result was twofold. First, Adamson and his patrons came to power at a time when they were able to sow seeds in the fertile mind of a precocious young king. As will be seen in what follows, Adamson's ideas on church and state took deep root in James and resurfaced in the later 1590s. Second, the distorted character of the archbishop debased and discredited episcopacy from which abyss it was unable to raise itself. His ambition, inconstancy, and obsequiousness before the crown confirmed all the fears of episcopacy voiced since the mid-1570s. Instead of leading the kirk he poisoned it and blazed the way for James to use the episcopate to serve his own purposes. Had he attempted to employ his archiepiscopal status to safeguard the interests of the kirk and to reconcile conflicting factions, the subsequent history addressed in the ensuing chapters might have been altogether different.

CHAPTER 5

'The Declyneing Aige of the Kirk of Scotland'[1]

In 1590 Robert Rollock, principal of the college in Edinburgh, published his *In epistolam Pauli apostoli ad Ephesios . . . commentarius.*[2] When writing upon Ephesians 4:11 Rollock accomplished two things — a demonstration of the artifices of 'puritan' exegesis, and a summation of the anti-episcopal dogma which had inflamed the kirk for fifteen years.

Rollock wrote, in accordance with his text, that Christ had appointed apostles, prophets, evangelists, pastors, and teachers (*doctores*) to work in the church. But before dealing with this list Rollock laid down the three components of the presbyterian view of the ministry — preaching and administering the sacraments; the exercise of discipline; and the care of the poor. The first and most important task he assigned to pastors and doctors, the second to elders (*presbyteri*), the third to deacons. Even to Rollock's preconditioned mind this format was not to be found in its complete state in Ephesians 4:11; thus it was necessary when writing of the elder to refer to I Timothy 5:17—'De presbyteris & diaconis non est nunc dicendum'. What Ephesians supplied was only a discussion of 'those who work in the word', the first order in the presbyterian scheme of ministry. What, then, of apostles, prophets, and evangelists, offices not found in the second Book of Discipline's agenda for contemporary ministry? Rollock resolved the dilemma just as Thomas Cartwright and the discipline had done, by making a distinction: 'Ministers of the word are partly extraordinary, and partly ordinary'.[3] The extraordinary ministry originated outside the customary manner of calling, invoked immediately by Christ (not *via* the mediation of a congregation). It existed only for a temporary period (*non in perpetuum sed ad tempus*) and was directed toward serving the church in a sense broader than local congregation or parish,[4] particularly in time of crisis. Such was the office of the New Testament apostles but also later giants of the faith including Wycliffe, Hus, Luther, and Zwingli, all of whom, beyond possessing an ordinary ecclesiastical vocation, had an additional calling which was not only extraordinary but even miraculous. Apostles planted, while evangelists, also possessed of an extraordinary appointment, built up the infant congregations.

Ordinary officers were called by ordinary means and endowed with ordinary gifts, but their office was perpetual (*ad finem mundi*). They were two in number, pastors and teachers (doctors), corresponding to the priests and levites of the Old Testament.[5] Again exceeding the bounds of his text, Rollock described them as not only preachers of the word but also as those who *applied* the word as distinct from preaching; they furthermore administered the sacraments, and presided over church discipline.[6]

In effect Rollock was discoursing upon a theme the content of which was already determined, rather than providing a careful exegesis of a biblical locus.

Thus he turned to one remaining question: 'cur non numeravit Apostolus etiam Episcopus inter ministros verbi?' The answer was simply that bishop (*episcopus*) in the Scriptures was equivalent to presbyter or elder, which might refer to the pastor, the doctor, or the ruling elder who was not a labourer in the word.[7] To this assertion Rollock appended a handful of scriptural proofs including Titus 1:5, Acts 20:17, Philippians 1:1, and I Peter 5:2. In none of these was there any superiority of bishops over presbyters. Finally, Rollock returned to Ephesians, stating that Paul, in reviewing all the orders of servants of the word, had nothing to say of bishops (in fact *episcopus* does not occur in the passage) as if they were distinct from pastors. Rollock saw the hierarchical bishop as ambitious and devoted to his belly, originating outside the pale of divine blessing and providing the ground from which Antichrist (the pope) ultimately derived.[8] In all this treatment the writer was hardly original, but he provided a clear statement of the presbyterian mood.

In the same year that Rollock's work on Ephesians appeared, king James offered grounds for hope that his upbringing and the kirk's prayers had borne fruit. At the end of his speech to the August 1590 general assembly,

> his Majesty praiseth God that he was born in such a time, as in the time of the light of the Gospell, to such a place to be King, in such a Kirk, the sincerest Kirk in the world. The Kirk of Geneva, said he, keepeth Pasche and Yuile. What have they for them. They have no institution. As for our neighbour Kirk in England, it is ane evill said messe in English, wanting nothing but the liftings. I charge you my good people . . . to stand to your purity, and to exhort the people to do the same; and forsooth, so long as I brooke my life and croun, shall maintain the same . . . .[9]

A wildly ecstatic assembly gave itself over to a quarter-hour of praise and prayer.

Two years later, in the so-called Golden Act, the kirk in its presbyterian form obtained some degree of recognition. Yearly assemblies, or more frequently if required, were allowed, and other levels of church courts were likewise empowered.[10] Presbyteries acquired the right to admit ministers to benefices,[11] the bishops thereby losing a significant aspect of their ecclesiastical function. Lest there be further injury done to the finances of crown and kirk, no additional erections of temporal lordships from kirk lands were to be permitted, though there was no attempt to revoke grants already made.

But in spite of the presbyterian wind there was a cloud on the horizon. The episcopate seemed to the sanguine presbyterian to be in a fatal decline, but by no means had parliament extinguished the ecclesiastical estate.[12] It would have to be filled one way or another. And perhaps most ominous of all was that the Golden Act did not deprive the crown of a voice in the determination of time and place of general assemblies.[13] James was quick to confirm this royal right. At the April 1593 assembly he asserted 'that in respect he cannot of honour sie the priviledge of his crowne hurt, therfor he will have regard to have the act of his last Parliament keipit concerning the conveining of Generall Assemblies by his Majesties appointment'.[14] Thus the assembly was to send representatives to him, '*to desyre him* to appoint the day and place of their nixt conveining'.[15] This was actually in excess of the power reserved to the crown in 1592 where the king or his delegate should be present — and, presumably, consulted — when the assembly appointed the time and place for the succeeding convocation.[16] Such manipulation and expansion of power would become commonplace in the difficult years that followed.

The calling of subsequent assemblies became a major bone of contention between crown and kirk,[17] commonly dealt with under the heading of 'free assemblies', held when and where the kirk should appoint, its membership determined by the kirk, its decisions freely made without external interference, particularly from the crown and the court.[18] In fact, if the crown could determine the venue of the next assembly it could, with little extension of its power, also delay the meeting more or less indefinitely. With the assembly set aside James would be free to attempt some other means of governing a kirk which was in his eyes too often cantankerous and independent.

Similarly the freedom of the pulpit was brought under scrutiny.[19] Presbyterian preachers thought of themselves as prophets or mouthpieces of the Holy Spirit[20] — thereby making the extraordinary calling part of their own ordinary vocation — and consequently they believed their sermons to be outwith magisterial competence and review[21] which they consistently declined.[22] It was their readiness to rebuke public figures which generated the hostility that James directed at the preachers. John Davidson once said to the king, 'Nather ought your Grace to mak light accompt of our threatnings, for there was never yitt in this realme, in cheefe authoritie, that ever prospered after the ministers began to threattin them'.[23] And threaten they did. James Gibson preached a sermon in Edinburgh in 1585 attacking those ministers who had submitted to the Black Acts and identifying James with Jeroboam: if he did not cease his persecution and perversion of the kirk, he would be the last of his house to rule in Scotland.[24] James had been trying since 1584 to control sermons,[25] and in 1593 he succeeded in having the assembly pass what amounted to a rather mild act restraining anti-government sermons.[26] But even as the 1584 act failed to restrain Gibson, the later attempt was equally futile when thrown in the faces of David Black and John Ross. Black, if the report is to be credited, labelled queen Elizabeth an atheist and denounced the church of England; he described all kings as the 'devillis childrene', the Scottish nobility as 'degenerat, godles, dissemblaris, enemeyis to the Kirk', and royal councillors as atheists, holyglasses, and cormorants.[27] John Ross accused the king of treason and hypocrisy, damned his French ancestry, and warned that without amendment James would 'fill out the nomber of his prediccessors wha have bene extraordinarlie tayne away'![28] Another declaration against presumptuous pulpiteers was announced on 2 December 1596[29] but it too proved futile. Fifteen days later John Welsh pronounced that James was possessed of a devil and he consorted with seven others, namely his council.[30]

Perhaps their insults were the least part of the preachers' indiscretions. In upholding public policy to censure they walked the fine line that bordered on sedition. Of course the presbyterians saw this as their proper, prophetic duty, but the crowned head at whom they took aim held that in setting policy he was actually

fulfilling his own divine commission. He was therefore not about to surrender his
supremacy in and over the kirk, whether the assembly, the pulpit, or the sentence
of excommunication. This latter point, which had come to a head in the affair of
Robert Montgomery, had been for some time a source of irritation between kirk
and state. Following the Ruthven Raid in August 1582 a declaration was made by
the perpetrators in which they gave their view of the realm's ills:

> Nixt the disciplene of the Kirk mair opinly impugnit, quhen as the Kings Majestie be
> the persuasion of thir enemeis to the Kirk was inducit to mak him selfe and his privie
> counsall Judges in the cognitioun & jugement of materis meir ecclesiasticall &
> concerning the doctrine of the preichouris & to tak upon him quhat sumever
> jurisdictioun the Paip usurped thairinto of auld, Yea & mair to dischairg the generall
> assemblie and haill pastouris within this Realme to proceid to the sentence of
> excommunicatioun, also to suspend the same sentence of excomunication maist
> justly and ordourly pronuncit and to decerne the samin of none availl force nor
> effect.[31]

The kirk claimed the right, through excommunication, to ban certain persons
from the royal presence, thus it might exclude individuals from providing counsel
and also dictate how the king ought to deal with papist earls and lords.[32] James
believed that there were some ready to disavow him as king if he failed to take
action against those who rejected 'the estableist religioun now professit'.[33]
Excommunication was intended to sequester offenders from civil as well as
ecclesiastical society – the king being no exception from liability to this dreaded
sentence[34] – raising once more the murky business of two ostensibly distinct
kingdoms which were quite obviously inseparably connected.

Third, there was the seemingly intractable problem of the ecclesiastical estate in
parliament. In July 1591 the assembly called for action against titulars who once
were in the ministry but now performed no authentic ecclesiastical function and
also failed to pay the stipends of ministers in kirks whose revenues they received.[35]
One year later it was decreed that no titular prelates should presume to vote for the
kirk in parliaments or conventions without the express consent and direction of
the kirk. It was recommended that consideration be given to a succession of
ministers in place of the prelates, though it would appear that the proposal
received no further attention at the time.[36] In the March 1596 assembly a proposal
was brought forward by John Lindsay, one of the royal financial advisers known as
the Octavians, whereby the prelacies were to be suppressed and the appropriated
tithes restored to their parishes. Thus might ministers' stipends be maintained at a
reasonable level. In the ticklish matter of the ecclesiastical estate, henceforth each
presbytery should send its own commissioner to parliament. From this contingent
the estates would choose a sufficient group to make up the proper number in
conjunction with the secularised prelacies. As the titulars died off, the commissioners would gradually take over the entire estate.[37] But vested interests prevailed
and the proposal died.[38]

Meddling with the episcopate meant that the kirk was impinging upon the
national constitution in which bishops and other prelates had long formed one of
the estates. To inhibit or depose them the kirk must necessarily find itself

imposing a political settlement upon the crown which looked to its prelatical appointees for support among the estates.[39]

These various considerations overlapped for they were different aspects of one central issue, the growth and stabilisation of the crown's jurisdiction. So long as the kirk could dictate to James, he could not truly be master, a 'universal king',[40] of a frequently unruly house. But he could see the solution — an episcopal kirk, its bishops the appointed servants of the crown.

In the years of upheaval that followed, the foundations of a historiographical tradition were laid down by a persecuted faction, the presbyterians. Much of the surviving material for the years 1596-1610 has been preserved in the diary of James Melville; therefore the telling of this story entails also the description of a partisan view of Scotland's post-Reformation ecclesiastical history.

James Melville was one of the formative influences upon the development of the presbyterian mind in the late sixteenth and early seventeenth centuries. Long in the shadow of his more famous uncle Andrew Melville, James merits a more prominent place in the history of the kirk under James VI. Not only did he write numerous letters and deliver thunderous speeches, he also collected materials and helped to lay the foundations of a presbyterian historiography. His importance to the cause was recognised by many contemporaries, hostile and friendly. King James called him to England in 1606 and long refused him permission to return home. David Calderwood wrote that archbishop Spottiswood said James Melville was crafty and a greater source of anxiety than Andrew,[41] while Calderwood himself stated that the younger Melville 'was one of the wisest directours of kirk affaires that our kirk had in his tyme'.[42] Youngèr co-religionists set themselves into a filial relationship with their 'most loving father'.[43]

A son of the manse, James was born in 1556 or 1557 and studied at St. Andrews University. In 1574 he went with Andrew to teach at Glasgow and later accompanied him to St. Andrews. He likewise shared Andrew's exile in England before assuming the pastoral charge of Anstruther in Fife in 1587.[44] James Melville died at Berwick in 1614 while journeying to Scotland on a trip licensed by archbishop George Gledstanes.[45]

The most salient feature of these memoirs is their uncompromising presbyterianism which entailed a parallel anti-episcopalianism. Melville's reason for setting down the history of those years, especially 1574-1610, the substance of his adult years, was to describe a battle between God and Antichrist, church government according to the Bible *versus* human invention. Of the homecoming of his uncle and close colleague Andrew he wrote, 'then the quhilk, I, nor Scotland nather, receavit never a graitter benefit of the hands of God',[46] whereas the creation of bishops at Leith in 1572 was 'the warst turn that ever was done for the kirk leiving'.[47] From this pattern he never deviated, and it was reported that on his deathbed he declared:

> The Roman hirarchie will schortlie undo religione in Scotland; I pray the Lord oppin the Kingis eiis, that he may sie it, and grant him grace to amend it. In my lyff I ever deteastit it, and resistit the same as ane thing unlawfull and antechrystiane, for the quhilk I am heir in exyll; and now, I tak yow all to witnes I die in the same judgment this day.[48]

There was real continuity for Melville between the kirk's struggles under the regent Morton and under king James. For both of them the church of England proved to be a tempting vision of a subservient Scottish kirk. It was Morton's intention, wrote Melville, to reduce the general assembly and to 'bring in a conformitie with Eingland in governing of the Kirk be Bischopes and injunctiones; without the quhilk, he thought, nather the kingdome could be gydet to his fantasie, nor stand in guid aggriement and lyking with the nibour land'.[49] In 1590, perhaps still inflamed by Bancroft's sermon, Melville called upon his colleagues to study and practise presbyterian polity with all diligence because, in part, the perverted English bishops 'be all moyen, yea and money, was seikand conformitie of our realme with thairs, till invert and pervert our Kirk, as did Achaz and Urias with the King and Altar of Damascus'.[50]

The watershed year in Melville's history was 1596 and the first three months of 1597. Of this time he wrote that it 'may be markett for a speciall periodic and fatall yeir to the Kirk of Scotland', and it was accompanied by the appropriate portents of a ferocious rainstorm and the beaching of 'a monstruus grait whaale'.[51] Viewing the years 1596-1610, Melville wrote their history under the rubric, 'A True Narratioune of the Declyneing Aige of the Kirk of Scotland'. Casting backward from 1610 for a brief survey of Scotland's reformed past, he described the years from 1560 when the kirk 'wes brought out of the darkness of Paperie to the Reformation begun in Scotland, the clear light of the Gospell, has been now sa perfect jubilee of sevin sevine [seven times seven] yeares'.[52] Applauding the kirk's infancy, exulting in its incomparable perfection, Melville deplored 'this doolfull decay, in this almaist dying aige, most pitifull and most lamentabill'. He believed that the kirk's perfection was grounded upon

> the paterne schawin by God to the Prophettis and Apostelles upon the Montaines of Sinay and Sion: In doctrine and discipline, without any mixture from Babylon, or that city sett on seven hills, or from the policie of man's braine, hath bein, for sinceritie, truth, and libertie, thaise mony yeires, of all Kirks, in all kingdoms of Europe, with admiration beholding and looking upon; faire as the morneing, cleir as the mone, pure as the soone in the eyes of hir freinds, and dreidfull as ane armie feghting under ane banner, to all hir enimies![53]

But after this triumphant beginning Melville had then to narrate the kirk's 'declyneing aige', commencing with 'that Evill Synod' of 17 December 1596, thereafter deteriorating steadily to the time of writing, c.1610.

The year 1596 brought to a head certain tensions which had been festering for several years. As far as the leaders of the kirk were concerned, the Catholic threat had to be suppressed, and they agitated for action against the papist earls and called for 'universall repentance'.[54] The March assembly engaged in lengthy soul-searching to root out all forms of unfaithfulness and thereby avoid the otherwise certain descent of God's wrath. Ministers must henceforth be tried more stringently before admission and they must be more diligent in their imposition of discipline. There were many aspersions on the behaviour of some ministers.[55]

John Davidson's call for repentance led to an extraordinary outpouring of sorrow such as had not been witnessed since the Reformation.[56] Subsequently there were recorded criticisms of behaviour elsewhere in the realm. Even James's personal piety was considered to be in decline. He swore too frequently, while his queen not only neglected the services of the kirk but also devoted herself to frivolous and unseemly entertainments.[57] Among numerous other defections from the truth it was again complained that 'sacrilegious persons, as Abbots, Pryours, dumb Bischops' voted in behalf of the kirk in parliaments, 'contrair to the lawis of the countrye, quherby the cause of the Kirk is damnified'.[58]

The effect of this spiritual inventory was the renewal of the covenant, a fresh promise to God that the kirk would follow His ways more fervently and precisely.[59] At the strongly presbyterian synod of Fife in May the renewal was preceded by a number of exhortations. The moderator, apparently James Melville, recalled God's blessings upon the kirk 'in planting and garding the saming from the Castalians, Obenittes [Aubignites, pertaining to Esmé Stewart, seigneur d'Aubigné], Spaniarts, Bischope Balaam, and lait Conspiracie of the Papist Erles'.[60] Later, Andrew Melville expressed fear of defection from the truth in that by subscribing to the Black Acts of 1584 out of anxiety over the prospect of losing their stipends many ministers 'war brought to a sort of denying Jesus Chryst'. He warned against the persistent threat of the Spanish who could easily sail into the Firth of Forth and 'essay our constancie with fyre and exquisit torments of thair Inquisitioun'.[61]

James Melville rued the failure of Edinburgh to renew the covenant, and attributed to this 'the effect of a feirfull desolatioun, gif we dar judge!'[62] The reference was of course to the 17 December riot fostered by prominent preachers out of fear of a Catholic plot when James was in Edinburgh for a conference. The outcome was that James treated the city as a conquered foe. He banished its ministers and then called for a convention of the kirk at Perth beginning the end of February 1597, though Calderwood remarked that the ensuing alterations had been plotted for at least a year, making the riot just a pretext for royal intervention.[63] From this point on the presbyterians saw their beloved kirk in decline and in defection from the truth.

Before the meeting of the kirk convention James set forth a list of fifty-five questions he desired to have discussed. They ranged from the external government of the kirk to the imposition of hands in ordination to the application of discipline. But over all hung the shadow of a Christian king who conceived an idea of his own exalted place in the kirk as well as in the state. In the preface to *The questions to be resolvit* he claimed for himself the office of ensuring that God was 'richtly honoured in his Land', and therefore as the nursing father of the kirk and custodian of both tables it was his rightful place

> to strengthen and assist be the concurrance of his civill sword, the saidis spiritual office-bearers in the dew execution of thair calling, and on the uther pairt, to compell thame to exercise faithfully thair office, according to the rule prescrivit to thame be the word of God, not suffering thame to transgresse the limites thairof in ony sort.[64]

James observed an overly free use of the pulpit and both obscurity and novelty in polity, thus he had determined to emulate 'the lovable example of the Christian Emperours of the primitive Kirk' and to summon a council

> to treat, ressoun, consult, and determine, (according to the word of God as the onley rule) upon the clearing and distinguishing of the spirituall jurisdictioun, alswell in applicatioun of doctrine, as in the haill pollicie and government of the house of God.[65]

The convention at Perth was to see a new godly Constantine presiding at a Scottish Nicaea.

In anticipation of the formal gathering the delegates from the synod of Fife convened at St. Andrews to air their opinions about the royal queries. Responding to the first, whether the kirk's policy might be brought once more under discussion, it was replied that the current polity was of divine origin, established by law (an excessively favourable interpretation of the Golden Act), 'and mair nor threttie years possessioun', a somewhat remarkable and oft-repeated claim that would years later elicit an energetic denial from non-presbyterian historians. Furthermore, both papists and 'our nibour enemies of the discipline, the Bischopes of Eingland'[66] were then seeking to undo the reformed kirk as it stood in Scotland. It was consequently rebellion against God and a senseless invitation to malignants to re-open the matter. So far as the Davidsons, the Blacks, and the Melvilles were concerned, the issue of ecclesiastical government had been settled by Jesus himself:

> Christ being Maister of his owne hous, has sett doun the rules of the regiment of his owne hous and houshold familie; which may no more be altered, than Moses might have altered the forme of the tabernacle sett down to him, (Exod. xxv. 40.)[67]

What could there possibly be left to say on the matter?

Further to James's view of himself, the St. Andrews gathering had other ideas about a king. In the preceding September Andrew Melville had made a presbyterian legend of himself when he shook the king's sleeve and called him 'God's sillie vassall', proceeding to point out that 'thair is twa Kings and twa Kingdomes in Scotland'.[68] Christ's kingdom was the kirk, and of it James was a member, not any kind of head. He might only assist the proper governors of the kirk. This was the background to the comments made in February just before the Perth convention to the effect that the civil authorities, particularly James, should only lend support to what pastors and doctors interpreted as the divine will.[69] But even without royal assent, ecclesiastical acts possessed a 'sufficient authoritie from Chryst' which was superior to any other power, 'yea, even sic as sould command and overruell Kings, whase graittest honour is to be members, nuris-fathers, and servants to the King, Chryst Jesus, and his spouse and Quein, the Kirk'.[70] Further assertions were made concerning free assemblies by divine, not royal, warrant,[71] and the king was denied the right to nullify even a grossly unfair act of excommunication.[72]

This gathering of the prickly synod of Fife instructed its commissioners not to accept the forthcoming Perth convention as a genuine assembly since it had not been summoned through the proper channels '*as hes bein the practise of the Kirk at all tymes befor within this realme,* warranted be the Word of God and lawes of the countrey'.[73] It was furthermore stipulated that these commissioners might not deal with matters of kirk polity because these had already been handled by a general assembly. If deliberation was called for, they must insist upon the liberty of the kirk and seek a delay until the next true assembly in April. All they could do, it appears, was deliver the judgements of their synod and protest against intrusions into the kirk's jurisdiction, meaning that only an assembly could make determinations. The presbytery of Edinburgh reacted similarly.[74]

James, of course, wanted the Perth convention to be regarded as an assembly. If he could not gain acquiesence in this point he would fail to establish his power of determining time and place for future assemblies. The selection of Perth was significant in that assemblies had generally been held in either St. Andrews or Edinburgh where the radicals held sway.[75] But James removed the assembly from that prejudicial environment, and through 'the diligent Apostle of the Northe', sir Patrick Murray, he exploited the resentment of the northern ministers, now present in larger numbers than usual, against 'the Poprie of Edinbruche'.[76] Predictably, Melville called these northerners courtiers and identified Edinburgh as 'the Sion of our Jerusalem'.[77] It was also reported that James had threatened the termination of all assemblies unless the convention complied with his demand that it metamorphose itself into an assembly[78] — a constitutional impossibility because each assembly was to be appointed at the preceding one. After much discussion, and a two-day debate,[79] the king had his way, the decision justified on grounds which included the power of the magistrate and the imperial precedent in antiquity.[80] James Melville protested that the Perth assembly and its proceedings were considered invalid by 'the best and most godlie'.[81] But resistance was in vain. Robert Pont was joined by a few others at St. Andrews in April in order to keep the regularly appointed assembly, now prorogued, where a gesture of independence and liberty was made.[82] The king, however, called his own assembly at Dundee in May where the Perth convention was again upheld as a legitimate assembly of the kirk.[83]

After all the preparations and rhetoric the outcome at Perth was less than decisive, but James was not dissatisfied at his gains and the (relatively?) 'willing mynd' of the ministers, demonstrating his pleasure by, among other things, proclaiming his protection of all ministers and their families.[84] The list of fifty-five questions was reduced to eleven.[85] Most significant among the assembly's final responses was that questions of polity might be raised in assemblies, but only those which were 'alterable according to circumstances', a phrase which would receive a very constricted scope in the hands of presbyterians. Pulpit comment on state affairs was subjected to some control, but perhaps the only real benefit to the crown was that the assembly agreed, if only by failing to make any positive claim, to subject the calling of assemblies to the royal will.[86] This was quite sufficient, however, to elicit a strong reaction from James Melville. He contrasted the two kinds of assemblies, the kirk's and the king's:

In end, the end of the Assemblies of auld was, whow Chryst's kingdome might stand in halines and friedome: Now, it is whow Kirk and Relligioun may be framed to the polytic esteat of a frie Monarchie, and to advance and promot the grandour of man, and supream absolut authoritie in all causses, and over all persones, alsweill Ecclesiasticall as Civill.[87]

James's usurpation of power in the kirk was likened by some to that of Uzziah, a comparison strengthened by the occurrence of a notable earthquake in the north.[88] Someone composed a poem of admonition to the king, concluding thus:[89]

> King James the Saxt, this yeir thow fast aspyrs,
> Ou're Chryst his Kirk to compas thy desyrs.
>   O wey this weill, and heire exemple tak,
> Lest Chryst, wha this yeir schuk thy north-wast parts,
> And withe eclipsed Sun amasde the harts,
>   For kings to com thie just exemple mak!

The assembly consented to the appointment of commissioners who were empowered to deal between assemblies with the king concerning various matters including the appointment of ministers in the chief towns and royal households, the planting of kirks, the 'constant platt' for ministerial stipends, 'and generally to give thair advyce to his Majestie in all affaires concerning the weill of the Kirk, and intertainment of peace and obedience to his Majestie within this realme'.[90] The interim delegation of authority was not innovative, for the assembly had commonly required some sort of representation between its meetings.[91] But the potential for independent action was now dramatically augmented. Assemblies might be suspended for lengthy periods according to the king's pleasure, thus granting opportunity for entrenchment of the commissioners' power due to the necessity of action by them in lieu of deliberation by the assembly which found itself increasingly stripped of power and initiative. Of the newly appointed fourteen commissioners, any seven would suffice for a quorum.[92] Maurice Lee, Jr. has pointed out that only four of the whole number were antagonistic toward James,[93] thus it would prove a simple matter for crown supporters to hold sway. The four dissenters could easily be outvoted or ignored.

For Melville these commissioners were generally (he was one of the fourteen) 'the deid-stroake and baine of the Kirk',[94] while another termed them 'his Majestie's led horse'.[95] Melville complained that with their elevation to easy access to the king and their sitting with James in council they 'began soone to chaing thair maneres and luik doun on thair breithrin. They reulit as they list', and were the occasion of a torn kirk. Melville wrote that most ministers followed the commissioners, implying that the majority were well disposed toward James, while, in a comment which revealed his own rather elitist view of the good and faithful ministry, 'the best stood to the Kirk hir establischit constitutioun'. The commissioners 'were the very neidle to draw in the Episcopall threid', a trojan horse through the acceptance of which the kirk effected its own defacement.

A partisan retrospective is a suspect historical source, but for what it is worth, and there is good reason to credit the report on account of its precise reference,

Melville wrote that it was during a conversation with sir Patrick Murray, James Nicolson, and Peter Blackburn on a northern visitation in October 1597 'I smeld out the purpose of erectioun of Bischopes againe'.[96] Probably they were discussing plans for the forthcoming parliament.

At that time the kirk's commissioners petitioned the estates, without the consent of the general assembly but with the king's encouragement, that ministers might vote in parliament[97] though without the trappings of bishops.[98] This, however, would have altered the structure of the estates, so it was rejected. The only way to acquire a voice in parliament was acceptance of episcopacy. One report claimed that the king would have agreed to the ministers' proposal but was opposed by the council.[99] This was undoubtedly an astute political move by the nobles who had no desire to see ministers placed in the 'great benefices'.[100] Both Melville and an English observer believed that the nobles insisted upon an episcopal format because they doubted that any self-respecting Scottish minister would ever accept such an arrangement given the length and vehemence of the kirk's opposition to episcopacy.[101] But James, surely delighted with these convoluted developments causing one to wonder whether he somehow orchestrated the whole affair, persuaded the commissioners to accept the bargain so that it was enacted on 13 December 1597[102] that in accordance with earlier custom, 'sik pasturis and ministeris . . . as at ony tyme his majestie sall pleis to provyid to the office place title and dignitie of ane bischoip abbot or uther prelat sall at all tyme heirefter haif voitt in parliament'. These prelacies with their attendant parliamentary seats were to be given only to qualified ministers, thereby disallowing in the future any more lay members from voting with the kirk's voice. The question of ecclesiastical power pertaining to these new quasi-bishops was remitted by parliament to the king in consultation and agreement with the general assembly.[103]

As a result of this parliament the commissioners issued a letter to the presbyteries, dated 22 December 1597, calling for an assembly to be held in March instead of May as originally scheduled. Prominent on the agenda was consideration of the ecclesiastical vote in parliament. They attempted to allay suspicions by denying any subversion of the existing discipline, explaining that the king intended by this means to redeem the ministers from penury, and that they had been pressured to accept the arrangement in behalf of the kirk or else lose all hope of an agreement that might alleviate the financial embarrassment of the ministry.[104]

Predictably, the synod of Fife was outraged by these proceedings and in February 1598 vented its collective hostility. The historian himself said in a speech that the granting of prelatical seats in the ecclesiastical estate would amount to the erection of bishops, 'quhilk we haid bein all our dayes dinging down'. David Ferguson, the senior minister in the kirk, related 'whow the corruptiones of that office of Bischopes haid bein espyed by the Kirk of Scotland from the beginning' and the efforts that had been made to keep them out.[105] He too saw in the current developments a renewed attempt to recreate episcopacy in Scotland through the tactics of the trojan horse whereby craftiness would bring the kirk itself to institute bishops. John Davidson then offered his famous remark: 'Busk, busk, busk him as bonilie as ye can, and fetche him in als fearlie as yie will, we sie him weill aneuche, we sie the hornes of his mytre!'[106]

It was this strident opposition that caused the crown to relent somewhat at the March 1598 assembly at Dundee.[107] James sought to quieten suspicion and mistrust aroused by the parliamentary bishops, declaring it was not his intention to introduce 'Angelicall nor Papisticall Bischoprickes, but only the best and wysest of thair Ministeres, apoyntit by the Generall Assemblie' to reason and vote on matters of concern to the kirk.[108] Given the substance of his literary activities later that year, there is justification for doubt concerning the sincerity of the protestation.

Whether through lack of time[109] or fear of negative reaction[110] this assembly did not define the manner of the kirk's representation in the estates, particularly election, stipend, length of office, title, and cautions to keep the office from tumbling into corruption.[111] The most it agreed to was that there should be fifty-one ecclesiastical representatives in the estate, and that crown and kirk should share in the election.[112] The king obtained his wish that commissioners of assembly be granted 'full power and commission'.[113] Furthermore, the assembly

allowit the honest and godlie intention of the Commissioners in craving vote in Parliament for the Ministerie, as conforme and aggrieing to sundrie uther acts of the Assemblies preceiding, in the quhilk it hes bein found expedient that the Kirk sould sute vote in Parliament.[114]

Thus, even though James did not get all that he wanted, in spite of the unease of some ministers he had fared not too badly and might have felt rather pleased at the outcome. Conversely the presbyterians could only worry about the darkening future.

Further discussion was had at Falkland in July 1598,[115] the conclusions of which were referred to the Montrose assembly held in March 1600. But between these two gatherings there was another at Holyroodhouse in November 1599 called by James, constituted 'of all sortes of the ministerie, zealus and fyrie, modest and grave, wys and indifferent',[116] with the intention of paving the way to a subsequent harmonious assembly. The prognosis was not good for the king. The presbyterians reacted strongly to the whole concept of ministerial entanglement in 'effears of this lyff',[117] including parliamentary representation. This was condemned by the word of God, as was anything which distracted preachers from their vocation, though this by no means precluded sermons about worldly, civil, or royal matters.[118] The presbyterians repudiated the notion of the 1598 assembly that any previous assembly had called for ministerial representation among the estates.[119] Comment was offered on two fundamental issues — the perpetuity of the voters in the ecclesiastical estate, and the title of bishop. With respect to the first, perpetuity was seen as the means of bringing in an 'Antichristian Hierarchie' and establishing the 'hie way to Paprie',[120] reducing the general assembly to nothing more than an episcopal chapter. As for the title of bishop, let it be used properly or else altered to 'Judas Episcopatus'.[121] The presbyterians were convinced that if the title were used, the substance of pre-eminence and inequality would soon follow and, given the longstanding opposition to the term, to do an about-face would 'offer just occasioun of sklander'.[122]

James was exasperated. Unable to sway the opposition, he terminated the conference and referred all to the next assembly which could decide whether or not it would receive his magnanimity and protection. 'As for him, he could nocht want an of his esteattes; he wald put in that roum, and these offices, sic as he thought guid, wha wald accept thairof, and do thair dewtie to him and his countrey'.[123]

At the assembly in March 1600 the presbyterians presented eighteen arguments[124] against ministers having parliamentary votes, most of the points in reference to mingled and confused jurisdictions. The function simply could not be reconciled with a polity based inflexibly upon the concept, however unworkable and naive, of two distinct kingdoms. But in spite of their assiduous efforts the principle of parliamentary representatives accepted by the 1598 assembly was upheld and enhanced. Selection of ministers for the ecclesiastical estate was to be through nomination of candidates by the kirk and election from the list by the king. Parliamentary ministers would retain the revenue of their prelatical benefices so long as the kirk was well planted and no harm was done to any educational institution dependent upon the same resources.[125] Thus the interests and ambitions of the reformed kirk were not to be hindered by the disposition of prelatical revenues.

The assembly sought to ensure its control over its parliamentary representatives through a series of cautionary conditions. They must speak only with the kirk's direction, and they must not keep silence when the kirk's place was imperilled; they must report to assembly and subject themselves like all other ministers to the terms of their calling; parliamentary office added nothing to their ecclesiastical jurisdiction, and if deposed from the ministry they would also lose their votes; 'and farther cautions to be made as the Kirk pleases and finds occasioun'.[126]

As for the name of these officers, the assembly proposed 'Commissioner of such a place'. No agreement was reached on the length of term, thus the question was deferred to the next assembly. However, it reappeared before the end of the current assembly when an annual term of office was accepted.[127] This, of course, presumed an annual assembly at which the voters should render accounts of their dealings. But the annual nature of their office was mitigated in that new nominations were not made each year. If a commissioner to the estates had done well his term would be continued, thereby effecting a compromise of sorts which actually came very close to the king's desire for a term *ad vitam aut culpam*.[128]

Also at the 1600 assembly it was clarified that a parliamentary commissioner had no *ex officio* right to vote in the general assembly and one guilty of *crimen ambitus* was liable to deprivation. In recognition of the strong tide of opposition ministers were warned against criticising the conclusions of the assembly from their pulpits. Once again commissioners were appointed to advise the king on ecclesiastical affairs until the subsequent assembly.[129]

At a convention of commissioners from synods held in October 1600 at Holyroodhouse the process of creating parliamentary commissioners was consummated, if not exceeded. For three *bishops* were elected — David Lindsay of Leith for Ross, Peter Blackburn for Aberdeen (he had actually been appointed in September),[130] and George Gledstanes for Caithness. They were appointed to vote in the next parliament, 'without anie regard', Melville complained, for the cautions previously agreed upon.[131]

Maurice Lee, Jr. has shed light on the methods by which James sought the subjugation of pulpit and assembly to his own will during the period 1596-1600.[132] The king dangled the incentive of improved ministerial stipends, he ensured the attendance at assemblies of more moderate and tractable ministers (usually from outside Fife and the Lothians), and he made personal contacts with ministers to allay their fears and to solicit their support. The upshot of Lee's study, however, is that, contrary to received opinion,[133] James did not plot the restoration of episcopacy from the outset of his interference. What the king sought was control, and episcopacy was by no means the sole method of establishing it. Only when he failed to get full satisfaction at Montrose in 1600 concerning the appointment of parliamentary commissioners did he decide to appoint bishops.[134]

Professor Lee's paper presents two major problems. First, he seems to have seriously underestimated James's capacity for consistent and premeditated action.[135] A contemporary, John Row, thought otherwise, calling James 'a wittie politick Prince, whose far-fetched drifts and politick plotts the more simple did not espy'.[136] Indeed his intellectual pretensions may have been both narrow and shallow and his demeanour thoroughly 'unkingly',[137] yet he was no fool, and some modern historians have spoken well of his ability as a ruler.[138] Second, Dr. Lee has depended too heavily upon Calderwood and has not appreciated sufficiently the contemporary comment of James Melville and even the *Historie and Life of King James the Sext* which claimed that as early as 1593 James had renewed his quest for bishops.[139] He has also failed to give due weight to the publications of the king himself. One must be careful to differentiate between James's ultimate goal conceived presently in only a general fashion and his decision to actually implement a measure. That is to say, the decision in favour of episcopacy in mid-1600 ought not to be read as a hasty and precipitate change of direction. In fact the king's treatises would suggest a prior attachment to episcopacy which was probably firmly embedded in his mind years before the final, inexorable, move.

To attempt an analysis of the royal mind concerning the kirk and its faith necessitates a detailed consideration of just what James meant when he promised in 1597 to defend the 'trew religioun'.[140] The most salient features of James's thought were his self-image as a Christian king with all the attendant privileges and responsibilities, along with an apparent dichotomisation of theology and polity, of confession and constitution. He regarded doctrine[141] as the more fundamental since to it pertained matters essential to salvation, while the structure of the kirk he discussed within the context of the political and social institutions of the particular time and place. Thus only faith was immutable while external form was a relative matter, quite contrary to what the presbyterians had to say on the issue.

In attempting to elucidate this problem one is confronted with the difficult task of making sense out of words spoken by a political figure who must conciliate even in the act of pressing forward his own aims. Of course there were doubts concerning the sincerity of his religious pronouncements. In 1586 Robert Pont praised God for the king but in the same breath added, 'we trust your Majestie speaketh without hypocrisy'.[142] Nor might James be expected to go out of his way to correct errors of interpretation — if people wished to read his remarks in such a light as rendered him palatable to them, then so be it. He did nothing to dampen the enthusiasm of those who called attention to his 1589 promise to uphold the kirk's discipline, though in the absence of any fuller report one is left to wonder exactly what James did say. The account of the speech may embody wishful thinking, for he never dissociated himself from the infamous *Declaration,* nor did he ever renounce royal control over the kirk or the right to appoint bishops.[143] Even in his stirring speech in 1590 when he expressed his views on the kirk's purity and superiority James said nothing about episcopacy. He condemned English worship but contributed nothing to James Melville's aspersions on the 'belli-god Bischopes in Eingland'.[144] One can, however, appreciate how ecstatic presbyterians might have interpreted James's words as an oath of allegiance to presbytery, an impression strengthened by the favourable legislation of 1592. At Hampton Court in 1604 he explained that even though he had been raised among puritans, as he referred to the presbyterians, 'yet, since hee was of the age of his Sonne 10. years old, he ever disliked their opinions; as the Saviour of the world said, Though he lived among them, he was not of them'.[145] In his 'Premonition' (1609) he claimed that the puritans had persecuted him even before his birth, a reference to the Riccio murder and their approval of it. Since thirteen years of age he had opposed them, and even at the tender age of eighteen (*i.e.* in 1584) he had restored bishops, and for six years before entering England he had devoted himself to suppressing parity and restoring bishops.[146] Other sources would seem to verify his claims. It was reported in 1586 that the twenty-year-old sovereign had said, 'he had bene brought up amonge a company of mutinous knave ministeres, whose doctrine he had never approved'.[147] A decade later this arm's-length relationship with the presbyterians was noticed by Roman Catholics:

> Although he was educated in Calvinism, he does not agree with the Calvinists in many opinions, whence it is not impossible that he might be brought by learned men to the Catholic faith.[148]

There can be little doubt that the presbyterians believed their own good seeds were crowded out by tares sown by men such as Morton, Adamson, Lennox, and Arran who had access to a young and impressionable monarch and filled his mind with seductive thoughts of universal and free monarchy.[149] 'Pernicious pests and monsters of men' had inculcated in James 'that devillish opinioun of absolute power' which would despoil Jesus Christ of his own proper authority.[150]

In 1598 James published his *True lawe of free monarchies* in which he declared, against John Knox and George Buchanan, that kings of Scotland 'were the authors & makers of the lawes, and not the lawes of the Kings'.[151] Knox's *History of the Reformation in Scotland* included several particularly unacceptable passages on political relationships. John Willock was cited to the effect that although magistrates were God's representatives, 'he did never so establish any but that, for just causes, they might have been deprived'.[152] Knox approved, and later, in a dispute with William Maitland, he declared that God had armed subjects against their own kings and authorised them to use force to resist offending monarchs.[153] John Douglas and John Craig gave at least qualified support to Knox's contention.[154] Buchanan's *De jure regni apud scotos* had already been condemned by the Scottish parliament,[155] by Richard Bancroft,[156] and by king James himself, while Buchanan's defence had been conducted by Andrew Melville,[157] an advocate not likely to impress the king. The great humanist had written that 'the law is stronger than the king and the people than the law',[158] and, building upon a contractual theory of government,[159] had approved of the deposition of wayward Scottish kings in times past.[160] Earlier, a work entitled *Ane discourse tuiching the estait present in October, 1571* declared that to permit rulers to do as they pleased made the people traitors to God. Written as a dialogue between George and Thomas and treating of the deposition of Mary, it suggests a relationship with Buchanan's *De jure regni* and may well be a hitherto unrecognised work of Buchanan. There was no one, wrote the anonymous author, exempt from the law:

> we mon farther understand that the violatioun of the lawis of God ar not only craifit to be punischit in private men, bot evin in Papis, Empirouris, Kingis, Quenis, and all estatis of Princessis, forsamekle as in the geving of the Law na libertie was gevin to sic transgressioun nouther ony exemption of thame quhairby thay may be privilegit.[161]

James looked also to the Bible wherein he ascertained that kings were gods by virtue of their sitting upon the deity's earthly throne.[162] They were responsible only to God, and no matter how wicked, there were not to be rebelled aginst but rather accepted as God's punishment of the people's evil.[163] Reacting to the insecurity of his throne, he denounced the 'shamles presumption' whereby contemporary Christians should now lay claim 'to that unlawfull libertie, which God refused to his owne peculiar and chosen people'.[164] Sharing his social group's antipathy toward an outspoken clergy, James was not a monarch who would willingly suffer the independence of ministers who presumed to call in question his manner of ruling. He could conceive of only one jurisdiction in Scotland, and that belonged solely to himself. If he were a tyrant, God, not presbyterian ministers (whom he did not regard as oracles), would deal with him.

The Scottish king's most significant composition was his *Basilikon Doron*, written during the summer or early autumn of 1598,[165] and printed privately in seven copies in 1599.[166] James composed the work as counsel for his son and heir, prince Henry, advising him to rule the kirk as *custos utriusque tabulae*.[167] This was predicated upon the dual role of a Christian king who stood astride the ecclesiastical and civil realms, 'for a King is not *mere laicus*, as both the Papistes and Anabaptists would have him, to the which errour also our puritanes incline over-far'.[168] Thus the crown should rule the pulpit as there could be no peace in the land so long as preachers meddled in affairs of state. He furthermore warned his son to 'suffer no Conventions nor meetings among Churchmen, but by your knowledge and permission'.[169]

In this treatise James vented his bitterness toward his presbyterian tormentors. He wrote of 'vain proud puritanes, that thinke they rule [God] upon their fingers';

'vaine people passing the bounds of their calling', in need of kingly correction; 'verie pestes in the Church and common-weill of Scotland'; worse than highland and border thieves.[170]

James by no means rued the Reformation. Even though he was plagued with an abundance of personal shortcomings and infirmities, there is no reason to doubt the sincerity of his attachment to the Christian faith, and that of a reformed type. This much of his Scottish religious heritage and upbringing took root. He did, however, express regret concerning the directions pursued by some Scottish Protestants. Whereas England had been fortunate to find its reform flowing 'from the Princes ordour',[171] the Reformation in Scotland was the disorderly offspring of 'a popular tumult & rebellion', to which James added as a parenthetical comment, 'as wel appeared by the destruction of our policie'.[172] The outcome was that some 'fyerie ministers' tasted political power, and liking it, they dreamed of democratic government. This led to their opposition to the queen regent and queen Mary[173] and their usurpations during James's minority, hoping to become '*Tribuni plebis: and so in a popular governement by leading the people by the nose, to beare the sway of all the rule*'.[174] James opined that the presbyterians were on the wrong side of every conflict, and so antagonistic toward him that they abused him simply for being a king, 'which they thoght the highest evil'.[175] Parity of ministers was introduced by the seditious as a means of silencing their fellows who disavowed presumption against the crown, and thereby 'the ignorantes were emboldened (as bairdes) to crie the learned, godlie, and modest out of it'.[176] But ministerial parity is a subject filled with irony. The presbyterians made it dogma, then complained that the king should undo the better ministers by drawing in pastors from the far reaches of the realm to vote in assemblies. Therefore those who upheld parity in their theory ended by deploring its implementation, while he who repudiated it as the source of distemper in the kirk and, ultimately, subversion of the state, made astute political use of it.

Not unreasonably, James fretted about any apparent challenge to his exercise of power as a free, unlimited, monarch. Thus, while acknowledging the benefits of historical study, he excluded 'such infamous invectives as Buchananes and Knoxes chronicles', and advised prince Henry to use the law against possessors of such seditious documents.[177] His concern about contrary political opinion was so great that this became one of James's reasons for acceding at Hampton Court in 1604 to the request for a new translation of the Bible. Of all the English Bibles, he regarded the Geneva translation as the worst.[178] Among its marginal notes he had found some which were

> very partiall, untrue, seditious, and savouring, too much, of dangerous, and trayterous conceipts: As for example, Exod. 1.19. where the marginall note alloweth *disobedience to Kings*. And 2 Chron. 15.16 the note taxeth Asa for deposing his mother, onely, and *not killing her*.[179]

At Hampton Court James also gave further expression of his view of the seditious possibility of presbytery, saying that it 'agreeth with a Monarchy, as God, and the Devill'.[180] The famous parallel statement of 'No Bishop, no King'[181] summed up what James had earlier written in the *Basilikon Doron*. He was confident of a solution to the intolerable situation which confronted him in the kirk. As an antidote to presbyterian poison he advised Henry to

> interteine and advance the godlie learned, and modest men of the ministerie, whom of (God be praysed) there lacketh not a reasonable number: And by their prefermente to Bishoprickes and Benefices (annulling that vile Acte of Annexation if yee find it not done to your hande) yee shall not onelie bannish their Paritie (which can not agree with a Monarchie) but yee shall also reestablishe the olde institution of three Estates in Parliament, which can no otherwaise bee done. [182]

More than any other, this statement demonstrates the difficulty associated with Professor Lee's interpretation. James knew what he wanted – bishops – and other officers such as parliamentary commissioners were just intermediate steps along the way to his final goal which he could foresee, even if the timetable were uncertain.

James wanted a well ordered kirk, and to that end he commended it to his son's loving care. Henry should be its 'loving Nurish-Father', ensuring a supply of properly paid ministers, and maintaining the doctrine and discipline of the kirk. The ministers should 'reverence their superiors' as their parishioners did them, thereby creating a climate of peace and order in the kirk. But if James thought that bishops were the key to this royal programme of reform, not just any bishops would do. Even as vain puritans had no place in the Jacobean idyll, neither had 'proud Papall Bishoppes'. Therefore they must be chained 'with such bonds as may preserve that estate from creeping to corruption'. [183] They were not to assume the superiority borne by the presbyterians, but to subject themselves to James and acknowledge their dependence upon him. Even in 1604 James disputed Jerome's assertion that episcopacy lacked divine institution [184] and would later affirm it as 'an Apostolike institution, and so the ordinance of God'. [185] But even the context of his rebuke of the patristic writer was only a prelude to his identification of episcopacy as a condition of monarchy. Indeed, as Godfrey Davies stated, James 'was a bigot, not for a religious doctrine but for a political theory'. [186]

James's view of the matter, at least in his Scottish years, was that there was no polity instituted in Scripture which must be followed without deviation, unlike the presbyterians who saw their system of kirk government inscribed in tablets of stone and delivered by no less a prophet than Christ himself. At the November 1599 conference at Holyroodhouse they demanded to see the lawfulness of certain propositions demonstrated from Scripture, 'els Ethnik, Turkishe, and Jewishe polecie might stand withe the Gospell'. The response came back that whatever was not repugnant to the word was acceptable. [187] And so it was in the *Basilikon Doron*. Henry must 'learne wisely to discerne betwixt poyntes of salvation and indifferent thinges, betwixt substance and ceremonies', and between genuine divine obligations and the inventions of men (read presbyterians). Of course, one might not abrogate a positive or a negative biblical command, 'but as for all other things not contayned in scripture, spare not to use or alter them as the necessitie of the time shall require'. [188] James had no hesitation about what the time called for: adiaphorism was the Christian king's best friend.

Despite its intended secrecy[189] the *Basilikon Doron* still managed to escape into the wider world where it caused, with good reason, a stir among the presbyterians on account of its 'Anglo-pisco-papisticall Conclusionnes'.[190] The leak and the ensuing furor necessitated a public edition to clear up suspicions aroused by the first, to which was prefaced an explanatory letter to the reader. The first item that required clarification was 'grounded upon the sharp & bitter wordes, that therin are used in the description of the humours of Puritans, and rashe-headie preachers, that thinke it their honour to contend with Kings, & perturbe whole kingdomes'. These aspersions on the leading presbyterians he sought to play down by the absurd definition of puritans as members of 'that vile sect' of Anabaptists known as the Family of Love, identifying even Robert Browne and John Penry with that despised company. But what he pretended to retract he as quickly restored by saying that he also called puritans those 'bransicke and headie preachers' who behaved in a similarly offensive manner.

James then arrived at a profoundly important statement of his religious mentality. Earlier he had defended the integrity and conformity of his faith: in the 1599 edition he had professed his belief, 'calling it the Religion wherein I was brought up, and ever made profession of', and encouraged prince Henry to persevere in the same 'as the onely true forme of Gods worship'. It is noteworthy that James spoke here of worship, not polity, as the object of his affection and protection. Returning to his discussion of the puritans, one finds that the king complained about their exclusive cast of mind 'in accounting all men prophane that sweares not to all their fantasies'. It was not worship or theology *per se* that created rifts; rather, these puritans had made 'for every particulare question of the policie of the churche, as great commotion, as if the article of the Trinity were called in controversie'.[191] James would protect what he thought of as the essentials of the kirk — its worship and its doctrines fundamental to salvation — but not its accidental (and unfortunate) features, particularly its presbyterian polity.

Puritan attachment to a wrong-headed reading of the Bible led them to tread upon any who differed, the king not excepted. But even on this point James was not so intransigent as his opponents. He was fully prepared to take a benign view of those who preferred the relatively inelaborate worship of the kirk in comparison with that of England which he himself had once impugned, very possibly in all sincerity. Similarly he accepted those 'that are perswaded, that their Bishops smels of a Papall supremacie, that the Surplice, the cornered cap, and such like, are the outward badges of Popishe errours'.[192] He was willing to 'love and honour' those who held such views. But the extent of his tolerance was the *peaceful* maintenance of non-conformist opinions. 'We all (God be praised) doe aggree in the groundes', *i.e.* on doctrine, but bitter discord over these other, clearly non-essential, matters only served to bring division and discord into the church, giving 'advantage and entry to the Papists' — a rationalisation repeated later for his repressive actions between 1600 and 1610. Given that the law was contrary to their views, the puritans (presbyterians) must abide by it, falling into neither unlawfulness nor schism. Persuasion was to be the only means at their disposal, though James quite naturally entertained the possibility that they would be enlightened and converted to his side in the matter. He did not, however, demand that his ministers agree with his views on polity — he knew that they practically all opposed 'the forme of the Englische churche' — but he did demand submission to their Christian king who bore a divine mandate and from whom flowed laws which must be obeyed as a Christian duty. Time would prove that his modest toleration of dissent was of an impatient sort.

By the time that James wrote his *Basilikon Doron* his anticipation of the English throne was in full flight — as David H. Willson wrote, 'With all his soul he yearned for the English succession'.[193] He expressed his hope that before he died he might be as well acquainted with England as with Scotland,[194] and he alluded to prince Henry's succession to more than one throne.[195] His earlier aspersions on the church of England were quickly forgotten: 'He found it exactly to his taste'.[196]

In England James entered a different world. The church was adequately supplied with admiring clergy, its leading lights committed to upholding his royal privileges and rights. Even as a young man a report of his biblical acumen had been passed on to London.[197] In 1600 another writer commented favourably on the erudition exhibited in the *Basilikon Doron* and exalted James as the first king since Solomon to attain such heights of learning and understanding.[198] Matthew Hutton, archbishop of York, described James as 'a passing wise King, and the best learned Prince in Europe',[199] while William Laud, a future archbishop of Canterbury,[200] and John White a royal chaplain, also offered their praises.[201] But this was subdued in comparison with what followed.[202] William Barlow's report on the Hampton Court conference dripped with the obsequious rhetoric of the courtly prelate. James's words, he enthused, were as 'Apples of gold with pictures of silver'.[203] Though raised among the imperfectly educated puritans of Scotland, James was 'as expedite and perfect as the greatest schollers, and most industrious Students, there present, might not outstrip him'.[204] The chancellor commented to Barlow, 'I have often hearde and read, that Rex est mixta persona cum sacerdote, but I never saw the truth thereof, till this day'.[205] Someone thought that James spoke under inspiration of the Holy Spirit,[206] though another opined that 'the spirit was rather foule mouthede'.[207] Even the learned Isaac Casaubon was impressed by James's real, if somewhat narrow,[208] learning. In 1613 he wrote that

> I enjoy the favour of this excellent monarch, who is really more instructed than most people give him credit for. He is a lover of learning to a degree beyond belief; his judgment of books, old and new, is such as would become a professed scholar, rather than a mighty prince.[209]

The new king of England knew how to reciprocate to his fawning English admirers. At the 1604 conference he thanked God for having brought him

> into the promised land, where Religion was purely professed; where he sate among grave, learned and reverend men; not, as before, elsewhere, a King without state, without honour, without order; where beardles boyes would brave him to his face.[210]

Hutton of York, in a letter to Whitgift of Canterbury, expressed his hope that James would leave the church of England much as Elizabeth had settled it, praying that he would maintain the dislike for both papists and puritans once expressed in the *Basilikon Doron*.[211] Indeed there was no cause for concern, and at Hampton Court James demonstrated his fundamental loyalty to the church of England as it was, the alterations emerging from the conference being of a minor variety.[212] Altogether James was disappointed and disgusted by the puritan representation.[213]

James quickly adapted his rhetoric to new circumstances. If once he thought that the Scottish kirk was the earthly apex of the church, he now proclaimed that the church of England had been for forty-five years the most flourishing church on earth.[214] Leaving no doubt at Hampton Court that, in spite of a few negative comments, he was wholly aligned with the bishops, James criticised the puritans for their repudiation of anything once used superstitiously under popery, such as the sign of the cross in baptism. 'By this argument, we might renounce the Trinity, and all that is holy, because it was abused in Popery', not to mention shoes and socks which papists also wore.[215]

Crossing the Tweed did nothing to abate the royal hatred for presbytery. When the word was mentioned at Hampton Court James immediately but erroneously[216] assumed an English movement parallel with Scottish presbyterianism: 'And when I meane to live under a presbitery, I will goe into Scotland agayn. But while I am in England, I will have Bishops for I had not been so quietly settled in my seate but for them'. Thus it seems most unlikely that the theory of divine right episcopacy flourished as a result of fear that James, bred among presbyterians, might alter the structure of the church of England. William Lamont writes: 'Even in the year of the Armada, some bishops were becoming more exercised at the thought of James than at that of Philip'.[217] He attributes, quite remarkably, Bancroft's 1589 sermon to this very anxiety. But the future archbishop's fear was not based on the king whom he had little reason to doubt, but rather, as J. W. Allen noted, on the English lower house which attempted to subject ecclesiastical authority to its own purview.[218] Patrick Collinson suggests that confidence rather than insecurity was the ground from which episcopacy *jure divino* sprang, and he also directs attention to the strongly Calvinistic minds of men like Carleton and Downame.[219] What urged Calvinist presbyterians to protest for the church's liberty and integrity also bore fruit in Calvinist episcopalian minds, however much the two differed from one another. J. P. Sommerville points out that even John Jewel and John Foxe upheld the position that spiritual powers pertained only to ecclesiastical officers.[220] He concludes: 'Foxe's distinction between the offices of a king and a clergyman is indistinguishable from that drawn by the proponents of *jure divino* episcopacy'.[221] The divine right of bishops was nothing more than a bold assertion of an inherent tendency within the church of England and would have been expressed even without the shadow of a Scottish pretender. William Barlow knew his man, and when he came to preach for bishops in 1606 it was not to counter unhappy tendencies in his king but to support his sovereign's attempt at browbeating recalcitrant Scottish presbyterians into submission to episcopalian sanity.

If James could have his way, another regiment of bishops would provide a similar service in troubled Scotland. It would be their unhappy task to impose the king's delight in things English on an unreceptive kirk.

CHAPTER 6

The Rebuilding of Jericho

R. G. Usher made some extravagant claims for archbishop Richard Bancroft's responsibility in the erection of episcopacy in Scotland. To him Usher attributed 'the scheme by which Episcopacy was gradually established, and . . . the care of the administrative details which became necessary in connection with the appointment of the new officers, the management of their estates, and the extent of their powers'. Bancroft, according to this account, actually made episcopal appointments for Scotland and Usher called the new settlement of the kirk 'Bancroft's compromise'![1] One wonders how James ever managed as he did before 1603 apparently with no mind of his own and lacking Scottish servants competent to assist the progress of the royal programme. George McMahon allows that Bancroft played 'a considerable part' in Scottish developments,[2] but the contemporary basis for such statements is slender and comes from a hostile witness, James Melville.[3]

It would seem reasonable, nonetheless, to credit Maurice Lee, Jr.'s assessment that James's English succession certainly 'made the revival of prelacy in Scotland a success'.[4] No longer did he have to take the leading role in fending off the Melvilles. Now he had appreciative prelates ready to defend him and to support his own contentions about order and godly magistracy. At Hampton Court James had proved himself trustworthy. The Scottish Constantine posed no threat to the established church of England, and its leading lights were not at all reluctant to embrace the new king. His enemies were their enemies.

Arthur Williamson has argued that John Knox was the leading Scottish exponent of 'Britain', a union of Scotland with England seen within an apocalyptic worldview with a joint monarch governing the nation as Constantine's successor, devoted to the struggle against Antichrist.[5]

Nevertheless, even from the time of the Reformation, and even among the 'Britain-minded' Marian exiles who laboured in Scotland, there were expressions of an ambivalent attitude toward the English church. Christopher Goodman memorialised Cecil in 1559 about superstitious relics of ceremony including clerical apparel and the observance of saints' days.[6] John Knox expressed his dislike for the Book of Common Prayer since it contained 'things superstitious, impure, unclean, and unperfect',[7] but at the same time he related to Cecil his hope for friendship between the two kingdoms, a cause which he claimed to have served unstintingly.[8] The role of England in the success of reform in Scotland was no barrier to further complaint. In 1566 Knox was commissioned by the assembly to write a letter to the English bishops in behalf of those oppressed in the vestments controversy 'because ther conscience will not suffer them to take upon them, at the comandment of the authoritie, sick garments as idolaters in the tyme of blindnes have usit in the tyme of idolatrie'.[9] Over the ensuing twenty years England presented a continuing source of anxiety while Morton, Arran, and Adamson sought conformity between the churches. In 1586 James Carmichael wrote back from his English haven of his fear that if some Scottish ministers were prepared to consent to bishops they would also bow before English vestments and the Book of Common Prayer.[10] But polity was the greatest worry and Bancroft's sermon in 1589 intensified the distress. One of the letters addressed to queen Elizabeth in the wake of the offensive sermon stated that 'it hath pleased God to joyne these two Realmes in a most joyfull and fruictfull amitie' which the wicked Bancroft had recently injured.[11] Anyone who supported his sentiments was 'no friend to the Gospell, no favourer of the amitie between the two landis, but a sworne ennimie to them both'.[12] The Scottish presbyterian could hardly avoid seeing England as the Protestant bulwark against popery, but its church was in patent need of purgation. Thus it was promised that reform of the church of England along presbyterian lines would tend to the glorification of God 'and sure establishing of amitie betweene the two realmes, through Christ Jesus our Lord. Amen'.[13] The zeal of presbyterians in Scotland blinded them to the obvious possibility — not that the kirk would ultimately prove to be the pattern for reformation of the church of England, but that English-style episcopacy would find a home north of the Tweed, and with it a lay head of the kirk, English Erastianism.

James Melville's anti-English bias has already been remarked upon. This was shared by his co-religionists in the years of the kirk's supposed decline. It was argued in 1600 that 'the experience of the Kirk in all ages sen that corruptioun enterit in, and namlie, in our awin age, nocht onlie amangs the Papists, bot in our nibour land of Eingland, and amangs our selves, cleirlie proves, and loudlie cries' that a true, spiritual bishop could not survive when elevated as a prelate with all manner of civil entanglements. 'Therfor the Quein of Eingland's *dictum* is, when sche makes a Bischope, 'Alas for pitie! for we have marred a guid Preatchour to-day.''[14] The experiences of 1606 would do nothing to convince presbyterians of the maxim's error.

The so-called union of Scotland and England in the person of James VI and I evoked some joyous responses. As Dr. Williamson states, 'The imperialists' hour arrived with the union of crowns in 1603. At that moment apocalyptic enthusiasm for Great Britain and the new emperor lately risen knew scarcely any bounds'.[15] An anonymous poet wrote:

> The English, Scots, and Irish true,
>   Of three are now combin'd in one,
> Their hartes a true love knot fast knit,
>   All former malice now is gone.
>
> As visage and the phrase of toung,
>   Twixt Scots and English neere agree,
> So guidet of all hartes, their hartes
>   Conjoyne, that loyall they may bee.[16]

Preachers joined the happy throng. Miles Mosse, who had played host to the fugitive Mar at Norwich twenty years earlier,[17] welcomed James as a new Joshua, 'by whom we conceive great hope to enjoy the perfect beautie and complements of the Gospell'.[18] His education, his record as king of Scotland, and his Protestant religion all commended James to Mosse.[19] John Gordon, son of the bishop of Galloway but long absent from Scotland, wrote two treatises on the union. In his *Panegyrique of congratulation* he attributed the confluence of Scotland and England to the merciful work of God, predicated upon the rise of true religion in both realms.[20] Henceforth armies which once fought each other would, under James, Constantine's successor, subdue Roman 'idolatry and abomination'.[21] In the *Henotikon*, preached before the king in 1604, Gordon pursued the blessings of union, investigating the esoteric etymological values of place names presumed to be derived from Hebrew, the language of the covenant. Britannia meant, 'in this Iland the covenant of God was to be established'. Anglia spoke of God's revelation, Scotia of God's peace, Hiberniah of 'the passing over of the Sonne of God', and Wales meant either God's river or revelation. Gordon summed up the argument thus:

> So that ye may see all these names are propheticall, and doe foretell that the covenant of God signified by the generall name *Brit-an-iah* should make this happy and blessed Union in one Religion, and one Kingdome.[22]

Only eighty years after Christ the Britons became the first of the nations to receive him, but the covenant had been subsequently broken with the advent of the idolatrous, *i.e.* Roman, mass. However, God had restored true worship and the covenant, thus James's restoration of the name of Britannia was by no less an authority than the Holy Spirit.[23]

James, who brought Gordon home to England from France where the *Panegyrique* was written and made the preacher of such esoteric doctrines dean of Salisbury,[24] was also brimming with joy over the union. He revelled in the expressions of many who met him on his triumphant journey to London in 1603,[25] and in his speech to his first English parliament he asked, 'Hath not God first united these two Kingdomes both in Language, Religion, and similitude of Manners?'[26] Like the preceding panegyrists James did not comment upon differences of religion between Scotland and England, but he did castigate the 'Novelists' in England who agitated for the amendment of church government and who were 'impatient to suffer any superioritie, which maketh their Sect unable to be suffered in any well governed Common wealth'.[27] There could have been no doubt concerning the identity of this 'sect'.

The Scottish writer Thomas Craig (1605) did recognise the historical bifurcation whereby there had developed presbytery in the north and episcopacy in the south of the shared island. But polity was not the fundamental consideration; rather, both countries were of reformed religion, which fact had produced an unprecented era of peace between them. Behind superficial differences of worship was agreement upon the essentials of doctrine. With respect to the Lord's supper he declared that both churches had tried to get back as close as possible to the 'original institution'.[28] Acknowledging Scotland's anti-episcopal sentiment, he seems to have written from the standpoint of acceptance of the political changes which James had thus far effected in the kirk, but he was sympathetic toward the suspicion and hostility of his countrymen:

> Scotsmen perhaps were somewhat excessively, but not without cause, prejudiced against the retention or restoration of the old ecclesiastical hierarchy; for they bore it a grudge, since to its influence and counsel they attributed not only the burning and ruin of many of our fairest cities, but also the fatal disaster of Pinkie, when the ecclesiastical order exerted its utmost influence to hinder the marriage between the heirs of the two kingdoms, lest the religion of the English, who had abjured the Roman Pontiff, might gain an entrance in Scotland.[29]

All told, however, Craig saw the two realms as one in religion and their king as the international champion against popery.[30]

Craig was certainly no presbyterian agent devoted to preserving the kirk's distinctive polity, while Robert Pont, a moderate presbyterian, published in 1603, *cum privilegio,* a treatise on the union in which he termed a calumny that opinion which emphasised the differences of religion between England and Scotland. The faithful would not be inhibited by external rites and order from joining with those whose doctrine was sound: God, Christ, justification by faith, the right administration of the sacraments (presumably in a non-idolatrous and non-superstitious fashion).[31] It was a dangerous and damnable opinion that refused to recognise as a church that body which was not entirely pure.[32]

But this moderation was by no means characteristic of Scottish presbyterianism.[33] Fearing what union might entail, the kirk demanded a general assembly before the meeting of the 1604 parliament which was to deal with uniting Scotland and England. Promises were given that religion would not be handled by the estates[34] but the kirk remained unconvinced 'becaus the realmes could not be united without the unioune of the Kirk; neither could the Kirkis be united in discipline, the ane being Episcopall and the uther Presbyteriall, unless that the ane sould surrender and cede to the uther'.[35] The commissioners of the previous assembly, then convened in Edinburgh (the proposed 1604 general assembly was suspended), were cautioned that, despite a recognition of the two realms' unity in one gospel,[36] kirk polity was not 'indifferent and alterabill, but substantiall pairtis of the Gospell', equal to any other tenet of the faith.[37] James had far to go to quench the ardour of Scottish presbyterians.

In 1606 James brought south to England eight of the leading Scottish presbyterians — Andrew and James Melville, James Balfour, William Watson, William Scot, John Carmichael, Robert Wallace, and Adam Colt.[38] Ostensibly this was to consult on remedies for the unhappiness of the kirk[39] but the king's real purpose was to remove their leadership at a critical juncture in the process of extending episcopacy; secondarily, he hoped by subjecting them to English preaching and worship to perform the miracle of transforming presbyterian water into episcopalian wine. Beyond an undoubted confirmation of James's contentment with his new crown and church little else was accomplished, as the presbyterians were only strengthened in their suspicions about the distemper in the church of England.

Prominent in this royal conspiracy were four sermons which were presumably intended either to seduce or shame the presbyterians into submission. James Melville wrote of the first occasion that, upon arriving at the chapel, 'we fand a place prepairit for us hard besyd the Pricher, Bischop Barlo, quhom, befoir the King, Quein, and Nobilis, we patiently hard mak a long or well-joyned sermone, writtin, and fynely compactit in a lytle buik, quhilk he had allwayis in his hand, for help of his memorie'.[40] William Barlow, then the bishop of Rochester, chose as his text Acts 20:28 wherein *episcopoi* were commanded to care for their flocks. Taking the term to signify 'bishops' (the Geneva Bible has 'overseers'), he was enabled to prove that even in the primitive, apostolic, church episcopal convocations of the clergy were the rule.[41] He also described the emergence of degrees of ministry in the New Testament, noting particularly that the apostles appointed bishops to succeed them in order to deal with dissension and confusion.[42] To these apostolic successors were reserved the ordinal rite of imposition of hands[43] and the authority to administer discipline.[44] In the published edition of his sermon Barlow added a letter 'to the Ministers of Scotland, my Fellow Dispensers of Gods misteries', an irenic note, perhaps not altogether genuine, which would have evoked little reciprocal tenderness in Scotland. He complained that Scottish detractors of episcopacy had offended against a Petrine injunction (I Peter 4:15) by making themselves *allotrioepiscopous*, 'Bishops and Censurers of other Provinces, by intituling the Church-governors among us, Papisticall English Bishops'.[45] He protested that this identification was a false and unchristian slander since English bishops had died for their religion 'in defiance of Papistrie'.[46] By way of a presbyterian evaluation of the spoken word, Melville remarked that 'the judicious termed it a confutatioune of the text'.[47]

The second sermon was by Dr. John Buckeridge, earlier a tutor of William Laud and subsequently the bishop of Rochester. Taking as his text Romans 13:5 — 'Wherefore you must needs be subject, not onely for wrath, but also for conscience' — Buckeridge followed in the steps of Thomas Bilson in his argument for the necessity of obedience to the prince.[48] Nothing less than complete submission was required for 'peace and tranquillitie, and Religion in This life, and life everlasting after death'.[49] He argued that the law of nature, wherein king and priest were united, indicated that one man customarily possessed jurisdiction in all affairs both civil and ecclesiastical.[50] In the Old Testament, Moses the magistrate had authority above Aaron the priest;[51] likewise among Jewish kings. Josiah

> purged Juda and Jerusalem from high places, groves, and Images: he gathered all Israel, reade the Law, renewed the covenant, and caused all Israel to stand to the covenant, and hee compelled them to serve the Lord: he kept the famous Passeover, and reduced the Priests and Levites to their courses set by David and Salomon. These and many more are the Acts of famous Kings in the time of the Law, done by their Royall authoritie, not at the appointment and command of the Priests . . . .[52]

Upon his conversion to Christianity Constantine resumed this authority over the religious life,[53] for which he was not lacking Christ's sanction: 'When Emperors command that which is good, it is Christ and no man else that commandeth by them'.[54] Of course kings had no priestly rights nor the authority to grant these to priests and preachers,[55] an opinion which James had expressed twenty years earlier.[56] Kings must, however, reform the church, convene its councils, proclaim its laws by their royal authority, and act as a court of appeal in matters of an ecclesiastical nature.[57]

It ought not to be thought remarkable that James Melville concurred in general with Buckeridge, as both presbyterians and Calvinist Anglicans wished the magistrate to support the church and both would put certain restrictions upon what a prince might do in the church.[58] Undoubtedly, if push came to shove the presbyterians would have proved to be much more virulent opponents of royal encroachments, and furthermore, English bishops certainly had no reason to quarrel with king James — he created (or maintained) them, he approved of them, they responded appreciatively. It was a mutually satisfying arrangement whereby bishops defended the crown and James upheld their office. Melville might have pointed out, though, that Buckeridge's argument that Moses the secular figure stood above Aaron the ecclesiastical officer had been rejected by the kirk in 1600. The one was not superior to the other; rather they were brothers, 'everie an to be about thair awin office and calling for uther's mutuall weilfear'.[59]

Melville did set one limit upon his approbation — Buckeridge erred in comparing presbytery and popery, 'as though the ane had beine joynit in the same judgment with the uthir'.[60] This identification by English clergy was not uncommon, including two other Hampton Court preachers, Barlow and King. King James had done the same in his *Basilikon Doron* and, before him in 1585, Patrick Adamson. The royal theologian would later call Jesuits 'Puritane-Papists'.[61] The adversaries of presbyterianism saw in that polity a form of ecclesiastical independence which reeked of papal claims to rebuke and even excommunicate — with uncertain political potential — disobedient and unfaithful monarchs. Melville may have thought that he and Buckeridge had found some common ground, but the preacher would not have been deceived. Popery and presbytery were, politically, all one to him: 'the Bishop of Rome, or the Presbytery, one Pope, or many Popes'.[62]

The bishop of Chichester, Lancelot Andrewes, was the third to mount the pulpit against the Scots. His text was Numbers 10:1-2 concerning Moses' two trumpets which were blown to summon the people of Israel.[63] The trend was the same as that which Buckeridge's sermon betrayed, the authority of the king in matters ecclesiastical, with special reference here to the calling of assemblies. Andrewes took the two trumpets to represent the two jurisdictions of state and church, and both were in the power of Moses, thus he and his magisterial successors were keepers of both tables.[64] This superiority of the prince was a perpetual law of God and was not abrogated by Christ.[65] The magistrate summoned all the great councils of the church, and so matters remained until the pope's theft of one of the trumpets.[66] But with the return to godly rule the second trumpet was restored to its divinely appointed custodian who should rule the church and call its clerical convocations. Presumably the presbyterians were now attempting a repetition of the papal larceny.

Andrewes' sermon did terrible violence to the text, even in identifying the two trumpets as church and state, for in the passage itself the sound of one trumpet called the leaders, two trumpets meant that the whole people of Israel should gather (vv. 3-4). Competent Bible students such as James Melville could hardly miss these blatant exegetical improprieties and excesses. He noted that Andrewes made his point 'directly against his text, quhilk sayis, that the sones of Aaron [*i.e.* priests] should blow the trumpets'[67] (v. 8). But this was the nature of theological debate complicated by loyalties and politics.

The fourth sermon at the 1606 conference was delivered by Dr. John King, later the bishop of London, who in most respects rehashed the preceding three sermons. Using Canticles 8:11 as his homiletical springboard, King discussed the keepers of the vineyard which was widely regarded as a type of the church. There were, predictably, two keepers, the magistrate and the minister,[68] and the former was by no means subjected to the latter, nor were they equal since a realm with two authorities would be like a twin-headed body.[69] With respect to the clerical keepership King at one point granted a certain mutability to ecclesiastical polity,[70] yet he also argued for the antiquity of episcopacy.[71] The corollary to this statement was the novelty of presbytery, 'this late formed discipline'.[72] The episcopal keepers of the church having been thrown out, a new kind of keeper had intruded, bearing 'a strange composition and concretion, part of cleargy, part of Laity'.[73] King derided the ruling elders: 'today a tradesman, tomorrow a churchman, today an artificer, tomorrow an elder'.[74] Melville, understandably, described this final oration as 'a most violent invective againes the Presbyteries, [the preacher] cryeing to the King, 'Doune! Doune with thame all!'',[75] words lacking from the printed text but a not implausible rhetorical embellishment in the chapel.

Private conversation likewise availed nothing for the king's cause. James Melville argued with James Montague, dean of the chapel royal, over the antiquity and nature of episcopacy, and concerning the royal supremacy over ministers. The conversation ended abruptly when Melville asserted that in Scotland the law did not set the crown above the kirk, to which Montague replied peremptorily, 'But ye must haiff it sua in Scotland!' A similar episode occurred with the bishop of Durham.[76] Several discussions were had with the archbishop of Canterbury, though Bancroft was hardly a welcome face among Scottish presbyterians, having piled additional offences upon his infamous sermon of 1589.[77] Andrew Melville 'tuik occasioune plainely in his face, befoir the Counsell, to tell him all his mynd, quhilk burst out as inclossit fyre in watter!'[78] He complained to the prelate about persecution of true preachers, maintenance of an 'Antichrystiane Hierarchie and Popische Ceremonies',[79] then with dramatic flair he shook Bancroft's rochet sleeves and denounced them, in language as old as the reformed kirk,[80] as 'Romishe ragis' symbolic of nothing less pernicious than the apocalyptic beast.[81] The final conference was again with the archbishop who spoke gently, even flatteringly, to James Melville and William Scot. He sought to establish the grounds of religion common to both sides. 'Our difference is only in the Governeing of the Kirk and sume ceremonies.' He added that during the months that the Scots had been in London the kirk had been brought to virtual conformity with England. When Scot attempted to declare his own mind Bancroft intervened, whether out of impatience or condescension: 'Tush, man! Tak heir a coupe of guid seck!'[82] With a draught of ale ended the project for persuading or overawing the eight presbyterians. The episode concluded, James Melville finished his life in exile at Newcastle and Berwick, while Andrew, following several years in the Tower on account of some offensive lines he had written in London,[83] was released to teach at Sedan where he died in 1622.

James tried also to exert English influence within Scotland itself. He advised Patrick Galloway in 1608 that John King, George Abbot the future archbishop, and Anthony Maxey along with some other English preachers were being sent north 'to spende some short time amongst you there in preaching of gods worde'.[84] There might have been some dispute over whose word they spoke, but they did endeavour to convince the Scots that polity and ceremony were matters of indifference, and therefore, by implication, alterations in these areas ought not to generate opposition. Also in 1608 a sermon by George Downame, later the bishop of Derry, was sent north. Preached originally at a service for consecrating a bishop, it rehashed the typical episcopal arguments. Downame may have been thought a good author for the persuasion of stiff-necked presbyterians as he himself had been one earlier in his life.[85] The sermon, which did not lack for scholarship, was a discussion of Revelation 1:20 in which are described the angels of the seven Asian churches. Downame followed the common allegorical interpretation of the angels as bishops and proceeded to prove episcopal superiority in pre-eminence, power to ordain, and jurisdiction over other ministers.[86] He concluded that episcopacy had 'apostolicall and divine institution', and therefore no other polity was defensible.[87] It is most unlikely that Downame's words bore much fruit among presbyterians; perhaps some beleaguered Scottish bishops took heart in the preacher's assurance that while they performed their office faithfully 'they may expect, that [God] will blesse, defend, revenge, and reward them'.[88]

From the Tower Andrew Melville responded with 'A short confutatioun of Dr Downam's apologetick sermoun for the dignitie of the episcopall office'.[89] He began somewhat sarcastically, describing the unhappy state of decline into which the seven Asian churches had fallen. If this was the condition of the ecclesiastical angels-come-bishops only sixty-three years after Jesus' death, what state might one anticipate among the bishops after 1600 years?[90] Melville regarded Downame's biblical exegesis as nonsense, and without the £14,000 sterling which also were sent to Scotland, *tanquam aureus hamus,* no one would ever be persuaded of its truth.[91] He rebuked the method whereby Downame identified the seven angels with the seven churches, *i.e.* one angel for each church. Melville recalled the text of Revelation 1:20, 'the seven starres are the angels of the seven churches', suggesting perhaps an indeterminate number of angels to agree with his assertion of many angels in Ephesus. This he predicated upon Acts 20:17, but the word there is *presbyteros,* which the presbyterian thought to be interchangeable throughout the New Testament with *episcopos.*[92] But beside this leap Melville conveniently overlooked the letters to the seven churches which are invariably addressed 'To the angel of the church in . . . .' To be sure, Downame had no monopoly on texts drawn violently 'by the haire'. If there were those in Scotland capable of reading Downame critically, might they not also be able to see through presbyterian arguments and perhaps to join themselves to the king?

While two English doctors taught during the time the 1609 parliament was being held,[93] three other English preachers, George Meriton, Christopher Hampton, and Phineas Hodgson were sent to preach at the general assembly held at Glasgow in June 1610. Two of these sermons were printed. Meriton, chaplain to queen Anne and finally dean of York, delivered his thoughts upon the theme of conscience according to which, ostensibly, presbyterians resisted bishops. This patent error of conscience Meriton attributed to 'fearfulness of minde' for which there was no genuine basis.[94] After all, episcopacy was no innovation but was of apostolic institution and, unlike disorderly presbytery, conveyed order to the church.[95] In case such historical and theological material might fail in its appointed task Meriton also appealed on the ground of needful obedience to the king.[96] Certainly James had been sufficiently troubled by papists,

> but will his Protestants also resist him? Will you gainsay the godliest, the wisest, the lovingest King, that ever you enjoyed? no; you will not, for howsoever an erronious conscience, may make no conscience of disloyaltie, yet your holy consent in this publique business, declares your consciences to be better informed.[97]

That is, acceptance of episcopacy was the sign of good conscience duly obeyed. For good measure Downame also berated papal sins including that of usurpation of royal power. His auditors and readers were undoubtedly welcome to draw parallels.

Christopher Hampton, who would three years later become the archbishop of Armagh, preached a rambling sermon to the printed edition of which he prefaced a note which claimed the sermon had succeeded in satisfying its hearers, even those who at first were of another mind.[98] Hampton upheld the king as a person both civil and ecclesiastical and who therefore had power to take order with religion, even in ceremonial matters.[99] No one, 'etiamsi sis Apostolus',[100] could claim an exemption from the crown. With respect to ecclesiastical government, bishops were upheld as essential to the succession of true doctrine in the church.[101] Concerning the equality of ministers Hampton asked, 'why should equalitie, that is found intollerable in all other societies, be obtruded onely to the Church?'[102] Indeed that was a very pertinent question, the implications of which seem not to have bothered presbyterians. Might not a 'democratic' kirk foster similar tendencies in the state? Obviously the king thought so. As long as he or his successor might have his way, the kirk would be ruled by bishops. There was never a chance they could be persuaded to think otherwise.

In 1600 James had laid the groundwork for his resuscitation of the Scottish episcopate. There were, of course, many obstacles to be removed or circumvented and not only those in the minds of obstreperous presbyterians. Aristocratic claims and the usage of bishoprics to provide for expense accounts contributed to a thorough dilapidation and debasement of the sees. In 1590 Huntly and Moray had disputed over the possessions of the bishopric of Moray, and in 1603 the earl of Moray was promised the episcopal lands.[103] In 1598 archbishop James Beaton, for nearly forty years an exile in France and since at least 1587 Scottish ambassador to

France,[104] was restored 'to his heritages, honoris digniteis benefices offices landis rowmes possessionis actiounis', without having to subscribe the reformed faith.[105] Robert Bowes stated that Dunkeld was so divested of its revenues that its titular, Peter Rollock, held his parliamentary seat more by favour than by right.[106] Years later archbishop John Spottiswood summed up the situation in 1600:

> Aberdene and Argile had their own incumbents at the time, both actual preachers; S. Andrewes and Glasgow were in the hands of the Duke of Lennox; Murray possessed by the Lord Spinie; Orkney, by the Earl of Orkney; Dunkeld, Birchen, and Dumblane, had their own titulars, but these were not ordinary preachers; Galloway and Isles were so dilapidated, as scarce they were remembred to have been.[107]

Two sees, Ross and Caithness, had some revenue left, thus David Lindsay and George Gledstanes were appointed though they remained at their respective charges of Leith and St. Andrews 'for as yet they could not find any setling in their Dioceses'. It is unclear whether shortfall of financial resources or perhaps the threat of physical danger or some other cause was implied, though one suspects both poverty and intimidation, along with Lindsay's age, were important contributing factors. Spottiswood might have added that by the time Lindsay and Gledstanes were elevated, David Cunningham of Aberdeen had died and Peter Blackburn, minister in the city, had become bishop in his place.

In these early years the episcopate was, as Walter Foster writes, 'an almost purely civil office' bearing no more ecclesiastical authority than the parochial ministry.[108] It remained for the king to secure the place of these ministers by uniting several functions — the ecclesiastical duties of the traditional monarchical episcopate (*e.g.* ordination, confirmation, visitation), a voice in the estates, the power of commissioners of assemblies, and the presidential jurisdiction of moderators in presbyteries and synods.

In May 1601 a number of ministers were appointed to visit and plant kirks throughout Scotland.[109] Among them were George Gledstanes for Caithness, Sutherland, and Aberdeen; and David Lindsay for Clydesdale. Both of them were also appointed to consult with Catholic lords with an eye to bringing them into the reformed fold.[110] Lindsay, Gledstanes, and Peter Blackburn were placed upon the commission to represent the kirk's interests until the following assembly.[111] Already James had gained partial success in uniting the diverse elements of a resuscitated episcopal establishment.

At the November 1602 assembly at Holyroodhouse the three were once more appointed to visit: Gledstanes for Caithness and Sutherland, Lindsay for Ross, Blackburn for Moray.[112] All were again appointed commissioners of assembly along with Alexander Douglas who since 1600 had been titular bishop of Moray and would in a matter of days be formally appointed to the see.[113] Two more appointments followed in 1603: George Grahame to Dunblane and John Spottiswood to Glasgow. In 1604 Gledstanes was promoted to St. Andrews, being replaced in Caithness by Alexander Forbes, and in 1605 Gavin Hamilton was appointed to Galloway, Andrew Knox to the Isles, and James Law to Orkney. Thus by 1605 ten of thirteen sees had bishops, though it is difficult to ascertain precisely what sort of bishops they were — not simply titular or 'notionall'[114] because they had to fulfil certain ecclesiastical standards to be eligible, but not exactly 'reall' ecclesiastical bishops for they were just ministers, retaining their parishes and exercising other functions on a temporary rather than *ex officio* basis. Theirs was for the moment a transitional form of episcopate while on their way to becoming full-fledged hierarchical and diocesan bishops.

Unrest continued to beset the royal programme for the kirk. In 1604 it was complained 'that the Commissiouneris last chosine be the Generall Assemblie, or rathir a very few of that numbir, arrogatis to thame the haill governement of the Kirk and power of the Generall Assemblie'[115] — no doubt just as James intended. The commissioners responded that there had been no assembly since 1602, thus their warrant was still valid. The presbyterians believed, presumably, that the commissioners ought to have withstood prorogation and to have surrendered their office when the July 1604 assembly was inhibited.

In 1605 a letter concerning the bishops was sent to Dunbar expressing concurrence with the episcopacy designed at Montrose in 1600 whereby bishops should stay within certain jurisdictional bounds, which, 'if thai sall keipe and observe, we look for nothing but guid peice and quietnes among us'.[116] Breaches of the cautions would, however, lead to disquiet in the kirk and the blame would settle upon the young men — in 1605 one was under forty, David Lindsay was about seventy-four, most were in their mid-forties — now become bishops who were 'easily puft up with the auctoritie and countinence of so wyse and mychtie a King'. Episcopal tyranny would be opposed to the death as 'hight treassoune against Christ and the King',[117] the presbyterians insisting upon the illusion that somehow the king was being undone in all this proceeding. The writers claimed the support of the superior ministers. Perhaps good morality and theology were on their side, but with every passing year the ardently presbyterian share of the ministry was in decline.[118]

The 1606 parliament at Perth concluded an act which acknowledged 'his majesties soverane authoritie princelie power royall prerogative and privilege of his Crowne Over all estaittis persones and causes quhatsumevir within' Scotland.[119] Certainly the presbyterians knew what the waxing power of the crown portended and consequently they submitted to the parliament a Protestation in which they defended the full authority of Christ and threatened trespassers with temporal and eternal judgements.[120] This was intended to discourage the parliamentarians from advancing toward any alteration in the 'portrature' of the kirk and especially permission for the exercise of episcopal supremacy over other ministers. Episcopacy was

> the ground of great idlenes, palpable ignorance, unsufferable pride, pitiles tyrannie, and shameles ambition in the Kirk of God. And finally to have been the ground of that *Antichristian Hierarchie* which mounted up on the steps of preheminence of *Bishops* until that man of sinn came forth as the ripe fruite of man his wisdome, *whom God shall consume with the breath of his owne mouth*.[121]

H

Episcopal pre-eminence was Dagon (the Philistine idol Dagon fell 'upon his face on the grounde before the Arke of the Lord', I Samuel 5:4) who had already fallen once, and nothing would again stand him up securely.[122] The government authorised by Christ would stand firmly when the human invention of episcopacy was shown the door.[123]

The Protestation offered to prove that episcopacy was contrary to the Bible, the church fathers, the best present-day theologians and 'the doctrine and Constitution of the Kirke of Scotland since the first reformation of religion'.[124] William Scot's *Course of conformitie* includes a document that fulfilled this offer. Not only did the composition make an appeal to the history of the church in general and in Scotland in particular, it also attempted to incite hostility to bishops by pointing out how prejudicial they might prove to various interest groups in the realm:

> is it not his Majesties weale and honour to be safe and free from the falshood, flatterie and crueltie of ambitious avarice, which hath brought so many notable Emperours, Kings and Princes to tragicall ends, corrupted sincere Kirkes, and overthrowne flourishing Commounwealthes?[125]

Popish (was there any other kind in the presbyterian view of the world?) hierarchy, wielding two swords, led inexorably to servitude.[126] But perhaps most significantly an appeal was made to the honour and wellbeing of the estates then gathered at Perth.

W. R. Foster has argued that the nobility had more or less abandoned the presbyterians from the later 1590s, but its positive support for episcopacy was dubious until after 1606;[127] in fact, one must question whether the aristocracy could ever have accepted the new episcopal foundation with its claim on episcopal temporalities and its growing civil power. The tension may not always have been overt, but one suspects it never vanished. Symbolic of hostility between nobles and bishops was their dispute about honours in the parliamentary procession, which, according to Melville, caused the nobles to detest the bishops 'as soone as they had maid thame and sett thame up, perceiving that thair upelyfting wes thair awin douncasting'.[128] Of greater substance is a letter written in January before the Perth parliament from lord Fleming, soon to be earl of Wigton, to king James. Somewhat defensively Fleming responded to a royal letter, sent *via* the bishop of the Isles, which remarked upon his reported 'scrupulous judgment in this intenditt erection of Bischopis'. Whatever his opinion had been in the matter, he strenuously declared his loyalty to James's intentions and announced that any divergence at all 'is nott to be excusit'.[129] Two months later some bishops wrote to James of their attempt to settle the dispute between themselves and the council. Apparently the disharmonious state had arisen when some persons thought that by 'anoying us thai pleased the Statesmen'.[130] In 1605 Spottiswood had informed the king that the warding of refractory ministers was done by those who wished to bring the bishops into obloquy, for it was they who bore the blame for the oppression.[131] The suggestion is one of hostility, even if commonly sublimated, between lords and prelates, particularly Dunfermline and Spottiswood.[132] Once the lords had owned the bishops, but the king had supplanted their control.

Apparently the presbyterian writer thought to play upon these undercurrents of jealousy. Turning from warning the king against episcopal turpitude, he proceeded to caution the nobles that bishops were the 'Princes Ledhorse'.[133] 'Because they have their Lordship and living, their honour, estimatioun, profit and commoditie of the King',[134] they would carry through the king's plans, however despicable. With their superior knowledge they could be used to undermine the other estates and see themselves, and by implication their manipulative sovereign, victorious in all affairs. Crown officials should beware the bishops for they would soon ascend to the highest places of the realm, just as they had in the days of popery.

The episcopal future was a horror. Bishops would go along with whatever policies successive monarchs favoured — if popish, they must alter with kings. 'So there sall bee nothing amongst men but atheisme, licentiousness and profanitie'.[135] One may accuse the rhetorician of over-statement, but the ensuing thirty-odd years would prove him a not altogether worthless prophet.

Passionate outpourings, however, availed nothing and the parliament enacted a restitution of the ecclesiastical estate designed to undo the deleterious effects of the 1587 act of annexation which 'greatumlie Imparit and almost subvertit' the traditional political structure of three estates. So dilapidated were the sees that the possessors were unable to provide the necessities of life for their families, 'Mekill less to beir the charges of thair wonted Rank in parliament and generall counsaillis'.[136] Restrictions were placed upon feuing of episcopal lands to ensure there would be no further injury done to the financial resources of the sees.[137] The lords and nobles were sent away with assurances and confirmations to the effect that only episcopal temporalities were being restored. An embarrassed James felt it necessary to explain to the Scots soon after called to London that although parliament had erected seventeen temporal lordships from prelacies, kirks in those prelacies must be provided with adequate stipends by the new lords.[138] But finally, parliament failed to ratify the one point which might have assuaged presbyterian fears, the cautions set down by the general assembly in 1600. Scot reported the chancellor's rejection of them: 'We enter not Bishops according to an act of Assembly, but according to that they were an hundred yeares syne'.[139] This apparent compliance notwithstanding, aristocratic distate for a powerful episcopate was reiterated in 1609 when a convention of the estates rejected a proposal that would have necessitated an episcopal certificate of conformity before a noble inheritance was confirmed. Maurice Lee, Jr. notes that the underlying sentiment was a refusal by the landed classes to submit themselves in this manner to the episcopate.[140]

With the eight presbyterians in London and other prominent men of that stripe in exile following the abortive and prohibited July 1605 assembly in Aberdeen, James appointed a convention[141] of the kirk to meet at Linlithgow in December 1606. His desire was not at all in doubt since he had in February presented a series of articles to the provincial synods in which kirk polity was brought into question. Bishops were to have power over other ministers, against the caveats of 1600. Commissioners of assembly were to be continued and their actions and decisions were not to be subjected to review by the assembly. The final article read: 'That the King be acknawledgit suprem reuler of the Kirk undir Christ; and that from him the power of Ministeris assembling and spirituall meitingis doe lawfully flow'. [142] No doubt to assuage anxiety aroused by these threats to the kirk's view of itself James issued a disclaimer at the assembly denying any intention 'to subvert and overthrow the present discipline'; rather, he sought 'to augment and strenthen' it. [143] The bishops denied tyrannical ambition and offered to resign if the assembly requested and the king permitted. [144]

What the king wanted in 1606 was to erode the liberties of ecclesiastical courts at the levels of presbytery and synod, just as he had already accomplished with the general assembly. The ostensible reason was that annual changes of moderators brought in men who lacked experience in proceedings against papists. [145] Thus James proposed constant moderators for presbyteries, and wherever a bishop was resident in one of his diocesan kirks, he should moderate the local presbytery. Furthermore, because of their greater financial resources and 'their credit and place in counsell', bishops should also moderate provincial synods whenever resident. [146] So reads the register, but later it was disputed by some, the usually loyal Patrick Galloway and John Hall among them, that the article making bishops constant moderators of synods 'wes nevir spokin of in that Assemblie'. [147] Indeed the fact that specific mention of this office was made only in one place — 'It is therfor his Majesties advyse and pleasure that the moderation of the Provinciall Assemblie' [148] — and that these words are not found in Melville's version of the act render the presbyterian accusation not improbable. Doubts about authenticity were also fostered by the refusal of the authorities to give out copies of the act. [149]

After much discussion constant moderators were approved for presbyteries, though not without a lengthy list of caveats designed to prevent any diminution of the rights and liberties of the kirk as a whole, [150] though Scot claimed that the bishops set down that an assembly might relax any which seemed too strict. [151] In the actual event presbyteries were more than reluctant to accept their constant moderators, and in January 1607 letters were sent out commanding acceptance under pain of horning. [152] The attempt to intrude constant moderators upon synods met with equal resistance, and some in Fife were ready to respond to horning with excommunication of the archbishop of St. Andrews. [153]

The continued appointment of bishops to vacant sees eventually provided a full complement of men representing the new establishment. In 1607 Andrew Lamb was appointed to Brechin, James Nicolson (briefly) and Alexander Lindsay to Dunkeld, while in 1608 John Campbell succeeded his father Neil in Argyll. This appointment smacked of the old tulchan episcopate and there is no evidence that John was ever a preacher. By implication, the see remained the virtual possession of the Argyll family of Campbell.

Only Campbell and George Grahame of Dunblane were missing from the episcopal ranks when commissioners of assembly were appointed at Linlithgow in July 1608. Many of the commissioners had also been appointed at the previous assembly, thus it was stated by way of reservation that the virtual continuation

salbe no wayes prejudiciall to the libertie of the Assemblie in choosing and electing Commissioners quhom they sall think most meitt and expedient; neither sall this electioun induce or import any perpetuitie of the office in the persons electit.[154]

The assembly appointed several bishops, *inter alios*, to visit and plant kirks, and to try and deprive ministers.[155]

The increasing power of the bishops was evident not only in the kirk but also through their restoration to places in the civil realm. A number of bishops were admitted to the council, beginning with David Lindsay in 1600 and George Gledstanes in 1602.[156] In 1609 jurisdiction over commissariat courts was restored to the archbishops, granting them power in ecclesiastical, testamentary, and divorce cases.[157] Archbishop Spottiswood regarded this accretion as of fundamental importance for 'the reformation of our Church governement' and looked forward to full restoration of episcopal authority through the return of seats on the court of session whence much opposition to bishops came.[158] Finally, in March 1610 two courts of high commission were erected, one for each archdiocese then amalgamated in 1615.[159] These new courts were to deal with 'offenders either in life or religion, whom they hold any ways to be scandalous', and in the absence of reformation they might command preachers in appropriate parishes to pronounce excommunication. Among those subject to punishment were preachers who dared to speak against 'the established order of the Kirk'. Such public disputation on polity was deemed to be 'no matter of doctrine' and those guilty should be punished more harshly since their pontifications had distracted them from instructing their hearers in the way of salvation.[160]

One preacher who felt the strength of episcopal wrath, exercised through the council, was John Murray of Leith. His sins were plural, but that which the bishops lighted upon was a sermon he preached at a synod in Edinburgh in 1607.[161] Murray provided a litany of presbyterian rhetoric. He blamed Catholic activity on the alterations of polity since these may have given ground for 'perceiving that we were inclyning their way in our Church goverment'.[162] Alteration was wrong since polity was 'fixed and immoveable',[163] and innovation was leading down a slippery slope just as the ancient church fell into a yoke of bondage going from something similar to 'our new moderators' to bishops to archbishops to patriarchs to the pope and his 'Antichristian greatnes'.[164] Only by removing bishops might the kirk be preserved; only by standing firm in Christian liberty (*i.e.* presbytery) might God's wrath be averted.[165]

The final stroke in the resuscitation of episcopacy came in 1610. The nominated[166] assembly which met at Glasgow did so against a backdrop of discord on account of kirk polity to the extent that an earlier date had been set aside in order to await a more auspicious climate.[167] Moderated by archbishop John Spottiswood, this assembly marked the full jurisdictional restoration of episcopacy. King James sent to the assembly a letter outlining his own powers and intentions which were in any event no secret. He described himself as the 'Principal Opposits on earth'[168] to Antichrist, the pope. As the 'Nourish Father of [God's] Church here on earth' he took it as his duty to establish tranquillity in the kirk which had been distressed by disorderly behaviour. Most of all, the kirk needed leadership which would be provided through episcopacy of ancient institution. James had written in 1589 that

'David doth nothing in matters appertaining to God without the presence and speciall concurrence of Gods ministers, appointed to be spirituall rulers in his Church',[169] but time had brought the king to a rather higher view of what a Christian prince could do. He now asserted his right and duty to reform all distempers, and it was probably because of episcopal importunity that he decided to call an assembly, however unnecessary, and to gain the approbation of the ministers.[170]

The Glasgow assembly approved a number of articles 'for satisfaction of his Majesties will'. Bishops were to moderate twice-yearly diocesan synods, supervise excommunications, admit and depose ministers in conference with other local ministers. Ordination and visitation were the province of bishops, as was the moderation of exercises. The king was asked to grant yearly assemblies,[171] and bishops were to be subject to them in matters pertaining to 'lyfe, conversatioun, office, and benefice'.[172] As it turned out, there were to be only four assemblies over the succeeding twenty-eight years, and the fourth, also at Glasgow, would overthrow the decrees of 1610. But this paucity was actually permitted in that the assembly acknowledged that the calling of assemblies belonged 'to his Majestie be the prerogative of his royall crowne'. All ministers had, at the time of admission, to swear an oath of obedience to the king, an oath identical with the form of 1572.[173] With respect to qualification for bishops, no one might be elected (appointed, in reality) under forty years of age and who lacked at least ten years of pastoral experience.[174]

The assembly was followed by a proclamation on 19 June forbidding any opposition to the determinations concluded by 'the nobilitie and faderis of the Churche, and a nomber of the most learned and best affectit of the ministeris'.[175] James Melville was unimpressed. He had interpreted the restoration of episcopal jurisdiction in the commissary courts as a return to the old papal constitution, while the high commissions elevated James's bishops 'far above any Prelatt that ever wes in Scotland'.[176] But the *coup de grace* was the Glasgow assembly which in the space of a single day cast down the labours of *seventy* years.[177]

Melville included in his history a letter which described proceedings at the Glasgow assembly.[178] It may well have been this document which underlay the anonymous work, *A briefe and plaine narration of proceedings at an assemblie in Glasco.* Written by someone restrained in England,[179] not unlikely James Melville, it began auspiciously with three verses on its cover, including Luke 19:37: 'Those mine enemies, which would not that I should reigne over them, bring hither, and slay them before me'. The author complained of no less a disaster than that the glory of the Lord, alluding to the Old Testament *shekinah*, had departed, 'that part of Israell touching outward administration of Christ his Kingdome by his owne Office-bearers'.[180] He not only deplored the 'reliques of Antichrist' which continued in England but taunted those of all ranks who had submitted to the English pattern pressed upon Scotland by the archbishop of Canterbury, the old foe Richard Bancroft.[181]

The 'dissemblie' of 1610 was fraudulent. It was not free from external pressure, since its membership included thirteen bishops, thirteen nobles, and forty gentlemen who were not the authenticated delegates of presbyteries. Furthermore the outcome was attained by devious means — bribery and intimidation.[182]

In 1612 parliament ratified the conclusions of the Glasgow assembly which consummated that process begun in the 1597 parliament whereby the king should consult with the general assembly on the powers of bishops.[183] Parliament also included 'ane explanatioun' of some of the 1610 conclusions. It was, apparently, by way of explanation that the oath (of 1572) laid down in 1610 was enhanced in 1612 by a promise of obedience to the minister's ordinary:

> And als That everie Minister in his admissioun Sall sweare obedience to his ordinar according to this forme following. I A. B. now admitted to the kirk of C. promisis and swearis to E. F. Bischop of that diocie obedience and to his successors in all lauchfull thingis. So help me God.[184]

A presbyterian would have echoed the concluding appeal to the Almighty. After all, his bishop was a minion of Antichrist.

For good measure parliament rescinded the Golden Act of 1592 and anything else which might be construed in a sense contrary to this resuscitated episcopacy. But Calderwood's concern was that the articles of 1612 were not identical with those of 1610. He pointed out that bishops were not subjected to the assembly as dictated in 1610 and noted alterations in various practices and also the deletion of episcopal requirements in age and experience. He concluded, after measuring the sins of the bishops, that 'we are to stand to the acts of the kirk in kirk matters'.[185] And ultimately he was not referring to the assembly of 1610.

Finally, in 1617 parliament clarified the procedure for electing a new bishop by the diocesan chapter. The act stipulated that only a minister might be chosen, but this was of no real consequence because the chapter had no power whatsoever under the Christian magistrate:

> The deane of the said chaptoure with sa mony of thame as salhappin to be assembled sall proceid and chuse the persoun quhome his majestie pleased to nominat and recommend to thair Electioun.[186]

Constantine would delegate this power to no one.

The early years of the seventeenth century witnessed the loss of presbytery in practice, but not in theory. The editor of *Informations* included 'A treatise of kirk governement consisting of two partes, whereof this former conteineith a demonstration of true Christian discipline according to the word of God used in the kirke of Scotland'.[187] Christ was the sole head of the kirk; he had left its constitution clearly defined; parity was a dominical ordinance; episcopacy was Antichristian; the two horns of the second beast in Revelation 13: 14 represented the civil and ecclesiastical jurisdictions of bishops.[188] The author called for courage and constancy: 'let us hold fast the true profession of *Doctrine & Discipline* according to the word, without wavering, or halting, praying continually'.[189]

These were the words of present defeat, even if those who read them might have hoped for some later reversal of the kirk's condition. 'Thir are dayes of decay and mourning; the Lord restore again to us the favour of his countenance, and give peace unto Jerusalem',[190] wrote John Johnston from St. Andrews to Robert Boyd at Saumur. However, as Melville remarked, it was Jericho that was being rebuilt.[191] Jerusalem was under siege, if not being dismantled, and the presbyterians knew they were powerless to resist.

The learned presbyterian layman, David Hume of Godscroft, wrote an open letter to Patrick Simson in which he deplored the lack of zeal in defending the truth[192] while a correspondent of James Melville bemoaned 'the weakenesse and ignorance of manie'.[193] Melville himself composed a lengthy poem on the recent events from his place of exile in 1611, published in an abridged form in 1634 as *The black bastel, or, a lamentation in the name of the kirk of Scotland.* The lines are steeped in apocalyptic imagery and the title page bears three verses from Revelation 2. In apocalyptic style the writer describes a vision. The kirk is represented, as in Revelation, as a woman who has been dressed anew according to the will of the red lion rampant (James VI), an outrage carried out by thirteen wolves (bishops). The shepherds (pastors) have now become careless and fearful, 'snar'd with geare'.[194] The woman speaks for herself:

> I was of late a Queen of great renowne,
> My fame was spred abroad all Europe through,
> In everie province, and in everie towne,
> I was well served both in land and Burgh.
> No person high or low, so rude, so rough,
> My lawes or precepts rashly vilipended.
> All stood such aw that I should be offended.[195]

She then provides a litany of the presbyterian kirk's greatness and a lamentation over the distress which has recently overcome her:

> Me to comfort there is none of my lovers,
> My friends are fled, and look to me a farre,
> Yea many of them are become reprovers,
> They turn aside, and glance on me a skarre,
> And some, like barking dogs, begin to gnarre.
> By craft, by coin, by Kings authoritie,
> What pleases men, is brought to passe on me.
>
> I cry as if I felt some sharp incision,
> When I beholde the present miserie,
> I cry as if there were some great division
> Into my bones, with pain to torment me.
> Wilde Boar and swine dwell in the sanctuarie,
> Even bastard Bishops, worse than Moabites,
> And more malicious than the Ammonites.
>
> Like subtile foxes they have entred in,
> Pretending me to honour and enrich,
> Wild wolfs well wrapped in a weathers skin,
> Have dealt by craft till I fell in the ditch:

Now on my belly they their tents do pitch,
And reign like lyons o're my sheepe and hogs.
Convert them Lord, or let them die like dogs.[196]

The poem concludes with the woman being chased away by 'a fierie dragon' before the angel Michael and his host 'beat him down for all his fearfull boast'.[197] For Melville these were the end times and the identity of the great foe was blurred to the extent that it included not only Rome but also the episcopal and Erastian government forced upon the kirk. It was against this apocalyptic outlook that episcopacy's defenders would have to wage literary war.

Only one consideration remained in order to fully restore episcopacy. Up until 1610 the bishops depended solely upon royal warrant, but whatever ecclesiastical capacity James might have attributed to himself and however much he might have deemed himself responsible for the external health of the kirk, he did not claim to be able to perform authentically spiritual functions such as ordinations and consecrations. He could authorise bishops to function in a legal sense, but he could not give them spiritual jurisdiction. Only bishops could mediate this power to other bishops. Therefore, not long after the Glasgow assembly John Spottiswood of Glasgow, Andrew Lamb of Brechin, and Gavin Hamilton of Galloway were called to London for episcopal consecration by English bishops. So might 'the adversaries' mouths be stopped, who said that he [James] did take upon him to create bishops, and bestow spirituall offices, which he never did nor would he presume to do, acknowledging that authority to belong to Christ alone, and those whom he had authorized with his power'.[198]

Upon returning to Scotland the three proceeded to consecrate their fellows. James had fulfilled his goal. The kirk was episcopal. Whether or not it was happy was unimportant to Constantine.

CHAPTER 7

Attack and Counter-Attack

On 22 March 1605 archbishop John Spottiswood wrote to king James a letter in which he described the ugly anti-episcopal mood in Edinburgh. He complained of daily dosages of invective and contempt and that nothing seemed capable of abating the flow. 'Nether laws of Assemblies nor intimation of your Majesties displesure, nor our innocent and upricht procedingis, can worke us peace at their handis.'[1] Indeed the archbishop had good cause for feeling injured if he had sensed but a fragment of what John Welsh would soon unleash against him from his confinement in Blackness Castle:

> As for that instrument Spotswood, we are sure the Lord will never bless that man; but a malediction lies upon him, and shall accompany all his doings . . . . here I denounce the wrath of an everlasting God against him, which assuredly shall fall except it be prevented. Sir, Dagon shall not stand before the ark of the Lord; and these names of blasphemy that he wears of Lord Bishop and Archbishop will have a fearful end . . . . he has helped to cut Sampson's hair, and to expose him to mocking; but the Lord will not be mocked: he shall be cast away as a stone out of a sling; his name shall rot, and a malediction shall fall upon his posterity after he is gone.[2]

The presbyterians themselves brought this prediction to fulfilment when sir Robert Spottiswood, the archbishop's son, was hanged in 1646 with a covenanting noose.

Most of the men who donned Scottish mitres between 1600 and 1638 had come up through presbyterian ranks, and for that reason they were regarded as traitors to the great cause. Nearly the entire number were graduates of Scottish universities where many had been exposed to Andrew and James Melville at Glasgow and St. Andrews or to Robert Rollock at Edinburgh,[3] but presbyterian lessons had failed to impress some students. The future bishop of Argyll, Andrew Boyd, wrote in 1608 that since he completed his philosophy at Glasgow twenty-three years earlier, 'I have approveit and wissit the constitutione off *Episcopatus*'.[4]

David Lindsay, minister of Leith and bishop of Ross, had something of a chequered career but he had been sufficiently close to the presbyterian way for Andrew Melville to demand of him how he, as 'an of the antient fathers of the Kirk', could now find himself opposed to the word of God as a bishop.[5] Lindsay in fact declined so far as to send his son to be ordained at the hands of the bishop of London.[6] Peter Blackburn was remembered for having recanted the 'verie guid doctrine' he delivered to assembly in 1600 before bringing profound distress to the brethren by his reversal under duress.[7] Even John Spottiswood had been earlier identified with the presbyterians, giving his support to the Edinburgh ministers caught up in the maelstrom of royal displeasure following the December 1596 riot.[8] He won further approbation when he effectively rebuked David Lindsay with the battle cry, 'Lett us not seeke worldlie ease, with the losse of the libertie of Christ's kingdom'.[9] Soon enough he and his father-in-law would be linked as 'Caiaphas and Annas'.[10]

The 1606 anti-episcopal Protestation to parliament was undoubtedly justified in remonstrating about the confusion wrought by preachers who had recently condemned episcopacy but were now accepting that very 'dignitie, Pompe, and superiority in their owne persons'.[11] They were fit only to be cut off as rotten members from Christ's body.[12] But worse was yet to come. Within eleven years three of the Protestation's signatories, John Abernethy, Adam Bellenden, and William Cowper would become bishops.[13]

The presbyterian Patrick Simson is reported to have said that should he ever join with the defectors to episcopacy it should then be recalled that he had uttered his own condemnation: 'I had fallen fra Christ and from his trueth in that poynt'.[14] There was no shortage of prophets ready to remind the fallen of their 'desertioun' and slander of the truth.[15]

James Nicolson had been regarded as a pillar, therefore 'it was not credibil that that man, quho had bein so farr againes that corruptioun all his tyme', should go over to the other side.[16] His defection was an exceptional blow in that he had been an intimate friend highly esteemed by the brethren,[17] though as early as 1597 he had shown himself willing to listen to the king.[18] In 1607 John Dykes wrote to James Melville that 'the devill raigned never more in flesh nor in Mr James Nicolsone, *graviter impudens,* a horrible exemple of apostasie running to the highest degree'.[19] Similarly the author of *A briefe and plaine narration* wrote of 'perjured hyrelings, and apostate betrayers of Christ his kingdome'[20] and in bitter playfulness transmogrified 'Apostolicall' into 'Apostaticall' prelates.[21]

George Grahame, a bishop since the previous year, declared in 1604 that anyone who broke the cautions set down for parliamentary bishops should be hanged 'above all theeves'.[22] But no bishop ever resigned over the crown-inspired abrogation of these 'terms of employment', and Adam Bellenden reproached him for his actions:

> I see nothing in thee but thou art a mensworn man; thou art the excrements of all the ministrie; and thou hes imbraced the excrements of all the bishopricks in Scotland: if the brethren would follow my counsell, we should presentlie give thee over to the devil; but because they pitie thee, let this advertisement move thee, that thou mayest cast off that unlawfull place and calling, whilk thou hes taken thee to.[23]

Graham rejected the advice and in 1615 was translated to Orkney. His successor at Dunblane was Adam Bellenden.[24]

The controversial literature of the time was replete with challenges to the bishops to demonstrate the new light they had seen. David Hume called upon bishop James Law in 1608 to cease all rigours against non-conformists 'till suche tyme as there had beene some evidence to perswade the conscience' of the rectitude of changes in polity.[25] James Melville demanded that the bishops explain their change of heart. Given that they had been of 'ane judgment and practise with us in tyme bypast, now by a cleir lycht quhilk hes schynit to thame in thair gryt studie' that episcopacy, though condemned by the kirk, was 'the ordinance of God', let them now offer a clear statement of their reasons. Failure to do so would amount to sin against God, themselves, and their brethren of the ministry.[26] Alexander Hume, minister of Logie, had no doubts concerning what new light had dawned upon the bishops: 'Indeed, I grant ye see now thrie thingis, whiche befoir ye saw not: to wit, the object of warldlie commoditie, the object of warldlie promotioun, and the blandischements of ane eloquent Prince'.[27] He dismissed any nobility of purpose in the bishops' minds and proceeded to demolish, with typical presbyterian force, pro-episcopal arguments from the Bible and early Christian practice. Surely king James's bishops might be excused if they appeared reluctant to tangle with these relentless advocates of presbyterian history, exegesis, and logic.

The burden of episcopal defence fell to two men — James Law and William Cowper. Law, then the bishop of Orkney, engaged in an epistolary debate with David Hume, and even though the bishop's letters have perished, some of his arguments are preserved in the letters of his antagonist. A much more substantial body of material is found in two apologetic works of William Cowper, the bishop of Galloway. Cowper was a prolific, though generally non-controversial, writer, but the bitter attacks he sustained after accepting a bishopric in 1612 moved him to a response. His *Apologie*, printed perhaps in 1613, replied to an anonymous 'lying Libeller', while the much longer *Dikaiologie* (1614) was for the most part a reply to a manuscript work by David Hume which attacked the *Apologie*. The *Dikaiologie*, containing a reprint of the *Apologie*, was a rigorous confutation of Hume's aspersions from which the bishop quoted extensively. It is an impressive piece though it suffers from a verbosity which at times suggests the anxiety and uncertainty of the author who was undoubtedly not cut out for such vitriolic confrontation.[28] Hume replied to the *Dikaiologie* — one is awed to consider how lengthy it might have been, given the geometric progression customary in pamphlet wars — but it was never printed 'becaus the gentleman wanted the commoditie of the presse'.[29]

Cowper was generally accused of departing from that discipline 'whilk now your second light has altogether defaced'.[30] He would qualify the criticism but even if it were true, he countered, change to a better opinion ought to be regarded as a virtue.[31] The pressure he felt, however, must have been considerable, for his past contained a number of incidents some of which he explained, while some others he ignored. In about 1612, before he became a bishop, he felt compelled to write to the king that reports were circulating which recalled Cowper's earlier anti-episcopal sentiment. His admission of a former opposition, based upon his 'weak judgment', was unlikely to have been a revelation to James, for if contemporary reports are correct, Cowper had once told the king that he would 'rather be hanged at the markat cross ere ye know any man take a bishoprick'.[32] He could, nonetheless, still claim never to have reproached his royal master; on the contrary, his speeches always 'favored of a dewtifull affection' for the sovereign. But at the time of writing he sat on an anxious perch. Presbyterians repudiated him as a turncoat, and if the king cast him off he would be 'a losser at all handis'. [33] This was exactly where James wanted his bishops to be, utterly dependent upon his own pleasure.

In the *Apologie* Cowper defended himself by declaring that he had always regarded ministerial parity as 'the Mother of confusion', while in the matter of ministers having the vote in parliament he had likewise consistently favoured the arrangement as 'reasonable and necessarie', voting to that effect in the 1598 assembly at Dundee. [34] He noted scornfully that he had not participated in the abjuration of episcopacy in 1580, being then but twelve years of age. [35]

Cowper rejected a story repeated by David Hume that he had cast aspersions upon the procession of prelates at Perth in 1606. [36] In fact, the year 1606 proved ultimately to be remarkably difficult for the later prelate. He had, during the time of parliament, preached a sermon on kirk polity which in Melville's words had brought 'gryt confort and contentment'[37] to the godly. Hume claimed that Cowper had denounced 'the very stile of Bishops', [38] and another presbyterian stated that the remarks were remembered both by parliamentarians and Cowper's Perth parishioners. [39] The bishop's contention was that he had not condemned episcopacy in his sermon and he stood by the words he had spoken which could still be seen in the 'just copie' of the speech. [40]

A portion of the 1606 address was published by David Calderwood in 1636 and it confirms Cowper's assertion — unnoticed by detractors — that he desired a preservation of the older polity in conjunction with some presumably modified and unpretentious episcopate. But if Calderwood's extract may be credited — acceptance of it as legitimate is not difficult and goes far to explain the subsequent confusion — Cowper did make a pellucid reference to the wrongfulness of episcopacy. He described, first, how the apostle Paul adopted no title to make himself superior to Timothy, a mere evangelist:

> This may serve to make these men ashamed, who being partakers of one office of pastorship with the rest of their brethren, will bee separated from them by stately stiles. Order is good, I grant, but away with such order, as hath bred that Romane Hierarchie, the tyrannie of Antichrist. [41]

Though he was slow to make his point clear, Cowper was apparently prepared to consider episcopacy united with presbytery, and this would again explain his subscription of the 1606 Protestation. He signed it without reading since 'they tolde mee it contained nothing but a supplication for continuance of Church-government, that then was'. [42] He was at that time concerned that kirk polity was in danger of subversion but he had since learned that it was only to be made better and more firmly established.

It would appear, however, that this new appreciation of events did not emerge in 1606, for his November letter to bishop Grahame deplored the present developments and Grahame's participation in them: 'your course wherein ye are entered I never loved'. He recognised the bishop's good intentions but warned, 'it is hard for you to worke miracles'. [43] Eight years later, upon Cowper's own elevation, a presbyterian writer recalled these words and threw them in his teeth:

'Whither is it more hard for you or Mr George Grahame, to work miracles?' Cowper was taunted to send to James a copy not only of his apologetic *Dikaiologie* but also of his letter to Grahame so that the king might see 'how much he is beholden to you for all your Apology'.[44] Apparently Cowper had also compared bishops to stinking candle snuff, and this imagery was likewise remembered: 'I pray yow, how is your nose wyped now, in the times of your second light, that yow feel not the savour ye felt before'.[45]

Cowper had once sounded like an ardent anti-episcopalian. He rode high on the presbyterian crest and if he harboured doubts before c.1610-1612 he was careful to moderate them to the extent that the brethren had no inkling of the ferment of intellect and conscience within. It seems doubtful that one should attach any importance to the 'vile, slanderous, and abominable speeches' made by one William Hay against Cowper in 1604 that the minister was going to London 'and ere he came home would wear a surplice and a four-nooked bonnet'.[46] Cowper was a presbyterian and if he had really disliked parity the substance of his complaint was probably a reaction against disorderly proceedings in church courts rather than evidence of a liking for a stratified ministry with a rigid and sacramentally derived differentiation of function. But he came, without benefit of any unholy motives, to appreciate the advantage of obedience to royal authority so that by 1610 he was counselling others to wait and see what God would do.[47] Ultimately this troubled soul found resolution for his doubts in the will of a Christian king whose pious mind was the means of grounding the kirk upon a more ancient and honourable government. Presbytery, Cowper finally believed, had nothing to lose and everything to gain in co-operation with bishops and subjection to king James.

Like Cowper and Gledstanes, James Law also defended the proposition that 'there is nothing altered, or to be altered, in anie essentiall point or part of our discipline'.[48] But what was essential? Though Hume referred, perhaps disingenuously, to Law 'as one whom I count of to have greattest abilitie amongst them of that opinion',[49] his reply to the bishop's assertion did little to mask the underlying contempt. If bishops and constant moderators were to be regarded as non-essentials, *i.e.* offices not pertinent to the essence of kirk government then in force, 'I wote not what to call *essentiall*'.[50]

Cowper's reasoning was that the amendments were not of substance but of details, 'as time required, to make them serve for the greater edification of the Church'.[51] Were not kirk sessions, provincial synods, and general assemblies in place? Had ecclesiastical censures been abolished? No, he replied, 'they are rectified, roborated, but not removed'.[52] Furthermore, a different polity by no means entailed a new religion; in fact, 'Christian people might be ignorant of this disputation about Discipline, & come to heaven neverthelesse, if so it might please some of their Pastors'.[53] For it was no sign of a good pastor to trouble his flock with disputes about polity.[54] Here lies a key for understanding the mind of Cowper the episcopalian — his deep pastoral sense, which pervaded his devotional writings, elevated peace in the kirk high above disputes about external order so long as the word might be proclaimed and the sacraments rightly administered.[55] Security for the kirk lay not in a particular external form, but in a godly monarch. To this significant point there will be occasion to return at greater length.

William Cowper's vision of the kirk was of government by bishop-in-presbytery. Why ought they not to 'be reunited, the one of them being ordained to honour and strengthen the other, and being reduced to that order and use, for which anciently it did serve in the Primitive Church'?[56] Elsewhere he described the two aspects as head and body,[57] thus neither was more important than the other; in fact, they needed each other to be whole.

Brief consideration must be given to the extent to which Cowper's version of polity actually existed in Scotland c.1610-1638. Walter Foster's researches in presbytery records indicate that the kirk courts were by no means suppressed after 1610, although three months before the Glasgow assembly Spottiswood had written to James of his desire to leave the presbyteries 'a bare name, quhiche for the present may please, but in a litle tym sal evanische'.[58] This was utterly contrary to Andrew Boyd's recommendation whereby the synods, presbyteries, and kirk sessions, 'according to our bypast consuetude', should be continued under episcopacy, along with general assemblies, though these were to be restricted in scope.[59] The fact of the matter was of course some diminution of the presbyteries' independence, 'but those bodies continued to function, to increase in number and effectiveness, and to be vigorous and vital agents in the pastoral and disciplinary work of the Church'.[60] Bishops controlled excommunication but they by no means pre-empted presbyterial responsibility. Actually, even though bishops might act to soften a sentence, they could also initiate a process or give support to the efforts of the lower courts.[61] Sometimes bishops performed ordinations without regard for other ministers, but there are numerous instances on record of bishops and presbyteries co-operating, as at Bedrule where the ordination of the new minister was performed 'by the Bishop of Cathnes and Presbiterie of Jedburgh in the kirk of Bedreul with consent of the gentlemen, elders, and hail congregatioun'.[62] Presbyteries are also found bearing responsibility for the visitation of parishes and for the admission of readers and schoolmasters.[63]

Spottiswood's dream of diocesan episcopacy untramelled with the ballast of presbytery was not to be fulfilled, and the attempt represented by the canons of 1636 helped to wreck the kirk. For if George Gledstanes wrote at all reliably, most ministers approved of the 'hybrid' polity.[64] Thus presbyteries persisted, and to this extent bishops could justifiably protest that there were no substantial changes in the polity.

Bishop Cowper admitted quite freely that in his younger years he had not been a friend to episcopacy, but upon more mature deliberation he had come to regard it as best for the kirk, 'having the best warrants of all other governement'.[65] He maintained that episcopacy was an aid to the preservation of unity and to strengthening of censures, and he followed Jerome's appreciation of bishops as a remedy for schism which now threatened Scotland as it once had the church of the fourth century.[66] People such as David Hume who made sweeping condemnations of ancient bishops were guilty of abusing many 'worthie lights',[67] and Cowper remonstrated further that to condemn episcopacy because the papal hierarchy emerged from it was akin to damning truth because it gave rise to heresy. 'Because the Pope is a Plague in the Church, is the Bishop so also? If this be a proofe of your best Logicke, what will the rest be?'[68]

In his sermon to the Glasgow assembly bishop Law reportedly avoided basing his pro-episcopal argument upon divine right but predicated it instead upon 'antiquitie, universalitie, and perpetuitie'.[69] Cowper stood on the same ground, though he was also able to state that he had no quarrel with either Hadrian Saravia or George Downame, both of whom were supporters of episcopacy *jure divino*. In a lengthy discussion in the *Dikaiologie* he laid down a series of points detailing his argument for the lawfulness of episcopacy, though he was careful to point out that churches lacking bishops were not to be condemned.[70] The Bible itself maintained bishops while their prominence in all the churches through so many centuries likewise authenticated them.[71] Cowper was also able to remind Hume that bishops existed long before the emergence of popes, they had been energetic in their condemnations of Rome, and they of all men had been the most severely persecuted by the 'Romish Hierarchie'.[72]

But across all these theological and historical attempts to establish the lawfulness of episcopacy, which might well have been culled from the English sermons and treatises referred to in the preceding chapter, there lay the shadow cast by Scotland's 'gude, godlie, and learned Prince'.[73] A presbyterian account of bishop Law's 1610 sermon gave his concluding reason for episcopacy thus:

> it hath the commaund of our mightie King, who for knowledge of Theologie, *exceedeth farre all the Doctors of Divinitie.* Therefore what ingratitude shall it be to us to refuse so necessarie a law, a burden to us Bishops, but to the Kirk of God the onely perfection of hir libertie in this life.[74]

Barlow and Meriton could hardly have done better.

Unlike his brother John who once threatened James with divine judgement,[75] William Cowper had a history of tractability. In a sermon preached on 24 August 1600 following the Gowrie conspiracy he not only cleared James of guilt but called upon people to speak well of him: 'I exhort yow, in the name of God, to thinke reverentlie of your Prince, remembring that Salomon binds your consciences not to speake ill of him, even in your secreit chalmers'.[76] The furthest extent of admonition in the king's direction was to wish that the fright would be used of God to move James to greater support for the gospel.

Cowper's writings are replete with expressions of submission to the royal will. His retreat from anti-episcopacy was due to his sight of 'a Christian King most carefull out of his rare pietie and wisedome, to see it used unto the right end',[77] a God-sent monarch who was 'a Professor, a Confessor, a Semi martyr, a Protector, a Preacher, a Propagator of the Gospell with us, whose power, for any thing I can yet learne, is greater in the externall government of the Church, then we have well considered of'. He observed the king labouring to promote the evangel, thus it would have been against good conscience to withstand the godly work. Cowper was appalled that royal subjects should effectively line up with foreign enemies.[78] He was therefore in a position to accuse presbyterians of lacking due regard for their Christian king,[79] whereas he could present himself as a true friend of the magistrate who led the faithful into battle against the adversaries of truth.[80] At bottom, it was this appreciation for the work of a Christian prince along with a personal predilection for peace in the kirk which motivated a man like Cowper to brave the calumnies of the presbyterians.[81] The theological proofs bear the appearance of justifications after the fact.

Cowper and Law were not the only bishops to articulate their political views concerning submission to the will of a godly magistrate. Gledstanes preached to the 1607 parliament to the effect that the sovereign had jurisdiction over ecclesiastical assemblies and was by no means secluded from spiritual concerns.[82] In his sermon to the Glasgow assembly archbishop Spottiswood stated

> that Religioune must not be intertaineit after the manner it wes brought into the land. It was brought in be confusioun — it must be intertaineit be order: It wes brought in the land againes auctoritie — it must be intertaineit by auctoritie![83]

That authority was the crown. Spottiswood gave further proof of his political loyalty during the treason trial of John Ogilvie, a Jesuit priest executed in Glasgow in 1615. Ogilvie claimed that his own belief that the church was not subject to royal control was similar to that of the presbyterian ministers who convened the illegal assembly at Aberdeen in 1605. The archbishop retorted that 'our Religion' taught that the king was the supreme authority in all matters of state, and also in the kirk 'to maintaine Religion and God's pure worship'.[84]

These ideas were given further expression by David Lindsay, minister at Dundee and soon to be bishop of Brechin, who published his *Aphorisms* on the powers of the magistrate in 1617 as part of the celebration of James's solitary hegira to Scotland. Though not in possession of episcopal authority, the king was *summus gubernator* in the kirk and, according to ancient examples of Israelite kings and godly Constantine, had power to purify corrupt religion and also to make determinations in matters of worship,[85] an obvious allusion to liturgical changes then under consideration. James's bishops had learned their royal political lessons well and saw their views consolidated in the new Confession produced in 1616. It reiterated the usual descriptions of kings as nursing fathers of the kirk and drew the inference of the subject's necessary duty 'to obey them in all things they command lawfully, not repugnant to the will of God'.[86]

William Cowper may have been at an early time a troubled or even a confused man, but he could hardly be accused of ineptitude. His writings, if unspectacular, are not the products of an imbecile; similarly, the books of the highly regarded Patrick Forbes of Aberdeen. John Spottiswood and Andrew Boyd were not without literary gifts, and a modern historian has spoken well of the political capabilities of Andrew Knox and James Law.[87] Thus there was probably little substance to the aspersions of the presbyterians. David Hume deprecated the bishops in 1611 who, he alleged, possessed 'noe excellencie of anie gift' beyond the ministers whom, in his judgement, the bishops now dominated and oppressed.[88] Likewise, Alexander Hume queried whence these inferior men acquired the audacity to accept offices which their betters had refused. Was their continuation in their sees becaus the Prince counteth it good service? Know ye not quhat conceate the Prince hath of you? It appeareth by his answer giffin concerning you, that when it was motioned to his Majestie, that seing he wald needes haif bischopes set up in Scotland, why did he not mak electioun of the best men? his answer wes, That the best he could not gett, and thairfoir, must tak such as he culd haive.[89]

Calderwood claimed that James Melville was offered Dunkeld, but instead of accepting he quoted Beza to the royal messenger.[90]

Of course it is not to be expected that the presbyterians would ever have recognised the moral, intellectual, or spiritual superiority of any bishop over the brethren.[91] Yet the king did not fare all that badly, and if the bishops ranged from the excellence of some to the bumbling of a Gledstanes,[92] so the presbyterian party also covered the spectrum, and the truth of the matter was that even apparently staunch members of that fraternity were not immune to conversion. Archibald Simson prayed: 'Lord give us that gift [of perseverance] in thir dayes of defection, wherein the starrs of heaven fall continually, and those that seemed to be fixed in the firmament of God for fear or gain fall into earthly dispositione'.[93] Presbyterian broadsides were the expressions of anguished and frustrated spirits.

It must be recognised, however, that some bishops wavered, casting uncertain backward glances at what they used to be. Peter Blackburn was in a quandary about accepting the see of Aberdeen in 1600,[94] and in 1607 he was cited by James for having made manifest 'his froward and evill inclynnit dispositioun' toward the king's management of ecclesiastical affairs.[95] In 1611 Andrew Knox, bishop of the Isles, was translated to the Irish see of Raphoe. When the presbyterian John Livingstone could not find work in Scotland he went to Ireland where Knox received him in 1630 in spite of non-conformity and told him 'that he thought his old age was prolonged for little other purpose but to doe such offices', *i.e.* to make room for dissenters in the life and work of the church.[96] Alexander Lindsay, bishop of Dunkeld, attended an ordination in 1619 and, knowing the strong presbyterian sentiment of the candidate, declared that he participated only as a member of presbytery and that he would make no further demand than what was set forth in the old Psalter which knew nothing of episcopal ordination.[97]

It may be true that such men were unlikely to prove pillars of episcopacy or to promote an image of the strength of their order. But after all, episcopacy was the king's programme, not the result of petitions by assemblies and ministers. As James himself wrote, the restitution of episcopacy 'hes bene Oure owen proper motioun, not subgested or procured by importunitye or suiteing of otheris'.[98] At best, James's labours served only to bring crypto-episcopalians out of their closets. But he did have bishops, even if a fully convinced hierarchy was slow in emerging. They were not necessarily good table companions, elegant preachers, or celebrated theologians, but they did not need to be. James was making only a beginning, and the essential requirement in his bishop was obedience. For the most part he got what he wanted.

James's ecclesiastical ambition was 'the quyet estate'[99] of the kirk and 'a good, solid and perfect order in the discipline'[100] for which he held himself accountable before God. The achievement of this end necessitated the suppression of the 'malicious obstinancy'[101] of 'those evill disposed, turbulent, and contentious spiriteis',[102] *i.e.* presbyterians, and papists, 'falsly called Catholikes',[103] who refused to accept the inviolability of royal authority.[104] Bishops were the chosen instruments of this policy. Whether or not Andrew Knox's soft-heartedness to presbyterians was the result of soft-headedness in his dotage,[105] the fact remains that when he was sent to Ireland he took with him a glowing commendation based upon good service to the kirk and to the crown by 'reduceing of the ignorant and wicked people of oure Yllis to the acknowlegeing of God and obedyence to the Kings Majesteis lawis'.[106] The two belonged together in an indissoluble and harmonious unity — obedience to God *and* Caesar. What was owed to one was owed to the other, for Caesar was now a Christian, hence he ruled as a David or a Solomon or a Josiah. Whether attacking the king in kirk or in state, presbytery and papistry were sources of disorder, and thus they were an affront to the appointed structure of creation.

The bishops were indeed 'answerable to your Majestie for performance'.[107] They swore obedience to the king at the time of admission and again when they joined the privy council, 'acknowlegeing with most humble thankis his Majesteis gratious favour' in advancing them.[108] These were the king's men, and he relied upon them both in the kirk and in the civil realm through their prominent role in the selection of the lords of articles in parliaments.[109] That he could depend on them was because, as Gledstanes put it, 'there is none whose standing is so slipperie'.[110] If they fell from royal favour there was no safety net to catch them.

This subservience and pliability may have caused the bishops to be abhorred by presbyterians as apostates and by some aristocrats as intruded royal lackeys destined to undo noble power. But it was precisely these qualities which rendered the bishops useful to James. David Lindsay had felt James's indignation when he supported the view that the kirk might excommunicate the sovereign,[111] and the king could not have been pleased when in 1605 Lindsay, now the bishop of Ross, complained in council that the presbyterians Forbes and Welsh 'wer hardlie keiped and mair straitlie used nor aither Jesuites or murthourares'.[112] But generally he demonstrated an attitude of moderation for which Andrew Melville and John Davidson rebuked him.[113] Once imprisoned for opposing Adamsons's schemes,[114] he was subsequently among those who acquiesced to the Black Acts. He later premitted himself to be placed as moderator at the disputed assembly at Perth in 1597[115] and he also presided over the 1599 conference at Holyroodhouse.[116]

George Gledstanes showed his potential in 1597, for no self-respecting presbyterian would have consented to take the place of the deposed David Black in St. Andrews.[117] Almost immediately a presbyterian gave him a new title, 'the ravening gled [kite]'.[118] At Dundee in March 1598 he argued *for* ecclesiastical representation in the estates and soon found himself doing battle with the irrepressible Davidson.[119]

Historians have long noted that many future bishops served on the commissions of general assemblies.[120] On these interim boards their tractable dispositions might be noticed and even cultivated. Of eighteen bishops appointed during the years 1600-1618, only three had not on at least one occasion acted as commissioners.

The bishops were subjected to a variety of abusive characterisations, and as the materials for this period are limited both in quantity and in origin, it is not possible to pass final judgement on the veracity of the several allegations. Presbyterians did not seek out the good in their episcopal enemies, but one may not compensate for their bias by simply dismissing all the complaints. In the end what is of first importance for the purposes of this study is to understand the accusations and the defences. Some assessment will be attempted, but this will be both tentative and secondary. In 1638 all that mattered was conviction, not truth. Doubtless this division would have aroused a presbyterian whirlwind of fury, but for the historian it has its uses.

Alexander Hume cited two major sources of complaints against the bishops. The one was their behaviour as ecclesiastical officers — lack of zeal in sermons and prayers, toleration of wrongful administration of marriage and baptism, and disgraceful management of kirk meetings: 'No questioun the grace and glorie of our ministrie, of our Presbitreis and Assembleis, is notablie decayed; and farr is all declined from that measour of perfectioun quhilk it haid, sone after the beginning of Reformatioun'.[121]

The other was of a more personal nature. 'These apostats are craftie tods, and filthie dogs and swyine', wrote one libeller after remarking upon drinking to excess, whoring, sport, wealth, and fame.[122] James Melville commented upon the bishops' dancing, card playing, dicing, 'and worse exerceisses'[123] which he was perhaps too decorous to describe more luridly. Reflections upon deceitfulness were also made, as might have been anticipated concerning Balaams, Judases, Esaus, and Shemaiases.[124] Hume added references to pride, covetousness, anger, impatience, 'craftines and partialitie', willingness to believe false reports (!), financial irresponsibility, and unseemly levity. With a considerable display of presbyterian magnanimity Hume allowed that not all were guilty of every vice, though everyone was tainted to some greater or lesser degree, 'except a few secreit ones, whome I doubt not but the Lord hathe sanctifeit and separated to him self'.[125]

William Cowper fought back valiantly, responding with the wrath born of righteous indignation. Apparently some of his detractors had gone to the extreme of seeing God's judgement against him in the death of some of his children,[126] and he was subjected by David Hume and other anonymous writers to character assassinations, 'the lyke hes never bein written against a man not condemnit of heresie'.[127] But here was a bishop who could answer in kind. To those who damned his motivation he retorted:

> But yet by some carnall and contentious spirits, who live as if they were Demi-gods, and in their tongues God had set his tribunall, or had made them Judges of the consciences of their brethren, it is objected, published, and carried from hand to hand, in a Libell, as full of lies as lines, that corrupt respects of gaine & glory hath moved me to embrace it – a fearfull crimination, if I were as guiltie of it, as they are bold to affirm it.[128]

Cowper, whose writings have left a legacy of piety not inferior to anything the presbyterians produced, attempted to repose confidently and serenely upon a heavenly judge in these skirmishes. He denounced the allegations Hume made concerning the quest for 'Gaine and Glorie' since only God knew a man's conscience — who was Hume to judge secret things? Cowper protested that of all the sins, covetousness had the least place in his heart, and in all these injustices Hume played the devil to Cowper's Job.[129]

He similarly denied that ambition underlay his actions.[130] Recognising that he was not likely to find believers among his adversaries,[131] he declared that he was not at all anxious to gain preferment and would much rather have submitted to someone else as bishop. His preference was for the quieter life of a parson, and his acceptance was only because of the obedience he owed to king and kirk.[132] As it was, he waited eighteen weeks before acceding to the appointment.

Hume criticised Cowper's conduct in pastoral office,[133] criticisms which the bishop could not leave unchallenged in view of his professed dedication to the work. To one of his anonymous detractors he confessed with characteristic humility that he was 'the chiefe of sinners', but he would not stand silent in the face of unjust attack: 'but where you will come in, and out of your pride, runne over mee, and treade my gift under your feete, I will not suffer you'.[134] He regarded his gift for ministry as from God, and his work had certainly not been without fruit. In his brief autobiography he protested, 'My witnesse is in heaven, that the love of Jesus and his People, made continuall preaching my pleasure, and I had no such joy, as in doing his worke'.[135] He wrote to king James in 1615 that preaching was his 'greatest comfort' while idleness was the worst of fates, 'for it staineth the dignitie of our calling, and corrupteth our selves'.[136]

Cowper was apparently genuinely concerned for the integrity of the high office into which he had entered. In a sermon preached upon the occasion of Spottiswood's translation to St. Andrews in 1615 he expressed his deep conviction about the great responsibility which rested on the shoulders of the bishop. He must be a living example, bearing himself with 'integritie, gravity, sinceritie',[137] eschewing ambition and discontent arising from thwarted aspiration. Elsewhere he prayed that God would safeguard bishops from 'pride, tyranny, and idlenes'.[138] The episcopal office was precious to bishop Cowper and he laboured sedulously in spite of physical distress to fulfil its demands. He had planted, repaired, and built kirks and he professed that his work in Galloway had been for God, king, and country.[139] Such was the witness of a beleaguered man. The presbyterian case could succeed only by proving Cowper to be a pathological liar without religion or conscience. Frankly, that case could not succeed.

In 1608, before he became bishop of Argyll (1613), Andrew Boyd declared to James he would not accept any higher place than a parochial charge even though he was favourable to episcopacy.[140] When in 1613 Spottiswood commended Boyd to James for preferment to the episcopate he wrote to the archbishop, 'What am I, or what is in me, to procure such royall favour?' He denied having even wished for that office, but, in his horrendously recondite literary style, professed obedience to the king's will.[141] Two years later he again protested, this time to James, that advancement to a bishopric was 'far besyd ather thocht or appetite'.[142]

A minor actor like Andrew Boyd drew little comment, but it was otherwise with a former apparently convinced presbyterian, 'guid, godlie, and kynd Patrick

Forbes of Cors'.[143] Melville could afford to be complimentary since Forbes's elevation to the see of Aberdeen occurred in 1618, four years after the diarist's death. But his presbyterian brethren were rather less charitable. Forbes had been in exile in England with Andrew Melville thirty-five years earlier, but upon his return he was not prominent in kirk affairs until he began lay preaching which brought him to the king's attention in 1610.[144] His work was soon after regularised through episcopal ordination and he served at Keith until 1618.[145] Upon being called to the episcopate he declined, but not because of antipathy toward diocesan episcopacy. In his *Defence of the lawful calling* (1614) he showed himself agreeable to either episcopacy or eldership as reformed polities,[146] and by the time of his elevation he was more forthright in his approbation of episcopacy. Given proper election and a moderate spirit, episcopacy, he wrote, was 'not only a tolerable, but even a laudable and expedient policie in the Church, and very well consisting with God's written word'.[147] Indeed he recognised the 'tyrannical usurpation' of some former bishops, but thought it allowable and necessary that men of quality should now be advanced lest the sees fell to 'belligods, hirelings, and sycophants'.[148] As for himself his only reason for refusing was because of the looming storm of liturgical innovation which, as will be studied in an ensuing chapter, he thought undesirable. His 'calme, moderat, and equal carriage'[149] was not at all adapted to the tempest brewing at that very moment.

Nonetheless, the highly respected and exemplary[150] Forbes did accept the bishopric of Aberdeen and presbyterians unanimously abused him for insincerity.[151] William Scot and David Calderwood thought his letter a clever piece of manoeuvring, written 'after such a forme that the Bishops might easily know he wold accept the Bishoprick *nolens volens*'.[152] They likewise accused him of a mercenary motive, that of propping up an impoverished estate.[153] But such an accusation is without foundation and describes only the unhappy depths to which the embittered religious mind might plunge. Forbes knew well what awaited him as a bishop:

> If I durst choose my own course, I had rather have a cottage in some wilderness, wherein to drive out the remanent of my dayes, then to be brought any more unto the view of the world, and in the mouthes of men. And if I were so vain as to be set for honour, ease, or commoditie; yet, alas! what honour could I look for by accepting a Bishoprick, whereby the mindes of men, who now both honour and reverence me, above either my place or merit, shall be turned to account me a corrupted man, and ambitious aspirer? What ease might I expect in so toilsome a task and heavie a charge? What could be my commodity in so dilapidat and dissipat an estate?[154]

At least Forbes entered the episcopate with his eyes wide open.

The letter of selection to which Forbes replied was subscribed by six bishops, including Spottiswood and Law. They recognised that their adversaries thought bishoprics were virtual sinecures and were sought after on that basis. But they knew well this was not the reality. The profit and status were no ample repayment for the hardship, and except for the conviction of serving God through their labours they would much rather have lived the quieter lives of parochial ministers.[155] Of course there might be found exceptions such as Abernethy who actively sought Glasgow in 1615[156] (though he later sought to quit the episcopate), but Spottiswood was not anxious to move to St. Andrews upon Gledstanes's death.[157] David Lindsay, bishop of Brechin, taunted the presbyterians in 1621 with a sarcastic rebuttal of their criticism of episcopal ambition: 'None of you (forsooth) like to have promotions, and I warrant you would flie into deserts to hide your selves, if ye knew your selves to be sought to be placed in high roomes'.[158]

James Melville's reference to 'rych Prelatis' in 1609 was a groundless accusation.[159] In his own time and thereafter a bishopric was as likely to ruin a man as to raise him to luxury and ease.[160] In 1614 bishop Law wrote to the king that he was in danger of debtor's prison and would have to resign his 'most hurtfull titill' and find some distant refuge to shelter himself from 'trubill, shame, and miserabill povertie'.[161] Shortly after this he informed the council that he had spent the savings of his youth and had sunk himself and his friends in debt, and for this reason he must resign.[162] In another letter to James he described his see as a 'malefice'. The bishop of Moray, Alexander Douglas, was tied up in legal trouble with the lord Spynie, and the cost of litigation had so impoverished him he wrote to James that '[I] wilbe forcit betyme to reteir my selff, and nocht to appeir to do your Majesties service' without immediate relief.[163]

Even the primatial see of St. Andrews was in financial straits to the extent that Gledstanes could not fulfil his duties in 1606.[164] Pressing hard to enhance his revenues, he asked for a tax exemption[165] and drew James's ire when he tried to claim the customs paid in St. Andrews.[166] In 1621 Spottiswood reminisced upon his translation to St. Andrews whereby he was obliged to take to himself higher expenses with a lower income. The declining price of corn had badly eroded his revenue, 'and in qhat case I suld leave my children, if God suld visit me, he knowis'.[167]

Monetary problems, sometimes compounded by aristocratic thuggery, interfered with episcopal residence in the dioceses. John Abernethy could not collect his rents due to the behaviour of the earl of Caithness[168] and therefore continued to reside at his parochial charge of Jedburgh. Diocesan residence was impossible:

> The rent of that benefice is so small and far worse payed because of the people's barbaritie, that it wold not sustaine me and my familie there scantlie half a year together, beside that I have no resident place there: neither darre I hazared, under the feet and tyrannie of the Earl of Cathness and his sone.[169]

He visited Caithness in the summer and did his best, but he asked his correspondent in 1623 to represent him well to the king, noting that he was paying his diocesan taxes out of his own resources. Charles, who was determined to enforce episcopal residency, ordered him to remove to his diocese in 1634, and this appears to have had the desired impact.[170]

Non-residence, another presbyterian complaint though for the sake of consistency they might have thought it a blessing,[171] was both by financial necessity and by royal command as in the case of Gledstanes who was ordered to reside in Edinburgh where his high commission now met,[172] to his financial ruin. Cowper also was non-resident because the king appointed him dean of the Chapel Royal at

Holyroodhouse and, as with Gledstanes, the effect was economic hardship. His living accomodation was abominable — 'a man may not possiblie turne a halbert'[173] — but his request for tax relief[174] was ill received by sir Gideon Murray, treasurer-depute, who wrote James that many other bishops had problems as bad as those of Cowper.[175] This serves as a commentary less on the bishop's avarice than on the general penury of the episcopate.

The extant episcopal testaments, seven in number, have been examined by Dr. Foster.[176] It is difficult to know what to make of the rather disparate figures ranging from David Cunningham's net assets of £3,052 (1600) to Gavin Hamilton's £22,278 (1612). One difficulty is ascertaining how much of the money was drawn from diocesan or family sources, of particular significance in cases of bishops connected to landed families. Another is the rather large sums which appear as debts payable to the bishops which probably represent unpaid rents, though George Grahame was sufficiently solvent to have large sums set out as loans.[177] Gledstane's net assets of £15,104 included receivables of £14,209; Law's testament was valued at £13,096, but this was rather less than the £14,737 owed to him, meaning that he was still confronted with cash flow problems. Nor can there be certainty that the money owed to bishops would have remained in their own coffers as private fortunes. It is not unlikely that episcopal incomes were on their way to adequate levels like those of ministers,[178] but there is nothing in the foregoing to support an allegation that Scottish bishops generally lived like princes.

By no means were the financial concerns of the bishops purely for themselves. Six bishops petitioned James to have the 1606 parliament ratify a pension granted to the family of John Dury who had been minister at Montrose.[179] While minister at Eaglesham, Andrew Boyd had drawn James's attention to the 'miserable povertie' of the ministry.[180] Gledstanes sought to alleviate the hardships of two of his ministers[181] and complained to James when lord Sanquhar forced some ministers to grant him their teinds for an absurdly low sum.[182] Similarly the bishops in 1607 had opposed those who tried to gain their 'consent in the alienatioun of the Teindis from the Churche perpetuallie, and to content so mony Churchis with a smal provisioun',[183] while in 1609 they demanded that lords of erection either provide for the kirks in their lands or surrender their lordships.[184] William Cowper's sermons before the visiting king in 1617 denounced those who had committed the dread sin of sacrilege, leaving in their voracity 'not so much as the small teinds of the Vicarage for maintenance of a Pastor'.[185] Like the 1616 assembly which warned that poor stipends for ministers portended the kirk's desolation,[186] Cowper feared that the Scottish kirk, of so ancient foundation, was now in danger of expiring through impoverishment. The king, however, was not the responsible party, and the bishop praised James's concern for the kirk, calling him a Nehemiah and a Zerubbabel for his care.[187] Presumably the bishop of Galloway also excused himself, even though his brother Andrew held two places in the Chapel Royal at Stirling and a parsonage as titular while two nephews also possessed parsonages on the same non-serving basis.[188] Calderwood added that Cowper had extorted up to 200,000 merks from his diocese and other lands,[189] a most unlikely allegation.

King James was, of course, anxious to enhance the financial condition of the kirk and thereby to improve the stipends of the ministers.[190] Thus he was concerned to ensure that the work of restoring episcopal revenues was not undone 'by the dilapidationis of those who ar in present title of these Prelacies by there so hurting the Estaites of the same, there dilapidationis, as that there successoures shall want mantenance to beare out there rank, and so through povertie forced to relinquishe it'.[191] One wonders all the more, then, at Cowper's magnanimity to his family, but it does become clear why the bishop of Moray was so quick to defend himself against the rumour that he had dilapidated his see.[192]

Henry Spelman's treatise *De non temerandis ecclesiis* was published in London in 1613. A defence of the ecclesiastical patrimony against encroachments, the work was republished in Scotland in 1616 with a preface by 'I.S.' James Cooper considered likely candidates who might have written the introductory words 'to the Right Reverend Fathers and Brethren, the Bishops and Ministers of the Church of Scotland'.[193] One possibility was sir James Sempill who in 1619 set forth his *Sacrilege sacredly handled* on the same theme, but Cooper rejected him because his initials ought to have been 'S.I.S.', and in any event, the closing form would appear to indicate a cleric: 'Your Brother, and fellow-labourer in the Gospell'.[194] The process of elimination led finally to archbishop John Spottiswood whose 'care and zeal to procure a suitable provision for the clergy of Scotland . . . points to the same conclusion'.[195]

The preface protested bitterly about the wrong suffered by the kirk. 'Who seeth not th'estate of the Church of Scotland, as concerning the Patrimonie, to goe daylie from worse to worse? Sacriledge and simony have so prevailed, that it beginneth to bee doubted of many, whether there bee anie such sinnes forbidden by God, and condemned in His Word'.[196] The writer blamed the state of affairs upon kirkmen who set tacks, purchased benefices, courted 'corrupt patrons', behaving as if there were nothing distinctive about ecclesiastical concerns. He warned that this abuse represented the greatest impiety of the day, and without amendment the ministry and the kirk as a whole would soon decay. 'Repent, therefore, and amende your owne negligence in this behalfe, and call upon all others for amendement, whilest you have time'.[197]

Whether or not it was in actual fact the primate who wrote these heated words of commination, Spottiswood was impatient with those bishops who were poor husbandmen and guardians of the kirk's patrimony. Though he thought that the former archbishop of Glasgow Robert Montgomery was unjustly persecuted for accepting the episcopal office, Spottiswood did say that he had been 'pitifully corrupted' by his pact with Lennox 'for which justly he ought to have been repulsed'.[198] A lawful office could not coexist with an unlawful act. Spottiswood was a defender of Patrick Adamson but nevertheless admitted that the archbishop had been 'an ill administrator of the Church Patrimony'.[199] He likewise accused George Gledstanes of damaging the see by setting lengthy leases and

esteeming (which is the error of many Churchmen) that by this mean he should purchase the love and friendship of men, whereas there is no sure friendship but that which is joyned with respect; and to the preserving of this nothing conduceth more then a wise and prudent administration of the Church rents, wherewith they are intrusted.[200]

Spottiswood did not, however, offer any comment upon his receipt of New Abbey in 1612[201] which was in 1624 erected into a lordship for his son Robert.[202]

Patrick Simson declared that the bishops 'have trode the anointed of the Lord under their feet',[203] while his brother was forced to preach Patrick's funeral sermon at night, 'being silenced and stay to preach publickly by the persecution of the Prelats'.[204] It was natural that the bishops should be accused of oppression in that they bore down those opposed to the wishes of James, threatening to interfere with ministerial stipends[205] and sitting upon the high commission. Spottiswood replied to this accusation that a charge of 'excessive lenity' would be more accurate than that of 'domination and tyranny'.[206]

The analysis of the high commission undertaken by George McMahon indicates that under James fifty-four ministers were called before the court. Twenty-eight of these, including William Scot, were excused without further action. Of the twenty-six who suffered some form of penalty, six were confined temporarily to their parishes, among whom was John Row the historian. Five were suspended from the ministry and subsequently restored; seven, including David Dickson, were deprived but restored after a time; eight, including David Calderwood, were deprived permanently.[207] It was Calderwood who supplied much of the information about the high commission's proceedings, and since he terminated his work at 1625, the material for the reign of Charles I is not as full. At least ten ministers were sentenced to suspension, deposition, or warding. Among them was Samuel Rutherford who was suspended and warded in Aberdeen. David Dickson made another appearance but received only an admonition.

Presbyterians could not be expected to take kindly to any attempt to enforce conformity with respect to either polity or worship as these developed in the seventeenth century, but the disciplinary proceedings of the bishops, even as reported by a hostile party, do not describe a reign of ecclesiastical terror imposed by vicious and cruel men, despite Calderwood's scornful remark about a mitigated sentence: 'The merceis of the wicked are cruell'.[208] The bishops showed a strong inclination to persuade offending ministers to abjure their obstinacy and conform, and the bishop of Ross in 1606 prided himself on having brought ten of the seventeen charged after the illegal Aberdeen assembly to subscribe obedience.[209]

Indeed, John Spottiswood demonstrated periodic concern to see the refractory well disciplined, and in this he showed some insight into the politic need to uphold the integrity of authority. A number of bishops and future bishops had requested that John Murray be restored to his former pulpit at Leith[210] but Spottiswood was not among them. Perhaps he brought others to his own way of thinking because a later episcopal memorandum signed by him suggested only that Murray be released to the papist centre of New Abbey where the preacher would undoubtedly find useful distractions from anti-episcopal rhetoric.[211] The recipient of this document was to remind the king of the need for warded ministers to confess their faults before being granted liberty, 'otherwise they shall undoe all that hath beene hitherto followed for the peace of the Kirk'.[212]

The archbishop was, however, one who petitioned for Robert Wallace's restoration to Tranent and for James Balfour's to Edinburgh after the 1606 Hampton Court conference, and in 1610 he called upon the council to reduce a sentence against an Edinburgh merchant lest severity have an effect opposite to that which was hoped for.[213] The episcopal petitions were not without human caring. In behalf of Henry Blyth, minister of the Canongate then confined to Inverness, the bishops wrote to James of 'the seiknes of his children, want of moyen to entertain him self and his familie' and of his promise to behave satisfactorily.[214]

Of course James had the final say in the release of ministers from various forms of discipline, and when the bishop of Moray was suspected of acting independently in the tortuous Bruce affair he became the object of the king's personal attention.[215] James did grant Spottiswood's request and in 1613 released all confined ministers in the diocese of Glasgow.[216] On other occasions he might act without apparent prompting, only 'for certane reasonis thairunto moving Us'.[217] In sum, discipline of non-conformists was not remarkably oppressive for its day, even if the modern mind finds the whole issue of religious persecution altogether distasteful. The refractory were not physically abused or given a virtual death sentence by incarceration in insanitary holes. For the most part their sentence was not to leave their parishes or else to be sent to the end of the earth in Inverness. Nor were sentences irrevocable. A submissive individual might not be returned to his original place but he could be restored to the work of ministry. This did not necessitate conversion to the abjured article pressed upon him, but only agreement to keep his peace and obey his ordinary. Perhaps even this was too much, but beneath the growing weight of Stewart authority it was light treatment, and ungrateful presbyterians might have done well to reflect upon who their friends were.[218]

Presbyterian critics of the bishops were concerned at the apparent readiness to jump onto the anglophile bandwagon at the cost of loyalty to a distinctively Scottish kirk. James Melville recoiled in horror from the vision of a foreign and presumably English judge in a potential disputation between the episcopalian and presbyterian parties: 'quho can suffer it that is a true Christiane Scottisman?'[219] England was blamed as the source of the detested episcopacy then being forced upon Scotland,[220] and the tract entitled *A briefe and plaine narration* tried to shame Scotsmen:

> Are the Nobles, Barons, and Borroughes of Scotland (as well as the Bishopps and some Ministers there) corrupted by the treasure of England, to yeeld unto the overthrowinge of their Law, by directions from England, which proceed from the instigations of the Archbishop of Cantorbuie?[221]

Alexander Hume condescendingly described the religion of England as a partial reformation only where certain 'vestiges of idolatrie and superstitioun' persisted.[222] For Scotland to turn to the form of English episcopacy would therefore be a 'retrogradatione'.[223] David Hume appealed to James Law's patriotic sense in prognosticating that changes in polity could eventuate only in England's 'tyrannizing' over Scotland.[224]

But bad would soon get worse when in 1610 Scottish bishops received consecration from English hands in London of all places. David Hume wrung his own hands in despair when he heard the news: 'So oft I thinke I am dreaming that suche formes sould be used or avouched in Scotland by a Scotish man, a Protestant, let be a minister'.[225] Calderwood expressed his view that even one of the bishops from popish times would never have subjected himself to English consecration,[226] though he did record a rumour that some of the new bishops 'sturred at the forme and order of the consecration'.[227] John Spottiswood, too, was sensitive to the implications of the trip to London, fearing that the kirk, 'because of old usurpations',[228] might take the English consecration in bad part as indicative of a subjection he had no intention of accepting. But his wise sovereign had already thought of this and arranged it so that neither English archbishop participated.

Spottiswood also defended himself against anti-patriotic imputations in his sermon preached at the 1618 general assembly at Perth. He had heard that some opponents of the liturgical changes presented at that time accused those who obeyed of 'a betraying of the libertie of our Church and Kingdome'.[229] He shot back that the conformity at stake was not that with England but with the whole church before the coming of popery and its distortions. It was not he and his partisans who were poor Scotsmen but those who resisted the godly and Christian king. He went on to demonstrate his stalwart defence of the kirk's liberties, including his request for an assembly in 1618.[230] He also appealed to his actions in the case of the marquis of Huntly who had been excommunicated in Scotland and was subsequently absolved — in England. This caused real consternation in Scotland since the kirk's decree had been set aside by another church, but upon the representations of the bishops it was dictated that another absolution, made in Scotland, should be sought by the offender. Thus armed, the archbishop declared: 'If matters should thus come to be contested for [*i.e.* subjection to England], which is not to bee expected, wee should not bee found neglectful either of our Church or Country'.[231] He was true to his word — for a time at least. At the funeral for James, Spottiswood refused to stand with anyone other than the archbishop of Canterbury, which was granted on the proviso that he should accept English clerical garb for the occasion. To this

> he flatlie refuised, saying he wald carye him selff thair as primat of Scotland and go attyred according to the forme receaved and observit in his awne cuntry, and that he should never in his persone do that scandall to the Churche of Scotland as to assume thair apparelling and forgoe his awin . . . .[232]

The outcome was Spottiswood's withdrawal from the obsequies. However, at Charles's Scottish coronation in 1633 he acquiesced[233] while, according to one admittedly unauthoritative account, Patrick Lindsay, newly translated to Glasgow, was put out of the proceedings by William Laud because of his refusal to don the requisite trappings.[234]

William Cowper was made the butt of an abusive poem by sir James Sempill of Beltrees:[235]

An mystery most strange
of tailyeour Cowper his change.

Ane tailyeour once, an Cowper did beget,
 Two ticklish trades, and subject both to change.
Ye see the tailyiours mind is wholly set
 To chase the court, and follow fashions strange.
He chalkes, he cutts, he chappes he cutts short
 His needle can mend eache enormitie.
The Romish, Spanish, Inglish must be tryed
 and every cutt he calls conformity.

. . . .

But the reality was that Cowper was far from wanting to cut Scotland according to the pattern of England. His commentary on the Apocalypse was written, states Arthur Williamson, as 'a patriotic gesture'[236] to counter Thomas Brightman's 'Anglocentric' version of history and the future. A more visible protest against any English trend to swamp Scotland was Cowper's reaction to James's desire to have statues of the apostles erected in the Chapel Royal in 1617. Though at the cost of a royal rebuke[237] the bishops, Cowper wrote to Patrick Simson, had succeeded in having James withdraw the order. However, it appeared that the king would once again call upon his English divines to dispel the senseless fears harboured by the Scots. But Cowper was steeling himself to resist: 'God make us wise and faithfull, and keepe us from their usurpation over us, which now is evidentlie perceived, and hardlie taken by us all'.[238] Whatever their reason for joining the episcopal side, it was not because Cowper, Spottiswood, and their colleagues were striving to become English.

It was of great importance in the seventeenth century to die well, bearing one's self nobly, having a clear conscience, approved by the church, then fading confident of salvation having uttered quotable words on the moral life or the true church. An otherwise estimable character could be ruined by the appearance of unresolved mental and spiritual anquish on the deathbed, while the physical horrors which attended the demise of some miscreants added further confirmation to their evil lives.

The bishops had, therefore, to defend their departed brethren from the aspersions put forth by presbyterian writers. Spottiswood's predecessor at St. Andrews, George Gledstanes, was said by the hostile John Row to have died miserably, desiring that no one should visit him in his final days. When he died it was necessary that 'his filthie carion' be interred immediately 'be reason of the most loathsome case it was in'.[239] Calderwood added that the archbishop's 'fleshe fell off him in lumps'.[240] Spottiswood, however, recorded that 'he ended his days most piously and to the great comfort of all the beholders'.[241] Before death Gledstanes had set down an affirmation of episcopacy because he suspected that the presbyterians would circulate rumours that he was unsure of his episcopal course. Calderwood lived up to the expectation of slander, alleging that Gledstanes took pen in hand at the desire of his family 'to procure the king's favour to them'.

William Cowper was alleged to have died after a terrifying vision came upon him while playing golf. He expired repeating the phrase, 'A fallen starr'.[242] Scot stated that his death followed a conversation with 'a good Christian woman'.[243] Spottiswood concurred that Cowper had been much harassed by people, but suggested that the bishop of Galloway was inclined to take criticism too seriously and this contributed to his death. The archbishop thought highly of his colleague, but opined that he was too much concerned for 'the applause of the popular'.[244] Apparently a successful, or at least long-lived, bishop required a thick skin. Perhaps he would have advised that royal approval was all a bishop could hope for.

Spottiswood's defence of Cowper followed one published by bishop David Lindsay in 1621 who praised the bishop of Galloway's sermons and other works 'which will continue with the posteritie, will witnesse against all their malice, that he was inferiour to none of the Opposites in preaching, yea, in many degrees superiout [sic] to them all'.[245] Lindsay also came to the defence of James Nicolson who died in 1607 not long after his appointment to Dunkeld. The author of *A briefe and plaine narration* stated that Nicolson died a troubled man, disallowing his title in his will and excluding his episcopal rents (such as they were in his dilapidated see) from the final reckoning.[246] Calderwood, Row, and Scot perpetuated this picture, Row filling out the details.[247] When it was suggested a doctor be called, Nicolson declared that 'no physician but King James could cure his wound, (O atheist! could not Christ cure it better!) he had put a mitre on his head; he behooved to take it off againe'. Little wonder that Lindsay came to the rescue especially if he knew of the verses attributed to himself about Nicolson, who was married to Mrs. Lindsay's sister:[248]

> His wife and friends comforts in vaine, bids bring a doctor hither;
> None but King James can give me health, by taking off my mitre;
> My bodie doun into the grave, my soule to lowest hell
> It presseth doun, O take it off, or ells it will me kill.

Lindsay denied that there had been any forgery at Linlithgow where constant moderators were introduced under Nicolson's presidency, and he defended the dead bishop as 'a man for his Wisdome, Knowledge, and Holinesse in greater reputation, then that thy calumnies can touch him'.[249]

The bishops were not above human frailty. There remain questions about the conduct of some, particularly their 'jumping ship' and suddenly becoming bishops despite recent assurances of their loyalty to the presbyterian definition of truth. As a collective they did poorly in defending episcopacy, and by their primary allegiance to king James they can have done nothing to enhance the stature of their office or their persons. But at the same time it must be said also that they were not hopelessly evil men. Gledstanes was perhaps the least lovely of them all and the critics of his life were not only presbyterian by religion.[250] The lord Binning wrote to John Murray of Lochmaben, that he had heard tell of some things Gledstanes had spoken 'which I will be loath to believe, and will forbeare to express thame for the reverence of the place whairwith his majestie hes honored him'.[251] Murray received another letter at about the same time, just before the unhappy archbishop's decease, which indicated that all who knew him had grown quite tired of his behaviour.[252] But these excesses were not noted against other bishops, and studying the episcopal sins recorded in presbyterian calumnies tells more about the writers than the prelates. Many questions about the character and work of the bishops are yet unanswered and will likely remain so without the unanticipated discovery of diaries and other records. This much may, however, be proposed, that the presbyterian picture of the Jacobean episcopate is not to be taken at face value. The worth of these writers, who will be addressed directly in the following chapter, is that they illustrate a certain mood in the kirk, one which came to full flower in 1638. The truth of their accusations is of far less importance than their public expression. In propaganda wars, brutal slander is more effective than factual history.

CHAPTER 8

Defining the Past

The episcopal years after 1610 witnessed the development of competing historio-graphical camps, episcopalian and presbyterian. The first shots had been fired by the presbyterians, particularly James Melville, but with two exceptions their histories were not printed for more than two hundred years. The bishops, however, had no difficulty obtaining access to the press, thus William Cowper holds the distinction of having published the first attempt to use the post-Reformation history of the kirk to justify and authenticate a particular form of polity.

It was Cowper's contention that the kirk was governed episcopally at the time of the Reformation, and under that polity 'wee enjoyed the Gospell for many yeares', or to be more precise, for twenty years.[1] This period was for the bishop of Galloway the 'purest estate' of the kirk, and his primary means of sustaining the argument was the assertion that bishops and superintendents were one and the same, the latter a term of Latin derivation for *episcopos*, the Greek original.[2] Consequently Cowper leaped upon David Hume for uttering derogatory remarks against the episcopal churches of Europe:

> In like manner, you spet in the face of your Mother, affirming that our Church was in an errour twentie yeeres, all the dayes of John Knoxe, for all that time it had no governement, but Episcopall: all that time, there was not such a thing as a Presbyterie in the Church of Scotland: and if any truth be in you, all that time was our Church in errour?[3]

The bishop pointed out that superintendents were never appointed to oversee the dioceses of reforming bishops, suggesting the kirk's approbation of the old hierarchy when reformed and the identification of the two titles as one ecclesiasti-cal office. Furthermore the ratification of episcopal polity at Leith in 1572 was done 'willingly'. Against Hume's argument that superintendents were distinct in that they were responsible to the kirk Cowper asserted that bishops were also; and if bishops were chosen by the king, so superintendents were selected by the council. Therefore he appealed to the presbyterian, 'See you not here a constant forme of government in our Church? See you any other Bishops now then were in the days of John Knox?'[4] He also drew attention to the good works of bishops, for it was they and not presbyteries who planted kirks in Annandale and the Borders.[5] Episcopacy would be proved advantageous by a review of the reformed kirk's history.

For as long as episcopacy flourished the kirk was orderly and united, relations between crown and kirk were peaceable, and papists were unheard of.[6] Unhappily, this episcopal idyll fell into decay and in 1575 the original polity of the reformed kirk 'beganne first to be withstood'.[7] Cowper became rather less convincing, though, when he treated the demise of episcopacy. It was sheer obscurantism at work when he declared to Hume that the kirk's discipline never 'disalloweth the office of Bishops, but only fights against the corruptions thereof'.[8] In fact, if one were to search the kirk's records as Cowper commended, one would observe that hierarchical and diocesan episcopacy was commonly represented as the great pariah — it was corruption epitomised. Probably Cowper was nearer to the truth when he claimed that some ministers submitted to the new polity out of fear of schism and that the rejection of episcopacy in 1580 was against the will of those who had affirmed it in 1572. He argued that alteration of polity during the royal minority was contrary to the 1572 concordat, and in 1579 a royal missive called upon the assembly to cease meddling with the kirk's government.[9]

The effect of this glorious episcopal past was to provide Cowper with the material upon which he could mount a plaintive appeal for submission:

> Thinke it no shame to submit your selfe to Episcopall governement; to receive it in the Church, which the plaine evidence of truth forces your selfe to confesse, that it was set up in our Church by the oldest and best Fathers that ever our Church had.[10]

The first presbyterian retort came from David Calderwood (1575-1650) whose *De regimine ecclesiae scoticanae brevis relatio* appeared in 1618, printed most likely in Holland where the author would soon be exiled on account of his recalcitrant opposition to James's ecclesiastical manoeuvrings. This brief tract provided a perspective on the kirk's history rather different from that in Cowper's *Dikaiologie*. Instead of seeing an episcopalian continuum broken at 1580 by the machinations of wrong-headed presbyterians, Calderwood described a continuous reign of presbytery until 1597 when James began to undo the established polity. This view by no means originated with him. It was probably James Melville who wrote in 1585 that the Black Acts had in one day 'cast doun twentie-foure yeeres' bigging'.[11] The watershed in the development of the kirk's polity was not the second Book of Discipline but the Reformation itself.

Calderwood's perpetuation of this historiography was predicated upon several factors. First, he claimed that the original Book of Discipline had been granted authority by the council in 1561 and, moreover, that the second Book was but an enlarged version of the first.[12] There was, therefore, no presbyterian revolution in the 1570s and the second Book simply continued the work of its predecessor. Second, by means of this peculiar historical perspective Calderwood read back the existence of presbyteries to the beginning.[13]

The spirit of the earlier assemblies and other courts of the kirk was one of concord, in conscious opposition to prelatical tyranny.[14] But try as it might to innoculate itself against episcopal dangers, the kirk's progress was hindered by three kinds of bishops.

The discussion of the first kind of bishop began with the superintendency, though unlike Cowper, Calderwood made no equation of superintendent and bishop. In fact superintendents were appointed *ad tempus*[15] and bore only a delegated authority. Superintending power was not ubiquitous — kirks that were properly established cared for their own affairs. There was insufficient money to

K

supply more than five superintendents and therefore the assembly appointed commissioners or visitors to provide wider coverage. Among these, due to the lack of other qualified men, there were enrolled a few of the old bishops: 'Whence it it clear that the bishops of the first kind exercised not episcopal but temporary power, delegated by the assembly'.[16] The experiment turned out badly as the bishops meddled in civil affairs and generally neglected their ecclesiastical responsibilities.

The second group consisted of the tulchan bishops who were an aristocratic device for seizing kirk revenue. Calderwood chronicled, not without overstatement, the concern which followed the concordat of Leith and the movement of the assembly to reduce diocesan episcopacy to parochial cure. Bishops and superintendents were shortly thereafter superseded by commissioners, and finally in the second Book of Discipline hierarchy was forcefully condemned.[17] Presbyteries were erected with royal approbation and in 1590 all commissions for visitation were terminated, the power devolving upon the presbyteries. In 1592 parliament ratified the kirk's polity and as late at 1596 'we were running well'.[18]

But the devil would not be still and conspired to send a third episcopal plague upon the kirk. First there was the usurpation of civil power by ministers who could vote in parliament. This was followed by the breach of the cautions, domination over other ministers, intrusion of constant moderators, and manipulation of the 1610 Glasgow assembly. From these developments resulted division and confusion in the kirk and, furthermore, alterations in the administration of the sacraments and also the observance of festivals[19] — an obvious reference to the innovations represented by the Five Articles of Perth. The influence of bishops was thus altogether pernicious in Calderwood's eyes, and his treatise offered clear evidence that eight years had not sufficed to quieten anti-episcopal thought in Scotland. The number of the disenchanted may have been relatively small, but the faction was vigorous and rancorous.

The major episcopalian response to Calderwood came from archbishop John Spottiswood (1565-1639). The son of the superintendent of Lothian, he succeeded his father as minister at Calder before appointment to the archbishoprics of Glasgow and then St. Andrews. No one was more prominent than he in seeing through king James's designs for the kirk.

Spottiswood addressed his *Refutatio* to prince Charles so as to provide a true account of the history of the kirk since the Reformation and to give the heir to the throne ample warning about the turbulent spirit of presbyterians.[20] The book condemned Calderwood's abuse of history and the unsettling impact of presbyterians of whom Spottiswood held no higher opinion than they did of him. He argued that the reformers regarded an episcopal superintendency as essential to the life of the kirk, wherein it accomplished great things.[21] In effect the superintendents supplemented the work of reforming bishops, while commissioners did not share equal authority — a somewhat dubious assertion. Presbyteries, he contended, did not emerge for twenty-six years after the Reformation, and he attributed their arrival to the baneful influence of Andrew Melville who was saturated with the Genevan discipline.[22] As for Calderwood's idealised pictures of the general assemblies, the archbishop cited a Spanish observer who compared them with the market places of his homeland.[23] Spottiswood deplored the riot of 17 December 1596 as the work of the devil[24] — he was probably unaware that Alexander Hume had actually criticised it from a presbyterian perspective[25] — and, rather superciliously, demanded what occasion for offence had been given by king James's subsequent proceedings.[26] However doubtful the claim, Spottiswood thought that the three episcopal periods in the reformed kirk were of one kind.[27] By such reasoning the episcopalians could see themselves as reflecting the minds of the original reformers. But as the controversy showed, neither side was willing to abjure the kirk of Knox and his friends. Thus they were dressed and dressed again in the colours of factions of a later time. One suspects that for the most part the leaders of 1560 would not have been perfectly comfortable with either side in 1620.

As might have been expected, an inveterate presbyterian of Calderwood's constitution could not permit the *Refutatio* to circulate unchallenged. Therefore he wrote another treatise, entitled *Vindiciae contra calumnias Johannis Spotswodi Fani Andreae pseudo-archiepiscopi*,[28] which dissected the archbishop's arguments piece by piece. Calderwood was most likely also the force behind the 1621 edition of *The first and second booke of discipline*. In the preface is found a review of the kirk's history since the 'darke and dreadfull dayes of barbarous blindnesse, and superstition'.[29] The Reformation was the golden age of the kirk, a time when there was no hint of a pompous or lordly bishop arrogating to himself superiority over other ministers or failing to fulfil his duties:

> O Scotland! what was then thy felicity? Then didst thou sing and shout with the voyce of joy: God wil arise and his enemies shall be scattered; they also that hate him shall flye before him. Thou hast brought a Vine out of Egypt. Thou has cast out the heathen, and planted it. Thou madest roome for it, and didst cause it to take root, and it filled the land, &c.[30]

Continuing the Old Testament imagery, Calderwood complained that Delilah had cut Samson's hair, *i.e.* the discipline whereby ecclesiastical purity was maintained had been broken down.[31] This was the work of ambitious men striving under pretence of retrieving the kirk's revenues.[32] To these 'Apostates from Discipline'[33] was attributed virtually all the ills of the kirk: 'the disgracing of Pastors, ejecting of Elders, destroying of Assemblies, and fashioning, doctrine, discipline, Sacraments, confessions of Faith, formes of prayer, and all in a new shape'.[34] Episcopacy was equated with popery and the whore of Babylon, and was termed the 'greatest monster' ever to confront the kirk.[35] To disprove all the episcopal contentions was the purpose of publishing the Books of Discipline, and Calderwood clearly had in mind the works of Cowper and Spottiswood.[36]

The final sentence of Calderwood's preface went to the heart of the debate: 'either of the said books [of discipline] confirm the other, & neither of them abolish, or innovate the other'.[37] But the opposition was equally adamant, and bishop David Lindsay of Brechin in that same year (1621) was confidently citing the first Book of Discipline to disprove Calderwood's allegations.[38]

At about this time there was a renewed interest in archbishop Patrick Adamson.

He had made such an impression that the presbyterians were unable or unwilling to forget him. Spottiswood wrote some years later, while commenting upon Andrew Melville, that

> there cometh to my mind the hard and uncharitable dealing that he and his faction used towards Patrick sometimes Archbishop of St Andrewes, who not content to have persecuted that worthy man in his life, made him a long time after his death the subject of their sermons . . . .[39]

Spottiswood showed himself to be the defender of lost causes, but his statement about presbyterian interest was correct. In 1607 George Gledstanes was threatened with judgement by one of the ministers in attendance at the synod of Fife: 'Weill, Sir, your pride, I hope, sall gett a fall. I saw the judgement of God upon your predecessour, and if yee amend not, I beleeve to see the like upon you'.[40] Alexander Hume recalled Adamson's tearful recantation and then taunted contemporary bishops: if gifted Adamson had come to such an end, 'who ar ye litle ones to succede wittinglie in his vice?'[41] Andrew Duncan warned Spottiswood that 'hall binkis ar sliddrie' and added an example that could have referred only to Adamson: 'I have sein one richt high mounted in your roume and cours, that gatt a foull and schamefull fall'.[42] William Cowper was drawn by David Hume to comment upon the former archbishop, though unlike Spottiswood he did so as if walking on eggs. He praised Adamson's erudition but did not attempt to rehabilitate the man's life and work. Instead he rebuked Hume for passing by others 'who lived and died honest men'.[43]

Others shared Spottiswood's enthusiasm. In 1619 two books of Adamson's writing were edited by Thomas Wilson, Adamson's son-in-law and a former student under Melville.[44] One was entitled *Poemata sacra* and included most of the archbishop's compositions, accompanied by a number of panegyrics. One of these was addressed 'To the envious, or evill willer':

> Thy thoughts, thine hopes, and purposes ar gone,
> Thou buildis on clouds thy pallace all of stone.
> For this Arch'bishop is immortall made,
> By learned Workes that shall not after fade.
> Whom thou and thine did causles ever blame,
> Heere thy reward shalbe great endles shame.[45]

The second volume was *De sacro pastoris munere tractatus* which Wilson claimed had been suppressed by the archbishop's enemies.[46] In Wilson's *Vita Adamsoni*, included with the foregoing, Adamson was vindicated and Andrew Melville vilified.[47]

But the presbyterians fought back in 1620 in a book dubiously attributed to Melville.[48] In *Musae* there was published a brief life of Adamson which recorded the familiar presbyterian aspersions and attacked Wilson's 'impudence and lies'.[49] This was followed by a Latin translation of the *Recantation* entitled *P. Adamsoni palinodia*.[50] That same year Spottiswood defied gravity when he stated that Adamson's recantation was forced and that its published version was full of interpolations.[51] In his final word on the matter Spottiswood claimed that Adamson 'complained heavily of the wrong that was done him' in the affair.[52]

The brief historical works already referred to did not terminate the debate over the reformed past in Scotland, and particularly after 1620 writers on both sides devoted themselves to larger compilations and interpretations of the history of the kirk since the Reformation.

The larger body of material was produced by the presbyterians, four of whom merit our attention. John Forbes of Alford (c.1568-1634), brother of Patrick, bishop of Aberdeen, was one of the ministers exiled in the wake of the Aberdeen assembly of 1605. The date of his *Certaine Records* is unclear, except it was after 1606 when the story ends. Forbes's basic purpose was to describe the Aberdeen assembly and the trial that followed, but to set the stage he provided a brief survey of the kirk's history from the Reformation. He supplied no details of the early years but his presbyterian bias was made manifest from the first. When Scotland was delivered from popish darkness not only was doctrine made pure but also there was established 'that only lawfull, decent, and comly forme and ordour of government in the house of God, prescryved by Christ and practised by his Apostles',[53] while 'antichristian hierarchie' and every vestige of the beast were rejected. Forbes offered no comment on superintendent or tulchan bishop but focused his attention upon the troubled year of 1584 when the king, 'by oft suggestion of subtill flatterers, and godles Atheists',[54] turned against the established, *i.e.* presbyterian, order. In 1590 the kirk began to be restored to its proper polity but this lasted only until 1596 when more decay set in, leading again to the erection of 'the abjured and damnable disorder of that antichristian Hierarchie'.[55]

William Scot (1566-1642) was for many years the minister of Cupar in Fife. A participant in and contributor to many of the events and affairs described in his works, he paid for his presbyterian loyalty when summoned to London in 1606. Scot wrote two works, both of a historical nature. The first, *The course of conformitie*,[56] was published in 1622, probably in Holland. Episcopacy was the key to permitting the entry of the great evil which was papistry. It 'hath set up and holdeth up Papistrie',[57] and even if the Scottish bishops were themselves not favourers of Rome, their actions could serve only to encourage Antichrist. Scot's historical scheme saw the kirk ruined by degrees of which there were four.[58] First was division which occurred at Perth in the 1597 assembly. Second was the suppression of free assemblies, and third was the restoration of bishops which followed a six-step process — the parliamentary vote, constant moderation, the high commission, the grant of jurisdiction at Glasgow in 1610, consecration, and the regulations for elections and chapters in 1617. The fourth degree was innovation in worship:

> So our Prelats, after their preferment, not resting content with the destruction of the unitie, authoritie and order of the Kirk, nor with their precedencie before the Peeres of the Kingdome, and power over all the subjects, must make an on set upon the worship of God, esteemed the substantiall and fundamentall part of our profession . . . .[59]

Scot's longer work, *An Apologetical Narration,* lay unpublished until 1846. It related the kirk's history from 1560 to 1633 and appears to have been written in 1635,[60] though sections may have been prepared before then.[61] He began the *Narration* with the Book of Common Order in which four ecclesiastical offices were recognised — pastors, doctors, elders, and deacons.[62] Superintendents were added later both in the Book of Common Order and then in the first Book of Discipline which 'was not intended to be strictly observed in all tyme coming in every point, but liberty was reserved to the posterity to devise and establish a more perfect [book]'.[63] Those who drafted the discipline did not regard episcopacy as an apostolic institution, and superintendents were not one of the 'ordinary offices' of the kirk either. They were strictly temporary, necessitated by conditions in the infancy of the reformed kirk. In any event there was no substantial similarity between old bishop and new superintendent. Superintendents were itinerant preachers; they were freely chosen; they were admitted without elaborate ceremony and were thereafter subjected to censure; they were all of one degree and must not become entangled in the affairs of this life.[64]

In this analysis of the past, Scot divided the Protestant kirk's history into five 'courses', the first lasting until 1572. Its major feature was the 'power of Assemblies'.[65] The lack of ministers precluded the erection of presbyteries in the beginning, though Scot seems to have thought that these were planned for from the outset. It was the period of superintendents and commissioners, but 'Mr John Knox his ministry did more good then all the superintendents'.[66]

The second course began with the concordat of Leith in January 1572. Of these tulchans Scot wrote contemptuously that 'the bishop served to cause the bishoprick yeeld commoditie to my lord, who procured it to him'. The kirk accepted the arrangement only on an interim basis — Knox was implacably opposed in this version of the story — with the bishops permitted to function only as superintendents, though it is likely that the progenitors of the scheme harboured more ambitious designs.[67]

A third stage was reached in 1576 when the kirk abrogated the rule of bishops and superintendents and resorted to visitors. Then in 1580 episcopacy was utterly abolished:

Least any man should think that they damned not the office *simpliciter,* but the corruptions, he must know that these corruptions are the very essence of the office; so that to abolish the corruption of the estate of bishops, is to be abolish [sic] the corrupt state of bishops.[68]

These developments were crowned by the second Book of Discipline.

Presbytery reigned after 1581, even though troubled by the intrusion of bishops including Montgomery, 'a stolid asse and arrogant', and Adamson, brought low by 'gluttony and drunkennesse'.[69] Even the king was heard to praise presbytery for its suppression of heresy,[70] and Scot was sedulous to point out the contrast between presbyterian tranquillity and episcopalian disorder.

The fifth and final course dealt with the re-establishment of episcopacy after 1596. Four steps were identified — the parliamentary vote, constant moderation of presbyteries and synods, the high commission, and the restoration of jurisdiction in 1610.[71] Once in power the bishops commenced to alter the worship of the kirk.[72] It was clear from Scot's understanding of the lamentable state of the kirk that there could be no hope of renewal so long as episcopacy endured.

John Row (1568-1646), minister of Carnock, Fife, was the son of the reformer of the same name. For the edification of some young ministers[73] he described the kirk's history from the time of the Reformation in a work which first circulated in manuscript about 1634. It was later brought up to 1637,[74] and the work as published in 1842 contains passages interpolated after the Glasgow assembly of 1638.[75]

There was no anti-episcopal writer more acerbic than Row. Concerning George Gledstanes he wrote, 'Let that perjured apostat's filthie memorie stink, rot, perish!'[76] Proud prelates were sons and heirs to Antichrist, the first-born of the devil.[77] Like others of his faction he was firmly convinced of the kirk's superiority above all other churches. Even its unique name was better since 'kirk' was derived from a Greek word[78] while its constitution was utterly and perfectly biblical. Upon Mary of Guise's death

the Ministers that were, took not their pattern from any Kirk in the world, no, not fra Geneva itself; but, laying God's word before them, made Reformation according thereunto, both in doctrine first, and then in discipline, when and as they might get it overtaken.[79]

The kirk was clearly distinct from the church of England where reform was at royal command and according to the crown's pleasure, 'whilk hes bene the cause why other Kirks, professing the same trueth with us, yit had never the sinceritie of discipline amongst them'.[80]

Row described the contents of the Books of Discipline, the second of which was 'set downe . . . more succinctlie',[81] an implication of continuity that necessitated a discussion of the superintendents. He explained that they were visitors, they were admitted like other ministers, and they rendered account of their work to the assembly. Unlike the bishops who were also appointed to visit, the superintendents were 'verie faithfull, diligent, and holy men'.[82] The employment of bishops could be justified only on the ground that in the early years of reform there had to be toleration of some elements which must thereafter be suppressed. When bishops were reintroduced in the 1570s 'the sincerest of the ministers and good professors would faine have had them altogether removed out of the Kirk'.[83] The 'verie vitious and ungodlie' Adamson at least died well following his recantation, and Row hastened to draw a moral from the archbishop's renunciation of his avarice, eloquence, and love of royal favour: 'This should be a great warning to all men this day'.[84]

It was at Dundee in 1598 that there 'began the great change that came upon our kirk' through the creation of parliamentary ministers.[85] From there the path was swiftly downhill. Assemblies were manipulated by the exercise of the royal prerogative which Row called 'a small friend to the croune of Christ and libertie of his Kirk'.[86] When in 1604 the commissioners of assembly discarded their control by the assembly Row concluded that this gave evidence that 'my Lord Bishop exyled began to return fra his banishment out of this Kirk'.[87] Constant moderators were one step closer to 'a Diocesian Lord Prelat',[88] whom the historian held responsible for all the perversion of the kirk to 1638.[89]

The largest of the presbyterian histories came from David Calderwood, who has already been cited frequently in this study. He produced three different versions — a massive compilation no longer extant in its fullness; the manuscript, written in about 1627,[90] which the Wodrow Society printed and which is most commonly cited by students of the period; and the edition published in 1678 'which the Author desireth only to be communicat to others; and this [the largest of the three], with the other contracted in three volumes [Wodrow Society], to serve only for defence of the third, and preservation of the Storie in case it be lost'.[91] It was prepared c.1631.[92]

Calderwood was in the first place a compiler rather than a historian as understood in the modern sense. His contribution was the assiduous and careful collection and transmission of original sources many of which are not to be found elsewhere. His historiography, therefore, was generally not his own but that of his sources, some of which he named in another part of the explanatory passage quoted above: Knox's *History*, James Melville's *Autobiography and Diary*, the diary of John Davidson,[93] proceedings of general assemblies, acts of parliament, proclamations, and whatever other relevant materials he could lay hands upon. He did not commonly state whence he was quoting, but the wording of Knox and Melville was often taken over in its entirety. Actually there is very little of Calderwood in his *History*, and as a result it lacks the force of continuous first-hand narrative such as one finds in James Melville. When Calderwood does write his own material the effect is often unfortunate. He is given to gossip and rumour and is quite incapable of seeing good in his enemies. Dunbar is whispered to have been a homosexual,[94] the duke of Lennox and marquis of Hamilton were poisoned,[95] and Calderwood repeats allegations that king James was also the victim of a dirty deed.[96] He frequently records portentous events or places a theological interpretation upon the remarkable. He relates how in June 1623 James's portrait in the palace at Linlithgow fell and was smashed: 'The like befell the King of France his picture in that same place, sixe weekes before his death'.[97] He noted the birth of a monster,[98] the appearance of comets and meteors, even a 'fyrie dragon'.[99] In 1621 a great flood washed away the new bridge at Perth. He wrote that only one arch remained 'for a monument of God's wrath' against a city which had been so central to the devolution of the kirk.[100] Such general credulity must be borne in mind when reading Calderwood's gossipy aspersions on the lives of the bishops.

Although David Calderwood is remembered first as a historian, his temperament dictated that he should go through life as a controversialist of considerable force and effectiveness, whether against belly-god prelates or their Romanising ceremonies. Nor did he set aside this character when he came to his *History* which, consequently, is also fundamentally controversial. No quarter is given to the enemy, no opportunity is missed for Calderwood to wield the sword of the Lord.

He was a holy warrior committed to defending the purity of the kirk against the poison of Rome and its close relative the church of England.

The version of the *History* published in seven volumes (Volume 8 is devoted to editorial concerns) by the Wodrow Society gives fifty-five pages to the period up to 1513. In this small fragment of the whole work (about 1.1% of the total 4926 pages) Calderwood outlined a five-part pattern for understanding the pre-Reformation past: paganism; conversion to Christianity; the golden age of holy, learned, and humble non-diocesan bishops; the medieval decline which stemmed from clerical wealth, legal exemptions, and refuge behind papal authority; and the restoration which began in about 1422 with the martyrdom of one of God's 'owne secreit ones'. [101] This fifteenth-century opponent of Rome permitted Calderwood to disclaim the Lutheran origin of the reformed kirk. [102] Indeed, he was no admirer of Lutheranism in his own time. [103]

Further to his earlier writings Calderwood claimed that the first Book of Discipline was 'accomodat to the time' and was intended to be revised later in order to correct its deficiencies. These were, however, rather limited. Only the offices of superintendent, exhorter, and reader, along with a few other items were in need of amendment. [104] The 1678 edition includes a brief summary of the discipline but the Wodrow Society edition presents a confusion. Calderwood writes, 'We have thought expedient to insert the booke in this part of our Historie', now admitting it was refused by 'worldlings', [105] members of the council. He then sets down two headings, the preface and the section on doctrine, before launching into a seventy-page rendition of, not the first Book of Discipline, but the Book of Common Order! Obviously this edition was not carefully prepared and revised for publication, and this consideration is sufficient to explain the apparent mistake which would undoubtedly have been corrected had Calderwood gone on to send this work to press. One need not resort to the defensiveness of the editor who suggested that Calderwood thought it unnecessary to include the first Book of Discipline since he had published both Books in 1621. [106] Why, them, does the second Book appear in both editions of the *History* now under consideration? Calderwood was careful, nonetheless, to demonstrate that superintendents were subject to the whole order of the ministry. [107] He was in error, though, when he wrote that in the first fifteen years following the Reformation superintendents and bishops were never chosen to fulfil the office of moderator of assembly. [108] Unless he meant — obscurely — that all moderators were chosen simply as ministers, not on account of some higher office, he was sadly and remarkably mistaken. Between June 1563 and March 1575 superintendent John Willock was elected five times, superintendent John Erskine also five times, and archbishop James Boyd once. [109]

Calderwood included in the future Wodrow Society edition a document dated 12 April 1581, published at Edinburgh *cum privilegio*, and entitled 'A short and generall confessioun of the true Christian faith, sett furth by us archbishops and bishops', an obvious allusion to the document more widely known as the King's Confession or the Negative Confession, to be considered in the remaining chapters. The brief tract affirmed the Roman views of episcopal and Petrine authority, and of the seven sacraments. It was subscribed: 'P., St Andrewes.

James, Glasgow. D., Aberdeene'.[110] The historian made only a brief comment: 'This Confessioun of Faith was forged'. Indeed. None of the Confession's alleged signatories shared its beliefs and clearly it could only have been a humorous production, too clumsy even to have derogated from the bishops' then widely assailed repute. But where did Calderwood get it? There is no record of it in the relevant catalogues, and if he was copying a manuscript why would he introduce it as 'printed'? The puzzle persists, and recent communication with the National Library of Scotland sustains the judgement of Dickson and Edmond: 'We have neither seen nor heard of a copy of the tract'.[111]

Another problem is that of the forged recantation of James Lawson, one of the fugitive presbyterians in England who died in London in 1584. In what is given as Lawson's authentic testament — and there is no reason to doubt it — the dying man animadverted upon 'Satan and his supposts, *pseudo-episcopi*',[112] just as one might have expected. This document is followed by a reference to a forgery:

> The Bishop of St Andrewes, Mr Patrik Adamsone, forged a testament in Mr James Lowson's name, wherin he brought him in repenting of his former courses, and exhorting ministers, noble men, and others, to embrace the estat of bishops.[113]

It furthermore reproached sundry leading lights in the kirk for a variety of sins including adultery and misappropriation of kirk revenue.[114] The fraud is blatant, but the association with Adamson, though not impossible, is simply asserted by Calderwood who was no more charitable toward the hapless archbishop than any other presbyterian. The only other reference to the testament is also in Calderwood, in a letter sent by Bothwell to the ministers of Edinburgh in 1592 in an attempt to gain their sympathy for his cause against the king. Bothwell accused chancellor John Maitland of writing the forgery:

> Did he not first penne the infamous and hereticall accusatiouns sett out under the name of the Bishop of St Andrewes, against the faithfull servant of God, Mr. James Lowsone, and remanent godlie persons banished at that tyme, as the said bishop hath latelie confessed?[115]

The Wodrow Society edition portrays a generally uncritical antiquarian/controversialist pursuing his prey.

Calderwood's presbyterian view of the kirk's history was that the fundamental sin to which it was subjected was 'the erecting of the state of bishops, the beginning of defection, and ground of farther defection like to follow'.[116] He recorded the usual rumours about episcopal vice and misfortune, and took special delight, one suspects, in pointing at John Spottiswood, one of the three archiepiscopal arch-villains against whom he was most bitter, Gledstanes and Law supplying the remaining two-thirds of the evil threesome. In Edinburgh one day in 1595 sir James Sandilands, Spottiswood's patron, became engaged in a street brawl. The future prelate was with him and, wrote Calderwood, 'played the part manfullie that day in defence of Sir James'.[117] He also pilloried the archbishop's linguistic weaknesses. Suggestion was made in 1624 that those seeking admission to the ministry must undergo a test of their Hebrew, Greek, and Latin. 'The bishop himself was not able to do it'.[118] In 1619 Spottiswood crossed the firth of Forth on the Sabbath 'in time of sermon' and added to his offence by playing cards in the afternoon: 'And yit this profane villane, with an impudent face, darre seeke obedience and reverence, neither having lawful authoritie, but usurped, nor urging things lawfull, but superstitious and idolatrous'.[119]

Spottiswood did not retort in kind.[120] His *History* is a rather calm and mild piece in comparison to the works produced by the presbyterians, and its supercilious bearing might have proved more irritating to his antagonists than a stream of invective. The archbishop did not attempt a full rebuttal of presbyterian accusations. For the most part he simply ignored them, and in reality his 'church' history devotes most of its words to politics wherein the kirk is but one aspect of the Scottish political arena.

The *History* has, in fact, every appearance of a work composed by a man who deemed himself to be on not only the side of truth, but also on the side of victory. His prefatory letter to king Charles may have come 'from the place of my Peregrination' on 15 November 1639[121] when his life's work seemed to be sliding into an abyss, but the writing was done earlier. The *Refutatio* of 1620 referred to a more complete history even then under preparation.[122]

It must be remarked that Spottiswood's 'judiciousness of tone and moderation in the characterization of individuals are not the same thing as impartiality of spirit', as Maurice Lee, Jr. has rightly indicated.[123] Spottiswood's version of the past is no less tendentious and biased than that of Calderwood. Nor was he obscure about this. He informed Charles that the lack of an adequate history 'hath bred in our Church many strange mistakings: For did men understand how things went at our Reformation, and since that time, they would never have moved to think that Episcopacy was against the Constitutions of this Church'. The communication of that understanding was, of course, one of his purposes. The other was to affirm the royal care for the kirk. Since king Donald in the third century the kirk had never lacked a 'Nursing Father', and he concluded the *History* by eulogising James as 'the Salomon of this age'.[124] The archbishop's mind was a mirror of James's to the effect that episcopacy and monarchy belonged together, and even in admitting that James was a temporiser he perceived no wrongdoing in his royal paragon.[125]

The Reformation posed a considerable dilemma for Spottiswood. On the one hand it was a very necessary renovation of religion. Before its advent, the kirk was in a generally deplorable state with 'Ignorance and Impiety' commonplace. The difficulty for the historian, though, was that laymen took reform into their own hands and 'made that violent and disordered Reformation'.[126] He by no means offered a defence of the murdered archbishop Beaton but disavowed the act and stated that John Knox ought not to have joined himself with the castilians. Knox was a major embarrassment to Spottiswood. He and Willock were wrong in giving opinions about Mary's deprivation in 1559 since 'it is no where permitted to subjects to call their Princes in question or to make insurrections against them, God having reserved the punishment of Princes to himselfe'.[127] Spottiswood went so far as to deny Knox's authorship of certain offensive passages in the reformer's *History*.[128]

But Knox redeemed himself by composing the first Book of Discipline[129] which described superintendents whose 'power was Episcopal'[130] and whom Knox urged the ministers to obey.[131] These were halcyon years when ministers did not decline magisterial authority[132] and when the kirk continued in the episcopal way. Spottiswood cited the kirk's letter of 1566 to the English bishops concerning the vestiarian controversy. He did not comment upon the central issue but he did make episcopalian hay out of the positive view the kirk had of the English church: 'it will appear by the letter, in what esteem our reformers did hold the Church of England, and how farre they were from accounting the government thereof Antichristian'.[133] The point was the same at Leith in 1572, but here the archbishop went awry and ought to have copied out the agreement rather than offered his own, inaccurate, assessment. For Spottiswood insisted that the bishops appointed according to the terms of 1572 were to 'ordain' ministers.[134] But in choosing this term the archbishop was reading back his own episcopal powers whereby the hands of a bishop were necessary — legally if not theologically — to the empowerment of a minister. The concordat stipulated that bishops, like superintendents, would 'admit' ministers.[135] As Duncan Shaw has written, 'ordination' belonged to Roman Catholic theological language, and the Scottish reformers were anxious to distinguish themselves from its sacramental overtones.[136] In fact, Spottiswood did hold to a rather 'high' view of the ministry. When deposing a presbyterian in 1620, he agreed he could not unmake a minister, only suspend his function. Ordination bore a *character indelibilis* which marked a man for life.[137] But this was an overstatement of Reformation doctrine.

Similarly he should have been more accurate in transcribing the first Book of Discipline. He claimed in his *History* to be about to insert the discipline 'word by word',[138] but as David Laing observed, 'very little reliance can be placed' on this statement.[139] Laing listed a number of what he regarded as the more significant omissions and alterations. Figuring prominently among these was the section on the superintendents to which D. Hay Fleming also drew attention, citing Principal Lee's words to the effect that Spottiswood's 'account might almost appear to have been intended for the purpose of misleading negligent inquirers'.[140]

One finds in fact that the introductory part of the description of the superintendency has been radically abbreviated to about 16% of the original. The effect of this mutilation was, in Fleming's opinon, to obfuscate the otherwise obviously temporary nature of superintendency. But in view of the argument presented earlier in the present study, no defender of the intended perpetuity of the office would have had to resort to such devices since the first Book of Discipline in no way imposed a time limit upon the existence of superintendents since they were fundamental to the reform programme. Spottiswood's distortion of the original document was more likely an attempt to tone down its asperity toward pre-Reformation bishops with whom he believed superintendents and later bishops stood in continuity. It could have contributed nothing to his argument to describe, with the discipline, a widespread situation at 1560 where many 'have never heard Jesus Christ truely preached' and 'are dead in superstition and ignorance'.[141] Actually he had kind words for bishops Reid of Orkney and Lesley of Ross.[142] In the former instance, his favourable impression of Reid immediately preceded the paragraph on Walter Mill's martyrdom at the hands of the prelates.

It was not only the reformed church which created an interpretive dilemma for Spottiswood.

Elsewhere the archbishop garbled the instructions about itinerancy and omitted the section on the deposition of wayward superintendents;[143] he did, however, include directions on censure and deposition in a subsequent passage.[144] Thus if he was really seeking to give out a bowdlerised edition of the discipline to mislead readers, the attempt can only be labelled a disastrous failure, for the structure of the superintendency appears in the *History* in its same basic shape. It is impossible to say with certainty why he engaged in this unflattering nonsense. Perhaps it was only an attempt to abbreviate, but then one is left with his introductory remark on verbatim repetition. In any event, the effect is serious. It casts a shadow — a shadow which does not materially affect Calderwood's practically unimpeachable accuracy in transcription — over the reliability of the archbishop's *History* as a historical source book.[145]

Calderwood impugned Spottiswood by pointing to the father who as superintendent of Lothian promised to submit to the kirk's examination of his life and work, 'but his son Mr John Spotswood. afterward pretended Bishop of St. Andrews, has said plainly, that he will not be subject to such a crew'.[146] Earlier, James Melville recorded that superintendent Spottiswood's words were hurled at the archbishop to the effect that the confusion of civil and ecclesiastical offices in a minister was unlawful.[147] But John and his brother James had other uses for their father's controversial bequest. James Spottiswood (1567-1645) graduated from the University of Glasgow in 1583 and twenty years later entered the church of England under Whitgift and was admitted to the rectory of Wells, Norfolk. In 1621 he was consecrated archbishop of Clogher in Ireland.[148] When he was given the degree D.D. by the University of St. Andrews in 1616 he preached a sermon in which he recalled that his father, like Melanchthon, had foreseen trouble in the kirk should the old polity be removed.[149] Similarly, archbishop John quoted the elder Spottiswood,

> that the Ministers by their follies would bring Religion in hazard, and as he feared, provoke the King to forsake the truth: Therefore he wished some to be placed in authority over them to keep them in awe; for, the doctrine, said he, we profess is good, but the old policy was undoubtedly the better: God is my witness, I lie not.[150]

Elsewhere he repeated what was supposedly a common reproach of the presbyterian period, 'that of all men, none could worse endure parity and loved more to command, then they who had introduced it into the Church'.[151]

Whereas Calderwood defended his presbyterian predecessors and contemporaries while berating bishops and their supporters, Spottiswood, on a much smaller scale, reversed the polarity. Andrew Melville was the chief villain[152] and stirred up the estimable James Melville[153] and John Dury, though Dury later saw the error of his ways and made it his deathbed counsel that the kirk ought to have bishops.[154] Archbishop Boyd's fatal melancholy stemmed in great part from 'the ingratitude of Mr. Andrew Melvil and his uncourteous formes'.[155] Presbyterianism foreshadowed the dissolution of the archbishop's monarchical and episcopalian world. He would live just long enough to see the deluge.

As it turned out, the historical debate proved to be the substance of not just a religious shouting match but also an important ideological element in a revolution. The presbyterian view of the past was translated into a national commitment — presbytery, the only divinely sanctioned polity, was inscribed on tablets of stone and both kirk and nation were sworn to uphold it. To do less was to commit the sin of apostasy and to incur God's terrible wrath. When the dénouement arrived the presbyterian view of the past was the millstone which crushed episcopacy.

CHAPTER 9

'The sound of the feet of Popery at the doores'[1]

The rather more tranquil and amicable religious climate of England worked a transformation upon a king who once described English worship as the next thing to popery, a judgement shared by many of his Scottish subjects. Thus they were once pleased when James indicated that, as a sign of his great love for the Scottish people, it was not his purpose 'to lay upon them any new formes or ceremonies'.[2] But in spite of this declaration there was reason for opponents of innovation to be concerned, for only one year earlier, in 1605, a royal proclamation had recognised the great desirability that ultimately 'two Estaittis [countries] so inseparablie conjoyned sould be drawin to als grit conformitie' as could be attained. There was no promise to uphold the integrity of the Scottish kirk, only that changes would not be 'suddene or haistie'.[3]

By 1616 James had set aside all reserve and waxed eloquent in his estimation of his adopted church:

> I say in my conscience, of any Church that ever I read or knew of, present or past, [the church of England] is most pure, and neerest the Primitive and Apostolicall Church in Doctrine and Discipline, and is sureliest founded upon the word of God, of any Church in Christendome.[4]

In England James was surrounded by those who not only admired Erastian episcopacy but also prized the English liturgy and its ceremonial forms, and he readily fell under their influence.[5] He set about, then, to alter the way the kirk worshipped — part of a programme, which would be pushed even further in the succeeding reign, whereby the church of Scotland would be more or less absorbed by the church of England.[6] Thus in 1615 archbishop Spottiswood noted that a new Scottish confession should approximate that of England, the form used for translating bishops should be the English one, and the general assembly was to be remodelled according to the house of convocation.[7]

The story of liturgical change, first under James and then Charles, has been told by a number of historians and will not be repeated in detail here.[8] Rather, the present purpose is to consider the place and attitude of the bishops in these developments, and also to invesitgate how their enemies looked upon changes in worship and the accusations that flowed from hostile pens.

In the innovations which James brought to Scottish worship, he was the instigator and the bishops were to be the instruments of the royal will. Generally they were quite eloquent in their expressions of loyalty and obedience to one whom George Gledstanes once called 'our great Archbishop',[9] but neither the bishops nor others of James's Scottish servants at 1617 had experienced the benefit of extended periods under English tutelage. This lack of contact was reversed in the case of an absentee king who did not have to worry about the day-

151

to-day administration and imposition of the intended changes. Though James's Scottish bishops were ready to accept episcopacy as lawful and constructive, their 'Scottishness' became evident when worship came to the fore, and they not less than many others were offended deeply. Spottiswood and his fellows would soon find their political loyalty severely tested. That it did not break proved an important point to those who already found episcopacy prominent among the trappings of Antichrist.

The best known and historically most significant aspects of James's liturgical policy are to be seen in the Five Articles which were passed by a general assembly at Perth in 1618 and a parliament held in 1621. They included kneeling at communion, the observance of five holy days (Christmas, Good Friday, Easter, Ascension, and Whitsunday or Pentecost), episcopal confirmation, and private baptism and communion. The first two were the most troublesome, and the king's friends were among the unhappy. Patrick Galloway, minister at Edinburgh, wrote back to James that holy days were indifferent and were widely observed in other Protestant churches, 'bot with us the same will seeme more hard to be embraced'.[10] He feared the growth of superstitious abuse among the people and drew attention to the distraction posed to ministers who would have to labour sedulously to offset the deleterious effect of holy days. Private baptism possessed plausible grounds but he worried that some might regard it as an affirmation of the abjured doctrine of 'absolute necessitie'. Private communion might be allowed but only on the strictest conditions, particularly that of infirmity which kept the recipient from attending regular worship. If confirmation presented Galloway with no qualms, the thought of kneeling at the Lord's supper all but unnerved him. He could foresee nothing but woe from this divergence from the apostolic institution:

> Trewlie, Ser, I wolde faine be informed of your Majestie, how I might doe it myself? how I might informe otheris to do so? and how, be reasone, I might meete and mende otheris who ar of contrary mynd? And so for my awin opinione heerin, I think as yit that the best forme of taking it is, as we do, sitting . . . .[11]

Viewed historically, kneeling was closely associated with pope Innocent III's decree of transubstantiation, thus it represented an idolatrous adoration of the elements. A presbyterian might have replied more vociferously than Galloway, but not differently in substance.

The bishops experienced similar tension and felt obliged to retreat from pressing the immediate acceptance of the Articles at an assembly held in November 1617.[12] James, shortly returned from his only visit to Scotland, called their actions 'a disgrace no less than the Protestation itself',[13] a document which reacted against a rumour that henceforth ecclesiastical laws might be made by the king, prelates, and 'a competent number of the ministrie'.[14] This protest, against what sounded rather like the English house of convocation, was signed by such diverse individuals as the future bishops Thomas Sydserff and Walter Whitford, along with the presbyterian David Calderwood.[15]

It has been suggested that in the affair of the Five Articles James's 'intelligence system'[16] failed to inform him of the trouble likely to arise from his policy. This is true to a point in that the bishops had actually assured him that when he came to Scotland no hindrances would delay passage of the Articles.[17] But even without warning letters from the bishops, at least the friendly Galloway had issued a sharp caution just before the 1617 assembly. Furthermore, James was a Scot and his thirty-seven years of experience in Scotland had not failed to impress upon him the intransigence of his people and their ingrained dislike for English forms. He also knew of William Cowper's misgivings about the Chapel Royal. Together these indications ought to have moved a wiser or clearer mind to step back from the brink. It was anticipation of the kirk's coming distress which led Patrick Forbes at first to decline elevation to the episcopate in 1618. He wrote to Spottiswood that he did not want to argue about the Articles themselves but he did believe that 'if so wise, so learned, and so religious a King' were to know all the facts he would not press 'this intended conformitie'.[18] It says much of the Scottish episcopate that the king did not change his mind but Forbes did accept the see of Aberdeen and was consecrated three months later. Apparently the incitement of 'his Majestie's bitter indignation' was the pre-eminent evil.[19]

Despite Forbes's reluctance James had no occasion to be disappointed with his new bishop's performance at the assembly which met at Perth beginning 25 August 1618. Actually, James had intended to forego further assemblies after the fiasco of 1617 but had relented in the face of episcopal importunity.[20] He did, nonetheless, insist upon his own rights independent of an assembly's concurrence. To deny him the power to determine such matters as the Five Articles would be

> a misknowing of your places, and withall a disclayming of that innate power, which We have by Our calling from God, by the which, We have place to dispose of things externall in the Church, as we shall thinke them to be convenient, and profitable for advauncing true Religion amongst Our Subjects.[21]

Forbes evinced no greater affection for the Articles in August than he had in February, but in his assembly sermon he upheld royal jurisdiction and counselled acceptance to avoid the king's ire.[22]

Archbishop Spottiswood addressed the assembly and made clear his own unhappiness with the Articles, stating that the bishops would gladly have persuaded James to abandon them or else would have preferred simply to disobey them.[23] But Spottiswood and his fellows possessed a highly developed sense of responsibility to the crown. This by no means precluded advising James to follow a different path — one wonders, though, if they had had the courage to do so whether the king would have listened — but it granted, in the final analysis, no place to refusal or resistance. James was God's anointed and the archbishop confessed that it was contrary to the tenets of his faith to offend the king. Perhaps already aware of the need to do battle at a historical level he preached, 'Our Religion teaches us to obey our Superiours, in all things, that are not contrarie to the Word of God. So our Confession speakes, which is printed in the beginning of your Psalme bookes'.[24] Spottiswood did offer some words justifying the Articles, or better perhaps, consoling the kirk on having to accept them. The Lord's supper administered in private was solely for comfort; he cited Bucer to demonstrate that denial of baptism outside regular hours of worship would foster its contempt; episcopal confirmation was a legacy of the apostolic age (a useful argument, perhaps, if one accepted the lawfulness of episcopacy); other reformed churches observed holy days; kneeling was only a circumstantial consideration, and even Peter Martyr disclaimed the view that it entailed an improper adoration of the elements. But the anguish in his own mind could not be so easily subdued. He proclaimed the King's excellence in divinity and that James understood 'what is fit for a Church to have, and what not, better then we doe all'.[25] He must, however, have been choking as he spoke, for a moment later he reiterated that his personal choice would have been against such contentious measures. He was stuck with them, but at arm's length if possible: 'Therefore, let no man deceive himselfe; these things proceede from his Majestie, and are his owne motions, not any others'.[26]

The archbishop's arguments were the offspring of necessity and his sermon could hardly have convinced even waverers. Surely it was this obsequious behaviour against conscience and good judgement that justified presbyterian contempt for the bishops — the kirk's highest officers were impotent to exercise any substantial theological leadership, forced to bend their own beliefs about what was right and proper to suit the designs of a pretentious and declining monarch. One wonders whether the king could ever have done anything to cause some bishops finally to cease their hedging and become outspoken critics and active opponents of royal ecclesiastical meddlings.[27] Spottiswood reportedly stated in 1620 that if James reversed himself, the archbishop would obey immediately — 'the king is Pope now'.[28] Such ineffectual and mindless men can only have served well the presbyterians whose vigorous opposition offered the possibility of a kirk that was governed by a considered theology and not royal whimsy.

The presbyterian response of 'no surrender' was set forth in print by David Calderwood. He was by no means surprised by what had befallen his beloved kirk. Polity had been corrupted and now worship was going the same way: 'the insolent domination of Prelates hath entered in by unlawfull meanes amongst us; popish rites and superstitious Ceremonies have followed'.[29] He remonstrated against the 'Nullity' of the Perth assembly on account of a number of irregularities — Spottiswood took to himself the moderator's chair, unlawful commissioners were present and actually carried the vote, the Articles had to be accepted or rejected *en bloc*.[30]

Calderwood offered a variety of proofs against the innovations. He called kneeling a 'breach of the institution'[31] which had been of perpetual appointment.[32] Kneeling had not been practised in the ancient church but entered during the time of Antichrist.[33] On festival days he quoted William Cowper who had preached at Christmas 1618 that no one, whether in a place of civil or ecclesiastical authority, could make a day holy. God alone could do so as he did in setting apart the Sabbath.[34] One suspects, however, that Calderwood was quoting selectively since the bishop wrote at about that time that Christian rulers or churches could nonetheless set apart special days for preaching.[35] Calderwood denied that the imposition of hands in confirmation was a sacrament, and its performance by bishops was incongruous with a prior abjuration of episcopacy.[36] As for private administrations, there was no absolute requirement of the sacraments and their legitimate and hallowed place was in the public worship of the whole congregation.[37]

The king's side was represented in published work by three men including a bishop, a minister who was soon to be elevated to the episcopate,[38] and another minister whose ambition, wrote Calderwood, was for 'a fatt bishoprik'.[39] The least comfortable member of the trio was bishop Cowper who had only six months to live after the Perth assembly of 1618. Holy days, he wrote, were matters of circumstance only and were therefore to be accepted if they were not repugnant to the word especially since conformity would bring the kirk into harmony with 'the ancient and recent reformed Churches'.[40] He saw good in certain instances of private sacramental administrations, but acknowledged that 'the hardest point of all' was kneeling on account of its idolatrous associations.[41] Indeed, he had refused to kneel in the Chapel Royal in June 1617[42] but now found himself having to justify the practice. This he attempted by arguing that Jesus' sitting at the last supper was purely circumstantial in view of the occasion, meal time. Furthermore, the apostle Paul made no mention of sitting in his treatment of the Lord's supper. Three postures were possible, all of which were lawful according to Peter Martyr, and to condemn any one of them would be to injure a friend. As it was, Scotland would no longer sit, and in fact kneeling would contribute to an enhancement of reverence in observance of the sacrament.[43]

David Lindsay, minister of Dundee and bishop of Brechin from 1619, had to defend himself against a misquotation in Calderwood's *Perth assembly*.[44] He explained that he had not said at the assembly that the Articles lacked reason, Scripture, and antiquity, but only that these authorities did not *impose* a particular posture for receiving the Lord's supper.[45] He also repudiated the notion that kneeling was an act of idolatry and declared that it was contention rather than posture which wrought havoc with the piety of weaker brethren:

> When they see Cephas incensed against Paul, and Paul against Cephas, Pastor against Pastor, for Sitting and Kneeling; what can the simple people thinke, but that in these Ceremonies the substance of Religion consisteth, and that the change of these is the alteration of Religion, seeing we make so much adoe about them?[46]

Lindsay proved a tough opponent and Calderwood, though unmoved, allowed that the bishop had preserved the reputation of his party.[47]

Bishop Cowper reduced the issue to one point: 'the question heere is betwixt a Prince and his People'.[48] Lindsay took refuge in the same sanctuary of the Christian prince. 'Who is ignorant,' he queried, 'that all this alteration and change hath proceeded from the constant resolution, & the instant desire of a most wise and religious Prince, our gracious Soveraigne?'[49] Clearly, the argument was proved prior to the proofs. The great theologian had spoken and his bishops had listened as good pupils. One can only wonder whether any of these outwardly admiring prelates ever longed to subject their mentor to a theological examination or grumbled privately to each other about royal interference and ignorance.

On the other side presbyterians were slow to reject the king but could not share the bishops' adulation. John Murray thought that James did not know what was best for the kirk and that Scotland's David was in need of the guidance of another Nathan.[50] William Scot was far from granting to James credit for an infallible understanding and insisted that a royal decree must have a scriptural warrant.[51] Calderwood tried to preserve the king's honour and thought he might be persuaded, perhaps by the labours of right-minded nobles,[52] to help the kirk's (presbyterian) cause.[53] But the myth wore thin when he blamed ecclesiastical woes upon royal appointments of 'asses, swine Beares & Bulls'[54] and when he limited royal jurisdiction in the kirk to assisting it (cumulative power) as distinct from inhibiting the kirk's free exercise of its own rightful jurisdiction (privative power).[55] In 1627 Andrew Blackhall, minister of Aberlady, was in trouble with the high commission for denying the royal supremacy in the church and the agency of episcopacy.[56] Spottiswood reacted to this brand of presbyterian obstinacy by comparing it to that of the executed Jesuit, John Ogilvie,[57] and by accusing an opponent of calling James king, 'but he must be ruled by you'.[58]

If the historical and doctrinal proofs presented by the king's supporters were of superficial importance, the same might be said of Calderwood's assertions. For his view of the matter was also dictated by an ostensibly external authority, the sacred history of the reformed kirk. As he discussed the various Articles he pointed to the past and showed the rejection of certain practices at the time of the Reformation in Scotland. The 1560 Confession prohibited in general terms the adoration of the sacraments.[59] The first Book of Discipline was more explicit, declaiming against the observance of Christmas and the superstitious consequences of celebrating the Lord's supper at Easter.[60] Baptism was to be performed in conjunction with preaching, generally on Sunday, and it denied that children were damned without the rite.[61] The sacraments were to be observed according to the apostolic pattern, including sitting at communion,[62] while the definition of idolatry encompassed 'all honouring of God, not conteined in his holy word'.[63] All these points about worship, wrote Calderwood, 'were by Ecclesiasticall authority in free, full, and lawfull generall Assemblies, publicke confessions, and solemne protestations advisedly established,'[64] and by 1619 had been instituted for fifty-nine years.

Above all other considerations, these aspects of worship had received their full authentication in the oath sworn in 1581. This was the declaration published as *Ane shorte and generall confession* (Edinburgh, 1581), more commonly referred to as the King's Confession or the Negative Confession. It was issued by royal authority to calm the nerves of Scots during a time of pronounced anti-Catholic passion aroused particularly by the ascendancy of Esmé Stewart, duke of Lennox. The Confession's purpose was to secure universal public subscription to the Protestant faith besieged on every side by Romish abominations and papal usurpations, and also to drive recusants out of hiding.[65] It affirmed full agreement with the 1560 Confession and, pursuant to that, it declared that 'wee abhorre and detest al contrarie Religion and doctrine', including Roman teachings about the Scriptures, church, and civil authority. The reformed understanding of the sacraments was defended against the Roman Antichrist's 'fyve bastard Sacraments, with all his rytis, ceremoneis, and fals doctrine added to the ministration of the trew Sacraments without the word of God'.

On this basis Calderwood asserted:

Wee swore to keepe the same forme of worship that was used in the Kirk of Scotland, and specialie in the use of the sacraments. This specification . . . admitteth neither English, Lutherane, nor Romane rites in the worship of God different from our profession.[66]

The oath was binding on the original signatories and on posterity also,[67] and thus the kirk was effectively prohibited from accepting these innovations. Abrogation of its conditions was 'a high degree of perjury', and persecution of those who remained true to its terms exposed Scotland 'to a woefull vengeance, and perpetuall ignominy'.[68] Elsewhere he warned any oath-breakers to observe next Christmas in the light of 'this fearfull execration'[69] of eternal damnation.

The opposing view of the issue was presented by John Michaelson, minister at Burntisland, the third member of the king's trio of defenders, and once again bishop David Lindsay. If in fact the oath should be construed as Calderwood demanded — and Michaelson did not grant the point — then it must be unlawful because it denied the kirk's liberty to amend indifferent items and second, 'it taketh away that subjection which Gods word commandeth we should give to higher Powers'.[70] He pointed out that the oath cut two ways and could be used to hew down those who claimed to stand by and for the kirk defined by presbyterian measurements since it bound people to uphold this 'maine point' of doctrine; 'Let every soule be subject to the higher Powers'.[71]

Lindsay delved somewhat deeper into the structure of the historical documents upon which Calderwood depended. He claimed that the 1560 Confession and the second Book of Discipline both accepted the possibility of change. He pointed out that the original Confession of the reformed kirk included a statement that denied perpetuity to ceremonial forms:[72]

Not that we think that any policie and an ordour in ceremonies can be appoynted for al ages, times, and places: For as ceremonies, sik as men have'devised, ar bot temporall; so may and aucht they to be changed, when they foster superstition then that they edifie the Kirk using the same.[73]

Lindsay conveniently omitted to emphasise the clearly anti-Roman bias of the document whereby this passage was really intended to break with the past rather than to invite alteration in the future. He also noted that the second Book of Discipline granted the kirk authority 'to abrogat and aboleisch' anything in need of amendment.[74] Moving to the Negative Confession, Lindsay continued his denial that the kirk's historical documents prevented further development. In fact, submission to future changes was demanded, 'even as they who sweare to obey the government of a Kingdome or Citie, are by their oath not onely obliged to obey the present Actes and Lawes, but all, which shall afterwards bee made for the Common-wealth, howbeit the former be thereby discharged'.[75]

The bishop's contention was based upon authority. He actually doubted that others could be bound by the oath of an earlier time,[76] but in any event the key was authority, and to Lindsay that was the Christian king whose will was final.

Constitutional contentions such as a presbyterian relied upon were irrelevant to this political philosophy which saw legitimate power in terms of a living, speaking monarch whose words took precedence over earlier statements. The past might not bind the present in things indifferent, a category given a wide scope by the king and his servants.

It was James's strong determination which fuelled the effort to enforce the Five Articles. He wrote to the privy council of his 'firme and constant resolutioun'[77] to have them obeyed, under pain of severe punishment if necessary. After the ministers and council of Edinburgh had petitioned him to 'divert us, frome preassing any further the obedience of the Articles', James wrote back an angry letter to Patrick Galloway dated 27 June 1619 declaring that their hope was groundless and nothing more than an ill-advised ploy to ingratiate themselves with an unruly people.[78] His manner of addressing the bishops, by whom he had been much aggravated in the whole business, was admonitory[79] and then threatening. As a result of the passage of the Articles by parliament in 1621[80] James informed them that

> the sword is now putte in your handes; go on therefor to use it, and lett it ruste no longer til yow have perfited the service trusted unto yow; for otherwise We muste use it both against you and them [non-conformists]. If anie or all of you be false or fainte hearted, wee are hable aneugh (thankes be to God) to putte others in your places, who both can and will make thinges possible which yee accompte so difficile.[81]

Spottiswood may have been perfectly correct when he told the disobedient Andrew Duncan to keep silent 'least ye fall in the handis of wors burriois [hangmen] then I have bein'.[82]

Alexander Douglas, bishop of Moray, was able to write to James in an expansive spirit that his diocese was free of non-conformity and that he was anxious to keep it that way.[83] But not every part of Scotland was as tractable as the north-east, and the diocese of St. Andrews, including Edinburgh and Fife, proved a difficult area.[84] In 1619 the bishops, in conference with 'ane good number of the principall Ministers in thir parts',[85] said again they wished that the Articles had not been set forth[86] but they had before them a letter from James who had a flock of English clergy ready to send to Scotland to fill the places of those who might be deposed for non-conformity.[87] They replied with an expression of their willingness to serve the king by achieving his purpose but they also pleaded for time and patience,[88] commodities the aging sovereign was lacking.

It was thus under great pressure that Spottiswood began to take action against the disobedient. If he told Andrew Duncan that he would never feel remorse for action taken against the likes of him, these were probably words arising from the frustration and unease at having to persecute in a cause where his own heart was lacking — thus Duncan's sin was not his rejection of kneeling but of making Spottiswood's life unpleasant. Ultimately no fewer than thirty-nine ministers and six laymen were called before the high commission to answer for their refusal to accept the Five Articles.[89] In 1623 the archbishop expressed his utter frustration with the recalcitrant, noting that their opposition 'wil not be amendit with reproofis or benefites, qhairof the more thei get the worse thei growe'.[90] He stated the need for authority and some new measures, but the battle could never be won, a fact which did not altogether escape the notice of Charles I. While affirming his intention to have obedience done, he granted a dispensation to those who had been admitted to the ministry before the Five Articles were brought in, 'haveing befoir taught and instructed ther parochiners utherwayes'.[91] All others, though, had no choice in the matter. Since 1620 ordinands had been required to swear an oath of canonical obedience to yield to the presiding bishop 'in all lawfull causes, according to the lawes ecclesiasticall in that behalfe provyded'.[92] However, even this concession by Charles was insufficient for bishop Boyd of Argyll who saw the church threatened by schism on account of the Articles. Writing to Spottiswood in 1629, he called for an abrogation of the law or else liberty to perform or not to perform the practices in question. He recognised that other bishops, including Patrick Forbes, would not be in sympathy with his recommendation, but he believed that an episcopal supplication to Charles would be the best way of settling the undying controversy.[93] Boyd could have had little hope of royal agreement, however, since Charles had in 1628 responded angrily to a request from the ministers of Edinburgh for an exemption from the requirement of kneeling.[94]

William Law Mathieson discussed the episcopal period under the chapter heading, 'The Reign of the Moderates',[95] and while sympathising with their political impotence, credited the bishops with effecting 'what was little short of a revolution in the thought and character of the Church'.[96] The bishops moved the kirk away from fanaticism to an understanding that Christian faith resides, not in a 'mechanical rule', but in a renewed spirit. Similarly, E. G. Selwyn wrote, 'the substitution of forbearance and courtesy for fanaticism and violence, and of theological study and discussion for pamphleteering and the invective of the pulpit, was indeed the most permanent gift' of what he and others have termed, rather erroneously, the 'First Episcopate of Scotland'.[97]

Of course, there are some inviting features about certain of the bishops. They did not appear to be controlled by the strident spirit which possessed some presbyterians, and some left behind a legacy of godliness and piety not to be scorned. But this interpretation of the episcopate is surely superficial and naive. As has been shown, the apparent moderation of Spottiswood's *History* masked a one-sided and at times rather distorted picture of the kirk's history. People of the ascendant party can afford the appearance of moderation and magnanimity. Had the king been presbyterian, perhaps Calderwood and Row might have written in a calm and gentlemanly manner. But he was episcopalian — and that is why most of his bishops were. James, then Charles, created them, and they obeyed. It is this fact of political loyalty which threatens their appraisal as moderate men. Indeed, they may have been, like Patrick Forbes, disinclined to join a scrum, and yet they did. They may, like Spottiswood, have disliked the Five Articles, but mostly they did push their acceptance. Moderate men perhaps, but they were devoted to serving the causes of an immoderate monarchy. The public appearance, then, of their characters was that of a group of 'trimmers',[98] tailoring theological tendency and conviction to suit the needs of the royal master who was as much a bigot as Calderwood and Row. The real significance of the episcopate lay not in its moderation — even presuming moderation to be always a Christian virtue — but in its immoderate devotion to the ruinous policies of the crown, not least of all the Five Articles.

The impact of the Five Articles for the episcopate was altogether negative. The bishops had to choose between political loyalty and their better judgement (whether of a practical or a theological nature), and in choosing the former they identified themselves utterly and fatally with a monarchy which would grow increasingly unpopular in Scotland. Instead of maturing as a body and defining its own right and jurisdiction, the episcopate remained a wagging tail absolutely dependent upon its political creator. Therefore, its apologetic and defence were not, and could not be, theological in essence but political. Thus in 1618 Spottis-wood demanded of a minister about to be admitted that he first confirm his maintenance of 'his Hieness' right and prerogative in causes ecclesiasticall'.[99] But politics could not suppress theological conviction which might burn underground for years. It was as a result of the Five Articles, however much some parts of the country submitted without a murmur, that conventicles first surfaced.[100] They were encouraged by David Calderwood who wrote that attendance at kneeling communions was wrong,[101] and that even a lawful assembly, which Perth in 1618 had not been, could err and be therefore justly disobeyed.[102] In Dr. Foster's phrase, the innovations 'made possible the creation of a permanent non-conform-ing party'.[103] The episcopal presence in Scotland can only have suffered as a result. If the bishops forebore strong action they appeared indecisive and powerless; if they tried to suppress non-conformity they showed themselves to be tyrants, in intent if not in accomplishment. Either way their status was eroded.

The most that can be said for the bishops in general is that they tried to help the kirk make the best of the unhappy reality of absolute rule. Therefore, while accepting the crown's rights the bishops did commonly try to shelter the country from the full weight and impact of arbitrary power. But to some minds this was not wisdom but cowardice and treason, and one must not make the mistake of regarding all presbyterian opponents as half-crazed religious fanatics. They simply made a different choice than the bishops in the face of an oppressive political force which, until the 1630s, was painful to all concerned. Fortunately the historian need only to point out the alternatives and the consequences and, *qua* historian, leave aside the problem of good and bad, right and wrong.

The most significant result emerging from the disaster of the Five Articles was identification of them and their supporters with popery. Episcopacy had long since been associated with Rome by its presbyterian critics, and changes in worship simply augmented the interpretation and proved the accuracy of fears about the slippery slope presented by diocesan bishops. Even the bishops themselves were afraid that the Articles would nourish popery,[104] and in 1620 Patrick Forbes of Aberdeen advised James of the need to combat recusancy in order to counter accusations that he and his supporters were marching back to Rome:

As your Majestie would have a successe and happy settling of theise foolish broyles, which presently disturb the peace of this Church, and would vindicat your Majesties own upright intentiouns and our poor endeavours, who serve God and your Majestie in this bussines, from the pairtly ignorant, pairtly malicious calumnies of foolish and fanatik men, shew no les if not more vehemencie in correcting and repressing the peirt recepters of Jesuits and Preists, then in urging Conformitie to ceremonies inacted; for, otherwayes (I entreat your Majesties pardon for this boldnes), nather shal the one sort spair calumniously to avouch, that both your Majesty, and we who know your heart and therfor serve your Highnes heartely, ar but making way to Poprie . . . .[105]

There could be no more perspicacious comment about the construction that opponents would put upon the introduction of the Five Articles.

John Murray published a *Dialogue* on the new ceremonies and, speaking through Theophilus to the wayward Cosmophilus, declared, 'Ye have built a Kirk to your self, standing upon thritten rotten pillars, but painted with ceremonial colours, all of the workmanship of Rome'.[106] A presentation to the 1621 parliament saw the Five Articles as a return to popish worship and a breach of the oath.[107] Parliament was informed that usurping prelates had made polity Antichristian, the ceremonies before parliament were introducing Romish pollution into worship, and the future held out distortions of doctrine, 'and so all is gone'.[108] Scot, who recorded these materials, wrote the *Course of conformitie* with popery as the final doom to which episcopacy would lead.[109] He allowed that the bishops might not be consciously creeping toward Rome but their actions were nonetheless an encouragement to Catholics.

Calderwood feared the same outcome but emphasised the mediating role of the church of England by which Scotland would be corrupted. In his *Solution* he gave vent to his rampant fear of the neighbouring church. Accept one of its ceremonies, namely kneeling, and the rest would soon follow, 'and then when we shall be made fullie conforme to our neighbour Kirk, we shall turn in a trice to Papistrie, when it shall please authoritie by sound of trumpet to command us'.[110] His *Altar of Damascus*[111] was a relentless attack upon all the perceived faults in the English church — hierarchy, liturgy, ceremonies, mingled jurisdictions, high commission, pomp, pride, dispensations, non-preaching ministers. Calderwood savaged the whole structure from top to bottom. Now this corruption was being brought into Scotland with appalling result. In his *Speach of the kirk of Scotland* he opined that the ceremonies of England and Rome differed only in degree,[112] and his *Quares*, printed only in 1638 but prepared for the 1621 parliament,[113] stated that 'defection' in the direction of England would lead to conformity with Rome.[114] The *Altar* focused upon the 'perfidious violence'[115] which the bishops exercised through the high commission, identified here with the Spanish Inquisition![116] Scottish national feeling was canvassed by a description of the danger represented by the archbishop of Canterbury who, when union was achieved, would be vice-pope under the prince[117] — this at a time when Canterbury was occupied by the Calvinist George Abbot. But Calderwood was not anxious to blame the king and so he focused upon the cruelties of 'degenerate Clergimen' who usurped or accepted civil power in the high commission to commit violence against true religion.[118] However, God would finally triumph over the tyranny of bishops: 'As the Lord lives that sees them, he shal yet harden their hearts more, and at last shall tread them in the wine-presse of his wrath, and there shall be none to deliver them'.[119] In fact hard hearts became harder, but before describing the further misadventures of the episcopate it is necessary to pause and consider the accuracy of the charge of popery — were the bishops leading the kirk back to Rome, or were they faithful sons of reformed doctrine?

King James may not have satisfied presbyterian fervour in his attempts to eradicate recusancy in Scotland but he was not at all indifferent to the presence of Roman Catholics. Never inclined to spill blood on account of religious opinion, he nonetheless endeavoured to lead all his subjects to the pure light of reformed theology and practice.[120] His parliaments passed numerous acts against papists, and the parliamentary ratification of the Five Articles interpreted confirmation as a means of 'stayeing the Incres of Poperye'.[121] The rationale for constant moderators had been to better combat Catholicism, the resurgence of which James readily attributed to disputes among ministers, a pellucid reference to the debate over polity.[122] Charles reaffirmed anti-Catholic action in the estates[123] and he reassured the ministers in 1627 that the security of the true faith would be 'our chiefest care'.[124]

Bishops were important elements in this holy warfare for minds and souls. They were to keep track of all those in their respective dioceses 'who ar excommunicat for religioun and who ar appostatis and refuisis to subscryve swere and comunicat for religioun',[125] and in 1622 the archbishops were appointed to work with the council to suppress 'the new growthe of poprie'.[126] The bishops themselves proved to be willing supporters of James's measures against recusancy. Spottiswood led the case against John Ogilvie, and he was not alone in his zeal. Andrew Knox, bishop of the Isles, drew praise for his strivings against popery,[127] and bishop Boyd of Argyll called for yearly assemblies to combat the Romish plague.[128] Boyd also wrote a letter of encouragement to James to stand firm in the 'good cause' of opposition to 'Papists and sacrilegious persons'.[129] Later, in 1627, Patrick Forbes advised against any indulgence toward recusants for it would lead only to greater trouble in the future.[130] In the same year bishop Lamb of Galloway renewed his attention to increasing popery and directed the presbytery of Kirkcudbright to summon recusants for a hearing.[131]

But no matter how diligent the bishops might be, there was no satisfying presbyterian writers who regarded acts of parliament and fraudulent assemblies and episcopal sermons prejudicial to Catholicism as insincere.[132] One of the bishops thus libelled was William Cowper, a most curious and eccentric choice to be suspected of collusion with the enemy. Cowper took an active role in the struggle against recusants, and he also replied along the way to presbyterian aspersions. James Melville had blamed the growth of popery upon episcopacy,[133] but Cowper's argument was that without bishops papists might well have overrun Scotland.[134] In the early, episcopal, days of the reformed kirk in Scotland there were no papists to be found, but with the decline of episcopacy came the resurgence of popery, 'and by a false kinde of reasoning . . . it is imputed to

Bishops now, but as with decrease of Episcopall government it entred: so I hope in God with the credit, and authoritie thereof, it shall goe to the doore againe'.[135]

In replying to David Hume's criticisms Cowper marvelled that the presbyterian hatchet man actually accused him of holding to a point of Roman theology. He referred to his recent tract against papists as ample proof of his orthodoxy and attacked Hume's perversity.[136] Cowper's *Seven dayes conference* was a clear statement of Protestant argument against the supposed errors of Rome. It eschewed raillery but granted a presbyterian no opportunity to cry foul. Calderwood did criticise the work, but only for Cowper's use of an unreliable historical record in the process of proving the ancient kirk's existence independent of Roman influence. This much even Calderwood was ready to forgive as the product of ignorance.[137]

The bishop's literary dialogue repeated the usual Protestant polemics — Rome was the whore of Babylon and the seat of Antichrist. Papistry was 'a pernicious doctrine'[138] and 'a just punishment laied on reprobate men for their sinnes, and a forerunner of the wrath to come'. He criticised Roman innovation in the celebration of the Lord's supper, including the doctrine of transubstantiation.[139] The centrality of the Scriptures was defended, and the Roman teaching about meritorious acts added to Christ's blood was described as the 'rotten dregges of Papistrie'.[140] Prayers to saints were discarded and the faithful servant of king James directed an arrow at the papal teaching concerning the deposition of monarchs. Cowper, like presbyterians, was convinced of the greatness of the kirk which was among the last to fall under Roman tyranny and among the first to see the light anew.[141] Its worship was nothing other than that in use in the time of the primitive church. Cowper's kirk was authentic; Rome was spoiled by innovation.

Cowper's other works were no less combative, with anti-Roman comment emerging at any point where a reference might be made. Images and the immaculate conception were rejected, the Bible — without the Apocrypha —was upheld as the authority for faith, and Roman cruelties were abominated.[142] The same themes emerged in *Pathmos*, his commentary on the book of Revelation. This is hardly surprising since the introduction, though recognising divergent interpretations, declared that Protestant exegetes were agreed on the essential matter of the Apocalypse: 'The Pope is Antichrist, Rome is Babel, the Popish Church the Whore of Babel'.[143] What followed was not the work of a papist sympathiser.

Patrick Forbes was no less earnest against popery than Cowper. As G. D. Henderson said of Forbes, he 'was definitely, positively and pre-eminently a Protestant'.[144] Living in the north-east, Forbes had first-hand experience of resurgent Catholicism, and all his works dealt with some aspect of this situation. They were all composed before he became bishop of Aberdeen; *Eubulus*, printed in 1627 and again in 1638, was written c.1614,[145] at more or less the same time as the other pieces, but as its newly written letter to the reader demonstrated, elevation to the episcopate had done nothing to calm Forbes's anti-Catholic passion.[146]

Throughout his writings Forbes professed the desire to defend the Protestant faith against the 'emissary frogs'[147] of the Roman Antichrist who were undermining the progress of truth in the region where Forbes was a minister. The success of popery he attributed to 'the peert & perverse diligence of Romanistes' aided by numerous powerful patrons and the paucity of reformed ministers.[148] Writing as an apologist for Protestantism, Forbes denied that papal sanction or the Roman understanding of apostolic succession was essential to the church. He argued that the authentic succession was predicated upon true doctrine,[149] while ordination was a consecration to God and not a promise to obey the pope in all his sinful ways.[150]

Some of the bishops, whether before or after their elevations, also wrote theological works of a non-controversial nature, though periodic anti-Catholic blasts might still find a place. Little has been written about these treatises, and it is beyond the scope of this study to provide a thorough introduction since that would necessitate a full description of not only episcopal thought but of other contemporary opinion as well. Two works on Scottish theology all but ignore this material, but perhaps this is not a fault in that the bishops were not creative and impressive theologians; rather, they made a homiletical and pastoral usage of what amounted to standard reformed doctrine, and thus bishop Lindsay of Brechin could claim that in the midst of debate in the kirk, 'touching the truth of Doctrine, there is no controversie'.[151] This interpretation was echoed by John Macleod who offered a passing note on those whom he termed 'Episcopal Conformists': 'it is plain that in the first part of the seventeenth century they were as definite in their profession of the Calvinistic Faith as they came to be hazy and indefinite on the subject of doctrine in later days'.[152]

The several bishops reviewed here belonged to that group of religious writers and preachers whom William Haller characterised as 'physicians of the soul',[153] a term actually used by bishop Abernethy in his *Christian and heavenly treatise.*[154] This work, from a man who apparently dabbled in physic while a bishop,[155] contains more medicine than formal theology; likewise Andrew Boyd expressed his own concern for the ministry of the word in medical terms. What good was medicine, he queried, 'except it be layed unto the disease?'[156] This interest gave an obvious bias toward 'Practicall Divinity',[157] rather than a concern for metaphysical abstractions. Therefore these soul doctors 'set out to describe the warfare of the spirit, to portray the drama of the inner life, to expound the psychology of sin and redemption'. Doctrine was secondary, serving only to provide a systematic structure around which to shape a heartfelt appeal to men and women to repent and to cast themselves upon the mercies of God.

The largest share of this literature was produced by William Cowper. His critic John Row was reduced to finding fault with a trivial point of Greek exegesis in the bishop's commentary on Romans.[158] Cowper was not hesitant about defending the good effect of his publications and retorted that

> howsoever they be disesteemed by you and some of your humour, yet that they are in account with men of greater pietie and learning then you is evident, in that now the third time that Commentarie upon the eight to the Romanes, hath beene imprinted; others of them five times imprinted.[159]

Even the generally unsympathetic McCrie granted the superiority of Cowper's sermons and clearly approved of the 'vein of practical piety' that marked his writing.[160]

Beneath this unexceptionable homiletical exterior lay an equally orthodox soteriological construct — that of the 'Golden Chaine of Salvation'.[161] Bishops Patrick Forbes and John Abernethy made use of the same theology,[162] but it was left to Cowper to give a fuller explication of the significance of this theological commonplace.

William Perkins had published his *Armilla aurea* in 1590, followed by a number of other editions, and in 1605 the royal chaplain Anthony Maxey preached to James a sermon based on Romans 8:30 in which he explained the process of salvation:

> The auncient Fathers in the course of their writinges, they doe call it the goulden Chaine of our Salvation, because each one of these: Predestination, Calling, Justification and glorifyinge, are so coupled and knitte together, that if you hould fast one lincke, you drawe unto you the whole Chaine: if you let goe one, you lose all.[163]

The pre-eminent divine will was in clear view when Cowper described the chain:

> This reason is made clearer in the subsequent Verse [Romans 8:29], where the Apostle lets us see how the linkes of the golden chaine of our Salvation are knit together inseparably by the hand of God, that no power in heaven or earth can sunder them: wherof it comes, that he that is sure of one is sure of all.[164]

He then proceeded to a brief survey of election, calling, justification, and glorification. Elsewhere he demonstrated his Calvinist orthodoxy, affirming that 'this worke of Calling is the Lords onely, so he extends it to none but unto those who are chosen: it makes a particular separation of a few from the remnant', dividing without respect to 'ranckes and estates'.[165]

Cowper and his peers were extremely sensitive to the oppressive reality of human sinfulness. He himself warned of God's great controversy with the present generation,[166] and summoned his audience to break off 'the former course of thy sinnes'.[167] John Guthrie complained that 'our naughtie hearts sin after flying shadowes but despise the substantiall glory' of God.[168] Andrew Boyd cautioned the need to 'ken' both self and God and warned his hearers in 1604 of life's impermanence which indicated the need to repent.[169] Confronting the people's sins at a time of plague, he told them, 'Miserie is deserved, becaus man hes disobeyet'.[170]

But good physicians were not content to leave their patients without hope. 'To cut thee off from all hope of mercy, and so send thee to despaire; I have not that in Commission', wrote Cowper.[171] Proclaiming mercy, he believed, was both 'the highest, and most difficult' aspect of ministry.[172] Abernethy wrote to assist his readers to steer clear of sin and also to assure them that predestinarian doctrine ought not to deny hope, for virtually the only sure sign of reprobation was final impenitence.[173] Evangelical preaching pushed back the harshness of the double decree and implored people to attend to word and sacrament and thereby prove that God would be merciful to the penitent.

There can be little doubt that it was David Calderwood who was responsible for the 1628 publication entitled *The pastor and the prelate*. Once again the old arguments about the history of the kirk, the Negative Confession, and the corruption of episcopacy were rehearsed and even enhanced. Now the bishop was responsible for making the nation unready for war: 'By his oversight of ryoting and idlenes, their [Scotsmen's] bodies become weake and effeminate, and by his owne large rents, and his example of prodigalitie, which to them is a law, he enervates the estate, and cutts asunder the sinewes of warre'.[174] But in this overdrawn picture there could hardly have been any reason for Scotland to take up arms, certainly not on the Protestant side, since the bishops were already halfway to Rome. There were, he announced, some 'Catholick moderators' in the kirk who were engaged upon a reconciliation with Rome.[175] 'The Pope shall no more be Antichrist, Papistrie may be borne with',[176] since by permitting the flourishing of Catholicism the bishop was able to divert attention from episcopacy. This unprincipled behaviour, should it be widely emulated, portended that 'Antichrist & Machiavel would be our chiefest Maisters, and every Scottish man of spirit would prove another Caesar Borgia, or Ludovicus Sfortia'.[177]

This ludicrous bombast notwithstanding, there were those by the later 1620s who were favourable to some sort of rapprochement between hostile Protestants and even with Rome. This is not to suggest that advocates of Protestant moderation were plentiful, but their contribution had a wide impact, if only in a negative and reactionary sense. Philippe du Plessis-Mornay (d.1623), leader of the Huguenots for many years, desired a Protestant synod in order to settle theological differences then threatening the further disintegration of Reformation thought.[178] Isaac Casaubon sought a middle ground so that a comprehensive basis for church unity might be formulated. As Mark Pattison wrote, men of this outlook

> regarded the Reformation, not as a new religion, but as a return to primitive christianity. They desired to promote, not protestantism, but a religious revival, in which all christians should participate without quitting the communion of the church universal.[179]

In Germany, George Calixtus, professor at Helmstedt from 1613, was no ready convert to Catholicism but was nevertheless willing to see that not every theological problem impinged upon the essence of the faith, and thus he was able to look beyond the confines of a narrow Lutheran confessionalism. He still regarded the pope as Antichrist but argued that the Roman church must therefore be a true church for the Antichrist was to rule as a usurper.[180] Calixtus' irenic spirit expressed itself thus: 'I will not debar myself from the company of reputable people, be they Calvinists or be they Papists'.[181] Scots also were active in this 'movement'. John Cameron, a Glasgow graduate who lived and taught in France for many years interrupted by an unhappy year as principal of his alma mater, stated that it was still possible to be saved in the Catholic church and granted Peter's place as the first bishop of Rome.[182] John Dury (1596-1680), son of the exiled Robert who suffered for keeping the 1605 Aberdeen assembly, roamed across the length and breadth of Europe for fifty-two years in search of Protestant unity.[183]

Needless to say, there was little room for this brand of ecclesiological pacifism among men cut from Calderwood's cloth. They rejected all forms of moderation and innovation, and they were proud of what in their eyes, at least, the reformed kirk had always been — an example for other churches that hungered after doctrinal purity. Clarendon remarked that the kirk's religion amounted to 'an entire detestation of Popery, in believing the Pope to be Antichrist, and hating perfectly the persons of all Papists, and, I doubt [*i.e.* fear], all others who do not hate them'.[184] This unflattering portrait did, in spite of its one-sidedness, reflect the widespread sentiment of anti-popery in pre-Revolution Scotland, and the orators of such hostile sentiment would undoubtedly have concurred with those who termed Calixtus' ideas the 'excrements of Satan'.[185]

The all-inclusive term, in Scotland and England at least, used to deplore these feared developments of moderation was 'Arminianism'. Arminianism *per se* was part of a European phenomenon of liberalising reaction against the prevailing rigidity of Protestant scholasticism with its strong emphasis upon predestination.[186] In 1610 followers of Jacob Arminius (1560-1609), professor of Leyden, presented their Remonstrance in which they outlined the points at which they desired a modification of the predominant interpretation of Calvinist thought. The Remonstrants subjected the doctrines of grace and election to review and determined that although grace was essential to salvation, it was not irresistible. This undid the predestinarian decrees of salvation and reprobation, and accepted a general atonement (Christ died for all humankind) along with the possibility of falling from grace. Election thereby became related to belief and ceased to rest upon divine caprice.[187]

Though Arminius' name was applied to the emergence of similar teaching in England, men like William Barrett and Peter Baro at Cambridge had even before 1600 inflamed their university by calling 'orthodox' Calvinism into question.[188] T. M. Parker doubts, in fact, whether English 'Arminianism' was derived from the Netherlands at all,[189] but whatever the connection, the general trend of thought conquered the power centre of the church of England. Beginning in the later years of James I and then carried through under Charles I,[190] Arminianism dominated the church to the extent that in 1626 when Buckingham was appointed chancellor of self-consciously orthodox Cambridge, the teaching of predestinarian doctrine was prohibited.[191] The process was capped in 1633 when William Laud, 'the incarnation of the Arminian revolution',[192] succeeded George Abbot at Canterbury. This invasion of the hierarchy split the church wide open, for at least when Whitgift and Cartwright had battled, beneath their squabble about polity was a shared theology of grace and predestination.[193] The Arminian, Laudian, or Canterburian school severed this tie. No longer was the church of England theologically one.

There was much more to English Arminianism than a shift in theology. Like both Casaubon and Calixtus, the English thinkers who diverged from orthodoxy were warmly disposed to Christian antiquity, as suggested in Laud's comment, 'we live in a Church reformed, not in one made new'.[194] Parker remarks that 'much of the reaction to doctrinaire Calvinism can be traced to the spread of Patristic studies in England, and the consequent move away from the forensic approach to grace and salvation which had characterised most Reformation teaching'.[195] Instead the Arminians discovered channels of grace in the sacramental life wherein the two sacraments effected a displacement of the pulpit as the primary means of grace.[196] Baptism was not just a covenantal sign but the commencement of the process of salvation. The communion table became an altar set permanently at the east end of the chancel and the celebration was interpreted as a propitiation. The opposition, which was immense, saw Laudianism as the high road to popery. Peter Smart attacked John Cosin's alterations at Durham Cathedral, which included images, an overabundance of candles, genuflection, copes and the like, as an attempt 'to revive and set up Poperie once again'.[197]

This close identification of Arminianism and popery was perpetuated in Scotland. In 1638 Alexander Henderson, moderator of the Glasgow assembly, described two forms of the heresy. In the Netherlands it progressed in the direction of Socinianism while in England 'it runs to Papistrie, and is *inchoatus Papismus*'. Scotland's doctrine had been bent out of shape by Arminian tenets, 'and next consider how that the externall worship of God was in changeing by the Service Booke, I see nothing deficient for the whole bodie of Poperie but the Pope himselfe'.[198] Therefore when one considers Arminianism in Scotland it is this general application of the epithet rather than a narrow doctrinal connotation that must be regarded.

This is not to suggest a lack of evidence for doctrinal revision in Scotland c.1630. Even earlier than this David Calderwood had accused bishop David Lindsay of Brechin of supporting the Dutch Arminians,[199] and there were other allegations of a general sort.[200] Robert Blair, a stalwart Covenanter and protégé of Robert Boyd the erstwhile principal of the University of Glasgow, complained that John Cameron, Boyd's successor for a year, had taught that election was predicated upon God's foreknowledge of a person's faith, making election conditional.[201] These opinions were also known among the Aberdeen Doctors.[202] If these were not very advanced views, there were others who went further and there can be little doubt that presbyterian authors were correct in their allegations of Arminian teaching in schools and in the university burghs.[203] Walter Foster notes that in 1634 the Paisley presbytery objected that the local minister was teaching 'that a man once justified, might possiblie fall away from justifiing faith'.[204] Again in 1638 there was trouble in the town. The minister taught the general atonement and that predestination, the guarantor of theological purity and reliability, 'hath been hatched in hell'.[205]

This same injudicious minister also announced that those contentious points dividing not only Protestant from Protestant but even Protestant from Catholic were 'but a mouthful of moonshine, and if churchmen were peaceably set, they might be easily reconciled'.[206] There were bishops who shared at least a portion of this enthusiasm. Calderwood asserted that archbishop Spottiswood told the Perth assembly in 1618 that it was idolatry and not ceremonies *per se* which distinguished papist from reformed. If Catholics would abjure their offensive idolatry, Spottiswood 'would meet them mid-way, and joyne with them'.[207]

The archbishop's moderation of Protestant factional fighting was testified by his reception of John Dury in the mid-1630s. However, he knew the contemporary mood and Robert Baillie approved of his caution: 'I approve weill the Bishop's wisdome in concealing that from our people, for they would not fail to tak it for a policie of theirs, to bring us on that farr, to yeild first to the Lutherans, and then to the Papists'.[208] These were precisely the fears of Samuel Rutherford[209] who was thoroughly prejudiced against the work of bishops: 'the Lord take the keys of His house from these bastard porters!'[210]

But Spottiswood's waywardness was rather restrained when compared to that of some other bishops. The emergence of a Laudian faction invites comment upon a new breed of men. Henry Guthry, bishop of Dunkeld after the Restoration, thought that the troublemakers in the later years of the Caroline episcopate were younger men 'who in Wisdom and Experience were far short of the Elder'.[211] Whether or not lacking in experience, to call the later appointments 'younger', except by way of simple comparison, does violence to the term. Of eight bishops consecrated during the reign of Charles I, none was under forty. In the year of appointment John Maxwell was forty-two, Neil Campbell forty-four, James Fairlie and William Forbes forty-nine, James Wedderburn fifty-one, Thomas Sydserff fifty-three, Walter Whitford fifty-four, and John Leslie fifty-seven. Unless Guthry believed that Charles should have searched out septuagenarians as Spottiswood became in 1635, the suggestion proves all but empty. The Caroline bishops may have been younger than those already in place but they were hardly youngsters. If they were distinct as a group, the reason must be sought elsewhere, and in fact there are certain aspects in the careers of some that are worth underlining.[212]

John Leslie, a royal chaplain, was elected by royal command to the Isles in 1628. Then in 1633 he translated to Raphoe in Ireland and finished his long life as bishop of Clogher after the Restoration. He was much travelled on the Continent and before returning to Scotland had served in the church in England. He was brother to William Leslie, one of the scholarly and moderate Aberdeen Doctors. When some Scottish ministers complained about the publications of the English Arminian Richard Montague, they enunciated the kirk's general abhorrence of that deviation in a work entitled the *Anti-Montacutum*. But a representative of Arminianism had recently been appointed to the Isles by means of Buckingham's patronage. Leslie was described as

> a Bird of the Libertine Fether, and we doubt a Mountaguist: And they say he was so well beloved in his Parish of St. Martins in Vintree, that they rang the Bells when he was removed from them, and they of St. Faiths would have done no lesse, if they had any Bells to ring: but they did more; for they gave him mickle money to be rid of him.

His sins included prophane language, frivolous behaviour, and following Montagu's example in calling 'all honest Orthodox Ministers' by the name of puritan.[213]

Thomas Sydserff was consecrated bishop of Brechin in 1634 and translated to Galloway the year following. He was enrolled at the University of Heidelberg in 1609,[214] and although nothing more is known of his experience abroad, it may be presumed that he had ample opportunity to learn of doctrinal controversies current in European Calvinism. His elevation to the episcopate was upon Laud's recommendation;[215] clearly he had distanced himself by then from his subscription of the 1617 protestation in behalf of the kirk's liberties.[216]

John Maxwell was a minister in Edinburgh when appointed bishop of Ross in 1633. He was a beneficiary of Laud's favour[217] and the support of James Maxwell of the bedchamber.[218] In 1629 he met with Laud to discuss liturgical change in Scotland, and thereafter he functioned as 'Laud's agent', or as a contemporary put it, 'Curst Canterberries creture'.[219] The marquis of Hamilton thought him 'ane abill man', while Guthry regarded him as the only really impressive episcopal appointee of the time.[220] Lest it be thought that his ambition and innovation grated upon all the older men, Spottiswood named Maxwell the executor of his will, committed to him the publication of his *History*, and recommended that Maxwell succeed him at St. Andrews, 'as of all our number he is the most fit man, and most qualifeit'.[221]

According to Robert Baillie, Laud's two Scottish favourites were James Wedderburn and William Forbes. The archbishop of Canterbury persuaded king Charles, Baillie wrote scornfully,

> that of all our Church men these two, for every good quality, were the flower for learning, pietie, lecture of the ancients and especiallie for that rare jewell, and where it can be found in a learned divine in this intemperate age of a price inestimable, to wit, sobrietie, and moderation of judgment in our Controversies, with the Church of Rome.[222]

Though a graduate of St. Andrews, Wedderburn was deeply imbued with the spirit of the church of England. He studied in England and was a tutor in the family of Casaubon who was himself favourably impressed by the Jacobean church.[223] Wedderburn's ordination was English and he served as a rector before returning to teach divinity at St. Andrews in 1617. His departure, in 1626,[224] was on account of Arminian lectures which brought him under suspicion,[225] whereupon he resorted again to England. In 1635 he found his way back to Scotland as dean of the Chapel Royal,[226] and was then promoted to the bishopric of Dunblane in 1636.

Wedderburn left behind some unpublished hints concerning the nature of his ecclesiological thought in a notebook now in the British Library. Of uncertain date, the most significant part of this volume, a treatise on the church catholic, seems to have been carefully preserved in Aberdeen and was found there along with works of William Forbes by the Covenanters.[227] Segments of it were quoted in Baillie's *Large supplement*.[228]

Baillie accused the Canterburians of working for 'the reducing of the Protestant Churches to Rome, from which they esteeme that our Forefathers under the name of reformation, have made a needlesse Schisme'. The statement contains an element of truth, though it also overlooks some important reservations on the part of both Wedderburn and Forbes. Wedderburn was a severe critic of what he considered to be Roman errors such as images, the use of Latin in worship, denial of the chalice to the laity, celibacy (though he himself never married), transubstantiation, and the Roman claim to infallibility.[229] He thought the Roman church narrow and its claim to universality extravagant. Yet he also rejected Protestant attempts to prove that the pope was Antichrist[230] and believed that the Reformers ought not to have broken off communion with the pope.[231] He explained that

> we doe not relinquish the communion of the Catholique church, but of a Catholique church corrupted, & that only in so farre forth as she is corrupted, retaining still an internall communion with her *in fide fundamentali et charitate*, & an externall too, in the profession of one faith, one Baptisme, yea & in one Priesthood, & sacrifice or sacrament of the Altar, *exclusis erroribus et superstitionibus* . . . .[232]

Wedderburn wanted to be Catholic, but denied the necessity of becoming Roman to fulfil that wish, to which effect he was able to appeal to Casaubon's own experience with a Gallican friend who counselled him not to convert. The bishop thought that the true believers were 'the moderate, peaceable & charitable',[233] defined in an 'Anglo-Catholic' sense. Undoubtedly he was a sincere and well meaning individual, but many of his countrymen thought that the only true believers were those ready to shed their own blood to retain simplicity in worship and safeguard the kirk against all signs of popery. To such as these Wedderburn was only one, almost imperceptible, step outside the Roman fold. Even another bishop, William Cowper, had written 'that true Christians abhorre all fellowship with the Beast of Rome'.[234] However much the earlier episcopate had aroused pronounced hostility, its representatives had not prepared Scotland for the religion of the Canterburians.

William Forbes was a native of Aberdeen and earned the M.A. at Marischal College in 1601. He later studied abroad, including Helmstedt, 'a centre of Melanchthonian humanism',[235] and his reputation for learning was such that he was offered the chair of Hebrew at Oxford.[236] He preferred, however, to return to Scotland where he ministered in several places, among them Aberdeen where, briefly, he was also principal of his old college. In 1622 he moved to St. Giles, Edinburgh, ministering there for four somewhat stormy years. According to Calderwood, Forbes quickly upset the 'godlie' by his defence of the Five Articles which he termed 'maters of moonshine'.[237] He was also attacked for stating that reconciliation with papists was possible, 'especiallie, in the head of Justification'.[238] Forbes returned to Aberdeen in 1626, then in 1634 was consecrated the first bishop of Edinburgh. He died, however, less than three months later.

Forbes' major work was *Considerationes modestae et pacificae*, first published in 1658, and republished with a translation in the nineteenth century in the Library of Anglo-Catholic Theology. This extensive work was an attempt to compose differences between Roman and Protestant on justification, purgatory, the invocation of saints, Christ's mediation, and the Eucharist. His method of establishing peace was twofold. He eschewed extremism and advised that Christians should tread the *via media*.[239] Second, he preferred the ancient church fathers to 'a party of moderns'[240] and used antiquity to criticise both factions. He could speak favourably of many different writers including modern Romanists and Protestants, and especially some English authors. George Grub stated that the

Considerationes represented 'the first Scottish theological work in which the writings of the Anglican divines were constantly appealed to as authorities'.[241] But all later writers must be tried by older authorities: 'The Christian commonwealth stands altogether by holy antiquity, nor will it be more properly repaired when waste than if it be re-modelled by its original'.[242] Thus Forbes denied that purgatory should be maintained by Rome as an article of faith, but counselled Protestants to avoid damning it as heresy. They should, nonetheless, accept prayer for the dead as firmly established in the traditions of the church. Obedience to patristic example would restore peace to the Christian world.

Bishop Gilbert Burnet would write later in the century, 'I do not deny but his earnest desire of a general Peace and Union among all Christians has made him too favourable to many of the Corruptions in the Church of Rome'.[243] Forbes' contemporaries would have thought this a striking understatement,[244] for whatever the virtues of his thought, it was clearly out of step with the vast weight of opinion in the kirk which found expression in William Guild's *Compend of the controversies of religion* (1627). Guild was later principal of King's College under the Covenanters. His treatise was a simple Scripture-laden argument for some basic Protestant tenets. God alone, not the saints, was to be invoked in prayer;[245] predestination had nothing to do with 'fore-seene good workes';[246] there was, in view of Christ's all-cleansing blood, no need for purgatory which was concocted by the 'spirit of errour'.[247] This was the genuine voice of the kirk and it could not coexist indefinitely with the utterly contrary views of Wedderburn and Forbes.

Maurice Lee, Jr. states that there were two fundamental conditions that must be kept for episcopacy to be accepted by Scotland:

> There must be no change in the layman's experience of the church and religion which could give rise to an effective charge of Popery, and the bishops as individuals and as a class must pose no threat to the material interests of the powers-that-be and must integrate themselves into the governmental machinery without jarring it.[248]

Of course there were a number of outspoken persons like David Calderwood who kept alive the dogma that no form of diocesan episcopacy with or without ceremonies could ever find a rightful place in the kirk. Robert Blair wrote that 'Prelacy itself was the worst of all corrupt ceremonies',[249] though he also remarked that the opposition to bishops was limited until the introduction of the catastrophic Five Articles.[250] With them, the sins of episcopacy began to impinge rather more obviously upon ordinary church life and ensured a widespread campaign of non-compliance with episcopal rule.

The breach of the second condition gave firepower to the anti-episcopal party in the church, for the policies of Charles I alienated the nobility to the point of rebellion and cemented a 'fatal conjunction',[251] however unstable in the longer run, between presbyterian and noble.[252] Ever since James's departure for an English promised land, the nobility had been deprived of access to the royal presence in the traditionally informal setting of the Scottish court. Dignity was consequently divorced from influence. Meanwhile James's bishops were entering the privy council, ruling over the high commission, and directing parliament through their primary role in the selection of the lords of articles.

Charles, adamantly and blindly securing absolutist rule, set out to undermine further the power of the nobility throught the Revocation, which Calderwood said had been feared since 1617,[253] and a readjustment of teind payments, while enhancing the financial position of the kirk. William Lithgow wrote:

> Should Tythes belong to Laicks? should Church rent?
> Bee giv'n to temp'rall Lords; by Gods intent,
> Tythes were for Levits; not for Haulks nor Hounds;
> Nor no reward, of Sycophanting sounds.[254]

But the luckless monarch found even his bishops in opposition to the settlement[255] though their jealous reasons were not such as to impress a wounded aristocracy.[256] It was also feared by some that the abbeys were to be restored to the kirk, providing it with one-third of the lands in the realm and ensuring the king an unbeatable parliamentary bloc when the attached voting powers were transferred to the incumbent clergy.[257] These fears were both premature and exaggerated in that Charles was intent upon caution[258] and that the action was limited to four institutions — Kelso, Arbroath, St. Andrews, and Lindores.[259] In the case of Arbroath, it was destined to be annexed to the 'very poor Bishopric of Brechin',[260] while the priory of St. Andrews would be appropriated to finance the rebuilding of the ruined cathedral in the primatial see.[261] Good intent aside, the rumour promoted mistrust and suspicion about the manoeuvrings of an absentee sovereign.

Under Charles, the bishops came to new heights of prominence in affairs of state. In 1626 Spottiswood was appointed president of the exchequer and was by royal appointment to be henceforth the first subject of the realm,[262] a move which was strenuously and bitterly resisted by chancellor George Hay.[263] Then in 1635 the archbishop succeeded Hay, resulting in even greater animosity.[264] not least of all because Spottiswood's son Robert had shortly before been appointed president of the college of justice.[265] There was also real concern that Maxwell was out to gain the office of treasurer.[266] In 1634 all bishops received commissions as justices of the peace while their power as commissioners of exchequer and as privy counsellors grew significantly.[267] Thus, as the monarchy's unpopularity waxed, so did that of its foremost body of servants, the episcopate. A contemporary tract concluded that the great proportion of wars fought in Christendom during the preceding eight hundred years 'hes bene occasioned by the pryde and ambition of prelats'.[268] But soon there would be a formidable bloc poised to withstand an aspiring prelacy. Through the 1630s the theological predilections of presbytery were wedded to the social and political concerns of aristocracy. The one provided a satisfying apologetic, the other the needed clout.

It has been argued that the episcopate of the Caroline years lacked the social status of earlier bishops which had permitted men like Patrick Forbes to gain some degree of acceptance among the landed classes.[269] W. R. Foster allows that

Maxwell and Whitford were well connected but other Canterburians lacked the necessary relationships to carry through their reform programme.[270] G. I. R. McMahon has suggested that the differences were not radical, though merchant class connections do figure prominently among some of Charles's appointments.[271] But even if all the bishops at 1638 had been scions of noble houses, had they still been equally fervent in their loyalty to crown policy, one must doubt whether family connections could have turned the tide. At most, social standing was a peripheral issue.

If James VI had dealt clumsily in introducing the Five Articles, then Charles I's handling of his own innovations was positively ruinous. James, even if under pressure from his bishops, had permitted the calling of an assembly to approve the Articles. Of course, the deck was stacked and those persons who later upheld the legality or propriety of the Perth proceedings were treading on thin ethical ice, if not actually attempting to walk on water. Nonetheless, the appearance of consultation and participation was a sensible concession. Charles eschewed this method. He simply imposed canons and liturgy without the advice or consent of any representative body, whether assembly, parliament, or council.

With the publication of the canons and the liturgy in 1636 and 1637 respectively, the anglicised altar of Damascus had indeed taken up a Scottish domicile. The canons, issued 'by Our Prerogative Royall, and Supreme Authoritie, in causes Ecclesiasticall',[272] envisioned a thoroughly Erastian church on the English pattern,[273] administered by bishops who would rule over a graduated ministry of presbyters and deacons.[274] The canons necessitated episcopal licensing of ministers and their transfer to new charges, while bishops were granted wide discretionary powers in the imposition of penalties.[275] Diocesan synods were confirmed and even national synods were foreseen, although these were extraordinary and were entirely subject to the king's command. However, presbyteries and kirk sessions simply disappeared from sight, while conventicles were banned once again. Kneeling at communion was enjoined as it had been at the beginning of the reign, and vagrant attendance at kirks of dissenting ministers was clearly aimed at and prohibited. Henceforth a presbyter (minister) might not admit strangers to the sacrament without certification from their own parochial minister.[276] Juxon, bishop of London, predicted that at first the canons 'will make more noise then all the Canons in Edinburgh Castle',[277] a remark which demonstrated the insensitive attitude of Charles and his circle toward the mind of Scotland. It was equally significant that the recipient of Juxon's letter was bishop Maxwell who would later write disparagingly of the general assembly as the 'Great and High Sanhedrin'.[278] By then, however, it was clear that Juxon's prophecy of eventual acceptance of the canons was without foundation.

The canons anticipated, and assumed acceptance of, a new liturgy,[279] which appeared in 1637. Of course, royal attention to liturgical affairs in Scotland was no novelty, and in fact several liturgies were produced earlier[280] though none were printed. This was the price James was prepared to pay for gaining passage of his Five Articles.[281]

Charles, however, was determined to renew the question of liturgical revision, and in 1629 John Maxwell conversed with Laud about what direction it should take. The archbishop wanted the English Book of Common Prayer taken over in its entirety, while Maxwell replied that he and the Scottish bishops 'thought their Countriemen would be much better satisfied, if a Lyturgie were made by their owne Bishops',[282] undoubtedly one of the Jacobean drafts which proved 'too bare' to satisfy Laud.[283] The prospect of more change led William Struther, an Edinburgh colleague of Maxwell, to fear a conflagration. Writing on 28 January 1630, he recognised that two sore points were already hurting the kirk. One was episcopacy, the other kneeling:

> But if a third be inflicted, there is no appearance but of a dissipation of this church. In the first people were onely anlookers on Bishops state. The second touched them more in celebration of the holy sacrament, but yet lest arbitrarie to them, But this third will be greater, because in the whole body of publike worship they shall be forced to suffer novelties.[284]

But Charles was minded to agree with Laud, and even by June 1631 Samuel Rutherford had heard that the Book of Common Prayer was to be introduced.[285] Rumour was substantiated in October 1633 when the English service — which was by no means previously unknown in Scotland — was formally enjoined for use in the university chapel in St. Andrews, in episcopal residences for daily prayers, and in the Chapel Royal.[286] Bishop Andrew Boyd, at least, was impressed:

> Organes and musick voyces gives a sound,
> His repercussing Chappels gars redound.
> The Liturgie it hath the greater grace,
> Bishops, and divine doctors in the place.[287]

But the dean of the Chapel Royal, bishop Adam Bellenden of Dunblane, failed to follow the prescribed order and was therefore denied succession to William Forbes in Edinburgh.[288] Instead David Lindsay was translated from Brechin, Bellenden was sent to succeed Patrick Forbes in distant Aberdeen,[289] and James Wedderburn was given Dunblane and the Chapel Royal with promise of greater preferment to follow.[290] Thomas Sydserff first took Lindsay's place in Brechin and then, upon his translation to Galloway in 1635, Whitford succeeded him. Along with Maxwell's appointment to Ross in 1633, the 'new men' were all in place.

In October 1634 Charles renewed his instructions that the English service was to be used in specified places and on particular occasions until a new Scottish liturgy was completed, 'and that as neir as can be to this of England'.[291] Laud, of course, wanted strict conformity between the two prayer books, and even though he affirmed his appreciation of the final alterations in the Scottish version,[292] he was perplexed by them: 'And since I heare from others that some exception is taken, because there is more in that Lyturgy in some few particulars, then is in the Lyturgy in England, why did they not then admit the Lyturgy of England without more adoe?'[293] This letter contradicts the suggestion advanced in 1638 in a work composed for English consumption that the new Scottish liturgy was only a prelude to its imposition in England.[294]

Some changes made in the basically English liturgy were such as the bishops thought might mollify Scottish opposition, including the reduction of readings from the Apocrypha[295] and perhaps the consistent substitution of 'presbyter' for 'priest'.[296] But others, which have been ascribed to the influence of James Wedderburn, were of a more conservative nature, based upon the 1549 liturgy of Edward VI,[297] and so the new liturgy was in reality a Scotticised Edwardian prayer book.[298] Undoubtedly Laud's advice would have served better than the ill-conceived alterations whose overall effect was more of popery than patriotism.[299] Even the episcopate was divided and uncertain about the wisdom and desirability of the final draft.[300] Baillie reported David Lindsay's opposition to 'Surplice, Crosse, Apocrypha, Saints dayes, and some other trashe of the Inglish Liturgie', while in 1636 Spottiswood and some other bishops recommended a delay in the prayer book's imposition.[301]

The new Book of Common Prayer was authorised by a proclamation issued on 20 December 1636: all were 'to conform themselves to the said publike forme of worship, which is the only forme, which we (having taken the Counsell of our Clergie [*i.e.* bishops]) thinke fit to be used in Gods publike worship in this Kingdome'.[302] Charles was clearly determined to emphasise his use of the prerogative which circumvented any sort of representative body. Later accusations that the bishops forced the unknowing king's hand were nonsense.[303]

The Scottish Book of Common Prayer was introduced on 23 July 1637. Its reception had been long prepared, and not just on the basis of the week's notice announced from pulpits on 16 July.[304] Three months earlier a cadre under the guidance of Alexander Henderson, David Dickson, lord Balmerino, and sir Thomas Hope had formulated a response to the liturgy along with the assistance of some local Edinburgh women.[305] On 6 July another group which also included Henderson decided that 'quhen the service beginneth to be read all to start up and go foorth'.[306] In the actual event the reaction was rather more vigorous than a peremptory departure:

> Upon Sunday, the twentie thrid of July, that blak doolful Sunday to the Kirk and Kingdome of Scotland, the service book begoud to be read in the Kirks of Edr. At the beginning thairof thair rayse sik a tumult, sik ane outcrying quhat be the peoples murmuring, mourning, rayling, stoolcasting, as the lyk was never seien in Scotland . . . .[307]

Twice that day the bishop came close to serious injury.

If Maxwell had once desired the older Scottish draft liturgy, he had come to be an admirer of the 1637 prayer book, saying 'it is one of the most Orthodox and perfect Liturgies in the Christian Church'.[308] But presbyterians and many others of a generally less zealous disposition hated it. Archibald Johnston termed it 'this vomit of Romisch superstition'.[309] A brief tract by George Gillespie published in 1638 stated that the communion service 'hath all the substance and essentiall parts of the Masse, and so brings in the most abominable Idolatry that ever was in the world, in worshiping of a breaden God, and makes way to the Antichrist of Rome, to bring this Land under his bondage againe'.[310] An unpublished tract declared that the service book was paving the way for a full institution of popery — 'I meane not of errours in superstition and rite only, but of all the heresies that are maintained in poperie, at least the greatest part of them'.[311] Hysteria perhaps, but the liturgy had succeeded in fanning the flame of protest to white heat, and it was soon followed by a number of petitions requesting the recall of the service book.[312] One, dated 23 August 1637, by Alexander Henderson and two other ministers, complained that the book violated the kirk's liberties and approximated Roman practices.[313] Another document of the same day complained of the liturgy's 'many gross points of Poperie'.[314] When these approaches availed nothing the demands were augmented, as Robert Blair wrote, to include the Five Articles and the high commission.[315] The petition of 18 October accused the bishops of imposing the popish service book (which was against the 1581 Confession) and canons upon the kirk in contravention of the king's actual wishes.[316] By now animosity toward bishops was becoming more evident. Sydserff of Galloway was designated a 'Papist lowne, Jesuite loun, Betrayer of religione'[317] and was subjected to mob violence in Edinburgh.[318] The canons, liturgy, and high commission were all popish in their superstition and tyranny,[319] and the bishops were widely regarded as the villains who imposed the offensive measures. Thus the October petition asked that the bishops be 'takin order with according to the lawes of the realme and that they be not suffered to sitt anie more as our judges untill this cause by tryed and decided According to justice'.[320]

Before the end of 1637 the Scottish episcopate was a helpless ship among deadly rocks. In the immediate aftermath of the riot Spottiswood had apparently called for strong action but the council had withstood him.[321] In February 1638 he had turned about-face and advised the shelving of the prayer book 'and not to presse the subjects with it anie more'.[322] Spottiswood had reached the end of his tether and, in reality, neither option was at all viable. Suspension of the service book would no longer appease the appetites of many leaders in kirk and state, while the façade of Stewart absolutism masked an abject inability to take decisive military action.[323] Power had already shifted in Scotland and the bishops were left without a weapon. Their destiny was being plotted and would shortly be revealed. As David Hume had written to James Law in 1611, 'There must kythe [be made manifest] the full measure of miserie'.[324]

CHAPTER 10

Episcopacy Abjured

Modern historians agree that episcopacy was widely acceptable in pre-Revolution Scotland and that the decision to jettison the office was 'only a secondary development'.[1] Mathieson commented upon the strong approval many ministers gave to episcopacy and he also remarked that 'the majority of the ministers had become reconciled, if not positively attached, even to the Perth Articles'.[2] It is difficult to assess the scene and even harder to peer beneath external conformity where animosity may have been quietly nourished. One suspects that Mathieson's idealised picture was based less upon solid evidence than upon a predisposition to demonstrate that episcopalian moderation and good sense were making headway against presbyterian immoderacy and obduracy.

The Grievances prepared for submission to the 1633 parliament indicated unhappiness with the disregard shown the cautions set down for the kirk's representatives in the estates and also complained at the changes made in the parliamentary ratification (1612) of the terms of the Glasgow assembly (1610).[3] Superficially this evinced an acceptance of episcopacy. However, an episcopate thus reconstituted would be so narrowly constrained as to permit the resurgence and predominance of conciliar, *i.e.* presbyterian, forms of kirk government. This is clear even in Rothes' denial in February 1638 that he and his fellow Supplicants were aiming at the institution of episcopacy:

> Rothes answered, we creave no more but the discharge of the Service-book, Canons, and High Commissione; that no oath sould be taken of Ministers be their ordainatione bot that which is allowed be the Act of Parliament, which gave Bishops the power of ordination; that Bishops might be restrained be these caveats wheron the Kirk and King condiscendit, that they might not be incontrolable, bot lyable to censure as the rest of the leiges; and that a Generall Assemblie might be appoynted evrie yeir, that so errors and absurdities in all churchmen might be taken order with . . . .[4]

This vision of episcopacy drew its inspiration in part from another generation and had very little to do with the Jacobean programme; in reality, it was these limitations that James wrestled to set aside. With appropriate leadership this limited, impotent, hence innocuous, episcopacy was but one step removed from the second Book of Discipline, particularly when others would deny bishops the power to ordain.

The National Covenant, first subscribed on 28 February 1638,[5] 'that glorious mariage day of the Kingdome with God',[6] emerged as a response to the threat of charges of treason against the Supplicants.[7] It was based upon the Negative Confession of 1581 which, in addition to the sacramental concerns reviewed in the

previous chapter, condemned the pope's 'warldly Monarchie, & wicked hierarchie'. But how far did this abjuring of hierarchy go? Was there such a thing as a
benign or lawful episcopate? That of course depended, in 1581, upon whether one
asked the Melvillians or the king, his councillors, and the archbishop of St.
Andrews. Similarly there would have been more than one available interpretation
of the promise to 'continue in the obedience of the doctrine and discipline of this
kirk' since ecclesiastical polity was then passing through a period of animated
disputation.[8] The kirk had done everything but read the second Book of Discipline
into its acts of assembly, and even James would shortly stumble into an insincere
demonstration of compliance with the presbyterian agenda. This was made in spite
of his recent demand for a cessation of attempts to alter the polity, and he soon
renewed his work of establishing episcopacy in the kirk. Clearly, then, the
Negative Confession was capable of diverse interpretations, and the passage of
fifty-seven years did nothing to clarify the issue.

The National Covenant, drafted by Alexander Henderson and Archibald
Johnston, had an intentionally moderate tone in order not to alienate those whose
hostility was directed at various excesses but not at the underlying institution.
Robert Baillie was one such minister, and on his insistence the original version of
the Covenant was modified before subscription[9] and thus it avoided an open
renunciation of episcopacy, calling only for signatories to forbear 'aprobation of
the corruptions of the publike Governement of the Kirk or civill places and power
of Kirkmen, till they be tryed and alowed in free Assemblies, and in Parlaments'.[10]
Baillie wrote a letter of explanation to John Strang, principal of the University of
Glasgow, attempting to clear the way for the hesitant Strang's subscription.[11]
Baillie stated that he did not believe that the Covenant contained anything 'that
makes against the King's full authority, so farr as either religion or reason can
extend it, or against the office of Bishops, or any power they have by any lawfull
Assemblie or Parliament'.[12] This, of course, ought not to be read as evidence of
Baillie's support for the Scottish episcopate. He did once write, 'Bishopes I love',
then proceeded, 'but prid, greid, luxurie, oppression, immersion in saicular
affaires, was the bane of the Romish Prelats, and can not have long good succes in
the Reformit'.[13] Several years later he wrote that episcopacy was the source of 'all
the miseries schisms dangers wherwith our church since the reformation hath
been vexed'.[14] The only exception to his repudiation of episcopacy, and the source
of his modest dissent in 1638, was that he was not fundamentally hostile to the
bishops of antiquity or to those of the time of John Knox, *i.e.* superintendents.
Nonetheless, even these benign representatives of episcopacy were not expedient
for Scotland.[15]

The apparently moderate tone has led Donaldson to discount the anti-episcopal
interpretation of the National Covenant,[16] claiming that it intended only a
restoration of the earlier 'moderate episcopalian regime which had existed during
most of the period between the Reformation and King Charles's innovations'[17] —
a generalisation which passes by many debates and variations. The view advanced
here, however, is that the Covenant's avoidance of open anti-episcopal rhetoric
was contrived to ensure that less convinced or more critical minds would not be
put off, an opinion which was expressed in print by bishop Maxwell after the

Revolution.[18] Writing in 1639, even Baillie recognised the truth of the matter. He wrote first that 'any designe or hope to have gotten down Bishops altogether did appear in no man, to my knowledge, at that tyme [the original subscription in 1638]' — but then he made a significant admission: 'these few who then harboured such intentions in their breast did dispaire, in haste, to obtain the consent of the most part to any such proposition'.[19] Underlying the appearance of moderation, the unsuspecting Baillie then failed to appreciate, was a hard core of presbyterian opinion.[20] It was rooted in an earlier generation represented by James Melville and kept alive by individuals such as David Calderwood, who in 1636 was still fulminating about the dire effects of a heterodox and tyrannical episcopate,[21] and others who very quickly restored the power of ordination into the hands of presbyteries.[22] As Williamson puts it, 'the National Covenant unmistakably constitutes an assertion of presbyterianism',[23] and its advent was not a lucky accident that simply fell into the laps of unsuspecting presbyterian zealots. They knew from the outset exactly what they were about and were confident that once the National Covenant was subscribed they could demonstrate its essential presbyterianism by historical argument, and that Scotland was now bound by God to deliver itself from the plague of diocesan episcopacy and reinstitute the dominical polity of two kirk officers — elders (bishops) and deacons.[24] As the Covenant claimed, all generations of Scots were 'bound to keep the foresaid nationall Oath and subscription inviolable'.[25] Baillie himself recognised the power of the oath which, once taken, could not be recalled.[26] Thus all that was necessary to control the weight of history was to set upon the Negative Confession an authoritative interpretation which could be neither altered nor challenged even if signatories had previously entertained diverse opinions of its meaning. Therefore, whoever controlled the hermeneutical process could redefine and reconstitute the polity of the kirk.

Archibald Johnston of Wariston noted in his diary for 25 February a sermon by Henry Rollock in which the preacher 'pressed verry weal the breatches of the Covenant in doctrine, discipline, churche governement of ordinars quho he feared sould be found extraordinars, and the fyve articles'.[27] Johnston, who had expounded the meaning of the Negative Confession to his family in September 1637,[28] regarded episcopacy as 'the roote of papacie',[29] and when the nation accepted the Covenant which he had helped to compose, it placed in the hands of convinced presbyterians even if unwittingly, the weapon they needed to demolish the office of bishop.

The fact was quickly recognised by the Aberdeen Doctors. John Forbes of Corse, Patrick's son, issued his *Peaceable warning* only a few weeks after the Covenant was set forth.[30] As he had stated earlier in his *Irenicum,*[31] he denied that the Confession possessed the perpetual force which was claimed for it in the Covenant. He argued instead that it had only a royal mandate that expired not later than the time of death of the subscribing monarch, *i.e.* 1625.[32] Forbes also took a swipe at some other views of the Covenanters whereby both episcopacy and the Five Articles were described as 'Abominable, and Antichristian'.[33] A later document from the Aberdeen Doctors, *Generall demands concerning the late covenant,* showed that they, unlike Baillie, were never under any illusion as to the purposes of the Covenanters — that they were aiming their artillery at both episcopal government and the Five Articles through their use of the Negative Confession.[34]

A reply to Forbes was not long in forthcoming. Later that year, after 22 September,[35] there appeared *An answere to M. J. Forbes of Corse his peaceable warning*, not improbably from the pen of David Calderwood. The *Answere* argued again for the perpetual validity of the Negative Confession and maintained a specific interpretation of that work to the effect that it turned its back on all episcopacy in its words against hierarchy of which there could be no lawful or beneficial variety.[36] The writer then pointed out that the kirk had rid itself of episcopacy at the Dundee assembly in 1580 which came before the first subscription, hence the Negative Confession stood on this anti-episcopal ground.[37] Furthermore, the king himself was committed to the erection of presbyteries by his letter just three months after he signed the document. Thus 'the subscription of the Confession and erection of presbyteries went forward together the same yeare. So the discipline by presbyteries was sworne to, and not by diocesian Bishops, or yet Superintendnets [sic], which ceased in the yeere 1575'.[38] Scotland was committed irrevocably to the polity of presbytery, its Negative Confession answering the divine imperative. 'This much for Episcopacie', Calderwood asserted peremptorily, 'that it cannot consist with the Confession of Faith'.[39]

The author was able to conjure up an impressive pedigree from among his presbyterian forefathers for this view of the Negative Confession. He claimed that as early as 1585 a dialogue written 'by some learned and reverend minister' set the Confession against the plan to restore bishops and in 1606 both the Protestation and a supporting treatise evoked the Confession against episcopacy.[40]

In fact all of these claims are readily substantiated. The 1585 dialogue was 'Zelator, Temporizar, Palemon', probably written by James Melville. It stated that the 1581 Confession confirmed 'not onlie the doctrine but the forme of ecclesiasticall policie receaved and exercised in the kirk'.[41] The Protestation reminded the estates that they had the Confession 'to hold them backe from setting up the Dominion of Bishops', for it secured not only doctrine but also discipline.[42] The treatise on the Protestation, also perhaps by Melville, declared that the Negative Confession meant that if its signatories 'should (as God forbid) be about to sett up Bishops and Episcopall governement, they could not eschew the crime of horrible perjurie, execrable Apostasie, and most cursed repairing again of Jericho'.[43]

Melville confirmed these views elsewhere in his history, in a lengthy defence of the Blackness ministers, in the *Black bastel*, in a letter written to the synod of Fife in 1606, and once again — if he was the author — in *A briefe and plaine narration*.[44] Others followed his lead. Row stated that the Negative Confession was cited at the Holyroodhouse conference in 1599,[45] and Melville transcribed an 'Advyce' presented to the commissioners of the assembly before the 1604 parliament in which the same document was advanced against any alteration of polity.[46] During the trial of the ministers who kept the 1605 Aberdeen assembly John Forbes of Alford made numerous references to the Negative Confession both in his historical narration[47] and in his speeches. He reminded the jury before which he appeared 'to take heed of the Confession of Faith, which each one of you hath subscribed, . . . to maintaine the same Discipline of this Church, for the which we ar accused'.[48] The *Informations* included 'A Treatise of Kirke Governement' which disapproved of the acceptance of episcopacy in the shape of 'Conformitie with Eingland' by those who had previously sworn themselves to defend 'the true Discipline'.[49] John Murray set the oath against the perjury and apostasy of those who claimed now to see the greater light of episcopacy.[50] Alexander Hume's 'Afold Admonition' drew upon the same stock of ideas,[51] while in 1608 David Hume cautioned bishop Law that the presbyterian discipline, 'which we sware in the king's Confessioun', might not be altered because of the oath.[52] Another letter in 1610 pushed the matter further, declaring that the Negative Confession withstood all forms of imparity among the ministry. Hume no more accepted the English hierarchy than the Roman, 'for all is one, and they differ nothing in substance of the hierarchie and order sett doun in that Confessioun'.[53] The presbyterian mind made no allowances for a Protestant, as distinct from a Roman, hierarchy.[54] Law had apparently attempted to demonstrate that when the Negative Confession was subscribed in 1581 the kirk was governed by bishops and superintendents. Hume contradicted this and wrote that in any event superintendents bore only delegated authority, 'answerable for what they did, and subject to censures' — rather far removed, he thought, from the episcopacy then re-emerging.[55] There had never been any other understanding of the Confession, declared Hume, than that it renounced all hierarchy: 'I sie not how hierarchie is not contrare to that oathe; and, therfore, how can it be brought in that oathe safe?' This oath, which was equally binding on later generations, might be released only by God[56] — and Hume's God was the staunchest presbyterian of all.

The presbyterian historians bore the same banner. William Scot viewed the Negative Confession as a detestation of 'the degree and superiority of bishops'.[57] David Calderwood had discussed it briefly in his *De regimine*[58] and later put his party's position succinctly: 'The Discipline to be maintained by this Confession, is not the Episcopal Government, but the jurisdiction of Kirk Sessions, Presbyteries, Synodal Assemblies and General, agreed upon before, when the book of Policie [the second Book of Discipline] was approved in the Assemblie'[59] in 1578, before finally being registered in April 1581.

Several bishops replied to this presbyterian view of the Negative Confession. William Cowper, in his *Dikaiologie*, responded to David Hume's assertion that 'we may not receive Bishops, because the oath in conceived word is against Hierarchie'. Cowper complained that Hume had rather deceitfully suppressed the Confession's qualifying words, 'Papall, worldly, wicked'.[60] Like the bishop, John Hay, a judge on the court of sessions, could praise James for 'banishing that Romane and Antichristian Hierarchie' at the same time as he praised the king's maintenance and defence of the episcopal church.[61] Cowper, of course, believed that the reformed kirk had in the time of its infancy been hierarchical. Hume's opinion went contrary to the opinions of the early reformers — 'Did Mr. Knox and our Fathers set up Romish Hierarchie?' asked Cowper[62] — and the intentions of the king,[63] all of whose speeches before and since 1581 were clear statements of approval of episcopacy.[64]

David Lindsay, bishop of Brechin, had the audacity to suggest that in the Negative Confession the term 'discipline' referred specifically to 'the censuring of manners'.[65] Spottiswood chose somewhat higher ground for his defence. Placing his confidence in the civil realm rather than in unilateral ecclesiastical pronouncements, he asserted that in the Negative Confession,

> no other discipline is recognised than the one publicly received, undoubtedly the government of bishops and superintendents. Since their office had been damned by no sanctions of the kirk before 1581, nor was presbytery established before 1586, therefore in that Confession no one is bound to swear to the government of presbyteries.[66]

From their own constitutional and historical view of the matter, the presbyterians were correct in their allegations concerning the meaning of the Negative Confession, but so were their opponents who could also have pointed out that the Confession affirmed, if indirectly, the 'thre Estates of this Realme', one of which was the ecclesiastical, even though considerably secularised at the time. But to try to sort out the matter in this legalistic fashion is irrelevant. The question was not legal and rational. It was a passionate battle against Antichrist or else a loyal and obedient word against sectaries. When the final battle drew near all the historical rhetoric about polity was in place and had been for decades. The possibility of compromise, if it ever truly existed, was far away and the outcome was to be decided not by calm deliberation but by an unequal power struggle among men whose heated passions had already determined which way the tree would fall.

Even before the National Covenant appeared there had been demands for trial of the bishops. Then in April 1638 some 'Articles for the present Peace of the Kirk and Kingdome of Scotland' were produced by Alexander Henderson. Article six called for yearly, free assemblies which would be responsible for the good health of the kirk and which would as part of their duties care for the discipline of 'kirkmen', by which term bishops were clearly intended. For without this procedure, 'while kirkmen escape their due censure, and maters of the kirk of God, ar imposed without the consent of the free Assemblie of the Kirk, they will ever be suspected to be unsound and corrupt, as shuning to be tryed by the light'.[67]

Charles finally acquiesced to the demand for a free assembly in his proclamation of 28 June 1638, the date for which was set as 21 November in another proclamation dated 9 September. The inherent radicalism of the movement in the kirk was made somewhat more apparent in a brief tract entitled *Reasons for a generall assemblie*, published on 29 June. Assemblies were defended as existing by divine right, and though the godly prince might call them, he could not inhibit them. Among the reasons for calling an assembly at this time were the doctrinal deviations and the 'abuses and enormities' arising from rule by prelates: 'The Discipline of this Kirk established, by the acts of assemblies and by solemne oath, is not only perverted, but overturned'.[68] If this were not enough to demonstrate where the course of events was leading, another section of the tract denied that bishops were the representative kirk, rather than the general assembly, 'because they are not office-bearers of this Kirke, which since the time that the office of bishops was abolished, hath never to this day acknowledged any such office, as is now exerced by them'.[69] Again, on 5 July, the Covenanters admitted that from the outset their animadversions had been aimed primarily at the bishops 'as wicked instruments' of divisiveness.[70]

The Aberdeen Doctors, recognising the motivating force at work in the National Covenant, regarded the 'free' assembly with contempt since the presbyterian interpretation of the Negative Confession had effectively prejudged the case against bishops and the Five Articles, 'even before they be tried in a free assembly, and before they be heard who maintain and approve them as lawfull'.[71] Of course they wrote here of themselves for it was they who were leaders among defenders of the Five Articles and also of the 'lawfulnesse and venerable antiquity' of episcopacy.[72]

The covenanting brethren, Alexander Henderson and David Dickson, tried to outflank this objection from some rather formidable opponents and encouraged the Doctors to sign the Covenant and then come to the anticipated assembly and expound their views: 'wee urge not upon you our meaning but leave you to your own, till the matter be examined in Assemblie'.[73] After all, the Covenanters beckoned, the Covenant contained no express statement that the Five Articles and episcopacy were intended by the condemnation of 'Popish Novations'.[74]

But the Aberdeen Doctors proved too wily to be beguiled by this sort of insincere and deceptive argumentation. They insisted that the Covenanters did include the Five Articles and episcopacy in their condemnations, and they were no more prepared to accept the assertion that the intention was only to remove the unhappy consequences of the same items without actually laying the axe to the Articles and the episcopal office themselves.[75]

Their suspicions were well attested by the Protestation which responded to the royal proclamation of 9 September. Charles had attempted to divide the opposition by putting forth his own covenant, the 1581 Confession unadorned with contemporary material, and calling upon the whole realm to sign it. The Covenanters quickly rejected the alternate document and in doing so made patent their zealous presbyterianism:

> They [the king's party] seeme to determine, that in their Judgement the Confession of Faith, as it was professed in 1580. doeth consist with Episcopacie, whereas Wee by our oath have referred the tryall of this or any other question of that kinde to the generall Assemblie and Parliament.[76]

They reposed their confidence in these representative institutions only because they knew what the outcome would be. The apparent result of this abortive royal intervention was that by signing, the king's commissioner, the marquis of Hamilton, was held to have abjured episcopacy, necessitating a printed rejoinder.[77] When the Aberdeen Doctors signed at the king's call they made a declaration whereby they denied any intention of signifying a condemnation or forswearing of episcopacy and the Five Articles.[78] The King's Confession of 1638 also ensured that the impending assembly would enact a contrary interpretation of the Negative Confession's relationship to episcopacy.

John Forbes and his colleagues wrote of their conviction that bishops were lawful and they were consequently 'not ashamed, with Scripture, and Godlie Antiquitie, to call such as are advaunced to this Sacred Dignitie, Fathers, and Reverend Fathers'.[79] This echoed the defence of episcopacy set forth by Forbes in 1629 in his *Irenicum.* There he proceeded carefully and thoughtfully to delineate what amounted to a statement of episcopacy *jure divino*:[80] 'It is in agreement with divine law that, after the Apostles, who were Moderators in common of all societies, there should be one Moderator rather than many over each diocesan college of pastors'.[81] This individual should, except for poor conduct or broken health, be a permanent officer, though Forbes did expect him to rule in conjunction with the presbyters of his diocese and to continue to carry out the work proper to the office of presbyter since elevation to the episcopate entailed, not a change of responsibility, but additional burdens. Forbes was not at all inclined to unchurch non-episcopal ecclesiastical bodies. He simply advised that 'a bishop should be desired and striven for'.[82]

Forbes's exposition of the episcopal office was the only piece of pro-episcopal argumentation to reach print in Scotland in the final fifteen years of the pre-Revolution episcopate.[83] The apathy and negligence demonstrated by the bishops is astonishing and smacks either of indifference produced by uncertainty or else smugness born of contempt for the opposition. Instead of availing themselves of the Scottish press, which was in their control, to encourage acceptance of and support for their office and policy, they acted as if they could never fall, secure in the arms of an almighty Christian prince. The only energy shown in these years was almost entirely on the presbyterian side whether in pulpit rhetoric or in books published abroad and smuggled back into Scotland. The bankruptcy of the episcopal party can be observed in the case of John Maxwell while he was yet minister in Edinburgh. In 1631 he preached two sermons arguing for divine right episcopacy. But according to the presbyterian John Row, Maxwell 'got no thanks even from the prelats, who send for him and said to him, "Ye wrong us, for this is not our opinion, and it cannot be proven; we only say that *Episcopatus* is *Juris Positivi Ecclesiastici*"'.[84] By such reasoning any assembly might well undo them and annul their ecclesiastical function; thus they invited their doom.

It was not only the oracles of Aberdeen but also the bishops themselves who could sense which way the wind was blowing. On 26 June Rothes had told Hamilton that there was no place for bishops in a free assembly and three days later the Covenanter leaders

> thoght fitt, that the ministers and gentlemen of ilk Presbitrie sould meit and consider who in their Presbitries are fittest to be chosen commissioners for the Generall Assemblie; and when the Presbitrie is unsure, as wher the greatest part are Episcopall, that the ministers fittest to be commissioners be put in note, and that the ablest and best affected gentlemen in ilk paroch may be put on the kirk sessione, that so they may be in optione to be commissioners from the Presbitries.[85]

The Protestation which followed the royal proclamation of 9 September likewise rejected the accustomed place of bishops in the assembly. Lacking authentic warrant as officers of the kirk their presence might be only for trial on general complaints and on 'the particular accusations to be given in against them'.[86] Clearly the process of desposition was already underway; no wonder the bishops were 'infinitelie greived' by the prospect of an assembly.[87]

Recognising the drift six bishops drafted a *Declinator and protestation,* which, after being vetted by the king,[88] was presented to the November general assembly by Robert Hamilton, minister at Glasford and brother-in-law to bishop Walter Whitford.[89] For this act of superorogation he was rewarded with the succession rights to the see of Caithness, though he was never consecrated. Without a conquering army the promise of a Scottish episcopal see was worthless.

The episcopal remonstrance, published in 1639 first from the safety of London and then in Aberdeen,[90] was a reflection of the topsy-turvy times in that the bishops felt constrained to decline the authority of an illegal and prejudiced assembly. Just as the presbyterians had declined the bishops as judges because they were interested parties in controverted matters, the bishops declined the assembly because 'the most part, if not all of the said Commissioners directed to this meeting, have precondemned Episcopall governement'.[91] They animadverted upon a number of actions taken by the opposition. Presbyteries had been called upon to elect commissioners for an assembly even before the royal proclamation was issued; moderators of presbyteries had been deposed, thereby invalidating subsequent proceedings; laymen had elected the ministers who should attend; the tenor of opposition was lacking the appropriate deference to authority, especially toward the king.

The subscribing bishops also offered a belated apologetic for episcopal government, though the grounds were more practical than theological:

> We protest, that Episcopall governement in the Church is lawfull and necessary: and that the same is not opposed and impugned for any defect or fault, either in the Governement or Governours; but by the malice and craft of the Devill, envying the successe of that governement in this Church these many yeeres by past, most evident in planting of Churches with able and learned Ministers, recovering Church rents, helping of the Ministers stipends, preventing of these jarres betwixt the King and the Church, which in former times dangerously infected the same, keeping the people in peace and obedience, and suppressing of Popery, which in respect either of the number of their professors or boldnesse of their profession, was never at so low an ebbe in this Kingdome, as before these stirres.[92]

This explanation proved beyond doubt that there was no ground left for meaningful dialogue between bishops and presbyterians or between bishops and magnates. The one had no interest in the episcopal version of a peaceful kirk, while the other was counting the personal cost of ecclesiastical rents restored to the kirk. The views held by the bishops and by the presbyterian-aristocratic alliance were so utterly divergent that mutual understanding and compromise had not the slightest hope of realisation. If hitherto episcopacy had permitted, even if grudgingly, the continued existence of presbytery, affairs had deteriorated to the point where coexistence was no longer possible. Resurgent presbytery had been nourished in part under the wing of episcopacy. Now it was ready to devour its host.

The general assembly convened in Glasgow Cathedral on 21 November 1638. The king's commissioner was in attendance but the bishops were not. Spottiswood, whose life may have been endangered in February,[93] had apparently left the country for good by 9 September[94] and in November resigned the office of chancellor.[95] Charles, who refused to believe that episcopacy was in the dire straits depicted by Hamilton,[96] wanted the bishops at Glasgow,[97] but the closest any of them got to the assembly was the castle where Glasgow, Brechin, and Ross waited out events.[98] The presbyterians had sent out mixed signals. The presbytery of Edinburgh had on 24 October ordered the bishops to be present at assembly,[99] but two days later an unknown individual appealed to Johnston that should archbishop Spottiswood show up, 'some course may be taken for his terror and disgrace'. He continued, 'I fear that their [*i.e.* the bishops'] public appearance at Glasgow shall be prejudicial to our cause'.[100] The Protestation read at Glasgow 28 and 29 November called again for the prelates to appear,[101] but of course they did not.

The first week of the assembly's sitting was in great part given over to procedural wrangling, and only after it had secured its desired constitution[102] did it grant the reading of the bishops' declinature which proved to be an inauspicious source of mirth to the assembly's commissioners.[103] When the assembly's intention to try the bishops was made clear, Hamilton dissolved it and walked out, leaving behind a self-confident and assertive body to carry out its programme in open defiance of established authority.[104] Then commenced an orgy of religious radicalism which swept away the manipulated hence unlawful assemblies of 1606, 1608, 1610, 1616, 1617, and 1618, the canons, the service book, the high commission, and ultimately, episcopacy itself.[105]

The case against the bishops was delineated in a bill presented to the presbytery of Edinburgh in late October which was subsequently referred to the impending assembly. The bill complained of doctrinal corruptions, sacramental deviations, and tyrannical rule. Much was made, as in the Grievances of 1633, of the bishops' breach of the cautions appointed for them, and of the ills following from the lack of supervision of bishops by representative ecclesiastical bodies. Offence against the established social order was also noted:

> The pretended Bishops have usurped the place and precedencie before all Temporall Lords, the pretended Archbishops before all the Noble Earls of the land, and the pretended Primate before the Prime Officers of State in the land.[106]

Here coincided the presbyterian doctrine of the two kingdoms with aristocratic antipathy toward encroachments upon their accustomed role in the social and political structures of Scotland. Shortly after the conclusion of the assembly an observer wrote that, for the nobles' part at least, 'the prime reason of the removal of Bishops is the power they had in Parliament'[107] through their role in the selection of the lords of articles. Without the suppression of episcopacy the nobles could never regain their place of pre-eminence in free parliaments. Another commentator, bishop Maxwell, remarked upon this factor and also the question of revenue:

For, before Bishops were re-established, the Noblemen and Barons both possessed the substance of the Church rents, and also ruled the whole Estate at their pleasure in Councell and Parliament, by their own voyces, and voyces of the Gentry and Borroughs, who in those factious times did depend for the most part upon one Noble man or other . . . .[108]

Thus by involvement in two kingdoms, ecclesiastical and secular, the bishops were condemned by both sides. But already the pendulum of power and direction was swinging to the landed classes who were the moving force at Glasgow, and therefore the kirk gained not independence from secular control but fell under the influence of another ruling faction.[109] For the nobles could never willingly countenance an independent and self-sufficient religious organisation. They had not done so in 1560 or in 1572, while in 1606 they had shown considerable reluctance and would in 1638 reassert their claim to hegemony. The landed classes thus allied themselves with presbytery not because they had suddenly seen the divine light of a Melvillian polity but because the kirk courts of presbyterianism offered them an opportunity to re-establish the precedence of aristocracy. The alliance with the nobles, which some presbyterians actively sought,[110] gave freedom from bishops, but not independence. One may again wonder whether in condemning bishops the presbyterians did themselves a disservice.

The bill given in to the Edinburgh presbytery detailed a list of grievous personal faults committed by bishop Lindsay and his colleagues. Drinking, sexual immorality including everything from whoring to adultery to incest, gambling, swearing, Sabbath profanation, impiety, bribery, simony, and gross dishonesty were all flung at what appeared to have been an episcopate unparalleled for its wickedness since the apostolic foundation.[111] The abuse was summed up in a poetical diatribe written in 1638:[112]

> St. Andrews is an Athiest, and Glasgow is ane gouke:
> A Wencher Brechin: Edinburgh of avarice a pocke.
> To popery prone is Galloway: Dunkeld is rich in thesaure,
> A courtier Rosse: but glutton lyke Argyle eats out of measure;
> Dround Aberdein in povertie: vagge Murrayes subtile witt,
> Dumblaine the criple, loves the Coupe: Iylles for all subject fitt.
> Skill'd Orknay is in archerie, as Caithness is in droges,
> O quhat a shame Christ's flocke to trust to such unfaithful doges. [etc.]

The proceedings of the Glasgow assembly had little to add to these aspersions. The bishops were guilty, in general, of breaking the cautions and, thus uncontrolled, they had corrupted the kirk with Arminian doctrine, popish ceremonies, and hierarchical tyranny.[113] Baillie preached, 'The imposing of the Books on the Bishops part is an act of greater tyranny, than ever was used in this Nation'.[114] They were also accused of individual faults. Spottiswood, 'that pernitious weeid,

That cormorant of smouke',[115] was guilty of dilapidation to which charge some
nobles stated 'they tooke their pennyworthe of him'.[116] The charge served well
against the archbishop; that this self-incrimination rebounded not at all against
the nobles suggests something about who then controlled the assembly. Spottiswood was also accused of various personal faults including adultery, which
Calderwood in his *History* had alleged for the year 1617,[117] drunkenness, and for
good measure, 'preaching of Arminianisme and Papisticall doctrine'.[118] Even his
statement about meeting the pope midway was recalled.[119] These latter accusations, though extravagant to the point of absurdity, were understandable at least in
the case of Thomas Sydserff, 'that squint eyed stridling asse',[120] 'that Roman
snakie viper'.[121] James Wedderburn was cited for his nefarious influence on
Alexander Sommerville, a former student of Wedderburn at St. Andrews
subsequently suspected of preaching the dreaded heresy of universal grace.[122]
Walter Whitford was accused of adultery[123] which Baillie pronounced 'very
probable',[124] and David Lindsay of popish rites in bowing to an altar and
dedicating a kirk 'after the Popishe maner'.[125] Bellenden's ancient reproach
directed at George Grahame was remembered and flung back at him. The
evidence for many of these 'particular' faults was flimsy at best, but all that
mattered was the impact. Whether or not a given commissioner was fundamentally opposed to the institution of episcopacy, individual villains like these could not
be permitted to continue in office. Action against them was inevitable.

It was recognised even before the king's commissioner walked out that there
was an urgent need to make a clear and authoritative definition of the Negative
Confession.[126] A contemporary wrote,

> Therfor sieing, the doctrine, discipline, and use of sacraments ar sworne to as was
> then professed, and the contrarie abjured, necessar it is to be explained what was the
> doctrine, discipline, and use of sacraments then professed in the kirk of Scotland
> which wil be best cleired be the books of disciplin and acts of assembly at and about
> that tyme.[127]

Thus a committee was struck to determine what was intended when the Confession was first subscribed, 'what was abjured therein in doctrine, discipline,
worship, or government',[128] for it was this basis of historical continuity alone
which could be asked to grant legitimacy to the Covenanters' objectives. As
Loudoun stated, 'It must be the rule of all our proceedings', and therefore if the
radical presbyterians could prove their contentions about the original meaning of
the Confession, the religious revolution was theirs.

On 8 December, even as the trials of the bishops were in progress, answer was
given. The clerk of assembly, Archibald Johnston, who had already given his
opinion in committee,[129] read out acts of assembly from the years before the
Confession to the effect that the kirk had rejected episcopal government. On this
basis he declared, 'It is evident that, in all their Assemblies, the abrogation of
Episcopacie, the establishing of the [second] Booke of Discipline, and the
injoyning of the Subscription of the Confession, wer alwayes conjoyned'. Alexander Henderson, moderator of assembly, noted that, given these facts of history, the

meaning was clear, and to assert otherwise would be to 'deall deceatfullie' with God.[130] The imposition of episcopacy in 1610/1612 fell away on two counts — the parliament of 1612 did not actually ratify the intentions of 1610 having altered certain propositions, and in any event, the 1610 assembly had been repudiated as unlawful by the present assembly, and so its provisions were worthless.

When the assembly was called upon to vote on the meaning of the Negative Confession, hence of the National Covenant, one speaker summed up the longstanding presbyterian interpretation of the 1581 subscription, that there was 'a incompatibilitie betwixt Episcopall Government and Presbyteriall Power, that they [*i.e.* bishops] are to be removed and abjured out of this Kirk'.[131] Johnston later wrote that the unanimous view of the assembly was agreement with this declaration — 'Abjured and Removed'[132] — while other sources allowed one dissenting voice.[133] This belonged to Baillie, but despite his disdain for the manner of procedure[134] he was by no means opposed to the utter removal of the present episcopate and would before long defend the National Covenant and its rejection of episcopacy.[135]

Whatever the political nature of the event, the assembly, 'to whom belongeth properly the publick and judiciall interpretation of the confession of Faith', had delivered its peremptory judgement on the meaning of history and had claimed that all other views were false, and therefore contrary to the mind and will of God.[136] With this weapon in hand, the trials of the bishops' faults were really superfluous. Even had they been beyond reproach in morals and theology — as many of them probably were — their office was a sufficient source of condemnation.[137] Complaints against them did, nonetheless, serve to demonstrate once again that episcopacy was a rotten tree incapable of producing good fruit.

Against this backdrop there could be no outcome for the bishops but deposition. Their prelatical office was an act of covenant-breaking[138] and they had demonstrated themselves to be unsuited for the office of ministry. But there was also the sentence of excommunication to be considered, and it was in fact read against eight of the bishops. Of these, six including the two archbishops, Lindsay of Edinburgh, Sydserff of Galloway, Maxwell of Ross, and Whitford of Brechin, had subscribed the declinature. This was a particularly loathsome gesture in that it was held to be a 'banner against the setled order and government of this Kirk . . . fraughted with insolent and disdainfull speeches, lies and calumnies against the lawfull members of this Assembly'.[139] Bishops Bellenden of Aberdeen and Wedderburn of Dunblane were also excommunicated. The remaining six, who for one reason or another appeared less detestable in the sight of the assembly, were only deposed pending a period of grace in which they must submit themselves to the dictates of the assembly.

Of those not excommunicated, John Abernethy, bishop of Caithness since 1616, professed in a letter to assembly that his absence was the result of sickness. He stated that he acknowledged the assembly's legality and that he had 'willinglie' subscribed the Covenant.[140] Abernethy's strong pastoral care at Jedburgh seems to have benefited his appeal,[141] while some delegates also came to his aid. One told the assembly that the bishop had once attempted to demit his prelacy and return to his charge at Jedburgh but the high commission told him that he could quit only the two offices together — no bishopric, no ministry. It was concluded that should he repent he might be readmitted.[142] Probably nothing ever came of this, for the aged and infirm bishop died in 1639.

James Fairlie, appointed to Argyll only in the summer of 1637, received generous treatment since 'he sleipit but few nights in his Episcopall nest, and was not weill warmed in his Cathedrall chyre, whill both chyre and cushane was taken from him'.[143] He was rather fortunate that Baillie was not his judge:

> he seemed as worthy of censure as any: in his small tyme he had shown good will to goe the worst wayes of the faction, far contrare to the opinion that all men had of his orthodoxie and honestie: he was ane urger of the wicked oath on intrants, ane obtruder of the Liturgie upon them, ane oppressor of his vassalls, a preacher of Arminianisme, a prophaner of the Sabbath, and beginner to doe all that Canterburie could have wished.[144]

His submission was received, but others must have shared Baillie's estimation, for he was unable to find a parish to accept him, with the result that he fell into poverty.[145] Finally, he was received at Lasswade in 1644.[146] His death in 1658 forestalled an interesting problem which might have arisen had he survived until the restoration of episcopacy under Charles II.

Neil Campbell, bishop of the Isles, abjured episcopacy in 1640 and found employment in the charge of Campbeltown in 1642.[147] He died sometime between October 1643 and April 1647.

The recantations of two bishops, inspired by the memory of Patrick Adamson,[148] were published in 1641. Alexander Lindsay, bishop of Dunkeld since 1607, informed the Glasgow assembly by means of a letter that he had subscribed the Covenant and accepted the assembly's jurisdiction. He furthermore petitioned 'that he might die a Minister at Lyneydors [St. Madoes]'.[149] His plea had the backing of Argyll[150] and was also aided by the recollection that he had admitted some ministers 'without the band of conformitie'.[151] In spite of all this, he was received suspiciously and was directed to 'write a letter of his full dimission and repentance'. This was sent on 24 January 1639 and duly published, proclaiming his commitment never to take up the episcopal office again.[152] He was permitted to keep his parish church until his death in October.[153]

George Grahame of Orkney, a bishop since 1603, also sent a letter, by his son, to assembly stating his resolution that, 'if God spair his lyfe, he will be readie to doe and answer whatever the Assembly shall impose and requyre'.[154] His abjuration was written on 11 February 1639 and published with Lindsay's. He professed that he was 'sorrie and grieved at my heart that I should ever for any worldly respect have embraced the order of Episcopacy; the same having no warrant from the Word of God'.[155] Grahame professed no great desire to continue in the work of ministry, and one is left to ponder whether his letter was a cynical — and successful — attempt to save his lands.[156] He died in 1643.

Why, then, did these men ever accept bishoprics? Either they were not convinced of the theological authenticity of episcopacy or at least of its necessity, or else they lacked John Guthrie's courage to defend it.[157] Perhaps they had once followed the lead of men like Cowper who was desperate to obey his godly prince, but surely they were conscious of acting now in defiance of the royal will. Whatever the answer, Grahame's fall from episcopal grace was behind the English bishop Joseph Hall's work entitled *Episcopacy by divine right, asserted,* written in 1639: 'This uncouth act [abjuration] of his was more than enough to inflame any dutiful son of the church, and to occasion this my ensuing most just expostulation'.[158] The lengthy work which followed this note to king Charles included a study of the Scottish church and, along the lines of David Lindsay's *True narration,*[159] he identified bishops and superintendents as one and queried how an office approved by Knox himself could 'now become sinful and odious'. But Hall knew well the fate that awaited his treatise: 'what hopes can I conceive that these prejudged papers can have any access to your [Scottish presbyterian] eyes, much less to your hearts? My very title is bar too much'.[160] The bishop of Exeter understood his intended audience.

Only one non-abjuring bishop remained in Scotland. John Guthrie of Moray was portrayed at Glasgow as a Sabbath-breaker and 'a prettie dancer'. He had also encouraged a woman to perform barefoot penance.[161] Some thought he should be excommunicated immediately, and in the following year he was.[162] He preached until March 1639 and then took to his castle which he had provisioned with food and ammunition.[163] He was later placed under house arrest[164] and then passed some months in the Edinburgh tolbooth. Release was granted on 16 November 1641, 'with provisione he doe not returne to the diocie of Murray'.[165] Retiring to his own estate, he died in 1649.

The remaining eight bishops fled to England. Among them was the unhappy archbishop of Glasgow, Patrick Lindsay, for whom the 1638 assembly created a real dilemma. He attempted to avoid excommunication and sent to the assembly a message declaring his regret at having subscribed the declinature which he claimed he had been forced to do.[166] He offered his good work against papists and that he had not been energetic in pressing the recent innovations. This, however, evoked a strong reaction, the ministers of Glasgow testifying 'that there was no man more violent in urging the Service Book, &c'.[167]

Baillie was undoubtedly far too optimistic — or charitable — when he wrote that 'not three of the fourtein' would not have preferred to resign, repent, and return to the parochial ministry except for fear of Charles's anger and the hope of military victory over the Covenanters.[168] In all likelihood the archbishop of Glasgow was one who would have preferred that course, and in fact the assembly granted him an opportunity to submit. But it seems that he was too proud, or fearful. Baillie suggested he was afraid of poverty arising from the potential loss of a promised pension of £5000 sterling. As it was, penury came despite loyalty, and the archbishop was 'putt well near to Adamsone's miserie'.[169] He eventually found his way to England and died there in impoverished circumstances in 1644,[170] most likely forgotten and rejected by those he had betrayed in 1638.

Of the others who sought security near their king and maker, James Wedderburn died in September 1639 and was followed to the grave just two months later by archbishop Spottiswood. David Lindsay died in December 1641. Some lived to take up new careers. Walter Whitford was briefly a rector in Northamptonshire and died in 1647.[171] John Maxwell went to England in 1639, then in 1640 was appointed to the Irish see of Killala and Ackenry where he suffered a near-fatal assault during the rebellion. In 1645 he was translated to the archiepiscopal see of Tuam and died in Dublin in 1647 upon hearing of Charles's forlorn state.[172] Adam Bellenden of Aberdeen, fleeing finally on 23 May 1639,[173] was admitted rector of a Somerset parish in 1642 and died in 1648.[174] Only Thomas Sydserff of Galloway survived the Interregnum, passing some of his years in Paris where he continued to exercise his episcopal powers. Among those whom he ordained was the future archbishop of Canterbury, John Tillotson. In March 1662 he was appointed bishop of Orkney but lived in Edinburgh until his death in September 1663.[175]

Three bishops left written responses to the revolutionary upheaval which discarded them utterly. Spottiswood's last will and testament, published in 1655 with his *History*, gave approval to kneeling at communion and affirmed his belief 'that the Government Episcopal is the onely Right and Apostolick Form; Parity among Ministers being the breeder of all Confusion, as experience might have taught us'. He denounced ruling elders as 'a meer humane Device' who would ultimately destroy kirk and State.[176]

John Guthrie felt compelled to defend himself and his office:

> The service that I have born, these sixteen years, has been in Episcopacie; which throughout as many Centuries, has been esteemed a worthy work; but now mightily maligned and loaded with a world of Calumnies, whereby I am forced to speak, for my self . . . .[177]

Writing on 7 April 1639, he was unsure of his future, having heard the previous evening that an army was just six miles distant.[178] Guthrie was not the sort to fold under pressure and seemed more than happy with the prospect of meeting his divine maker with a clear conscience in the midst of such troubled days. He defended his work in terms already familiar to this study. He had done nothing to gain preferment to high office: 'I did never so much as dream of it'.[179] But like his peers, Guthrie had learned to obey those set above him, and it was this which motivated his various shifts from pastorate to pastorate and then to the episcopate. In Moray he found a deplorable state of affairs — rampant popery, dilapidation, simony, non-residency, ruined kirks. He was even the target of assassins. In spite of all, however, he laboured to rebuild the diocese both physically and spiritually. 'It was said by one and all (so far as ever I could learn) that I was a good Bishop a good man and a good Countery man'.[180]

But those whom he might have wished to persuade were past thinking that 'a man may be a Bishop, and a good man too',[181] and they would have found ample evidence of Guthrie's turpitude if they had known the contents of this autobiographical document. Indeed, they may well have known and been incited to incarcerate a man who had the temerity to affirm the bishops' declinature (which he had not signed, one suspects because of his distance from the centre of activity) and to deny the assembly's lawful authority.[182]

Had the bishop of Moray fled to safety, his composition might have found its way into print. That not being the case, the only bishop who entered the lists against presbytery by way of publication was John Maxwell. He compared the Glasgow assembly with the 'stacked' council of Trent and found that Trent had actually been more orderly than Glasgow — at least it had permitted bishops! Echoing earlier episcopalian views, he again identified superintendents and bishops, and consequently the second Book of Discipline was not a perfection but a reversal of the Reformation. [183] The early reformed kirk accepted episcopacy and therefore the Negative Confession must be tried against the antecedent of the 1560 Confession which assumed an episcopal view of the kirk, and against the episcopal mind of the king who proclaimed it. [184] But the real question confronting the Covenanters was not whether the Negative Confession abjured episcopacy, but whether episcopacy were lawful, [185] which in Maxwell's view it most clearly was, having been instituted by Christ. [186] This being the case, the oath as an anti-episcopal instrument was without force.

Maxwell was convinced that presbytery was a cover for sedition, and believed that the real intent of the Covenant was rebellion. After all, what could 'so many potent Noblemen and gentlemen' with all their followers have to fear 'from thirteen or foureteen Bishops, for the most part old decrepit and impotent men?' [187] Obviously they were rebelling against the king himself. Maxwell condemned the whole political tradition of resistance fostered by Knox and Buchanan and wrote that 'Presbyterian Government is not only inconsistent with Monaichie, but destructive of the Liberty of the Subjects person, and trade; encroaching upon all Authority, Soveraigne and delegate'. [188] His *Sacro-sancta regum majestas* (1644) argued at length the case for divine right absolutism, a suitably futile note on which to terminate the description of this historical episode. Maxwell's bolts were too late and too distant, backed only by an insensitive and alien regime that could have undone presbyterian polity and politics only with a force it did not possess or a respect it could not evoke.

Conclusion

For some, 1638 marked a great and victorious event in Scottish history, if not in the history of the church:

For in this great year of the Covenant
An all-embracing sweetnesse doth enlive
Each place a season, now all things do thriv
A sweet calme influence every where wee see,
As if each of the Stars had drunk a sea
Of nectar, and inebriat every flower
With their benigne aspects, and heavenly power.[1]

At the Glasgow assembly Andrew Ramsay announced the revival of religion now that winter was past: 'the floures appeare in the earth; and the tyme of singing of birds is come, and the voice of the turtle is heard in our land'.[2]

Others, however, saw an orderly cosmos in decay. Archbishop Spottiswood was reported to have said, 'Now all that we have been doing these 30 Years past is thrown down at once'.[3] John Guthrie lamented, 'I have laboured in vaine & have spent my strength in vain & for nothing, but my judgement is with ye Lord & my work with my god'.[4]

The unhappy story with all its disjunctions and continuities began with the discredited pre-Reformation episcopate. In England church reform was at least institutionally in the hands of the monarchy so that church and state moved more or less in tandem, whereas Scottish reform occurred parallel to political revolution. Indeed the lords of the congregation, with the assistance of queen Elizabeth, were the victorious party — but not in any absolute sense. The country would be Protestant, but the crowned head during the early years of the Reformation remained Catholic and consequently the reformers were not able to seize the episcopate which, for the greater part, remained attached to the religion of the sovereign, while the Reformers' own episcopacy of superintendents wallowed in financial distress. When, some years later, another rebellion brought the monarchy into the power of a Protestant nobility and with the crown also the old episcopal institution, the church was once again unable to control it, standing by helplessly while magnates pillaged the resources of the bishoprics.

The kirk's response was to articulate a strident presbyterian polity which also contained strong elements of anti-episcopacy. Not only did the kirk not require this office, hierarchical bishops were held to be the negation of what Christ had instituted. The succeeding decades would prove that this dogma would never be suppressed, finding vigorous new disciples in each generation. However, a young king, who in the midst of a number of vicissitudes was gradually emerging as the centre of Scottish political power, demanded the restoration of bishops to secure his control of the estates and also to silence the threat of presbytery which was regarded as synonymous with sedition. Social and political tranquillity were predicated upon an episcopate responsible only to the king.

This entailed three ultimately fatal factors. First, episcopacy was re-established not because the nation demanded it or even because there was a firmly convinced majority in the kirk which could envisage nothing but an episcopalian polity. Though episcopacy may have gained a basis in some areas of Scotland, it was never the result of popular pressure. Second, as royal creatures thoroughly disinclined to suffer the king's indignation, the bishops proved too pliable in administering crown policy, however much they may have abominated it. Some bishops attempted to lessen the impact of disastrous policies hatched in London, but the impression formed by too many Scots was that these were the lackeys of an increasingly alien absolutism. Third, one may ponder whether, without the 'union' of 1603, a truly Scottish monarchy might have upheld an episcopate untainted by the trappings of England's presumed near-approximation of popery, but as it was the fear of Anglicisation both in ostentatious and insincere religion (thought many Scots) and in a foreign and threatening form of political power led to a many-sided rejection of episcopacy in 1638.

Perhaps the fundamental problem for the latter-day bishops was the want of an appreciable historic institutional dignity. The late-medieval episcopate was awash in immorality and negligence, and the later Protestant bishops did not have the opportunity to sanctify their office through martyrdom as happened in England. The superintendency never gained a firm footing due to the secular power's lack of co-operation, and the tulchan bishops deserved very nearly the whole measure of contempt with which they were regarded at the time. Patrick Adamson stood at the crossroads and might have set the episcopate back on the road to respectability but lacked the strength and depth of character needed for such a difficult task. The restored Stewart episcopate numbered among its members some men of quality and ability, but its general submission to the crown eroded whatever ground bishops like William Cowper and Patrick Forbes retook. For undoubtedly many of the bishops appeared indecisive, arguing for episcopacy or the Five Articles not out of deep theological reasons but out of a sometimes unhappy sense of political loyalty — the king, right or wrong! Perhaps it might have gone better for the bishops had they been less reluctant hence compromised in their support of Stewart directives and had they laboured diligently whether by spoken or written word to build up a truly episcopalian kirk. But once again the apparent indifference, except on a very few occasions, contributed further to the lack of dignity of the institution and its officers. Not that they destroyed it by debased character, but in their general lassitude they accomplished little to counteract others who drew dark portraits of their lives and intentions.

One is impressed by the continuities over eighty years and more. The pre-Reformation bishops were accused — and were often guilty — of gross sexual immorality, pride, ambition, luxury, and neglect of ecclesiastical responsibilities, along with aberrations from Protestant doctrinal norms. These same aspersions were flung at the unfortunate bishops in 1638, though with rather less substance.

But the hostile view won the day — the supposedly Protestant bishops of James and Charles had brought the kirk full circle, back to the popery of 1560. Nonsense perhaps, but the direction of history is not dictated by careful distillation and assessment of fact. The allegation that episcopacy would lead the kirk backward was made unrelentingly for more than half a century, and too little was offered as an apologetic to disprove the slander.

Kirkmen themselves were to blame whether through the disastrous life of Adamson or the compromised values of Spottiswood or the unsettling practices of the Canterburians, but behind all the frustrations and dead-ends were two kings, James and Charles, who insisted upon imposing their own vision on the kirk. James had once understood it, and although he found himself fighting an ecclesiastical civil war, he knew his ground. In fact, had he left affairs as they were without the senseless Five Articles, perhaps episcopacy might have won the day. But these emanations of an English church, consolidated by Charles whose only claims to Scottishness were birthplace and family name, posed a challenge to the integrity of the life of the kirk, which had been blessed above all other churches, and to the independence of a self-consciously unEnglish country. Scotland belonged not to England nor to a once-Scottish monarchy, but to God who most assuredly had accepted the covenant made in 1581 whereby the whole people must always set religious loyalty above the bonds of political obedience. The seeds planted in 1581 were carefully watered and nourished by James Melville, William Scot, David Hume, and David Calderwood, and in 1638 the harvest was reaped. Episcopacy was laid bare, found wanting, and cast out:

> All things below in Earth's sublunar sphere
> Are changing still, unconstant every where,
> No state so stable heer can be this day,
> Which changes not, and quickly doth decay.
> That high seraphick ordour, which of late
> Bare church and kingdome down, overswayed the state;
> And domineird over all, as Lord and King,
> Pope-like who in their precints [sic] once did reigne;
> Now wonder strange, and greatest change of all,
> That tottering hierarchie begins to fall,
> Like Haman curs'd before blest Mordecai,
> Pointing out Sion's rysing, Rome's decay.
>   Scotland rejoice, those supports of proud Rome,
>   Ambitious Bishops, have received their doome.[5]

Notes

Chapter 1

1. See maps in *GDSR*, p. 112, and in Peter McNeill and Ranald Nicholson (eds.), *An Historical Atlas of Scotland c.400-c. 1600* (St. Andrews: Conference of Scottish Medievalists, 1975), p. 137.

2. Leslie MacFarlane, 'The Primacy of the Scottish Church, 1472-1521', *IR*, 20 (1969), 111-118.

3. *The Catechism set forth by Archbishop Hamilton printed at Saint Andrews, 1551* (Edinburgh, 1882), ff. clxi recto – clxiiii verso.

4. *Ibid.*, f. clxiiii recto. See also *SBD*, p. 165, n.9.

5. G.R. Elton, *England under the Tudors* (2nd ed; London: Methuen, 1974), pp. 303-304.

6. Richard W. Southern, *Western Society and the Church in the Middle Ages* (Harmondsworth: Penguin Books, 1970), p. 171.

7. Matthew Mahoney, 'The Scottish Hierarchy, 1513-1565', *IR*, 10 (1959), 28-36.

8. Gordon Donaldson, *Scotland: James V – James VII* (Edinburgh: Oliver and Boyd, 1978), p. 77.

9. Ian B. Cowan, *The Scottish Reformation: Church and Society in Sixteenth Century Scotland* (London: Weidenfeld and Nicolson, 1982), pp. 29-30; Mahoney, pp. 25-26.

10. I. B. Cowan, *Scottish Reformation*, p. 51.

11. Ranald Nicholson, *Scotland: The Later Middle Ages* (Edinburgh: Oliver and Boyd, 1978), p. 558.

12. Mahoney, p. 32.

13. J. A. F. Thomson, 'Innocent VIII and the Scottish Church', *IR*, 19 (1968), 31. See also MacFarlane, p. 129.

14. R. S. Rait, *The Parliaments of Scotland* (Glasgow: Maclehose, Jackson and Co., 1924), p. 166.

15. Robert Keith, *An Historical Catalogue of the Scottish Bishops down to the Year 1688* (new ed; Edinburgh, 1824), p. 34.

16. Donaldson, *Scotland: James V – James VII*, p. 42.

17. Mahoney, p. 44.

18. Donaldson, *Scotland: James V – James VII*, pp. 63, 68.

19. I. B. Cowan, *Scottish Reformation*, p. 51; Mahoney, p. 28; Nicholson, p. 559.

20. *GDSR*, p. 18; Mahoney, p. 43.

21. Duncan MacLean, 'Catholicism in the Highlands and Isles, 1560-1680', *IR*, 3 (1952), 6; *GDSR*, p. 26.

22. David Hay Fleming, *The Reformation in Scotland: Causes, Characteristics, Consequences* (London: Hodder and Stoughton, 1910), p. 47.

23. *Ibid.*, p. 51.

24. *Miscellany of the Spalding Club* (Aberdeen, 1849), IV, 59.

25. *CSPS*, II, 140; see also I, 592; II, 100.

26. John Durkan, 'The Beginnings of Humanism in Scotland', *IR*, 4 (1953), 17.

27. David I. Howie, 'Some Remarks on the Episcopal Ideal in Sixteenth Century Scotland', *Scottish Tradition*, 7/8 (1977/8), 51-55.

28. *Ibid.*, pp. 55-56.

29. Fleming, *Reformation*, pp. 41-45.

30. William Murison, *Sir David Lindsay: Poet, and Satirist of the Old Church in Scotland* (Cambridge: University Press, 1938), pp. 198-199.

31. Howie, pp. 57-59

32. *Statutes of the Scottish Church, 1225-1559*, ed. David Patrick (Edinburgh: Scottish History Society, 1907), p. 84.

33. *Ibid.*, p. 124.

34. *Ibid.*, p. 84.

35. *Ibid.*, pp. 124-125.

36. *Ibid.*, p. 98.

37. John Durkan, 'The Cultural Background in Sixteenth-Century Scotland', *IR*, 10 (1959), 410, 435-436; I. B. Cowan, *Scottish Reformation*, pp. 81-82.

38. *Catechism*, preface, no pagination.

39. *Ibid.*, f. lviii verso.

40. *Statutes*, p. 98.

41. *Ibid.*, p. 135.

42. *Ibid.*, p. 136.

43. *APS*, II, 370. Mention of James V's desire for reform was made in a letter to Thomas Cromwell by sir William Eure, 26 January 1540: 'that the King of scotts hym self with all

his temporall Counsaile was gretely geven to the reformacion of the mysdemeanours of Busshops Religious persones and preists within the Realme'. Sir David Lindsay of the Mount, *Works* (Edinburgh: Scottish Text Society, 1931-1936), II, 2.

44. *Statutes*, p. 156.

45. *Ibid.*, p. 163.

46. Robert Lindesay of Pitscottie, *The Historie and Cronicles of Scotland* (Edinburgh: Scottish Text Society, 1899-1911), II, 141. Gordon Donaldson, *All the Queen's Men: Power and Politics in Mary Stewart's Scotland* (London: Batsford Academic and Educational Ltd., 1983), p. 111, describes the bishop, Patrick Hepburn, as 'an aged, syphilitic reprobate'.

47. *Statutes*, p. 164.

48. *Ibid.*, p. 171.

49. *Ibid.*, p. 171, n.2.

50. See the discussion of authorship by James Murray in *The Complaynt of Scotland* (London, 1872-1873), pp. cvi-cxvi.

51. *The complaynt of Scotland* ([Paris], c 1550), f. 114v.

52. *Ibid.*, f. 115r.

53. William Lauder, *The Extant Poetical Works* (London, 1870), pp. v-x.

54. William Lauder, *Ane compendious and breve tractate, concernyng the office and dewtie of kyngis, spirituall pastoris, and temporall jugis* ([Edinburgh], 1556), sig. B3v.

55. Alexander Scott, 'Ane New Yere Gift', in *Ancient Scottish Poems. Published from the Ms. of George Bannatyne. 1568* (Edinburgh, 1770), p. 244.

56. Richard Maitland, 'On the Miseries of the Tyme', in *The Maitland Folio Manuscript*, ed. W. A. Craigie (Edinburgh: Scottish Text Society, 1919-1927), I, 41. Also in Richard Maitland, *Poems* (Glasgow, 1830), pp. 32-34.

57. Murison, pp. 80-119.

58. Both versions (1552 and 1554) are printed in Sir David Lindsay, *Works*, II, the earlier one on even-numbered pages, the later on odd-numbered. I have quoted throughout from the 1554 version, published in 1602. See Lindsay, *Works*, II, 1, 8-9; I. B. Cowan, *Scottish Reformation*, pp. 72-76.

59. Sir David Lindsay, *Works*, I, 129-143. It was written in 1547.

60. I. B. Cowan, *Scottish Reformation*, p. 88.

61. Brother Kenneth, 'Sir David Lindsay, Reformer', *IR*, I (1950), 91.

62. Quintin Kennedy, *Ane compendius tractive* (1558), in *WM*, p. 151.

63. Niniane Winzet, *Certaine Tractatis for Reformatioun of Doctryne and Maneris in Scotland. 1562-1563* (Edinburgh, 1835), p. 24. See Richard L. Greaves, *Theology and Revolution in the Scottish Reformation: Studies in the Thought of John Knox* (Grand Rapids: Christian University Press, 1980), pp. 73-75.

64. Winzet, p. 3.

65. *Ibid.*, pp. 4-5.

66. *Ibid.*, pp. 16-17, where Winzet quoted Ezekiel 22:17-18, 24-31, beginning: 'The worde of the Lorde come unto mee, saying thow Sone of man, the house of Israell is turnit into drosse, or roust'.

67. *Ibid.*, pp. 6-7.

68. *Ibid.*, p. 7.

69. *Ibid.*, p. 8.

70. John Knox, *History of the Reformation in Scotland*, ed. W. C. Dickinson (London: Thomas Nelson and Sons Ltd., 1949), I, 7.

71. *Ibid.*, I, 9. The parenthetical interpolation was the work of Knox.

72. *Ibid.*, I, 10.

73. *Ibid.*, I, 11.

74. *Ibid.*, I, 21.

75. *Ibid.*, II, 230-231.

76. *Ibid.*, I, 25.

77. Sir David Lindsay, *Works*, I, 133; Knox, *History*, I, 35.

78. Knox, *History*, I, 46-47.

79. *Ibid.*, I, 26.

80. *Ibid.*, I, 59.

81. *Ibid.*, I, 60.

82. *Ibid.*, I, 73.

83. *Ibid.*, I, 87. Earlier, some hope had been entertained for Hamilton by the Protestants. I, 48.

84. *Ibid.*, I, 104.

85. *Ibid.*, I, 130.

86. John Knox, *The appellation of John Knoxe from the cruell and most injust sentence* (Geneva, 1558), f. 11v. Also in John Knox, *Works* (Edinburgh, 1846-1864), IV, 465-520.

87. Knox, *Appellation*, f. 42v.

88. *Ibid.*, ff. 30v, 35r, 36r.

89. Knox, *History*, I, 87.

90. *Ibid.*, I, 114-115.

91. John Spottiswood, *History of the Church of Scotland* (London, 1655), p. 95. Republished in 3 vols., Edinburgh, 1847-1851.

92. *Ibid.*, p. 96; *DCH*, I, 340; Knox, *History*, I, 153.

93. Knox, *History*, II, 235.

94. *Ibid.*, I, 128.

95. *Ibid.*, I, 168. See also 'Extracts from "The Richt Way to the Kingdome of Hevine", by John Gau (Malmoe, 1533)', in *Bannatyne Miscellany* (Edinburgh, 1827-1855), III, 360-361.

96. *A Compendious Book of Godly and Spiritual Songs*, ed. A. F. Mitchell (Edinburgh: Scottish Text Society, 1897), p. 205.

97. *Ibid.*, p. 182.

98. Knox, *History*, I, 147.

99. *Ibid.*, I, 171-172.

100. *GDSR*, p. 53.

101. *APS*, II, 525.

102. Knox, *History*, I, 335.

103. Donaldson, *All the Queen's Men*, p. 45. But see *CSPS*, I, 592 where the bishop of Argyll was accused of sexual immorality which could hardly have endeared him to Protestants. On the other hand, there is a story that bishop Hepburn of Moray was prepared to join the congregation until his house was sacked and fired. In 'A Historie of the Estate of Scotland', *WM*, pp. 60-61. Robert Pont was empowered in 1570 to excommunicate Hepburn. *BUK*, I, 178.

104. *GDSR*, p. 67.

105. *APS*, II, 526.

106. Knox, *History*, I, 339.

107. *CSPS*, I, 465; see also pp. 462, 467.

108. *Scots Confession, 1560 and Negative Confession, 1581*, ed. G. D. Henderson (Edinburgh: Church of Scotland Committee on Publications, 1937), p. 39.

109. *Ibid.*, p. 57.

110. *Ibid.*, p. 75.

111. *Ibid.*, p. 77.

112. *Ibid.*, pp. 79-81.

113. *Ibid.*, p. 85.

114. *Ibid.*, p. 87.

115. *Ibid.*, p. 89.

116. Knox, *History*, I, 343.

117. *Scots Confession*, p. 89.

118. *APS*, II, 534-535.

119. Gordon Donaldson in *RPS*, V, Part I, p. iv; Donaldson, *All the Queen's Men*, p. 51.

120. *CSPS*, II, 174.

121. Gordon Donaldson, 'The Scottish Episcopate at the Reformation', *EHR*, 60 (1945), 353.

122. *GDSR*, pp. 55-58.

123. *CSPS*, I, 461.

124. *CSPS*, I, 486. As late as 1567 there was hope of St. Andrews' conversion. II, 371.

125. *CSPS*, I, 430.

126. Donaldson, 'Scottish Episcopate', p. 358. *GDSR*, p. 155.

127. *GSPS*, II, 296.

128. Donaldson, *Scotland: James V – James VII*, p. 123.

129. *FBD*, pp. 150, 161-162.

130. *APS*, II, 545-547; III, 3.

131. Gordon Donaldson, 'The Church Courts', in *An Introduction to Scottish Legal History* (Edinburgh: Stair Society, 1958), p. 367.

132. *BUK*, I, 88-89.

133. *BUK*; I, 36: see also I, 41-42, 56; and *RPS*, V, Part I, no. 1616.

Chapter 2

1. *FBD*, p. 85.

2. *FBD*, p. 209.

3. *CSPS*, I, 472.

4. Knox, *History*, I, 343.

5. *FBD*, pp. 210-222.

6. Cameron in *FBD*, p. 9; *GDSR*, pp. 61-63.

7. *FBD*, p. 115.

8. *FBD*, p. 122.

9. *FBD*, p. 123.

10. *FBD*, p. 127; *BUK* I, 14.

11. The old episcopal term, 'diocese', is used. See *FBD*, pp. 116-121, 176-177.

12. *FBD*, p. 115.

13. James Kirk, '"The Polities of the Best Reformed Kirks": Scottish Achievements and English Aspirations in Church Government at the Reformation', *SHR*, 59 (1980), 29. See *FBD*, p. 115.

14. Kirk, 'Polities', p. 30.

15. Thomas McCrie, *Life of Andrew Melville* (Edinburgh, 1899), p. 45; William Law Mathieson, *Politics and Religion: A Study in Scottish History from the Reformation to the Revolution* (Glasgow: James Maclehose and Sons, 1902), I, 285-286; Fleming, *Reformation*, pp. 273-275; Peter Hume Brown, *John Knox: A Biography* (London, 1895), II, 133-134; James L. Ainslie, *The Doctrines of Ministerial Order in the Reformed Churches of the 16th and 17th Centuries* (Edinburgh: T. & T. Clark, 1940), pp. 105-119; William Stanford Reid, 'French Influence on the First Scots Confession and Book of Discipline', *Westminster*

Theological Journal, 35 (1972), 13-14, and 'Knox's Attitude to the English Reformation', *Westminster Theological Journal*, 26 (1963), 12-16.

16. F. W. Maitland, 'The Anglican Settlement and the Scottish Reformation', *Cambridge Modern History*, II (1907), 594.

17. James Cooper, 'Superintendents and Bishops', in *Historical Papers submitted to the Christian Unity Association of Scotland* (Edinburgh: T. and A. Constable, 1914), p. 39. See also Alexander Moffatt, 'The Office of Superintendent 1560-1581', *RSCHS*, 4 (1932), 38.

18. Kirk, 'Polities', p. 44, See also I. B. Cowan, *Scottish Reformation*, p. 130; *GDSR*, p. 128.

19. *FBD*, pp. 161-162.

20. *GDSR*, pp. 102-129. See also Greaves, p. 81.

21. *FBD*, p. 115.

22. *BUK*, I, 18.

23. *BUK*, I, 42.

24. *BUK*, I, 39.

25. Even the temporary commissioners were not granted their requests to be permitted to resign. *BUK*, I, 39, 65, 77, 120, 183, 190, 205-206, 256, 287, 296-297, 302-303. Often the *BUK* records a resignation, but the man still holds his office at the next assembly. *E.g.*, for John Erskine, superintendent of Angus, *BUK*, I, 239, 242, 303.

26. *FBD*, p. 96.

27. *FBD*, p. 125.

28. *FBD*, pp. 123-125.

29. *FBD*, pp. 127-128.

30. Gordon Donaldson, '"The Example of Denmark" in the Scottish Reformation', *SHR*, 27 (1948), 63; James K. Cameron, 'The Cologne Reformation and the Church of Scotland', *JEH*, 30 (1979), 52, 62; Janet G. Macgregor, *The Scottish Presbyterian Polity: A Study of its Origins in the Sixteenth Century* (Edinburgh: Oliver and Boyd, 1926), pp. 45-46; Duncan Shaw, *The General Assemblies of the Church of Scotland 1560-1600: Their Origins and Development* (Edinburgh: Saint Andrew Press, 1964), p. 76; Brown, II, 133-134; Basil Hall, *John à Lasco 1499-1560: A Pole in Reformation England* (London: Dr. Williams's Trust, 1971); James Kirk, 'The Influence of Calvinism on the Scottish Reformation', *RSCHS*, 18 (1974), 167-168.

31. *GDSR*, p. 114.

32. George David Henderson, *Presbyterianism* (Aberdeen: University Press, 1954), pp. 32-52.

33. 'Draft Order of Visitation of the Country Churches', in John Calvin, *Theological Treatises*, ed. J. K. S. Reid (Philadelphia: Westminster Press, 1954), p. 74.

34. John Calvin, *Institutes of the Christian Religion*, ed. J. T McNeill (Philadelphia: Westminster Press, 1954), IV:3:8 (II, 1060).

35. *Ibid.*, IV:4:2 (II, 1069-1070).

36. On Calvin, see *GDSR*, p. 100. See also Moffatt, pp. 42-45, and Ainslie, *Doctrines*, pp. 92-95.

37. Martin Bucer, *De Regno Christi*, in Wilhelm Pauck (ed.), *Melanchthon and Bucer* (Philadelphia: Westminster Press, 1969), p. 284.

38. *Ibid.*, p. 285.

39. *Ibid.*, p. 284. Emphasis added to draw attention to what appears to be an assertion of *jure divino* episcopacy.

40. Maurice Lee, Jr., 'The Scottish Reformation after 400 Years', *SHR*, 44 (1965), 146.

41. *Statutes*, p. 86.

42. Knox, *History*, I, 15, 87.

43. Kirkwood Hewat, *Makers of the Scottish Church at the Reformation* (Edinburgh: Macniven & Wallace, 1920), p. 130.

44. Duncan Shaw, 'John Willock', in Shaw (ed.), *Reformation and Revolution* (Edinburgh: Saint Andrew Press, 1967), p. 61; *Fasti*, I, 50-51; I. B. Cowan, *Scottish Reformation*, p. 92.

45. Spottiswood, *History*, p. 344.

46. Robert Wodrow, *Collections upon the Lives of the Reformers and most eminent Ministers of the Church of Scotland* (Glasgow, 1834-1848), I, genealogical tree following p. 434. He may have died in 1591 or 1592. *Miscellany of the Spalding Club*, IV, lxxviii; *DNB*.

47. *DNB*; *Fasti*, V, 387. *JMAD*, p. 14 states that Richard Melville, Andrew's brother and James's father, accompanied 'James Erskine appeirand of Donne' as tutor, visiting Maccabeus in Denmark and Melanchthon in Wittenberg. McCrie, p. 5 took James Erskine to be John, later superintendent of Angus. But this cannot be, for, apart from bearing the wrong name, John was born in 1509 while his tutor was born in 1522. See W.J. Duncan in Wodrow, *Collections*, I, 430, 434; also *DNB*.

48. See, *e.g.*, Knox, *History*, I, 24: 'whom God in those days had marvellously illuminated'.

49. *GDSR*, p. 127.

50. The literature on Carswell is substantial, due especially to his 1567 translation into Gaelic of the Book of Common Order. For older views on the superintendent and bishop, see the introduction in *The Book of Common Order commonly called John Knox's Liturgy. Translated into Gaelic anno domini 1567 by Mr. John Carswell, Bishop of the Isles*, ed. Thomas MacLauchlan (Edinburgh, 1873), pp. xiii-xxvii; William J. Watson, 'Bishop Carswell's Liturgy', *Transactions of the Gaelic Society of Inverness*, 30 (1924), 287-312; Donald MacKinnon, 'John Carswell, 1520-1572: Superintendent of Argyle and the Isles', *RSCHS*, 4 (1932), 195-207; Angus Matheson, 'Bishop Carswell', *Transactions of the Gaelic Society of Inverness*, 42 (1965), 182-205; also printed in *Foirm Na N-Urrnuidheadh. John Carswell's Gaelic Translation of the Book of Common Order*, ed. R. L. Thomson (Edinburgh: Scottish Gaelic Texts Society, 1970), pp. lxxvii-lxxxix. The most recent study, which in part supersedes the foregoing, is that by Donald E. Meek and James Kirk, 'John Carswell, Superintendent of Argyll: A Reassessment', *RSCHS*, 19 (1975), 1-22. See also *GDSR*, pp. 127-128, 156-157.

51. Meek and Kirk, p. 9; Edward J. Cowan, 'The Angus Campbells and the Origin of the Campbell-Ogilvie Feud', *Scottish Studies*, 25 (1981), 30.

52. *GDSR*, pp. 127-128.

53. Meek and Kirk, p. 10.

54. *GDSR*, p. 128.

55. Meek and Kirk, pp. 10-11.

56. *Fasti*, VII, 417.

57. John Row, *History of the Kirk of Scotland, from the Year 1558 to August 1637* (Edinburgh, 1842), pp. 447-448.

58. *Contra* James L. Ainslie, 'The Scottish Reformed Church and English Puritanism', *RSCHS*, 8 (1944), 80; and W. S. Reid, 'Knox's Attitude', pp. 12-13.

59. Greaves, p. 78.

60. *CSPS*, I, 523.

61. John Knox, *The copie of an epistle sent by John Knox* (Geneva, 1559), pp. 97-98. Also in Knox, *Works*, V, 473-536.

62. Knox, *History*, I, 334.

63. *BUK*, I, 3-7.

64. *CSPS*, I, 555.

65. Robert Keith, *History of the Affairs of the Church and State in Scotland* (Edinburgh, 1844-1850), III, 10.

66. *CSPS*, I, 472.

67. Keith, *History*, III, 7, n.2.

68. *BUK*, I, 90.

69. John H. Leith (ed.), *Creeds of the Churches* (revised ed; Atlanta: John Knox Press, 1973), pp. 157-158.

70. Knox, *History*, II, 190; *Works*, VI, 547 (letter from John Douglas to Th. Beza); *BUK*, I, 90.

71. *BUK*, I, 179, 268, 344; *FBD*, p. 115.

72. *BUK*, I, 124.

73. *The CL. Psalmes of David in meter. For the use of the kirk of Scotland* (London, 1587), p. 16. Also in *DCH*, II, 56-62.

74. *CL. Psalmes*, pp. 25-26.

75. *Register of the Ministers, Elders, and Deacons of the Christian Congregation of St. Andrews. Part first 1559-1582.* Ed. David Hay Fleming (Edinburgh, 1889), p. 74.

76. *BUK*, I, 14.

77. *BUK*, I, 37. In March 1573 the penalty for absence was at one-half of the year's stipend. I, 263.

78. *BUK*, I, 25, 39, 43.

79. *BUK*, I, 266.

80. *BUK*, I, 29.

81. *Register, St. Andrews*, p. 168.

82. *BUK*, I, 195.

83. *BUK*, I, 33.

84. *Register, St. Andrews*, p. 75, for March 1561.

85. *BUK*, I, 318, for March 1575. See also I, 302-303.

86. Greaves, p. 81.

87. *BUK*, I, 14, 36.

88. *BUK*, I, 131; see also I, 191-192.

89. *BUK*, I, 34-35.

90. *BUK*, I, 60, 118, 143; *RPCf*, I, 675.

91. *BUK*, I, 162; see also I, 16, 26, 40.

92. *BUK*, I, 164.

93. *BUK*, I, 15; see also I, 14.

94. For examples of visitations, see *The Buik of the Kirk of the Canagait 1564-1567*, ed. Alma B. Calderwood (Edinburgh: Scottish Record Society, 1961), pp. 24, 32, 42-43, 62, 70; *Register, St. Andrews*, p. 75.

95. *BUK*, I, 27.

96. *BUK*, I, 50.

97. *BUK*, I, 61.

98. *BUK*, I, 8.

99. *BUK*, I, 19, 23.

100. *BUK*, I, 58.

101. *BUK*, I, 111.

102. *BUK*, I, 135, 175.

103. *BUK*, I, 30.

104. *Introduction to Scottish Legal History*, p. 367; I. B. Cowan, *Scottish Reformation*, p. 130.

105. *BUK*, I, 19; see also I, 23, 45, 146, 148, 306. But the kirk did not surrender its

judgement of causes for divorce. I, 187.

106. *RPCf*, I, 252. See also *Introduction to Scottish Legal History*, p. 368.

107. *FBD*, pp. 116-121; *GDSR*, pp. 111-113; McNeill and Nicholson, pp. 200-201.

108. *BUK*, I, 8.

109. *BUK*, I, 27-28; also I, 32 (June 1563). The general assembly was so confident of a positive outcome that it enacted that certain persons suited to the ministry be sent to the soon-to-be-elected superintendent of Aberdeen and Banff.

110. *BUK*, I, 53-54.

111. Spottiswood, *History*, p. 175. See also p. 150; *DCH*, I, 42: Richard Bannatyne, *Memorials of Transactions in Scotland, 1569-1573* (Edinburgh, 1836), pp. 185, 206-207. There were widespread complaints about the greed of the age. See *Complaynt* f. 115r; *Ancient Scottish Poems*, p. 242; David Ferguson, *Ane sermon preichit befoir the regent and nobilitie . . . in the kirk of Leith, 13 Januarie 1572* (St. Andrews, 1572), esp. sig. B5r, B8r; also in Ferguson, *Tracts 1563-1572* (Edinburgh, 1860), pp. 55-80; John Davidson, 'Ane Dialog or Mutuall talking betuix a Clerk and ane Courteour concerning foure Parische Kirks till ane Minister', in James Cranstoun (ed.), *Satirical Poems of the Time of the Reformation* (Edinburgh, 1891-1893), I, 303.

112. *BUK*, I, 53.

113. See *APS*, III, 37. Nothing came of the recommendation.

114. *BUK*, I, 300; see also I, 296-297.

115. *BUK*, I, 303. But in October 1580 he complained he had not been paid for nine years. II, 464.

116. *BUK*, I, 339; see also I, 128-129, 146, 148, 305.

117. *BUK*, I, 121.

118. *CSPS*, II, 421. He arrived in Edinburgh on 24 May.

119. *BUK*, I, 123.

120. *BUK*, I, 120.

121. *CSPS*, II, 454.

122. *GDSR*, p. 66.

123. Gordon Donaldson, 'Bishop Adam Bothwell and the Reformation in Orkney', *RSCHS*, 13 (1954), 86.

124. *CSPS*, I, 523.

125. Gordon Donaldson, 'Alexander Gordon, Bishop of Galloway (1559-1572), and his work in the Reformed Church', *Transactions of the Dumfriesshire and Galloway Natural History and Antiquarian Society*, 3rd series, 24 (1947), 111.

126. *Ibid.*, pp. 114, 128.

127. *APS*, II, 525.

128. *CSPS*, I, 482.

129. *FBD*, p. 211.

130. Knox, *History*, II, 73.

131. *Ibid.*, II, 189.

132. *Ibid.*, II, 194.

133. Donaldson, 'Alexander Gordon', p. 115; 'The Bishops and Priors of Whithorn', *Transactions of the Dumfriesshire and Galloway Natural History and Antiquarian Society*, 3rd series, 27 (1950), 142-143.

134. *GDSR*, p. 59.

135. *BUK*, I, 131.

136. *BUK* I, 32; see also I, 15, 28.

137. *DCH*, II, 224.

138. *BUK*, I, 17, 34, 44, 54, 190, 311-312.

139. *BUK*, I, 63. June 1565.

140. *BUK*, I, 377; see also I, 17.

141. *BUK*, I, 366-337..

142. *GDSR*, p. 129.

143. *GDSR*, p. 126.

144. *BUK*, I, 129.

145. *CSPS*, I, 575.

146. *CSPS*, I, 136, 190.

147. *BUK*, III, 854.

148. *BUK*, I, 112.

149. Sir James Melville of Halhill, *Memoirs of his own Life* (Edinburgh, 1827), pp. 178-179.

150. *BUK*, I, 114.

151. Sir James Melville, pp. 186, 205; *CSPS*, II, 376.

152. *BUK*, I, 162-163.

153. *BUK*, I, 166. But Alexander Douglas was refused admission to the parsonage of Glasgow since he was on the college of justice and the kirk feared he might be non-resident. *RPCf*, II 79-80.

154. *BUK*, I, 206. Emphasis added.

155. *BUK*, I, 264.

156. *BUK*, I, 267.

157. *BUK*, I, 207.

158. *BUK*, II, 589-590, 597.

159. *RPCf*, X, 289.

160. *BUK*, III, 802.

161. *BUK*, I, 131.

162. *BUK*, I, 150.

163. *BUK*, I, 261.

164. *BUK*, I, 273. See the report of one of his sermons in 1571 in *CSPS*, III, 609-610; *DCH*, III, 102-105.

165. *BUK*, I, 275-276; *Historie and Life of King James the Sext* (Edinburgh, 1825), p. 134.

166. *BUK*, I, 287, 309, 319-320.

167. *BUK*, I, 337.

168. *BUK*, I, 343.

169. Donaldson, 'Alexander Gordon', p. 128.

170. *OL*, I, 251.

171. *BUK*, I, 112.

Chapter 3

1. Keith, *History*, III, 10. See also D. E. R. Watt, *Fasti Ecclesiae Scoticanae Medii Aevi ad Annum 1638* (2nd draft; Edinburgh: Scottish Record Society, 1969), p. 150.

2. *BUK*, I, 244, 257, 261.

3. *Bannatyne Miscellany*, I, 254.

4. *BUK*, I, 25.

5. *Register, St. Andrews*, p. lix.

6. *WM*, p. 286.

7. *GDSR*, p. 156. See also David Hay Fleming, 'Scotland's Supplication and Complaint against the Book of Common Prayer (otherwise Laud's Liturgy), the Book of Canons, and

the Prelates, 18th October 1637', *Proceedings of the Society of Antiquaries of Scotland*, 60 (1927), 320-321.

8. *RPCf*, I, 511.

9. Meek and Kirk, p. 14. Maclean ambitions did not cease with Patrick's withdrawal. *RPCf*, III, 62, 124-125.

10. *BUK*, I, 144.

11. Meek and Kirk, pp. 20-21.

12. *FBD*, pp. 108-113; 156-164.

13. *RPCf*, I, 192-194; 201-202.

14. Knox, *History*, II, 29.

15. *GDSR*, p. 149.

16. *BUK*, I, 34.

17. *GDSR*, p. 151.

18. *APS*, III, 23.

19. *BUK*, I, 162.

20. *GDSR*, p. 172.

21. Kirk, 'Polities', pp. 36-37.

22. *GDSR*, pp. 177-178; I. B. Cowan, *Scottish Reformation*, p. 122.

23. *CSPS*, IV, 134; V, 180.

24. Bannatyne, p. 181.

25. *Ibid.*, p. 182.

26. Hamilton's execution was immediately memorialised by Robert Sempill in the style of Lindsay's work on David Beaton. In 'The Bischoppis lyfe and testament' the worldly prelate made his confession:

Gude pepill all, I pray yow to pray for me,
Quhat may my rent of riches now decoir me?
This far I speik in presence of yow all,
Complenand heir with pietie I deploir me,
Quha is the Lord to lyfe may now restoir me.
Heirfoir, go mark this in Memoriall,
Twyse being bischop with sic berial,
Hard to belief sum tyme to se me hing,
Gif I had servit my God and syne my King. (185-193) Cranstoun, I, 193-200.

27. *GDSR*, p. 160. Bannatyne, p. 178, has him 'maid bisshope' on 18 August.

28. David Hume of Godscroft, *The history of the houses of Douglas and Angus* (Edinburgh, 1644), p. 320.

29. *BUK*, I, 199.

30. *BUK*, I, 200; Bannatyne, p. 186.

31. Bannatyne, p. 183; see also pp. 185-186.

32. Cranstoun, I, 296-324.

33. *Ibid.*, I, xlv-xlvii.

34. *Historie and Life of King James the Sext*, p. 102.

35. Bannatyne, p. 183; *CSPS*, III, 670.

36. Bannatyne, p. 197.

37. *Ibid.*, p. 198. The correspondence is also located in *DCH*, III, 156-165.

38. Bannatyne, p. 199. In another letter written just one month later 'to ane faythfull brother', Erskine, in the course of a discussion about admission to benefices, referred only to 'sic of the ministerie as hes commissione and cuir to exeme the persone namit'. It is surprising that he made no reference to superintendents or bishops, but it is not contradictory. Here his concern was to define a high view of the ministry, not to articulate

the need for an episcopate. It does, however, suggest that Erskine held to an opinion of an episcopate closely identified with the rest of the ministry and one that was dependent upon and responsible to the kirk. In fact he proceeded to make that clear to the regent. *Miscellany of the Spalding Club*, IV, 92-101. The quotation appears on p. 100.

39. Bannatyne, p. 200.

40. *Ibid.*, p. 201.

41. *APS*, III, 65.

42. Bannatyne, p. 201.

43. *Ibid.*, p. 202.

44. *Ibid.*, p. 203.

45. *Ibid.*, p. 208. Also in Knox, *Works*, VI, 608-612.

46. Bannatyne, p. 213.

47. *Ibid.*, p. 217; *BUK*, I, 238.

48. *CSPS*, IV, 466.

49. *BUK*, I, 207. The kirk's representatives who actually conducted the negotiations included John Erskine, John Winram, David Lindsay, and John Craig. All but Winram would live to acquiesce to the episcopal polity of the 1580s, and Lindsay would become bishop of Ross in 1600.

50. *CSPS*, IV, 134.

51. *BUK*, I, 209.

52. *BUK*, I, 213.

53. *BUK*, I, 270.

54. *BUK*, I, 217.

55. *BUK*, I, 219.

56. *BUK*, I, 217.

57. *BUK*, I, 220-221.

58. *BUK*, I, 220. See the oath's use in *RPCf*, II, 129-130, 223-224, 301.

59. Bannatyne, p. 222.

60. *Ibid.*, p. 223.

61. *Ibid.*, p. 250; *BUK*, I, 247; *GDSR*, p. 169.

62. *JMAD*, p. 31.

63. Bannatyne, p. 251.

64. *BUK*, I, 248; *GDSR*, p. 170.

65. Bannatyne, p. 224.

66. *Fasti*, VII, 321-356, consistently errs on this point when it speaks of episcopal consecrations which were clearly lacking in the reformed kirk before 1610. David Cunningham was reported to have been 'consicratt' by archbishop Adamson in 1577, but once again this was not the formal consecration of an Anglican bishop in apostolic succession. *Miscellany of the Spalding Club* (Aberdeen, 1842), II, 46.

67. *APS*, III, 71; see also p. 82. *BUK*, I, 263, 272, 284.

68. *BUK*, I, 242; see also Bannatyne, p. 228.

69. *BUK*, I, 249; see also Bannatyne, p. 253.

70. *BUK*, I, 243-244.

71. *BUK*, I, 297, 317-318.

72. *BUK*, I, 264, 278, 297.

73. *BUK*, I, 270; see also I, 318.

74. *BUK*, I, 255.

75. *BUK*, I, 318.

76. *BUK*, I, 255.

77. *BUK*, I, 294.

78. *BUK*, I, 308.
79. *BUK*, I, 278-280.
80. *BUK*, I, 306.
81. *BUK*, I, 331, 348.
82. *BUK*, I, 314.
83. *JMAD*, p. 31.
84. *GDSR*, p. 172. Kirk, in *SBD*, pp. 33-35, has researched grants made by bishops.
85. *Fasti*, VII, 344.
86. Bannatyne, p. 224.
87. *Fasti*, VII, 339.
88. *BUK*, I, 270.
89. *BUK*, I, 300.
90. *BUK*, I, 315.
91. E. J. Cowan, p. 32; *BUK*, II, 593.
92. *BUK*, I, 332-335.
93. *BUK*, I, 340.
94. *BUK*, I, 164.
95. *BUK*, I, 350-351.
96. *BUK*, I, 352.
97. *BUK*, II, 454.
98. *CSPS*, VII, 291.
99. *Fasti*, VII, 350.
100. *BUK*, I, 288.
101. *BUK*, I, 164.
102. *BUK*, I, 323.
103. *BUK*, I, 349. Later he was imprisoned for some offence. *RPCf*, IV, 38.
104. *BUK*, I, 366.
105. *BUK*, II, 434.
106. *BUK*, I, 349.
107. *BUK*, I, 331-332; also for Dunblane, I, 349.
108. *BUK*, I, 255, 283, 300, 331.
109. *BUK*, I, 300.
110. *BUK*, I, 348.
111. *BUK*, I, 287; see also p. 270.
112. *BUK*, I, 309.
113. *BUK*, I, 314-317.
114. *BUK*, I, 332, 341.
115. *BUK*, I, 341.
116. See *Fasti*, VII, 321-356.
117. *BUK*, I, 132. See also Kirk in *SBD*, pp. 19-20.
118. *Miscellany of the Spalding Club*, II, 46.
119. *BUK*, I, 316. *Contra Fasti*, VII, 338 which prefers a doubtful statement in James B. Paul, *The Scots Peerage* (Edinburgh: David Douglas, 1904-1914), VI, 226. See also VI, 232-233.
120. Sir James Melville, p. 205.
121. Kirk in *SBD*, p. 21; *GDSR*, p. 161.
122. *BUK*, I, 246.
123. *BUK*, I, 246; see also I, 209, and Bannatyne, p. 217.
124. *WM*, p. 289.
125. *WM*, p. 290. See also *BUK*, I, 352.

126. *APS*, III, 89.

127. *BUK*, I, 325.

128. *BUK*, I, 316-317.

129. I Timothy 3:2, 'apt to teach'; Titus 1:9, 'able to exhorte with wholsome doctrine'; also Titus 2:1.

130. *BUK*, I, 326.

131. *BUK*, I, 349.

132. *BUK*, I, 326-327.

133. *BUK*, I, 356.

134. Kirk in *SBD*, p. 54.

135. *BUK*, I, 357.

136. *BUK*, I, 331.

137. *BUK*, I, 340.

138. *BUK*, I, 342.

139. *BUK*, I, 343.

140. *BUK*, I, 352-353.

141. *GDSR*, p. 190.

142. Kirk in *SBD*, pp. 45, 51.

143. Knox, *Works*, VI, 614. Cited in 1606; see *DCH*, VI, 509.

144. See Gordon Donaldson, 'Lord Chancellor Glamis and Theodore Beza', in *Miscellany of the Scottish History Society* (Edinburgh, 1951), VIII, 87-113. The letter is dated 1578 but both Donaldson (p. 99) and Kirk in *SBD*, p. 44 follow contemporary evidence and regard it as belonging to April 1576. Donaldson's edition is based upon a ms. copy of the Glamis letter, not the (partial) printed version in [Theodore Beza], *The judgement of a most reverend and learned man from beyond the sea, concerning a threefold order of bishops* (n.p., [1580?]). Donaldson omits Beza's preliminary remarks on the three kinds of bishops, commonly known as *De triplici episopatu* (p. 92). I have followed Donaldson for Glamis's letter and Beza's reply.

145. Beza, sig. A2v.

146. *Ibid.*, sig. A3r.

147. *Ibid.*, sig. B1r.

148. *Ibid.*, sig. B1v.

149. *Ibid.* See also *Miscellany of the Scottish History Society*, VIII, 103-104.

150. Beza, sig. B2r.

151. *Miscellany of the Scottish History Society*, VIII, 101.

152. *Ibid.*, p. 102.

153. *Ibid.*, p. 103.

154. *Ibid.*, p. 104.

155. *Ibid.*, p. 107.

156. *BUK*, I, 368-372.

157. See, *e.g.*, questions 14, 21, 28, 38, 41, 42.

158. *BUK*, 358-359, 361; *DCH*, III, 368. *GDSR*, p. 261 asserts that the superintendent of Angus, John Erskine, accepted a parochial charge. This is based, however, on a misreading of *RPS*, VII, 266 where another of the same name was to be admitted by the superintendent.

159. *BUK*, I, 360. *Cf.* a presbyterian version of Boyd's response in *JMAD*, p. 48.

160. *BUK*, I, 378; see also I, 209.

161. *BUK*, I, 379.

162. *BUK*, I, 386. He accepted a charge.

163. See Kirk's comment in *SBD*, p. 74: If commissioners and superintendents represent

a 'reduced form of episcopacy', then 'the debatable area between episcopacy and presbytery is considerably narrowed when it is recalled that the commissioner was by no means incompatible with a presbyterian structure'.

164. *SBD*, pp. 124-125; *APS*, III, 105. A supplication was sent to Morton wherein was expressed the fear that the lack of a kirk polity patterned after God's expressed will would entail a more or less inevitable decline in 'the sinceritie of his Word'. *WM*, p. 401.

165. *BUK*, II, 404.

166. *BUK*, II 408-409. Emphasis added.

167. *BUK*, II, 413.

168. *BUK*, II, 413; see also II, 423.

169. Apparently his non-residence and non-performance of duties led later to a sentence of deposition of 1594. *Fasti*, VII, 338. On Graham's case, see also Gordon Donaldson, 'Leighton's Predecessors', *Journal of the Society of Friends of Dunblane Cathedral*, 12 (1975), 9-11.

170. *BUK*, II, 420.

171. *BUK*, II, 423.

172. *BUK*, II, 425.

173. In 1580 he became earl of March. Paul, V, 335.

174. *SBD*, p. 124.

175. *BUK*, II, 487-488.

176. *BUK*, II, 428-429.

177. *BUK*, II, 456, 466. Robert Bowes wrote that Lennox subscribed the reformed faith for the sake of the king. *CSPS*, V, 520.

178. *BUK*, II, 475, 514, 519; *DCH*, IV, 272.

179. *DCH*, IV, 124-125.

180. Kirk in *SBD*, p. 46.

181. *GDSR*, p. 193.

182. *SBD*, p. 166.

183. *SBD*, pp. 169, 172.

184. *SBD*, p. 170.

185. *SBD*, pp. 195ff. See *BUK*, I, 146: 'That the jurisdictioune of the Kirk may be separate fra that quhilk is civille' (July 1569). Also, I. B. Cowan, *Scottish Reformation*, pp. 124-125.

186. *SBD*, p. 209.

187. *SBD*, p. 237; see also p. 243.

188. See Chapter 4.

189. *SBD*, p. 195.

190. *SBD*, p. 191.

191. *SBD*, p. 207.

192. *SBD*, pp. 17-189.

193. *SBD*, p. 176; also with the doctor, p. 187.

194. *SBD*, p. 177.

195. *SBD*, p. 181.

196. *SBD*, pp. 222-225.

197. *SBD*, p. 197.

198. *SBD*, pp. 223-224.

199. *SBD*, p. 226. See also *BUK*, II, 453, 474-475.

200. Kirk in *SBD*, p. 128. Also in McCrie, p. 72.

201. *BUK*, II, 526.

202. *RPCf*, III, 427, 770.

203. *BUK*, II, 524-525, 528.
204. David Moysie, *Memoirs of the Affairs of Scotland* (Edinburgh, 1830), p. 36.
205. Kirk in *SBD*, p. 135.
206. *BUK*, II, 533-534.
207. *BUK*, II, 528, 538, 543-544.
208. *DCH*, III, 595; *CSPS*, VI, 120.
209. *BUK*, II, 560.
210. *DCH*, IV, 111; Kirk in *SBD*, p. 132.
211. *RPCf*, III, 474. Also in *BUK*, II 571-573, though it mistakenly refers to James's 'minoritie'.
212. *RPCf*, III, 476-477. Also in *BUK*, II, 573-575.
213. *CSPS*, VI, 131; *DCH*, III, 621. On 23 May John Dury had denounced him as an apostate and traitor. *CSPS*, VI, 122.
214. *BUK*, II, 578, 580, 583, 590.
215. *BUK*, II, 581.
216. *BUK*, II, 607-609.
217. *BUK*, I, 374; II, 438, 450, 544, 632.
218. *BUK*, II, 593.
219. *BUK*, II, 604.

Chapter 4

1. *JMAD*, p. 293; see also pp. 121-122, 127-128.
2. McCrie, p. 461.
3. See *Fasti*, VII, 325-326; Cranstoun, II, 226-235.
4. *BUK*, I, 4.
5. *BUK* I, 44.
6. *BUK*, I, 51.
7. *Serenissimi ac nobilissimi, Scotiae, Angliae, Franciae, & Hyberniae principis, Henrice Stuardi illustrissimi herois, ac Mariae reginae amplissimae filii, genethliacum.* Reprinted in Patrick Adamson, *Poemata sacra* (London, 1619).
8. Cranstoun, I, 227.
9. *CSPS*, II, 303.
10. *CSPS*, II, 305.
11. *CSPS*, IV, 589; Patrick Adamson, *Gratiarum actio illustrissimae et potentissimae principi. Do. Elizabetae Ang. Franc. et Hyberniae Reginae, propter liberatem civili seditione Scotiam* (London, [1573]).
12. *DCH*, V, 118.
13. Cranstoun, II, 227.
14. *BUK*, I, 165.
15. *RPCf*, XIV, 40-41; Watt, *Fasti*, p. 385.
16. *BUK*, I, 193.
17. *BUK*, I, 198.
18. *JMAD*, p. 53.
19. *BUK*, I, 240-241; see also I, 317-318.
20. *JMAD*, pp. 31-32'; Bannatyne, p. 223.
21. *BUK*, I, 336.
22. *JMAD*, p. 53.
23. *JMAD*, p. 56.
24. *JMAD*, p. 47.

25. *BUK*, I, 367; see also I, 377.
26. *BUK*, I, 385.
27. *BUK*, II, 433.
28. *BUK*, II, 531.
29. *JMAD*, p. 121. James Lawson and Walter Balcanquhall also asserted that 'ye cursit bischopis' had subscribed the presbyterian polity. *CSPS*, VII, 219; *DCH*, IV, 75. See also *DCH*, IV, 316-317.
30. *DCH*, IV, 57.
31. *DCH*, IV, 58.
32. *DCH*, IV, 60.
33. *JMAD*, p. 120.
34. *CSPS*, VI, 644; Sir James Melville, p. 315.
35. *CSPS*, VI, 645, 649-651.
36. *JMAD*, p. 141.
37. *Historie and Life of King James the Sext*, p. 205.
38. *JMAD*, p. 152.
39. Sir James Melville, p. 315.
40. *DCH*, IV, 61. The poem is printed in Cranstoun, I, 346-390.
41. Moysie, p. 57.
42. *Extract from the Despatches of M. Courcelles, French Ambassador at the Court of Scotland, 1586-1587* (Edinburgh, 1828), p. 34.
43. *RPCf*, III, 690-691.
44. *CSPS*, VII, 185.
45. *CSPS*, VII, 205, 207.
46. *CSPS*, VII, 293.
47. *APS*, II, 292.
48. *APS*, III, 303, 312.
49. *APS*, III, 293.
50. *APS*, III, 312.
51. *APS*, III, 355.
52. *JMAD*, p. 187 indicates that the bull was issued earlier than August 1584.
53. *DCH*, IV, 143.
54. *JMAD*, pp. 194-196.
55. *CSPS*, VII, 278-279. Montgomery had experienced a violent reaction at an earlier time. Moysie, p. 37.
56. *DCH*, IV, 100.
57. *JMAD*, p. 194; see also p. 130.
58. *JMAD*, p. 194. On popery, see *DCH*, IV, 130, 133-134.
59. *DCH*, IV, 214; see also IV, 237-238.
60. *DCH*, IV, 216.
61. *DCH*, IV, 217.
62. *JMAD*, p. 199. See also *WM*, p. 433.
63. *DCH*, IV, 246; see also IV, 603-605.
64. *Miscellany of the Spalding Club*, IV, 70.
65. *Ibid.*, II, 47.
66. *WM*, p. 432. See the letter to Erskine from Montrose and Maitland calling upon him to be the king's agent for obtaining subscriptions. *Miscellany of the Spalding Club*, IV, 69-70.
67. *WM*, p. 436. Some were grateful for his efforts. *Miscellany of the Spalding Club*, IV, 71. James Melville wrote of Erskine as 'that notable instrument in the kirk, . . . of most

honourable and happie memorie'. *JMAD*, p. 39; see also p. 18.

68. *WM*, p. 434.

69. *DCH*, IV, 341.

70. *JMAD*, p. 200; *RPCf*, III, 703, 712.

71. *CSPS*, VII, 277-278.

72. *JMAD*, p. 200.

73. *JMAD*, pp. 200, 204; A. F. Scott Pearson, *Church and State: Political Aspects of Sixteenth Century Puritanism* (Cambridge: University Press, 1928), p. 123.

74. *JMAD*, p. 204.

75. *JMAD*, p. 55.

76. *JMAD*, pp. 211-212.

77. *JMAD*, p. 204.

78. *JMAD*, p. 212.

79. *DCH*, IV, 254.

80. *DCH*, V, 121, 124. See also Donaldson, *Scotland: James V -James VII*, p. 181. Patrick Galloway accused Adamson of acting upon instructions 'as he receaved from Arran and other godless courteours'. *DCII*, IV, 120.

81. *A declaration of the kings majesties intention and meaning toward the lait actis of parliament* (Edinburgh, 1585), sig. Aiir.

82. *Ibid.*, sig. B3v.

83. *Ibid.*, sig. A2v.

84. *Ibid.*, sig. A3r.

85. *Ibid.*, sig. A4r.

86. *Ibid.*, sig. A4v, B2v.

87. *Ibid.*, sig. B4v.

88. *Ibid.*, sig. Clr.

89. *Ibid.*, sig. Clv.

90. *Ibid.*, sig. C4r.

91. *Ibid.*, sig. Clr.

92. *Ibid.*, sig. C3v.

93. *Ibid.*, sig. C2r.

94. *Ibid.*, sig. Clr.

95. *DCH*, IV, 274.

96. McCrie, p. 107.

97. *DCH*, IV, 286-288.

98. *DCH*, IV, 283.

99. *DCH*, IV, 286.

100. *DCH*, IV, 294.

101. *DCH*, IV, 339.

102. *DCH*, IV, 338.

103. *DCH*, IV, 338; see also IV, 315: 'like a filthie dog, he turneth backe to his owne vomite'.

104. *DCH*, IV, 129.

105. *DCH*, IV, 309.

106. *JMAD*, p. 243.

107. *JMAD*, p. 241.

108. Thomas Erastus, *The Theses of Erastus Touching Excommunication* (Edinburgh, 1844), p. 160.

109. *Ibid.*, p. 163. See also *DCH*, IV, 524-525, 537-538.

110. Erastus, p. 164.

111. Knox, *Appellation*, f. 18v.

112. *CSPS*, I, 157.

113. Knox, *Copie*, p. 92. Emphasis added.

114. *Ibid.*, pp. 100-101.

115. *Miscellany of the Spalding Club.*, IV, 89.

116. *Ibid.*, IV, 91.

117. *Scots Confession*, p. 95.

118. *BUK*, I, 120.

119. *Foirm Na N-Urrnuidheadh*, p. 175.

120. *Ibid.*, p. 174.

121. Meek and Kirk, p. 20.

122. *Scots Confession*, p. 59.

123. Pearson, p. 62. See the dispute between the ministers and Morton in Robert Lindesay, II, 313-314; and Andrew Melville in *DCH*, IV, 5: God had appointed the king to be supreme in the 'civill governement of this countrie'.

124. *BUK*, I, 125. The book is listed in Harry G. Aldis, *A List of Books Printed in Scotland before 1700* (Edinburgh: National Library of Scotland, 1970) as no. 69. However, Robert Dickson and John P. Edmond, *Annals of Scottish Printing* (Cambridge, 1890), p. 307 indicate that no copies have been discovered.

125. *JMAD*, p. 162. See also Pearson, p. 70.

126. *The Bible and Holy Scriptures* (Edinburgh, 1579), f. iii recto. Emphasis added. Also in *BUK*, II, 441-448. See also *DCH*, V, 161. See the presbyterian agreement with Adamson on the king as the 'cheef and principall member' of the kirk. IV, 311. An allusion identifying ministers and the apostles was also uttered. V, 131.

127. *DCH*, IV, 507-508.

128. *CSPS*, VII, 227. At one point it was believed that Howeson might be executed for his homiletical indiscretion. VII, 232-233. See also *DCH*, IV, 146-148. John Davidson expressed a similar view in 1593. V, 279.

129. *DCH*, IV, 315.

130. *JMAD*, p. 130.

131. Row, *History*, p. 143.

132. *DCH*, IV, 491-494.

133. *BUK*, II, 647.

134. *BUK*, II, 652.

135. *BUK*, II, 653.

136. *BUK*, II, 653-654.

137. *BUK*, II, 667. Donaldson, *Scotland: James V -James VII*, pp. 199, 205, says that synods also were given episcopal moderators.

138. *SBD*, pp. 148-149.

139. Maurice Lee, Jr., *John Maitland of Thirlestane and the Foundation of the Stewart Despotism in Scotland* (Princeton: University Press, 1959), pp. 114-115, 121; *Government by Pen: Scotland under James VI and I* (Urbana: University of Illinois Press, 1980), pp. 5, 20.

140. *GDSR*, p. 217. See also Kirk in *SBD*, p. 151.

141. *GDSR*, pp. 218-219; I. B. Cowan, *Scottish Reformation*, p. 133; Gordon Donaldson, 'Sources for the Study of Scottish Ecclesiastical Organization and Personnel, 1560-1600', *Bulletin of the Institute for Historical Research*, 19 (1942/3), 199.

142. *Miscellany of the Spalding Club*, II, 52, 67-68.

143. *Fasti*, VII, 339.

144. *Fasti*, VII, 345.

145. *RPCf*, IV, 154.

146. *BUK*, II, 693.
147. *BUK*, II, 696.
148. *BUK*, II, 698.
149. *APS*, III, 431-437.
150. *JMAD*, p. 260. The kirk had continued to seek these funds to support education and to cover the expenses of presbyteries. *BUK*, II, 601-602. It desired the abolition of the act of annexation. II, 787.
151. *BUK*, II, 700.
152. *BUK*, II, 701.
153. *BUK*, II, 709.
154. *BUK*, II, 650-651, 689.
155. *BUK*, II, 699.
156. *BUK*, II, 717; *RPCf*, IV, 172.
157. *BUK*, II, 717; *RPCf*, III, 551-552; IV, 163-164.
158. *BUK*, II, 721. His licence to remain abroad had actually been revoked in 1567. *RPCf*, I, 563. Payment of his rents was inhibited at that time. I, 569-570.
159. The Stirling presbytery excommunicated him. *RPCf*, IV, 263-264.
160. *BUK*, II, 644-645.
161. *DCH*, IV, 497.
162. *BUK*, II, 657.
163. *DCH*, IV, 498.
164. *JMAD*, p. 247; *CSPS*, VIII, 328-329.
165. *DCH*, IV, 500. See also *JMAD*, p. 256.
166. *BUK*, II, 658.
167. *BUK*, II, 662-664.
168. *BUK*, II, 667.
169. *RPCf*, IV, 125.
170. *BUK*, II, 689.
171. *BUK*, II, 705.
172. *BUK*, II, 711.
173. *BUK*, II, 727.
174. *BUK*, II, 731-732.
175. *BUK*, II, 746.
176. William M. Lamont, *Godly Rule: Politics and Religion, 1603-60* (London: Macmillan, 1969), p. 36. On the contrary side, see Roland G. Usher, 'Bancroft and the Divine Right of Bishops', *Theology*, 1 (1920), 28-34; E. T. Davies, *Episcopacy and the Royal Supremacy in the Church of England in the XVI Century* (Oxford: Basil Blackwell, 1950), pp. 27-28; W. D. J. Cargill Thompson, 'A Reconsideration of Richard Bancroft's Paul's Cross Sermon of 9 February 1588/9', *JEH*, 20 (1969), 158.
177. W. D. J. Cargill Thompson, p. 265.
178. Richard Bancroft, *A sermon preached at Paules Crosse* (London, 1589), pp. 14, 69.
179. *Ibid.*, p. 9.
180. *Ibid.*, pp. 13, 15.
181. *Ibid.*, pp. 14, 16, 20, 23.
182. *Ibid.*, p. 89.
183. *Ibid.*, p. 15.
184. *Ibid.*, pp. 17-19.
185. *Ibid.*, p. 81; see also pp. 67ff.
186. Champlin Burrage, *The Early English Dissenters in the Light of Recent Research* (Cambridge: University Press, 1912), II, 131. Letter dated 23 December 1589.

187. Robert Browne, *A New Years Guift*, ed. Champlin Burrage (London: Congregational Historical Society, 1904), pp. 25-27. Also in A. Peel and L. H. Carlson (eds.), *The Writings of Robert Harrison and Robert Browne* (London: George Allen and Unwin Ltd., 1953), pp. 516-529 (esp. pp. 518-519). See Bancroft, pp. 75-76.

188. Bancroft, pp. 72-75.

189. *Treason pretended against the king of Scots . . . with a declaration of the kinges majesties intention to his last acts of parliament. Out of Skottish into English* (London, 1585), sig. A2r. Christopher Studley's letter was dated 20 February 1585. This would have been, presumably, Old Style, giving a publication date of 1586 New Style. However, A. W. Pollard and G. R. Redgrave, *A Short-Title Catalogue* (second ed; London: The Bibliographical Society, 1976), II, no. 21949.5, gives 1585 as does Edward Arber (ed.), *A Transcript of the Registers of the Company of Stationers of London, 1554-1640* (London, 1875-1894), V, 138, no. 3217. The discrepancy is puzzling but it seems best to retain the date as 1585. Had Studley sent the material south in 1586, it would have lost much of its 'hot-off-the-press' sensationalism.

190. Raphael Holinshed, *Chronicles* (London, 1807-1808), V, 713-720.

191. Bancroft, p. 75.

192. Burrage, II, 128.

193. [John Penry], *A briefe discovery of the untruthes and slanders . . . contained in a sermon . . . by D. Bancroft* ([Edinburgh, 1589]). Laing suggested either 1589 or 1590. *WM*, p. 471. Aldis, no. 209, gives the date as 1590, as does Gordon Donaldson, 'The Attitude of Whitgift and Bancroft to the Scottish Church', *Transactions of the Royal Historical Society*, 4th series, 24 (1942), 112. However, see Owen Chadwick, 'Richard Bancroft's Submission', *JEH*, 3 (1952), 59.

194. Penry, p. 11.

195. *Ibid.*, p. 27.

196. *Ibid.*, p. 30.

197. *DCH*, IV, 247.

198. [John Davidson], *D. Bancrofts rashnes in rayling against the church of Scotland* (Edinburgh, 1590), sig. A2r-A2v. Also in *WM*, pp. 503-520.

199. Davidson, sig. A4r-A4v.

200. *WM*, pp. 489-496; *DCH*, V, 73-77.

201. *DCH*, V, 72; *WM*, p. 471.

202. *WM*, p. 491.

203. *WM*, p. 494.

204. *DCH*, V, 77.

205. *Letters of Queen Elizabeth and King James VI of Scotland*, ed. John Bruce (London, 1849), pp. 63-64. 6 July 1590.

206. *WM*, p. 495.

207. Burrage, II, 128.

208. *Ibid.* Letter dated 12 November 1589. See also Donaldson, 'Attitude of Whitgift and Bancroft', p. 109; and Roland G. Usher, *The Reconstruction of the English Church* (New York: D. Appleton and Company, 1910), I, 56.

209. *WM*, p. 492; *BUK*, II, 745 for June 1589.

210. Davidson, sig. A5r.

211. *Ibid.*, sig. A5v.

212. Usher, *Reconstruction*, I, 58; Chadwick, p. 61; *CSPS*, X, 409-410.

213. *JMAD*, p. 85.

214. 'Assertiones quaedam' in Adamson, *Poemata sacra*. See also *DCH*, IV, 638-639.

215. *JMAD*, pp. 245-246, 256-257.

216. *JMAD*, pp. 281-282.

217. Prefatory letter to king James in *Apocalypsis S. Ioannis theologi, latino carmine reddita* in *Poemata sacra*, *JMAD*, p. 272.

218. *JMAD*, pp. 288-289. Lee, *John Maitland*, p. 116, says James and Maitland sacrificed Adamson for the sake of 'conciliation with the kirk'.

219. *JMAD*, pp. 289-290.

220. Row, *History*, p. 117.

221. *JMAD*, p. 290.

222. *CSPS*, XIII, 214, 219.

223. Patrick Adamson, *The recantation of Maister Patrik Adamsone, sometimes archbishop of Saint-Andrewes in Scotlande* ([Middelburgh], 1598), sig. A2v. Published in various other works. Row, *History*, pp. 118-129, has a complete rendition, with only a few different spellings. *JMAD*, pp. 290-292, has a partial text. *DCH*, V, 119-127, lacks the preface. There is a Latin translation in *Viri clarissimi A. Melvini musae et P. Adamsoni vita et palindoia et celsae commissionis ceu delegatae potestatis regiae in causis ecclesiasticis brevis & aperta descriptio* (n.p., 1620), pp. 49-56.

224. Adamson, *Recantation*, sig. A4r.

225. *Ibid.*, sig. C3r.

226. *Ibid.*, sig. C3v.

227. See Chapter 8.

228. *Historie and Life of King James the Sext*, p. 205.

229. Cranstoun, II, 235. Even the hostile McCrie, p. 370, granted that he was 'an elegant poet'.

230. *Confessio fidei et doctrinae* (St. Andrews, 1572).

231. In Adamson, *Poemata sacra*.

232. *BUK*, I, 310.

233. *DCH*, V, 118.

234. Patrick Adamson, *Catechismus latino carmine redditus* (Edinburgh, 1581). No copy of the 1573 edition is known to have survived. Dickson and Edmond, pp. 259, 264; Aldis, no. 122; *WM*, p. 305.

235. *JMAD*, p. 32.

236. Adamson, *Recantation*, sig. B3r.

237. *Ibid.*, sig. B3r, B4v.

238. Patrick Adamson, *De sacro pastoris munere tractatus* (London, 1619), pp. 50-53, 68.

239. 'Legitimam & orthodoxam Episcoporum authoritatem' in Adamson, *Apocalypsis* in *Poemata sacra*. The same phrase was used in his 1586 'Dilectis in Christo fratribus suis', *ibid.*, where he defended the view that the office of ecclesiastical visitation was better vested in a perpetual officer, not in an extraordinary commission. The letter was addressed to Robert Pont and Nicol Dalgleish.

240. *DCH*, IV, 337.

241. Adamson, *Recantation*, sig. B3r.

242. *JMAD*, p. 137.

243. *WM*, p. 417.

244. Adamson, *Recantation*, sig. A4v, B1r.

245. *JMAD*, pp. 153-154.

246. Adamson, *Recantation*, sig. A2r, B1v-B2r.

247. *Ibid.*, sig. A2v. John Forbes, *Certaine Records Touching the Estate of the Church of Scotland*, in William Scot, *An Apologetical Narration of the State and Government of the Kirk of Scotland since the Reformation* (Edinburgh, 1846), p. 350, blamed David Cunningham for actually tearing out the leaves.

248. *DCH*, IV, 84.

249. McCrie, pp. 480-481.
250. Patrick Collinson, *Archbishop Grindal 1519-1583* (London: Jonathan Cape, 1979), p. 242. In Scotland it was the presbyterians who cited Ambrose. *CSPS*, XII, 444.

Chapter 5

1. *JMAD*, p. 505.
2. Robert Rollock, *In epistolam Pauli apostoli ad Ephesios . . . commentarius* (Edinburgh, 1590). See reference in Row, *History*, p. 419.
3. Rollock, p. 158. See *SBD*, p. 178. On Cartwright, Donald J. McGinn, *The Admonition Controversy* (New Brunswick, N. J: Rutgers University Press, 1949), pp. 78-81.
4. Rollock, pp. 158-159. See Beza, sig. A2r.
5. Rollock, p. 160.
6. Rollock's generalisations blurred the distinction made in *SBD*, pp. 187-189 where the doctor elucidated the Christian mysteries but did not preach, celebrate the sacraments, or perform marriages. In practice the two offices were not clearly distinguished. Andrew Melville preached when he was at Glasgow and St. Andrews though his function was that of doctor. See McCrie, pp. 68, 127.
7. *SBD*, p. 191.
8. Rollock, pp. 160-161.
9. *BUK*, II, 771.
10. *APS*, III, 541. The legislation had been anticipated in 1590. *RPCf*, IV, 831.
11. *APS*, III, 542.
12. *GDSR*, p. 220; Lee, *John Maitland*, p. 249.
13. *APS*, III, 541.
14. *BUK*, III, 805.
15. *BUK*, III, 805. Emphasis added. See also III, 836, 845; *DCH*, V, 323-324.
16. *APS*, III, 541.
17. Shaw, *General Assemblies*, pp. 157-165.
18. *BUK*, I, 297.
19. *JMAD*, p. 536.
20. *DCH*, IV, 350, 485; V, 306, 600; *JMAD*, p. 358.
21. *DCH*, III, 625.
22. *E.g.*, *RPCf*, V, 326, 336.
23. *DCH*, III, 718.
24. *JMAD*, p. 253. See also *BUK*, II, 709-710; *RPCf*, IV, 40, 142.
25. *APS*, III, 296.
26. *BUK*, III, 806; see also III, 805, 837.
27. *RPCf*, V, 335; Moysie, pp. 127-128; *CSPS*, XI, 679-680, 682; XII, 352-353; McCrie, pp. 174-176.
28. *Historie and Life of King James the Sext*, p. 318.
29. *RPCf*, V, 340-341.
30. *RPCf*, V, 359.
31. *Ane declaratioun of the just and necessar causis, moving us of the nobillitie of Scotland & uthers ye kings majesteis faithful subjectis to repair to his hienes presence* ([Edinburgh], 1582), sig. AVr-AVv. Also in *DCH*, III, 651-665. See also *BUK*, II, 438; *RPCf*, III, 209-210, 237, 289, 852; IV, 264.
32. *DCH*, V, 282, 295.
33. *Historie and Life of King James the Sext*, p. 282.
34. *DCH*, V, 179.

35. *BUK* II, 781.

36. *BUK*, II, 787.

37. *BUK*, III, 882, 886.

38. *DCH*, V, 421, 423.

39. Donaldson, *Scotland: James V –James VII*, p.202.

40. *Ibid.*, p. 187.

41. *DCH*, VII, 46.

42. *DCH*, VII, 190.

43. *DCH*, VII, 48.

44. *JMAD*, pp. lvi, 13, 24, 48, 83-84, 257, *passim.*

45. *JMAD*, p. lvi. See also McCrie, pp. 329-330.

46. *JMAD*, p. 31; see also p. 38.

47. *JMAD*, p. 31.

48. *JMAD*, p. lix.

49. *JMAD*, p. 45; see also pp. 60-61.

50. *JMAD*, p. 281; see also p. 743.

51. *JMAD*, pp. 330-331.

52. *JMAD*, pp. 505-506.

53. *JMAD*, p. 506; see also p. 372.

54. *BUK*, III, 857.

55. *BUK*, III, 864-867.

56. *BUK*, III, 870.

57. *BUK*, III, 873.

58. *BUK*, III, 875.

59. *JMAD*, pp. 360-361.

60. *JMAD*, p. 354.

61. *JMAD*, p. 359.

62. *JMAD*, p. 368.

63. *DCH*, V, 557. See also Scot, *Apologetical Narration*, p. 71; *RPCf*, V, 332-333, 343-344 for evidence of state action against kirk liberties before 17 December.

64. *The questions to be resolvit at the convention of the estaits and generall assemblie, appointed to be at the burgh of Perth the last day of Februarie nixt to come* (Edinburgh, 1597), p. 1. The pamphlet is included in *BUK*, III, 903-908.

65. *Questions*, p. 2. In 1598 John Davidson told king James he was present at assembly not 'as *Imperator*, but as a Christian'. *DCH*, V, 683.

66. *JMAD*, pp. 390-391.

67. *DCH*, V, 599.

68. *JMAD*, p. 370.

69. *JMAD*, p. 391.

70. *JMAD*, p. 397.

71. *JMAD*, pp. 395-396.

72. *JMAD*, p. 401.

73. *BUK*, III, 908. Emphasis added.

74. *BUK*, III, 910; *CSPS*, XII, 476.

75. Maurice Lee, Jr., 'James VI and the Revival of Episcopacy in Scotland:1596-1600', *CH*, 43 (1974), 55.

76. *JMAD*, p. 403; see also pp. 439, 524.

77. *JMAD*, pp. 330, 523.

78. *CSPS*, XII, 483; *Analecta Scotica: Collections Illustrative of the Civil, Ecclesiastical, and Literary History of Scotland,* ed. James Maidment (Edinburgh, 1834-1837), II, 12.

79. J. Forbes, *Certaine Records*, in Scot, *Apologetical Narration*, p. 356.

80. *BUK*, III, 890; *APS*, IV, 110; *CSPS*, XII, 500.

81. *JMAD*, p. 410; see also p. 524.

82. *BUK*, III, 912.

83. *BUK*, III, 924.

84. *APS*, IV, 117.

85. *BUK*, III, 891-892; plus two other items, making a list of thirteen.

86. *BUK*, III, 895-896.

87. *JMAD*, p. 414.

88. *JMAD*, p. 420.

89. *JMAD*, p. 421.

90. *BUK*, III, 928.

91. Walter R. Foster, *The Church before the Covenants: The Church of Scotland 1596-1638* (Edinburgh: Scottish Academic Press, 1975), p. 11.

92. *BUK*, III, 928.

93. Lee, 'James VI', p. 57.

94. *JMAD*, p. 529. On the imagery of the trojan horse, see Row, *History*, p. 295.

95. *DCH*, V, 662.

96. *JMAD*, p. 434.

97. *JMAD*, p. 530.

98. *CSPS*, XIII, 136.

99. *CSPS*, XIII, 139-140.

100. *BUK*, III, 931. See also *CSPS*, XIII, 630.

101. *JMAD*, p. 530; see also p. 471; *CSPS*, XIII, 140, 719.

102. *BUK*, III, 932.

103. *APS*, IV, 130-131.

104. *BUK*, III, 931-932.

105. *JMAD*, pp. 436-437.

106. *JMAD*, p. 437. Again at the March 1598 assembly: 'Novus palliatus episcopus'. *DCH*, VI, 697.

107. John Davidson protested that this assembly was unlawful, but none were found to support him; *BUK*, III, 947.

108. *JMAD*, p. 531.

109. *BUK*, III, 946.

110. *JMAD*, p. 441.

111. *BUK*, III, 946.

112. *JMAD*, p. 534.

113. *BUK*, III, 943.

114. *BUK*, III, 945.

115. *BUK*, III, 954.

116. *JMAD*, p. 446.

117. *JMAD*, p. 448.

118. *JMAD*, p. 450.

119. *JMAD*, p. 453.

120. *JMAD*, p. 457.

121. *JMAD*, p. 460. Cupar presbytery was more tractable, accepting perpetuity and regarding the title as a matter of indifference. *DCH*, V, 724.

122. *JMAD*, p. 460.

123. *JMAD*, p. 462.

124. *JMAD*, pp. 471-485.

125. *BUK*, III, 954.

126. *BUK*, III, 956.

127. *BUK*, III, 958-959.

128. *JMAD*, p. 455; see also pp. 485, 537. Donaldson, *Scotland: James V – James VII*, p. 202.

129. *BUK*, III, 959.

130. *Fasti*, VII, 329.

131. *JMAD*, p. 489.

132. Lee, 'James VI', pp. 50-64.

133. Gordon Donaldson, 'The Scottish Church 1567-1625', in Alan G. R. Smith (ed.), *The Reign of James VI and I* (London: Macmillan, 1973), p. 50; Foster, *Church*, p. 12.

134. Lee, 'James VI', pp. 51, 63.

135. *Ibid.*, pp. 50-51

136. Row, *History*, p. 165.

137. Godfrey Davies, 'The Character of James VI and I', *Huntington Library Quarterly*, 5 (1941/2), 37-38, 63.

138. James Maidment in *Letters and State Papers during the Reign of King James the Sixth; chiefly from the manuscript Collections of Sir James Balfour of Denmyln* (Edinburgh, 1838), xiii-xv; Marc L. Schwartz, 'James I and the historians: Toward a Reconsideration', *Journal of British Studies*, 13 (1974), 114-134; Jacquelin Collins, The Scottish Episcopacy, 1596-1638 (Ph.D. thesis, Illinois, 1964), pp. 29, 45.

139. *Historie and Life of King James the Sext*, p. 283.

140. *APS*, IV, 117.

141. James professed allegiance to the Scriptures, the three creeds, and the first four general councils of the church. See his *An apologie for the oath of allegiance . . . together, with a premonition* (London, 1609), p. 50. Also in *The Political Works of James I*, ed. C. H. McIlwain (New York: Russell and Russell, Inc., 1965), where see under *A Premonition*, pp. 110-168.

142. *BUK*, II, 646.

143. The closest he came to approval of a non-episcopal polity was in 1586 when he promised to establish that kirk government which the ministers found to be 'most agreeable to the Word of God'. *BUK*, II, 646; *DCH*, IV, 548.

144. *JMAD*, p. 281.

145. William Barlow, *The summe and substance of the conference at Hamptom Court. January 14, 1604* (London, 1604), p. 20; see also p. 72. Also printed in Edward Cardwell, *A History of Conferences* (3rd. ed; Oxford, 1849), pp. 167-212.

146. James VI and I, *Apologie*, pp. 44-45.

147. *Extract*, p. 8.

148. *CSPS*, XII, 228. Of course, the hope was forlorn. The farthest extent of James's appreciation for Rome was his statement that it was 'our Mother Church'. James VI and I, *The kings majesties speech in parliament the 19. day of March 1604* (London, 1604), sig. B4v.

149. David H. Willson, *King James VI and I* (London: Jonathan Cape, 1959), pp. 29, 37-38. James Melville blamed Arran for putting the idea of absolute power in the king's head, *JMAD*, p. 119. Sir James Melville of Halhill, p. 281 described Arran as 'a scorner of religion, presompteous, ambitious, nedy and cairles of the commoun weall, and a dispyser of the nobilitie and of all honest men'. See also p. 275. On Adamson's role, see *DCH*, IV, 305; V, 489.

150. *DCH*, IV, 275-276.

151. James VI and I, *The true lawe of free monarchies: or, the reciprock and mutuall dutie betwixt a free king, and his naturall subjectes* (Edinburgh, 1598), sig. C7r. Also printed in

Political Works, pp. 53-70. See also *His majesties speech to both the houses of parliament the last day of March 1607* (London, [1607]), sig. B2v: 'Rex est Lex loquens'. Later he said that the just king observes the law, though rebellion was still inadmissible in the instance of a royal breach. *The kings majesties speech to parliament, 21 March 1609* (London, [1609]), sig. B3v-B4r. These documents are also in *Political Works*, pp. 290-305, 306-325.

152. Knox, *History*, I, 250.

153. *Ibid.*, II, 129.

154. *Ibid.*, II, 133-134. Later when Craig preached in favour of obedience he was answered by David Hume of Godscroft who upheld the right of deposition. *DCH*, IV, 466-483; Hume, *History*, pp. 413-429.

155. *APS*, III, 296.

156. Bancroft, p. 78.

157. *DCH*, V, 159.

158. George Buchanan, *The Art and Science of Government among the Scots [De jure regni apud scotos]* (trans. Duncan H. MacNeill; [Glasgow]: William MacLellan, 1964), p. 87.

159. *Ibid.*, p. 96.

160. *Ibid.*, pp. 64, 83.

161. *Ane discourse tuiching the estait present in October anno domini, 1571* (St. Andrews, 1572), sig. A5r. Aldis, no. 110; not listed in Pollard and Redgrave.

162. James VI and I, *True lawe*, sig. Blr. See also *His majesties speech in this last session of parliament* (London, 1605), sig. B2r where the biblical allusion is to Psalm 82:6; *Kings majesties speach, 1609*, sig. A4v. *His majesties speach in the Starre-Chamber, 20 June 1616* (London, [1616]), sig. Blr.

163. James VI and I, *True lawe*, sig. Clv, D7r. Sir James Melville, p. 271.

164. James VI and I, *True lawe*, sig. C5r.

165. James VI and I, *Basilicon Doron*, ed. J. Craigie (Edinburgh: Scottish Text Society, 1944-1950), II, 4. This treatise is also in *Political Works*, pp. 3-52.

166. James VI and I, *Basilicon Doron*, I, 13. *CSPS*, XIII, 373 has the number of copies as nine.

167. James VI and I, *Basilicon Doron*, I, 144.

168. *Ibid.*, I, 172.

169. *Ibid.*, I. 144-146.

170. *Ibid.*, I, 38, 50, 78.

171. *Ibid.*, I, 74. The 1603 ed. adds Denmark and Germany to the example of England. I, 75.

172. *Ibid.*, I, 74.

173. Barlow, *Summe*, pp. 80-82.

174. James VI and I, *Basilicon Doron*, I, 74.

175. *Ibid.*, I, 76. *Cf.* David Black's sermon, *supra*; also Gerald R. Cragg, *Freedom and Authority: A Study of English Thought in the early Seventeenth Century* (Philadelphia: Westminster Press, 1975), p. 91.

176. James VI and I, *Basilicon Doron*, I, 76; see also I, 140-142.

177. *Ibid.*, I, 148.

178. Barlow, *Summe*, p. 46.

179. *Ibid.*, p. 47. Emphasis in original. See also *OL*, I, 5.

180. Barlow, *Summe*, p. 79.

181. *Ibid.*, p. 36; see also p. 82.

182. James VI and I, *Basilicon Doron*, I, 78-80.

183. *Ibid.*, I, 82.

184. Barlow, *Summe*, pp. 35-36. On Jerome, see J. N. D. Kelly, *Jerome: His Life,*

Writings, and Controversies (New York: Harper and Row, 1975), pp. 147, 191, 212.

185. James VI and I, *Apologie*, pp. 43-44.

186. Godfrey Davies, p. 51.

187. *JMAD*, p. 448.

188. James VI and I, *Basilicon Doron*, I, 48. See also McGinn, p. 56. The same arguments were used in the Cartwright-Whitgift debate.

189. *CSPS*, XIII, 494. See also *DCH*, V, 744.

190. *JMAD*, p. 444. Those responsible were harassed for the indignity inflicted upon an anxious monarch. *CSPS*, XIII, 564; *RPCf*, VI, 34.

191. James VI and I, *Basilicon Doron*, I, 14-16.

192. *Ibid.*, I, 16-17. In fact, James warned his English bishops in these terms: 'If you should walke in one streete in Scotland, with such a Cappe on your head, if I were not with you, you should be stoned to death with your Cap'. Barlow, *Summe*, p. 77.

193. Willson, *King James*, p. 138.

194. James VI and I, *Basilicon Doron*, I, 72.

195. *Ibid.*, I, 116, 198.

196. Willson, *King James*, p. 197.

197. *CSPS*, IX, 166.

198. *CSPS*, XIII, 744.

199. John Strype, *The Life and Acts of John Whitgift, D.D.* (Oxford, 1822), III, 396. Also in Cardwell, p. 155.

200. Godfrey Davies, p. 51.

201. Patrick Collinson, *The Religion of Protestants: The Church in English Society 1559-1625* (Oxford: Clarendon Press, 1982), pp. 2-3.

202. Willson, *King James*, p. 199.

203. Barlow, *Summe*, sig. A4r.

204. *Ibid.*, p. 20; see also p. 62. Barlow, p. 84 called James, on account of his learning, 'a Living Library, and a walking Study'.

205. *Ibid.*, p. 84.

206. *Ibid.*, p. 83.

207. Sir John Harington, *Nugae Antiquae* (London, 1779), II, 228; Usher, *Reconstruction*, I, 328.

208. Mark Pattison, *Isaac Casaubon 1559-1614* (2nd ed; Oxford, 1892), p. 287.

209. *Ibid.*, p. 285. See also Godfrey Davies, p. 57.

210. Barlow, *Summe*, p. 4.

211. Strype, III, 401-402. Also in Cardwell, p. 160.

212. For recent literature on the Hampton Court conference and its significance, see Mark H. Curtis, 'Hampton Court Conference and its Aftermath', *History*, 46 (1961), 1-16; Patrick Collinson, *The Elizabethan Puritan Movement* (London: Jonathan Cape, 1967), pp. 448-467; Patrick McGrath, *Papists and Puritans under Elizabeth I* (New York: Walker and Co., 1967), pp. 346-353; Martin A. Simpson, 'The Hampton Court Conference, January 1604', *RSCHS*, 21 (1981), 27-41; Frederick Shriver, 'Hampton Court Re-visited: James I and the Puritans', *JEH*, 33 (1982), 48-71.

213. Cardwell, p. 161.

214. Barlow, *Summe*, p. 22.

215. *Ibid.*, p. 73. The exchange was a mirror of old arguments. McGinn, p. 28.

216. Usher, *Reconstruction*, II, 351. James could be forgiven if he was confused by the spectre of English puritanism. Usher wrote of the contradictions between it and the Scottish version: 'We left the English Puritans insisting that the Canons of 1604 must be confirmed by Parliament (that is, by the civil authority) before they could be binding upon

any one; and we find the Scotch ministers declaring warmly that the vote of the Kirk needed no confirmation by King or assembly [presumably he means the Scottish parliament for assent by the general assembly was certainly required] to bind every man in Scotland'. II, 154-155. He went on to contrast views of excommunication and the jurisdiction of civil authorities.

217. Lamont, pp. 35-36.

218. J. W. Allen, *English Political Thought 1603-1644* (London: Methuen, 1938), p. 127.

219. Collinson, *Religion of Protestants*, pp. 19-20.

220. J. P. Sommerville, 'The Royal Supremacy and Episcopacy *Jure Divino*, 1603-1640', *JEH*, 34 (1983), 549, 553. The article provides a convincing refutation of the Lamont thesis.

221. *Ibid.*, p. 553.

Chapter 6

1. Usher, *Reconstruction*, II, 161, 173.

2. George I. R. McMahon, 'The Scottish Courts of High Commission 1610-1638', *RSCHS*, 15 (1966), 193; The Scottish Episcopate 1600-1638 (Ph. D. thesis, Birmingham, 1972), p. 25.

3. *JMAD*, p. 804; *A briefe and plaine narration of proceedings at an assemblie in Glasco, 8. Jun 1610, anent the innovation of the kirk-governement* ([London?], 1610), sig. A3r-A3v; McMahon, 'Scottish Episcopate', p. 136.

4. Lee, 'James VI', p. 64.

5. Arthur H. Williamson, *Scottish National Consciousness in the Age of James VI: The Apocalypse, the Union and the Shaping of Scotland's Public Culture* (Edinburgh: John Donald Publishers, 1979), p. 11.

6. *CSPS*, I, 257.

7. Peter Lorimer, *John Knox and the Church of England* (London, 1875), p. 204. Also in Knox, *Works*, IV, 44.

8. *CSPS*, I, 218.

9. *BUK*, I, 86.

10. *WM*, p. 444.

11. *WM*, p. 490. See also *DCH*, V, 73-74.

12. *WM*, p. 495.

13. *DCH*, V, 77. See Williamson, p. 43.

14. *JMAD*, p. 480; see also pp. 449, 471.

15. Arthur H. Williamson, 'Scotland, Antichrist and the Invention of Great Britain', in John Dwyer, Roger A. Mason, and Alexander Murdoch (eds.), *New Perspectives on the Politics and Culture of Early Modern Scotland* (Edinburgh: John Donald Publishers, [1982]), p. 44.

16. *Englands wedding garment* (London, 1603), sig. A3v.

17. Miles Mosse, *Scotland's welcome* (London, 1603), sig. A3v.

18. *Ibid.*, pp. 60-61.

19. *Ibid.*, pp. 61-64.

20. John Gordon, *A panegyrique of congratulation for the concord of the realmes of Great Britaine in unitie of religion, and under one king* (London, 1603), pp. 3-4. Also published as *England and Scotlands happinesse: in being reduced to unitie of religion, under our invincible monarke king James* (London, 1604).

21. Gordon, *Panegyrique*, p. 6.

22. John Gordon, *Henotikon or a sermon of the union of Great Brittannie* (London, 1604), pp. 22-26.

23. *Ibid.*, pp. 26-29.

24. *Fasti*, VII, 344.

25. James VI and I, *Kings speech, 1604*, sig. A3v.

26. *Ibid.*, sig. B2r.

27. *Ibid.*, sig. B4v.

28. Sir Thomas Craig, *De unione regnorum Britanniae tractatus* (Edinburgh: Scottish History Society, 1909), pp. 286-287.

29. *Ibid.*, see also p. 429.

30. *Ibid.*, p. 464.

31. R[obert] P[ont], *De unione Britanniae, dialogus* (Edinburgh, 1604), sig. B1r.

32. *Ibid.*, sig. B1v.

33. *Letters and State Papers*, p. 60.

34. Confirmed by act of parliament, July 1604. *APS*, IV, 264.

35. *JMAD*, p. 555. See also Lee, *Government*, p. 34.

36. *JMAD*, p. 557.

37. *JMAD*, p. 559.

38. *JMAD*, p. 637. Some Scottish bishops stood in the shadows. *OL*, I, 60; George Grub, *An Ecclesiastical History of Scotland* (Edinburgh, 1861), II, 287.

39. *OL*, I, 365. See also *JMAD*, p. 645.

40. *JMAD*, p. 653.

41. William Barlow, *One of the foure sermons preached before the kings majestie, at Hampton Court in September last. This concerning the antiquity and superioritie of bishops* (London, 1606), sig. B1r.

42. *Ibid.*, sig. C2r.

43. *Ibid.*, sig. C3v.

44. *Ibid.*, sig. D2r.

45. *Ibid.*, sig. A2v. The presbyterians themselves had used *allotrioepiscopos* in 1599 to describe the false bishop who meddled in affairs beyond his own pastoral charge, thereby contradicting both parity and collective church government. Such men, it was noted in jest, should be numbered with murderers, thieves, and malefactors, according to the text. *JMAD*, p. 459. See also *DCH*, VI, 503. Actually the Greek term has nothing to do with episcopacy. It means 'busybody', one seeing over the affairs of others.

46. Barlow, *Sermon*, sig. A4r.

47. *JMAD*, p. 653.

48. John Buckeridge, *A sermon preached at Hampton Court before the kings majestie, on Tuesday the 23. of September, anno 1606* (London, [1606]), sig. B1v.

49. *Ibid.*, sig. C1v.

50. *Ibid.*, sig. C2r.

51. *Ibid.*, sig. C3v.

52. *Ibid.*, sig. D1r.

53. *Ibid.*, sig. D4v.

54. *Ibid.*, sig. E4r-E4v.

55. *Ibid.*, sig. D4r.

56. *JMAD*, p. 240.

57. Buckeridge, sig. E1r-E4v.

58. *JMAD*, p. 657; Collinson, *Religion of Protestants*, p. 19; Allen, pp. 130-135.

59. *JMAD*, p. 479.

60. *JMAD*, p. 657; Buckeridge, sig. B4r, C1r.

61 James VI and I, *Apologie*, p. 44.

62. Buckeridge, sig. B4r.

63. Lancelot Andrewes, *A sermon preached before the kings majestie, at Hampton Court, concerning the right and power of calling assemblies, on Sunday, the 28. of September, anno 1606* (London, 1606), p. 1.

64. *Ibid.*, p. 18.

65. *Ibid.*, pp. 17, 32-33.

66. *Ibid.*, pp. 34, 45.

67. *JMAD*, p. 663.

68. John King, *The fourth sermon preached at Hampton Court on Tuesday the last of Sept. 1606* (Oxford, 1606), p. 4.

69. *Ibid.*, p. 25.

70. *Ibid.*, pp. 28-29.

71. *Ibid.*, p. 10. This seeming anomaly of divine right within a relativistic ecclesiological context has been discussed by M. R. Sommerville, 'Richard Hooker and his Contemporaries on Episcopacy: an Elizabethan Consensus', *JEH*, 35 (1984), 177-187: 'Hooker stood at the centre of an Elizabethan episcopal consensus that held that Scripture recommended government by bishops but set forth no perpetual system of government for the Church' (p. 187).

72. King, p. 15.

73. *Ibid.*, p. 14.

74. *Ibid.*, p. 17.

75. *JMAD*, p. 667.

76. *JMAD*, pp. 693-694.

77. Stuart Barton Babbage, *Puritanism and Richard Bancroft* (London: SPCK, 1962), p. 36.

78. *JMAD*, p. 679. For the first meeting with Bancroft, see pp. 672-673.

79. *JMAD*, p. 679; see also p. 706.

80. *BUK*, I, 87.

81. *JMAD*, p. 679.

82. *JMAD*, pp. 699-700.

83. *JMAD*, pp. 682-683; James Melville, *The black bastel* ([Edinburgh], 1634), no pagination, end of book; Row, *History*, pp. 234-235.

84. NLS, Accession 7971, 2/6. See also *JMAD*, p. 748.

85. George Downame, *A sermon defending the honourable function of bishops* in *Two sermons* (London, 1608), 'To the Christian reader'. See also *JMAD*, p. 753.

86. Downame, p. 32.

87. *Ibid.*, pp. 94-95.

88. *Ibid.*, p. 99.

89. *DCH*, VI, 741. Calderwood stated that there was also a larger Latin treatise written by A. Melville. VI, 746.

90. *DCH*, VI, 742.

91. *DCH*, VI, 744.

92. *DCH*, VI, 742.

93. *JMAD*, pp. 780-781.

94. George Meriton, *A sermon preached before the generall assembly at Glascoe in the kingdome of Scotland, the tenth day of June, 1610* (London, 1611), sig. B1v.

95. *Ibid.*, sig. D1v, D2v.

96. *Ibid.*, sig. E1r.

97. *Ibid.*, sig. E2v.

98. Christopher Hampton, *A sermon preached in the cittie of Glasco in Scotland, on the tenth day of June, 1610. At the holding of a generall assembly there* (London, 1611), sig. A2v.

99. *Ibid.*, p. 3.

100. *Ibid.*, p. 22.

101. *Ibid.*, p. 19.

102. *Ibid.*, p. 29.

103. *CSPS*, X, 277, 839; *RPCf*, VI, 545.

104. *Extract*, p. 43; Moysie, p. 61.

105. *APS*, IV, 170; see also IV, 256.

106. *CSPS*, XII, 370. See also *OL*, I, 11.

107. Spottiswood, *History*, p. 456.

108. Foster, *Church*, p. 19. See also Donaldson, *Scotland: James V – James VII*, p. 202.

109. *BUK*, III, 972-973.

110. *BUK*, III, 966-967.

111. *BUK*, III, 971-972.

112. *BUK* III, 986. See also *JMAD*, p. 547.

113. *BUK*, III, 996; *Fasti*, VII, 350-351.

114. *OL*, I, 54.

115. *JMAD*, p. 567.

116. *JMAD*, p. 577.

117. *JMAD*, p. 578. See also *Informations, or a protestation, and a treatise from Scotland* ([Netherlands?], 1608), pp 11-12.

118. Foster, *Church*, pp. 27-29.

119. *APS*, IV, 281.

120. 'A protestation offered to the parliament at S. Johnstons 1. July 1606', in *Informations*, pp. 2-3. Also printed in [William Scot], *The course of conformitie* (n.p., 1622), pp. 15-19; *DCH*, VI, 485-491; *Select Biographies*, ed. W. K. Tweedie (Edinburgh, 1845-1847), I, 83-89. It may have been written by Patrick Simson. Scot, *Apologetical Narration*, p. 159; Row, *History*, p. 424.

121. *Informations*, p. 4. Emphasis in original.

122. On Dagon, see also *DCH*, V, 763.

123. *Informations*, p. 9.

124. *Ibid.*, p. 11.

125. Scot, *Course*, p. 40. Also in *DCH*, VI, 500-534. Written perhaps by James Melville. Scot, *Apologetical Narration*, pp. 159-160.

126. Scot, *Course*, p. 43.

127. Foster, *Church*, pp. 27-28.

128. *JMAD*, p. 640. See also *RPCf*, VII, 221, 423, 534; *OL*, I, 99.

129. *OL*, I, 34.

130. *OL*, I, 46.

131. *OL*, I, 24.

132. Lee, *Government*, pp. 41, 47-48.

133. Scot, *Course*, p. 44. See Williamson, p. 87.

134. Scot, *Course*, p. 45.

135. *Ibid.*, p. 46.

136. *APS*, IV, 282. The ecclesiastical estate was restored only in the persons of the bishops, the priories being erected as temporal lordships, thus the estate totalled only thirteen. McCrie, p. 250. The revocation of the act of annexation had been discussed by the parliament of 1600. *CSPS*, XIII, 714.

137. *APS*, IV, 283, 324.

138. *JMAD*, p. 654; *APS*, IV, 372-373. Melville saw the erections of temporal lordships and the restoration of bishoprics as a trade-off. *JMAD*, p. 640.

139. Scot, *Apologetical Narration*, p. 158.

140. Lee, *Government*, p. 94.

141. Donaldson, *Scotland: James V - James VII*, p. 205; Lee, *Government*, pp. 67-68; *JMAD*, p. 683.

142. *JMAD*, p. 627.

143. *BUK*, III, 1030.

144. Scot, *Course*, p. 50.

145. *BUK*, III, 1027, 1029.

146. *BUK*, III, 1030.

147. *JMAD*, p. 685; see also p. 719. *DCH*, VI, 624-627, 675.

148. *BUK*, III, 1030.

149. *E.g.*, *DCH*, VI, 650, 665-666; Lee, *Government*, p. 68.

150. *BUK*, III, 1032-1035.

151. Scot, *Course*, p. 50.

152. *BUK*, III, 1039-1040. See also *Letters and State Papers*, p. 98.

153. *DCH*, VI, 665-666. See also *JMAD*, p. 720.

154. *BUK*, III, 1059.

155. *BUK*, III, 1061-1062.

156. *RPCf*, VI, 187, 484.

157. *APS*, IV, 430-431. Diocese of Argyll was excepted. On the working of the commissariats, see Historical Manuscripts Commission, *Report on the Laing Manuscripts Preserved in the University of Edinburgh* (London: HMSO, 1914-1925), I, 114-120.

158. *The grievances given in by the ministers before the parliament holden in June 1633* (n.p., 1635), pp. 24-25. Included in *OL*, I, 187-190. See also I, 191, 197-198.

159. *BUK*, III, 1067, 1108-1113.

160. *BUK*, III, 1080-1081.

161. [John Murray], *A godly and fruitfull sermon preached at Lieth in Scotland* (n.p., 1607). The printer later confessed an error in stating the place of delivery as Leith. *Informations*, sig. *2r. The place was Edinburgh. *OL*, I, 123. See also *DCH*, VI, 690; *RPCf*, VIII, 72. According to Calderwood the sermon was published in London. *DCH*, VI, 691. *JMAD*, p. 763 has the location somewhere overseas. The publisher of *Informations* was in hiding, probably in the Netherlands where he may have fled after his press was blamed for Murray's sermon. *Informations*, sig. *1r.

162. Murray, *Sermon*, p. 18.

163. *Ibid.*, p. 23.

164. *Ibid.*, pp. 33-34.

165. *Ibid.*, pp. 55-58.

166. *OL*, I, 250-251.

167. *BUK*, III, 1083.

168. *BUK*, III, 1093. Also in *OL*, I, 248-250.

169. James VI and I, *A meditation upon I Chron. 15:25-29* in *The workes* (London, 1616), p. 84.

170. *BUK*, III, 1094; Spottiswood, *History*, p. 512.

171. *BUK*, III, 1095-1096. See also *OL*, I, 138.

172. *BUK*, III, 1097.

173. *BUK*, III, 1096-1097; I, 230-231.

174. *BUK*, III, 1098. See also *OL*, I, 139.

175. *RPCf*, VIII, 472.

176. *JMAD*, p. 770.

177. *JMAD*, p. 792.

178. *JMAD*, p. 800. The date should read 8 June.

179. *Briefe and plaine narration*, sig. A2r, A3r.

180. *Ibid.*, sig. A2r.

181. *Ibid.*, sig. A3r-A3v.

182. *Ibid.*, sig. A5r-A5v, A7v, B1r, *passim*. See *OL*, I, 425.

183. *APS*, IV, 469; for 1597, see IV, 130.

184. *APS*, IV, 470.

185. *DCH*, VII, 171-173.

186. *APS*, IV, 529. The St. Andrews chapter was reconstituted in 1607. *APS*, IV, 372. The full restoration of chapters began in 1613. *OL*, I, 312.

187. *Informations*, p. 15.

188. *Ibid.*, pp. 54-55.

189. *Ibid.*, p. 72. Emphasis in original.

190. James K. Cameron (ed.), *Letters of John Johnston c.1565-1611 and Robert Howie c.1565-c.1645* (Edinburgh: Oliver and Boyd, 1963), pp. 239-240.

191. *JMAD*, p. 804.

192. David Hume, *Patricio Symsono* (n.p., 1609), sig. A1r-A1v. This curious tract of seven pages lacks a title page, having only its recipient's name at the top of the first page. It is listed in Aldis as no. 412.3. Not in Pollard and Redgrave. On Hume's importance, see McCrie, p. 329; and Williamson, p. 174.

193. *DCH*, VI, 787.

194. Melville, *Black bastel*, [p. 2].

195. *Ibid.*, p. 4.

196. *Ibid.*, p. 8.

197. *Ibid.*, p. 10.

198. Spottiswood, *History*, p. 514. On the consecrations in London, see Thomas Hannan, 'The Scottish Consecrations in London in 1610', *Church Quarterly Review*, 71 (1911), 387-413; E. G. Selwyn, 'The First Scottish Episcopacy', *Church Quarterly Review*, 180 (1920), 198-199; Norman Sykes, *Old Priest and New Presbyter* (Cambridge: University Press, 1956), pp. 101-102. All three wrote from an episcopalian viewpoint and treated the topic for contemporary ecclesiastical reasons.

Chapter 7

1. *OL*, I, 16.

2. *Select Biographies*, I, 27.

3. On episcopal backgrounds, see *Fasti*, VII, 321-356; *DNB*; John Dowden, *The Bishops of Scotland* (Glasgow: James Maclehose and Sons, 1912); McMahon, 'Scottish Episcopate', pp. 51-74.

4. *OL*, I, 135.

5. *JMAD*, p. 461.

6. Gordon Donaldson, 'Foundations of Anglo-Scottish Union', in S. T. Bindoff *et al* (eds.), *Elizabethan Government and Society* (London: Athlone Press, 1961), p. 305. See also Donaldson, 'David Lindsay, c.1531-1613', in Robert S. Wright (ed.), *Fathers of the Kirk* (London: Oxford University Press, 1960), p.34, n.6.

7. *JMAD*, p. 469.

8. *DCH*, V, 560.

9. *DCH*, V, 738.

10. *JMAD*, p. 763.

11. *Informations*, p. 7. See also Row, *History*, p. 296.

12. *Informations*, p. 8.

13. *DCH*, VI, 491; *Select Biographies*, I, 89; Row, *History*, p. 430.

14. Row, *History*, p. 440.

15. *WM*, p. 573.

16. *JMAD*, p. 702; *DCH*, VI, 647.

17. *JMAD*, p. 674.

18. *JMAD*, p. 403; *DCH*, V, 606.

19. *DCH*, VI, 666.

20. *Briefe and plaine narration*, sig. A3v. See also Murray, *Sermon*, p. 45.

21. *Briefe and plaine narration*, sig. A5v.

22. *DCH*, VI, 272.

23. Row, *History*, p. 305. *Miscellany of the Scottish History Society*, II (Edinburgh, 1904), p. 234 prints a bowdlerised version.

24. Scot, *Apologetical Narration*, p. 239.

25. *DCH*, VI, 730.

26. *JMAD*, pp. 736-337.

27. *WM*, p. 574.

28. *OL*, I, 347.

29. *DCH*, VII, 180. See also William Cowper, *The bishop of Galloway his dikaiologie: contayning a defence of his apologie* (London, 1614), p. 175.

30. GUL, Ms. General 1212, Wodrow's Biographical Collections, vol. 18, Life of Cowper, p. 11 [Hereafter, 'Life of Cowper']. Also in NLS, Wodrow Mss., Quarto LXXXIV, no. 18.

31. William Cowper, *The bishop of Galloway his apologie* ([London? 1613]), sig. A2r.

32. 'Life of Cowper', p. 11; NLS, Wodrow Mss., Quarto LXXVI, f. 14r.

33. *OL*, I, 302.

34. Cowper, *Apologie*, sig. A2r. See also Andrew Boyd in *OL*, I, 135.

35. Cowper, *Dikaiologie*, p. 108.

36. *Ibid.*, p. 101.

37. *JMAD*, p. 638. See also [David Calderwood], *Perth assembly* (n.p., 1619), p. 7.

38. Cowper, *Dikaiologie*, p. 105.

39. 'Life of Cowper', p. 11.

40. Cowper, *Dikaiologie*, p. 106.

41. [David Calderwood], *A re-examination of the five articles enacted at Perth, anno 1618* (n.p., 1636), [p. 239] (see end of work).

42. Cowper, *Dikaiologie*, p. 106.

43. *Grievances*, pp. 21-22; *DCH*, VI, 600-601; *Miscellany of the Scottish History Society*, II, 234-235.

44. 'Life of Cowper', p. 6. Also in NLS, Wodrow Mss., Folio XLII, no. 80.

45. 'Life of Cowper', p. 11; Row, *History*, p. 255. The letter in 'Life of Cowper' was by a John Michaelson, probably the same man who was soon to be an outspoken defender of the Five Articles.

46. *Spottiswood Miscellany* (Edinburgh, 1844-1845), II, 283.

47. *DCH*, VII, 122; Cowper, *Dikaiologie*, p. 29.

48. *DCH*, VI, 749; VII, 119-122.

49. *DCH*, VII, 147.

50. *DCH*, VI, 750. Emphasis in original.

51. Cowper, *Dikaiologie,* p. 13.

52. *Ibid.,* p. 89; sig. A3r-A3v.

53. Cowper, *Apologie,* sig. A2v.

54. Cowper, *Dikaiologie,* p. 41.

55. Cowper, *Apologie,* sig. A2v: *Dikaiologie,* p. 36.

56. Cowper, *Apologie,* sig. A2r-A2v.

57. Cowper, *Dikaiologie,* p. 117.

58. *OL,* I, 235.

59. *OL,* I, 139. J. B. Craven, *Records of the Dioceses of Argyll and the Isles 1560-1860* (Kirkwall: William Peace and Son, 1907), pp. 63-67 includes a manuscript (NLS, Wodrow Mss., Folio XXVII, no. 5) entitled, 'An Humble Advice to His Majesty for making Bishops, meerly agreeing to the Apostolick rule and for Continuing of them so, To the Honour of God, Good of the Kirk, avoiding of corruptions, and Joy and Contentment of his Majestie'. There is neither date nor author given, nor is it included among Boyd's papers though on account of internal evidence Craven suggests it may have originated with the bishop. In any event, the document calls for more bishops and who would be resident teachers (of particular flocks), moderate the local presbytery, rule with a council of ten or twelve ministers of high quality, visit annually, conduct synods twice in a year, and be answerable to (preferably) annual assemblies.

60. Foster, *Church,* p. 110; see also p. 106 and Donaldson, *Scotland: James V - James VII,* p. 207.

61. Foster, *Church,* pp. 53-56, 105. *E.g., RPCs,* II, 242; VIII, 394.

62. Foster, *Church,* p. 53. W.G. Sinclair Snow, *The Times, Life, and Thought of Patrick Forbes, Bishop of Aberdeen 1618-1635* (London: SPCK, 1952), pp. 155-156, has attempted to demonstrate that after 1610 'the Bishops made no attempt to impose episcopal ordination, and the presbyteral form remained in common use'. To this effect he cites several examples, but none of the three most pertinent supports his case. George Gillespie's ordination by divine right action of the presbytery was dated 26 April 1638 – two months following the signing of the National Covenant. Similarly, Robert Ker was ordained 11 April 1638. As for William Forbes, the future bishop of Edinburgh, the action taken in his behalf on 29 October 1616 was that of admission, not ordination, upon his transfer to Aberdeen from the charge at Monymusk. See *The Presbytrie Booke of Kirkcaldie,* ed. William Stevenson (Kirkcaldy, 1900), pp. 129-130; Sir Archibald Johnston of Wariston, *Diary 1632-1639* (Edinburgh: Scottish History Society, 1911), p. 338; *Selections from the Records of the Kirk Session, Presbytery, and Synod of Aberdeen,* ed. John Stuart (Aberdeen, 1846), p. 85. In 1611 several ministers were confined for the offence of admitting a minister without the 'consent and presence' of the bishop. *OL,* I, 274. See also McMahon, 'Scottish Episcopate', p. 144; Foster, *Church,* pp. 65, 151-153.

63. Foster, *Church,* p. 109.

64. *OL,* I, 245. See also Lee, *Government,* pp. 99-100.

65. Cowper, *Dikaiologie,* p. 39.

66. Cowper, *Apologie,* sig. A3v; *Dikaiologie,* pp. 82-83.

67. Cowper, *Dikaiologie,* p. 77.

68. *Ibid.,* p. 90.

69. *JMAD,* p. 801.

70. Cowper, *Dikaiologie,* p. 149.

71. *Ibid.,* p. 129.

72. *Ibid.,* p. 142; *Apologie,* sig. A2v.

73. *A trewe description of the nobill race of the Stewards* (Amsterdam, 1603), no pagination.

74. *Briefe and plaine narration,* sig. A6v. Emphasis added.

75. *DCH*, IV, 606.

76. *Bannatyne Miscellany*, I, 152.

77 Cowper, *Apologie*, sig. A2r.

78. *Ibid.*, sig. A2v, A3v.

79. Cowper, *Dikaiologie*, p. 87.

80. *Ibid.*, p. 81.

81. Williamson, p. 34.

82. *DCH*, VI, 669-670.

83. *JMAD*, p. 800.

84. [John Spottiswood], *A true relation of the proceedings against John Ogilvie, a Jesuit* (Edinburgh, 1615), p. 27.

85. David Lindsay, *De potestate principis aphorismi* (Edinburgh, 1617). Also in [John Adamson], *The muses welcome* (Edinburgh, 1618), pp. 203-207. There is in the BL, Royal 17A XXXVI, a manuscript entitled 'Ane glasse for Christiane subjectis'. Very anti-Catholic in tone, this treatise hinged upon II Peter 2:13 and defended the government of monarchs who, whether good or evil, should be obeyed and under no circumstance rebelled against. The good king was a paternal figure and as God's anointed held power over the kirk, though this was only hinted at by the author: 'Sall Christianitie be ane hinderance to the libertie to the autoritie to the honour of civill government in the person of a Christiane prince?' (f. 19r)

The author gave his name as 'David Lindesay' and the catalogue assumes the later bishop of Brechin, c.1617. However much this individual could have stated such sentiments, I believe the identification to be incorrect. The sole autobiographical note in the work describes Lindsay as having been minister at St. Andrews, where the future bishop of Brechin never held a charge. But David Lindsay, son of the bishop of Ross, was minister there 1597-1606 (*Fasti*, I, 161; V, 238). He was the author of two devotional works published in 1622 and 1625. It seems most likely that he was the author of the manuscript.

86. *BUK*, III, 1139.

87. Lee, *Government*, pp. 81-82.

88. *DCH*, VII, 148.

89. *WM*, p. 583.

90. *DCH*, VI, 684-685.

91. Cowper, *Dikaiologie*, p. 44.

92. Lee, *Government*, pp. 96, 99-100.

93. *Select Biographies*, I, 125.

94. Row, *History*, p. 204.

95. *RPCf*, VII, 532; see also p. 411; *OL*, I, 103-104. He refused to ride in pomp at the 1606 parliament. *DCH*, VI, 493-494.

96. *Select Biographies*, I, 141. J. M. Barkley, 'Some Scottish Bishops and Ministers in the Irish Church, 1605-35', in Shaw (ed.), *Reformation and Revolution*, p. 148.

97. Row, *History*, pp. 326-327.

98. *OL*, I, 406.

99. *OL*, I, 26; see also p. 87.

100. *BUK*, III, 1092.

101. *OL*, I, 48.

102. *RPCf*, VII, 371.

103. James VI and I, *Speech, 1604*, sig. B4r.

104. See Peter Hay, *An advertisement to the subjects of Scotland* (Aberdeen, 1627), p. 124. The work was to be reviewed by the bishops and published if approved. Sir James Balfour, *The Historical Works* (Edinburgh, 1824-1825), II, 145.

105. James B. Leslie, *Raphoe Clergy and Parishes* (Enniskillen: privately published, 1940), p. 5.

106. *RPCf*, IX, 570. See also *APS*, IV, 281-282.

107. *OL*, I, 241.

108. *RPCf*, X, 319.

109. Rait, pp. 368-371; McMahon, 'Scottish Episcopate', pp. 103-108; *DCH*, VII, 250; *State Papers, and Miscellaneous Correspondence of Thomas, Earl of Melros* (Edinburgh, 1837), II, 416.

110. *Grievances*, pp. 27-28. Also in *OL*, I, 295.

111. *DCH*, V, 162.

112. *RPCf*, VII, 105.

113. *JMAD*, p. 61; *DCH*, V, 283; VI, 104.

114. *JMAD*, p. 198.

115. *JMAD*, p. 410; *RPCf*, V, 368.

116. *JMAD*, p. 461.

117. *JMAD*, p. 419.

118. *DCH*, V, 668. See also McCrie, p. 289.

119. *DCH*, V, 694.

120. Scot, *Apologetical Narration*, p. 101; Foster, *Church*, p. 15.

121. *WM*, p. 588.

122. *DCH*, VII, 2; Row, *History*, pp. 293-294.

123. *JMAD*, p. 763.

124. *DCH*, VII, 50. On Gledstanes, see *JMAD*, p. 644; on Spottiswood, see Row, *History*, pp. 298-299.

125. *WM*, p. 586.

126. Cowper, *Dikaiologie*, p. 171.

127. *OL*, I, 346.

128. Cowper, *Apologie*, sig. A3r.

129. Cowper, *Dikaiologie*, p. 23. Murray, *Sermon*, p. 54, termed covetousness and ambition 'the two banes of the church'.

130. Cowper, *Dikaiologie*, p. 180.

131. Cowper, *Apologie*, sig. A4r; *Dikaiologie*, p. 56.

132. Cowper, *Dikaiologie*, p. 56. *The life and death of the reverend father and faithfull servant of God, Mr William Cowper, bishop of Galloway* (London, 1619), sig. B4r. But even Cowper's life as pastor was vexed, sig. B3r-B3v. Also in *The workes* (London, 1603), pp. 1-10.

133. Cowper, *Dikaiologie*, p. 32.

134. *Ibid.*, p. 180. See also *OL*, I, 346.

135. Cowper, *Life and death*, sig. B2v.

136. *OL*, II, 426.

137. William Cowper, *Phosphoros or a most heavenly and fruitfull sermon, preached the sixt of August. 1615* (London, 1616), pp. 52-53. Also in *Workes*, pp. 797-809.

138. Cowper, *Life and death*, sig. B4v.

139. *OL*, II, 426.

140. *OL*, I, 133.

141. *OL*, I, 303.

142. *OL*, II, 422.

143. *JMAD*, p. 18.

144. *OL*, I, 227-228; *Miscellany of the Spalding Club*, I, 153-154.

145. Snow, pp. 47-49.

146. Patrick Forbes, *A defence of the lawful calling of the ministers of reformed churches, against the cavillations of Romanists* (Middelburg, 1614), pp. 5-6.

147. *OL*, II, 545-546.

148. *OL*, II, 547.

149. *OL*, II, 546.

150. *OL*, II, 518. See also the comments by [Gilbert Burnet], *The life of William Bedell, D.D., bishop of Kilmore in Ireland* (London, 1685), sig. a2r-a3r; also the laudatory contributions to *Funerals of right reverend father in God Patrick Forbes of Corse, bishop of Aberdene* (Aberdeen, 1635; reprinted Edinburgh, 1845).

151. Snow, pp. 63-64.

152. Scot, *Apologetical Narration*, p. 254.

153. Row, *History*, p. 260, similarly accused Adam Bellenden.

154. *OL*, II, 547.

155. *OL*, II, 544; also p. 551.

156. *Fasti*, II, 125.

157. *OL*, II, 644. Allegations of Spottiswood's political ambition were made. Historical Manuscripts Commission, *Report on the Manuscripts of the Earl of Mar and Kellie* (London: HMSO, 1904), p. 49. See his denial in *OL*, II, 690. Also, Allen B. Birchler, 'Archbishop John Spottiswoode: Chancellor of Scotland, 1635-1638', *CH*, 39 (1970), 318.

158. David Lindsay, *A true narration of all the passages of the proceedings in the generall assembly of the church of Scotland, holden at Perth the 25. of August, anno dom. 1618* (London, 1621), pp. 108-109.

159. *JMAD*, p. 781.

160. Lee, *Government*, p. 64; John Hill Burton, *The History of Scotland* (2nd ed; Edinburgh, 1873), V, 445-461.

161. *OL*, 1, 324.

162. *OL*, I, 325-326. For a presbyterian view, see *DCH*, VII, 203.

163. *OL*, I, 304.

164. *OL*, I, 41.

165. *OL*, I, 131.

166. *OL*, I, 418-419.

167. *OL*, II, 644.

168. *OL*, II, 707-708, 710-711.

169. *Correspondence of Sir Robert Kerr, first Earl of Ancrum and his son William, third Earl of Lothian* (Edinburgh, 1875), I, 30. See also *RPCf*, XIII, 125, 151.

170. Balfour, II, 144; *The Earl of Stirling's Register of Royal Letters*, ed. Charles Rogers (Edinburgh, 1885), II, 793; *RPCs*, III, 248; *Fasti*, II, 125; *Correspondence of Sir Robert Kerr*, I, 61.

171. Foster, *Church*, pp. 45-47; *DCH*, VI, 626-627; VII, 282-283, 349; *BUK*, II, 1027.

172. *OL*, I, 270, 436-438.

173. *OL*, II, 510.

174. *OL*, II, 558.

175. *OL*, II, 560. But he was successful in his suit, p. 819.

176. Foster, *Church*, pp. 43-44.

177. Donaldson, 'Leighton's Predecessors', pp. 12-13.

178. Foster, *Church*, 45, 167-169.

179. *OL*, I, 47. This petition may have resulted from Dury's latter-day support for episcopacy. See Chapter 8.

180. *OL*, I, 137.

181. *OL*, I, 350.

182. *OL*, I, 300.

183. *OL*, I, 101.

184. *Grievances*, p. 24. Also in *OL*, I, 187-190.

185. William Cowper, *Two sermons* (London, 1618), p. 21. Also in *Workes*, pp. 777-791.

186. *BUK*, III, 1131.

187. Cowper, *Two sermons*, p. 41.

188. *OL*, II, 717-718. Charles Rogers, *History of the Chapel Royal of Scotland* (Edinburgh, 1882), p. cxxx. But in 1616 Cowper had written to James of his intention to restore the rents to support musicians in the Chapel Royal and pastors for impropriated kirks. *OL*, II, 466.

189. *DCH*, VII, 350.

190. Foster, *Church*, pp. 156-172. Also in Shaw (ed.), *Reformation and Revolution*, pp. 124-140.

191. *OL*, I, 413. See also *RPCf*, VIII, 601.

192. *OL*, I, 264.

193. James Cooper, 'Archbishop Spottiswood 1565-1639', *Transactions of the Glasgow Archaeological Society*, n.s., 7 (1924), 94.

194. *Ibid.*, pp. 96, 98.

195. *Ibid.*, p. 99.

196. *Ibid.*, p. 94.

197. *Ibid.*, p. 96. See also the complaint in William Struther, *Scotlands warning, or a treatise of fasting* (Edinburgh, 1628), pp. 26-29.

198. Spottiswood, *History*, p. 316.

199. *Ibid.*, p. 385.

200. *Ibid.*, p. 523. See a similar accusation in Wodrow, *Collections*, I, 316-317.

201. *DCH*, VII, 164.

202. *RPCs*, I, cxlv.

203. *Select Biographies*, I, 103.

204. *Ibid.*, I, 115.

205. *OL*, I, 91; II, 524, 586.

206. John Spottiswood, *Refutatio libelli de regimine ecclesiae scoticanae* (London, 1620), p. 88.

207. McMahon, 'Scottish Episcopate', pp. 143-145.

208. *DCH*, VII, 53.

209. *OL*, I, 44.

210. *OL*, I, 172.

211. *Grievances*, p. 25. Also in *OL*, I, 187-190.

212. *Grievances*, p. 24.

213. *OL*, I, 170-171; *JMAD*, p. 803.

214. *OL*, II, 652. See Blyth's letter to a friend, pp. 639-640.

215. *RPCf*, IX, 624, 627.

216. *RPCf*, IX, 550.

217. *OL*, I, 453.

218. William Row, *The Life of Mr. Robert Blair, Minister of St. Andrews* (Edinburgh, 1848), p. 137.

219. *JMAD*, p. 744.

220. *Informations*, p. 16.

221. *Briefe and plaine narration*, sig. A3r-A3v.

222. *WM*, p. 581.

223. *WM*, p. 582.

224. *DCH*, VI, 730.

225. *DCH*, VII, 146.

226. *DCH*, VII, 150.

227. *DCH*, VII, 154.

228. Spottiswood, *History*, p. 514.

229. Lindsay, *True narration*, p. 44. The sermon is also in *Spottiswood Miscellany*, I, 63-88.

230. Lindsay, *True narration*, p. 40. The archbishop elsewhere wrote that the bishops requested that the king should not exclude ministers from the making of ecclesiastical laws. Spottiswood, *History*, p. 531.

231. *Ibid.*, p. 45. See also *OL*, II, 475-478; Grub, II, 304.

232. *RPCs*, I, 650.

233. *Miscellany of the Spalding Club* I, 17.

234. John Rushworth, *Historical Collections. Second Part* (London, 1680), p. 182. McMahon, 'Scottish Episcopate', p. 237, doubts the story's veracity.

235. 'Life of Cowper', p. 9.

236. Williamson, p. 35.

237. *OL*, II, 496-499. James explained that withdrawal of the order was for practical reasons.

238. *OL*, II, 500. Also in *Select Biographies*, I, 95; and *DCH*, VII, 244-245.

239. Row, *History*, p. 303.

240. *DCH*, VII, 197.

241. Spottiswood, *History*, p. 523.

242. Row, *History*, p. 259.

243. Scot, *Apologetical Narration*, p. 238. See also *DCH*, VII, 342.

244. Spottiswood, *History*, p. 540.

245. Lindsay, *True narration*, p. 69.

246. *Briefe and plaine narration*, sig. B3r.

247. *DCH*, VI, 630; Scot, *Apologetical Narration*, p. 196; Row, *History*, p. 242.

248. Row, *History*, p. 243; NLS, Wodrow Mss., Folio XLIII, no. 70. I have not discovered any reference of Lindsay's to these lines.

249. Lindsay, *True narration*, p. 100.

250. Row, *History*, pp. 303-304.

251. *State Papers, Melros*, I, 195-196.

252. *Analecta Scotica*, II, 65. See also Lee, *Government*, pp. 147-148.

Chapter 8

1. Cowper, *Apologie*, sig. A2r; *Dikaiologie*, p. 129.

2. Cowper, *Dikaiologie*, pp. 76, 162.

3. *Ibid.*, p. 80.

4. *Ibid.*, p. 131.

5. *Ibid.*, p. 69.

6. *Ibid.*, pp. 133-134.

7. Cowper, *Apologie*, sig. A2r; *Dikaiologie*, p. 134.

8. Cowper, *Dikaiologie*, p. 15; see also pp. 90, 135.

9. *Ibid.*, p. 136.

10. *Ibid.*, p. 175.

11. *DCH*, IV, 305; see also pp. 289, 331, 338.

12. [David Calderwood], *De regimine ecclesiae scoticanae brevis relatio* (n.p., 1618), p. 2. This work also appears in his *Altare Damascenum* (n.p., 1623) as an appendix.

13. Calderwood, *De regimine*, p. 3.

14. *Ibid.*, p. 4.

15. *Ibid.*, p. 6.

16. *Ibid.*, p. 7.

17. *Ibid.*, p. 11.

18. *Ibid.*, p. 14.

19. *Ibid.*, pp. 27 28.

20. Spottiswood, *Refutatio*, sig. A2r-A6r. Also printed in *Spottiswood Miscellany*, I, 33-62.

21. Spottiswood, *Refutatio*, pp. 4-5, 23.

22. *Ibid.*, pp. 7, 31.

23. *Ibid.*, p. 9.

24. *Ibid.*, p. 69.

25. *WM*, p. 585.

26. Spottiswood, *Refutatio*, pp. 84-85.

27. *Ibid.*, pp. 89-90. John Spottiswood provided a list of worthies who disliked presbytery, pp. 43-45. This may be compared with a list offered by Alexander Hume in *WM*, p. 583 of those whom he thought would have been distressed by the state the kirk had fallen into by 1609. See also *DCH*, VI, 510-511.

28. Appended to *Altare Damascenum*.

29. *The first and second booke of discipline* ([Amsterdam], 1621), sig. A2r.

30. *Ibid.*, sig. A3r.

31. *Ibid.*

32. *Ibid.*, sig. A3v.

33. *Ibid.*, sig. A4v.

34. *Ibid.*, sig. A4r.

35. *Ibid.*, sig. A4v-B1r.

36. *Ibid.*, sig. B3r-B3v. *Cf.* Cowper, *Apologie*, sig. A2v; and Spottiswood, *Refutatio*, pp. 5-6.

37. *The first and second booke of discipline*, sig. B4v.

38. Lindsay, *True narration*, pp. 14-15, second series of arabic numbers.

39. Spottiswood, *History*, p. 500. McCrie, p. 128, n.3, calls attention to the fact that 'John Spotswood' was one of those who denied their assent to the reversal of Adamson's excommunication in 1586. See *DCH*, IV, 583. McCrie assumes here the future archbishop. But if this were so, he was at that time a callow minister aged twenty-one. However, there was another minister of the same name and there is no way of determining which one was the signatory. *Fasti*, I, 10, 356.

40. *DCH*, VI, 675; see also pp. 678-679.

41. *WM*, pp. 582-583.

42. *OL*, II, 699. For the picturesque phrase in the first citation, *cf. DCH*, V, 659.

43. Cowper, *Dikaiologie*, p. 43.

44. McCrie, p. 76.

45. Adamson, *Poemata sacra*, sig. B4v.

46. Adamson, *De sacro*, 'Lectori pio'. See also Spottiswood, *History*, p. 385.

47. Adamson, *De sacro*, p. 5.

48. McCrie, p. 448, n.11, suggests either David Calderwood or John Adamson as possible editors of *Viri . . . musae*.

49. *Viri . . . musae*, p. 48.

50. *Ibid.*, pp. 45-46.

51. Spottiswood, *Refutatio*, pp. 61-62.

52. Spottiswood, *History*, p. 385.

53. J. Forbes, *Certaine Records*, in Scot, *Apologetical Narration*, p. 345.

54. *Ibid.*, p. 349.

55. *Ibid.*, p. 398.

56. This work has been attributed to Calderwood. See Patrick Scot, *Vox vera* (London, 1625), p. 10. But for William Scot's authorship, see *Apologetical Narration*, pp. vi-vii. The phrase, 'The course of Conformity', appears in *Apologetical Narration*, p. 313.

57. Scot, *Course*, sig. A4r.

58. *Ibid*, p.9.

59. *Ibid*, p. 58.

60. Scot, *Apologetical Narration*, p. 123. He wrote after Lindsay's translation to Edinburgh (1634), p. 196; before Sydserff's translation to Galloway (1635); before Bellenden's translation to Aberdeen (1635).

61. *Ibid.*, p. 126. Daniel Wallace died in 1631. Unless Scot was unaware of this fact, the passage was probably written before that.

62. *Ibid.*, p. 3.

63. *Ibid.*, p. 5.

64. *Ibid.*, pp. 6-9.

65. *Ibid.*, p. 10.

66. *Ibid.*, p. 11.

67. *Ibid.*, pp. 25-26, 32.

68. *Ibid.*, p. 39.

69. *Ibid.*, pp. 49, 60.

70. *Ibid.*, p. 63.

71. *Ibid.*, pp. 96, 164, 218, 221.

72. *Ibid.*, p. 240.

73. Row, *History*, p. 3.

74. *Ibid.*, p. xiv.

75. *Ibid.*, pp. 78-79, 194, 258, 273, 281.

76. *Ibid.*, p. 304.

77. *Ibid.*, pp. 260-261.

78. *Ibid.*, p. 233.

79. *Ibid.*, p. 12.

80. *Ibid.*

81. *Ibid.*, p. 18.

82. *Ibid.*, p. 22.

83. *Ibid.*, p. 52.

84. *Ibid.*, p. 131.

85. *Ibid.*, p. 187.

86. *Ibid.*, p. 209.

87. *Ibid.*, p. 226.

88. *Ibid.*, p. 241.

89. *Ibid.*, pp. 411-414.

90. *DCH*, VIII, ix-x.

91. *DCH*, VIII, 129.

92. *DCH*, VIII, x.

93. *DCH*, I, 128.

94. *DCH*, VII, 163.

95. *DCH*, VII, 595, 630; also p. 243.

96. *DCH*, VII, 633-638.
97. *DCH*, VII, 576.
98. *DCH*, VII, 765; see also p. 164.
99. *DCH*, VII, 548, 585.
100. *DCH*, VII, 513. Cf. Scot, *Course*, pp. 101-102.
101. *DCH*, I, 47.
102. *DCH*, I, 55.
103. See Chapter 9.
104. David Calderwood, *The true history of the church of Scotland* ([Rotterdam], 1678), p. 25.
105. *DCH*, II, 50.
106. *DCH*, VIII, 161.
107. *DCH*, II, 303, 394.
108. *DCH*, VII, 108.
109. *Fasti*, VII, 436-437.
110. *DCH*, III, 515; see also IV, 398.
111. Dickson and Edmond, p. 510. Confirmed in a letter to the author, NLS, reference TAFC/DB, 12 December 1983.
112. *DCH*, IV, 204.
113. *DCH*, IV, 208.
114. The forgery is printed as an appendix. *DCH*, IV, 697-732.
115. *DCH*, V, 154. I do not know where Adamson confessed this.
116. *DCH*, VII, 577.
117. *DCH*, V, 361.
118. *DCH*, VII, 626. See also [David Calderwood], *The speach of the kirk of Scotland to her beloved children* (n.p. 1620), p. 40.
119. *DCH*, VII, 395.
120. But see the remarks attributed to him by Calderwood in *DCH*, VII, 425-426.
121. Spottiswood, *History*, 'To the King'.
122. Spottiswood, *Refutatio*, p. 2.
123. Maurice Lee, Jr., 'Archbishop Spottiswood as Historian', *Journal of British Studies*, 13 (1973/4), p. 141. See also Foster, *Church*, p. 58; A. Ian Dunlop, 'John Spottiswood, 1565-1639', in Wright (ed.), p. 60; Spottiswood, *History*, I, cxxxiii-cxxxiv; Mathieson, I, 325.
124. Spottiswood, *History*, p. 546.
125. *Ibid.*, p. 347, concerning Adamson in 1586. On the deception involved with the caveats, p. 453. See also Lindsay, *True narration*, pp. 4-5, where the bishop of Brechin expressed his wonder that any answer should have been given to the prejudiced. The Golden Act was passed 'in the most wary tearms that could be devised'. Spottiswood, *History*, p. 388.
126. *Ibid.*, p. 60.
127. *Ibid.*, p. 137.
128. *Ibid.*, pp. 85, 146, 267. See Calderwood's rejoinder. *DCH*, III, 277.
129. Spottiswood, *History*, p. 174.
130. *Ibid.*, p. 258.
131. *Ibid.*, p. 266.
132. *Ibid.*, p. 242.
133. *Ibid.*, p. 198.
134. *Ibid.*, p. 260.
135. *BUK*, I, 209.

136. Duncan Shaw, 'The Inauguration of Ministers in Scotland: 1560-1620', *RSCHS*, 16 (1969), 35-37.

137. *DCH*, VII, 423.

138. Spottiswood, *History*, p. 152.

139. Laing in Knox, *Works*, II, 587.

140. Fleming, 'Scotland's Supplication', p. 317.

141. *FBD*, p. 116. See Spottiswood, *History*, p. 158.

142. Spottiswood, *History*, pp. 95, 442.

143. *FBD*, pp. 122-123; Spottiswood, *History*, p. 159.

144. Spottiswood, *History*, p. 160; *FBD*, pp. 126-127.

145. Complaints were also alleged by Fleming against Spottiswood's recording of the acts of the assembly held at Glasgow in 1610. 'Scotland's Supplication', p. 346; Spottiswood, *History*, pp. 514-515. The deletions noted by Fleming suggest that Spottiswood was reading back the acts of parliament of 1612 to 1610. The error would be of gravest importance to a presbyterian. Supporters of the archbishop would see the 1612 acts as the consummation of the consultations of 1610, taking precedence over them. But once again, the historical reliability of the *History* is shaken.

146. Calderwood, *True history*, p. 27. See also Row, *History*, p. 417.

147. *JMAD*, p. 639. See also Scot, *Course*, p. 32; and *DCH*, VII, 54.

148. *DNB;* James B. Leslie, *Clogher Clergy and Parishes* (Enniskillen: privately published, 1929), pp. 10-11.

149. James Spottiswood, *Concio . . . ad clerum . . . pro gradu doctoratus* (Edinburgh, 1616), p. 30. Also in *Spottiswood Miscellany*, I, 92 (excerpted).

150. Spottiswood, *History*, p. 344. In 1617 the archbishop and Archibald Simson disputed the superintendent's opinions before the high commission. *OL*, II, 529.

151. Spottiswood, *History*, p. 386.

152. *Ibid.*, pp. 275, 289. See also *DCH*, VII, 285; Scot, *Apologetical Narration*, p. 285.

153. Spottiswood, *History*, p. 504.

154. *Ibid.*, p. 457.

155. *Ibid.*, p. 303.

Chapter 9

1. Scot, *Course*, p. 82.

2. *A declaration of the just causes of his majesties proceeding against those ministers, who are now lying in prison, attainted of high treason* (London, 1606), p. 28. Also in *DCH*, VI, 419-437.

3. *RPCf*, VII, 127.

4. James VI and I, *Speach in the Starre-Chamber*, sig. C2v.

5. See, *e.g.*, Joseph Hall, bishop of Exeter, to William Struther, minister at Edinburgh, in Joseph Hall, *The Works* (Oxford, 1863), IX, 120.

6 Lee, *Government*, p. 158.

7. *OL*, II, 445-446.

8. G. W. Sprott (ed.), *Scottish Liturgies of the Reign of James VI* (Edinburgh: William Blackwood and Sons, 1901); William McMillan, *The Worship of the Scottish Reformed Church, 1550-1638* (London: James Clarke, 1931); Gordon Donaldson, *The Making of the Scottish Prayer Book of 1637* (Edinburgh: University Press, 1954); William Maxwell, *A History of Worship in the Church of Scotland* (London: Oxford University Press, 1955); George B. Burnet, *The Holy Communion in the Reformed Church of Scotland, 1560-1960*

(Edinburgh: Oliver and Boyd, 1960); Ian B. Cowan, 'The Five Articles of Perth', in Shaw (ed.), *Reformation and Revolution*, pp. 160-177; Lee, *Government*.

9. *OL*, I, 295.

10. *OL*, II, 512.

11. *OL*, II, 513.

12. *OL*, II, 521-523; *State Papers, Melros*, II, 623-625.

13. *OL*, II, 524.

14. *DCH*, VII, 254.

15. *DCH*, VII, 256.

16. Lee, *Government*, p. 186.

17. *DCH*, VII, 272.

18. *OL*, II, 548.

19. *OL*, II, 552.

20. Lindsay, *True narration*, p. 49.

21. *Ibid.*, p. 50.

22. Calderwood, *Perth assembly*, p. 2; *OL*, II, 573-574; *Miscellany of the Spalding Club*, II, 159-160; *State Papers, Melros*, II, 627.

23. Lindsay, *True narration*, p. 21. The sermon is also in *Spottiswood Miscellany*, I, 63-88.

24. Lindsay, *True narration*, p. 22.

25. *Ibid.*, p. 39.

26. *Ibid.*, p. 41.

27. *DCH*, VII, 531; Lindsay, *True narration*, sig. B4r.

28. *DCH*, VII, 421.

29. Calderwood, *Perth assembly*, sig. A2r.

30. *Ibid.*, pp. 11-18.

31. *Ibid.*, p. 34.

32. [David Calderwood], *A solution of Dr. Resolutus, his resolutions for kneeling* (n.p., 1619), p. 28.

33. Calderwood, *Perth assembly*, p. 57; [David Calderwood], *A defence of our arguments against kneeling* (n.p., 1620), p. 53.

34. Calderwood, *Perth assembly*, p. 67.

35. Cowper, *Life and death*, sig. C4r.

36. Calderwood, *Perth assembly*, pp. 87, 92.

37. *Ibid.*, pp. 98-100.

38. *DCH*, VII, 396.

39. Calderwood, *Defence*, sig. A2v.

40. Cowper, *Life and death*, sig. D2r.

41. *Ibid.*, sig. D2v.

42. *DCH*, VII, 247.

43. Cowper, *Life and death*, sig. D3r.

44. Calderwood, *Perth assembly*, p. 9; also, *Solution*, sig. A2r; and Scot, *Course*, p. 153.

45. Lindsay, *True narration*, p. 70.

46. David Lindsay, *The reasons of a pastors resolution touching the communion* (London, 1619), sig. A4r.

47. Calderwood, *Solution*, sig. A2r.

48. Cowper, *Life and death*, sig. D2r.

49. Lindsay, *Reasons*, p. 182.

50. [John Murray], *A dialogue betwixt Cosmophilus and Theophilus anent the urging of new ceremonies upon the kirke of Scotland* (n.p., 1620), p. 29. On the authorship of this work often ascribed to Calderwood, see Row, *History*, p. 255.

51. Scot, *Course*, sig. A3v. See also *DCH*, VII, 531.

52. Calderwood, *Speach*, pp. 70, 115-125.

53. *Ibid.*, p. 53.

54. [David Calderwood], *The altar of Damascus or the patern of the English Hierarchie, and church-policie obtruded upon the church of Scotland* (n.p., 1621), p. 11.

55. *Ibid.*, p. 15.

56. *Earl of Stirling's Register*, I, 229-230.

57. *DCH*, VII, 537. *Cf.* Archibald Simson, *Heptameron* (St. Andrews, 1621), p. 157: opposition to the magistrate 'doeth greatlie smell of Antichristianisme and Poperie'.

58. *DCH*, VII, 539. *Cf.* David Ramsay, *A sermon, or litle treatise, upon the three last verses of the seaventeenth chapter of Deuteronomie* (Aberdeen, 1629), p. 13, where the king has no earthly superior.

59. *Scots Confession*, p. 89.

60. *FBD*, pp. 88, 183.

61. *FBD*, p. 182.

62. *FBD*, pp. 90-91.

63. *FBD*, p. 95.

64. Calderwood, *Perth assembly*, p. 24.

65. S. A. Burrell, 'The Apocalyptic Vision of the Early Covenanters', *SHR*, 43 (1964), 11; James Gordon, *History of Scots Affairs, from 1637 to 1641* (Aberdeen, 1841), I, 39.

66. Calderwood, *Perth assembly*, p. 31. See also [David Calderwood], *Parasynagma Perthensis et juramentum ecclesiae scoticanae* (n.p., 1620), pp. 26-40; and *OL*, II, 575, 619.

67. Calderwood, *Perth assembly*, p. 31.

68. *Ibid.*, p. 32. This became a permanent part of presbyterian rhetoric. See [George Gillespie], *A dispute against the English-popish ceremonies, obtruded upon the church of Scotland* (n.p., 1637), sig. Clr.

69. Calderwood, *Defence*, p. 72.

70. John Michaelson, *The lawfulnes of kneeling* (St. Andrews, 1620), pp. 85-86.

71. *Ibid.*, pp. 86-87. See *Scots Confession*, pp. 93-97; and *Ane shorte and generall confession* (Edinburgh, 1581).

72. Lindsay, *True narration*, pp. 3, 18 in the second sequence of pagination. Lindsay refers to article 21, but the statement is actually at the end of article 20. He was, presumably, following the faulty numbering of the act of parliament in 1567 which omitted the number 13, giving to that article the number 14, hence throwing the subsequent numbering into confusion. *APS*, III, 17.

73. *Scots Confession*, p. 83.

74. Lindsay, *True narration*, p. 4, second sequence; *SBD*, p. 198.

75. Lindsay, *True narration*, p. 16, second sequence.

76. *Ibid.*, p. 18, etc.

77. *OL*, II, 600; see also p. 623.

78. NLS, Accession 7971, 2/11. The king was thought to be after non-conformity again in 1624. Historical Manuscripts Commission, *Mar and Kellie*, p. 210.

79. *OL*, II, 620.

80. *APS*, IV, 595-597.

81. *OL*, II, 663.

82. *OL*, II, 700.

83. *OL*, II, 602.

84. Foster, *Church*, pp. 186-188; P. H. R. MacKay, 'The Reception given to the Five Articles of Perth', *RSCHS*, 19 (1977), 198. [David Calderwood], *A dispute upon communicating at our confused communions* (n.p., 1624), p. 72 claimed that three-quarters of the

churches ignored the Five Articles. Although that was perhaps a substantial overstatement, his party did not lack for support. The difficulty in assessing numbers is that even though a minister might conform when in the bishop's presence, the lack of rigorous enforcement would permit him to carry on in the accustomed style in his parish where his people were not at all likely to complain about evasion. See David Stevenson, 'Conventicles in the Kirk, 1619-1637. The Emergency of a Radical Party', *RSCHS*, 18 (1973), 100.

85. BL, Additional Ms. 19402, ff. 135-136.

86. *DCH*, VII, 397-398.

87. *OL*, II, 620.

88. BL, Additional Ms. 19402, ff. 135-136.

89. Foster, *Church*, p. 189.

90. *OL*, II, 713.

91. *Earl of Stirling's Register*, I, 63. See also *DCH*, VII, 533-534. On the need to conform, *Earl of Stirling's Register*, I, 63, 227.

92. *WM*, p. 607.

93. NLS, Wodrow Mss., Quarto XX, ff. 117r, 118r, 120r; *Funerals*, p. 200.

94. *Earl of Stirling's Register*, I, 271-272.

95. Mathieson, I, 321.

96. *Ibid.*, I, 343.

97. Selwyn, p. 199. Also in Selwyn's introduction to John Forbes of Corse, *The First Book of the Irenicum*, ed. E. G. Selwyn (Cambridge: University Press, 1923), p. 7. The term makes sense only to one who insists upon apostolic succession through episcopal consecration.

98. Hugh R. Trevor-Roper, *Archbishop Laud 1573-1645* (2nd ed; London: Macmillan, 1962), p. 400.

99. *DCH*, VII, 335.

100. Stevenson, 'Conventicles', p. 101. See also Gordon Donaldson, 'The Emergence of Schism in Seventeenth-Century Scotland', in Derek Baker (ed.), *Schism, Heresy and Religious Protest. Studies in Church History*, Vol. IX (Cambridge: University Press, 1972), p. 282.

101. Calderwood, *Dispute*, pp. 68-70; [David Calderwood], *An epistle of a Christian brother* (n.p., 1624), p. 15.

102. Calderwood, *Dispute*, p. 72.

103. Foster, *Church*, p. 192.

104. *OL*, II, 663.

105. *OL*, II, 635.

106. Murray, *Dialogue*, p. 28.

107. Scot, *Course*, p. 81. Also in *DCH*, VII, 480.

108. Scot, *Course*, p. 82.

109. *Ibid.*, sig. A4r.

110. Calderwood, *Solution*, p. 55.

111. The *Altar of Damascus* was published in 1621. A much expanded Latin edition, *Altare Damascenum*, followed in 1623. The title alluded to II Kings 16:10-11 and was by no means novel. See its use in *JMAD*, p. 281; *Informations*, p. 9.

112. Calderwood, *Speach*, pp. 60-61. See also [David Calderwood], *An exhortation of the particular kirks of Christ in Scotland to their sister kirk in Edinburgh* (n.p., 1624), p. 15.

113. [David Calderwood], *Quares concerning the state of the church of Scotland* (n.p., 1638), p. 15.

114. *Ibid.*, pp. 8-9.

115. Calderwood, *Altar*, p. 30.

116. *Ibid.*, p. 39.

117. *Ibid.*, pp. 13, 72, *passim.* Bancroft had once called Elizabeth 'a petie Pope' and Spottiswood had recently referred to James as pope, p. 7.

118. *Ibid.*, p. 28.

119. Calderwood, *Speach,* pp. 68-69.

120. *OL*, II, 498; *RPCf,* IX, 729.

121. *APS*, IV, 597.

122. *OL*, I, 389-390; *RPCf,* VIII, 25-26, *BUK,* III, 1059.

123. *APS*, V, 179-180; *RPCs,* I, 91-92, 157-158.

124. *Earl of Stirling's Register*, I, 127. See his letter to the bishop of Moray in SRO, GD 188/20/9/4 dated 3 July 1625.

125. *APS*, IV, 407; see also p. 429.

126. *RPCf,* XII, 730.

127. *RPCf,* IX, 569.

128. *OL*, I, 138.

129. *OL*, I, 304. See Boyd's anti-Roman manuscript in NLS, Wodrow Mss., Quarto XX, no. 12. His ms. writings are surveyed in Craven, pp. 71-75.

130. *RPCs,* II, 49.

131. Historical Manuscripts Commission, *Laing Manuscripts,* I, 177-178.

132. *DCH*, VII, 38, 218; Row, *History,* pp. 250, 273.

133. *DCH*, VI, 732, 739-740.

134. Cowper, *Dikaiologie,* p. 119.

135. *Ibid.*, p. 134.

136. *Ibid.*, p. 38.

137. *DCH*, I, 38; William Cowper, *Seven dayes conference, betweene a Catholicke Christian, and a Catholicke Romane* (London, 1613), p. 46. Also in *Workes*, pp. 645-682.

138. Cowper, *Seven dayes conference,* p. 118.

139. *Ibid.*, p. 147.

140. *Ibid.*, p. 171.

141. *Ibid.*, p. 63.

142. Cowper, *Works,* pp. 186, 191, 451, 590, 712, *passim.*

143. *Ibid.*, p. 820.

144. G. D. Henderson, 'The Influence of Bishop Patrick Forbes', *Religious Life in Seventeenth Century Scotland* (Cambridge: University Press, 1937), p. 34. See also Snow, p. 150.

145. Patrick Forbes, *Eubulus, or a dialogue* (Aberdeen, 1627), sig. A3r.

146. *Ibid.*, pp. 5-6.

147. Patrick Forbes, *An exquisite commentarie upon the Revelation of St. John* (London, 1613), sig. *1v. The frogs were identified with Catholic priests, especially Jesuits. See p. 243.

148. P. Forbes, *Defence,* p. 1.

149. *Ibid.*, pp. 6-8; Snow, p. 153.

150. Patrick Forbes, *An epistle to a recusant,* p. 27, bound with *Defence.*

151. Lindsay, *True narration,* sig. A2r.

152. John MacLeod, *Scottish Theology in relation to Church History since the Reformation* (Edinburgh: Publications Committee of the Free Church of Scotland, 1943), p. 57. James Walker, *The Theology and Theologians of Scotland chiefly of the Seventeenth and Eighteenth Centuries* (Edinburgh, 1888), passes the bishops by without a word.

153. William Haller, *The Rise of Puritanism* (New York: Harper and Brothers, 1957), p. 33.

154. John Abernethy, *A Christian and heavenly treatise containing physicke for the soule* (London, 1630), sig. A4r.

155. *Correspondence of Sir Robert Kerr*, I, 53; SRO, GD 188/40/2/13/72.

156. NLS, Wodrow Mss., Quarto CIV, f. 10v.

157. Abernethy, *Christian and heavenly treatise*, sig. A4v.

158. Row, *History*, p. 257; Cowper, *Dikaiologie*, p. 169.

159. Cowper, *Dikaiologie*, p. 169. For the many editions of Cowper's writings, consult Pollard and Redgrave.

160. McCrie, p. 390.

161. Cowper, *Workes*, p. 156.

162. P. Forbes, *Exquisite commentarie*, pp. 235-236; John Abernethy, *The dignity and duty of a Christian* (London, 1620), p. 16.

163. Anthony Maxey, *The sermon preached before the king, at Whitehall* (London, 1605), sig. A3r. In the *Basilicon Doron*, I, 36 James had referred to faith as 'the golden chaine that linketh the faithful soule to Christ'. The term was also heard at the synod of Dort in 1618. Archibald W. Harrison, *The Beginnings of Arminianism to the Synod of Dort* (London: University of London Press, 1926), p. 353.

164. Cowper, *Workes*, p. 245.

165. *Ibid.*, p. 165.

166. *Ibid.*, p. 152.

167. *Ibid.*, p. 156.

168. SRO, GD 188/2/3/2.

169. NLS, Wodrow Mss., Quarto CIV, f. 38v.

170. *Ibid.*, f. 50r.

171. Cowper, *Workes*, p. 249.

172. *Ibid.*, pp. 749-750.

173. Abernethy, *Christian and heavenly treatise*, p. 133.

174. [David Calderwood], *The pastor and the prelate* (n.p., 1628), p. 69.

175. *Ibid.*, p. 39.

176. *Ibid.*, p. 47.

177. *Ibid.*, p. 64.

178. Raoul Patry, *Philippe du Plessis-Mornay. Un Huguenot homme d'Etat (1549-1623)* (Paris: Fischbacher, 1933), pp. 546-547.

179. Pattison, p. 448.

180. W. C. Dowding, *German Theology during the Thirty Years' War: The Life and Correspondence of George Calixtus* (Oxford, 1863), p. 166.

181. *Ibid.*, p. 268.

182. Patry, p. 444; Brian G. Armstrong, *Calvinism and the Amyraut Heresy: Protestant Scholasticism and Humanism in Seventeenth-Century France* (Madison: University of Wisconsin Press, 1969), p. 7.

183. J. Minton Batten, *John Dury: Advocate of Christian Reunion* (Chicago: University of Chicago Press, 1944), p. 6.

184. Lord Clarendon, *History of the Rebellion and Civil Wars in England* (Oxford, 1888), p. 140. E. G. Selwyn, p. 196 remarked that Knox made the kirk 'irrevocably anti-Roman'.

185. Dowding, p. 333.

186. On this development, see Armstrong, p. 32.

187. Harrison, *Beginnings of Arminianism*, pp. 148-151.

188. Cragg, pp. 100-101.

189. T. M. Parker, 'Arminianism and Laudianism', in C. W. Dugmore and Charles Duggan (eds.), *Studies in Church History*, vol. I (London: Nelson, 1964), p. 29.

190. Archibald W. Harrison, *Arminianism* (London: Duckworth, 1937), p. 133.

191. Nicholas Tyacke, 'Puritanism, Arminianism and Counter-Revolution', in Conrad Russell (ed.), *The Origins of the English Civil War* (London: Macmillan, 1975), p. 133. See the complaint by the publishers of *Anti-Montacutum. An appeale or remonstrance of the orthodox ministers of the church of England; against Richard Montague* (Edinburgh, 1629), sig. A2r that 'orthodox' books could no longer find a press in England; thus it was printed in Edinburgh.

192. Cragg, p. 110.

193. Tyacke in Russell (ed.), p. 121.

194. William Laud, *Works* (Oxford, 1847-1860), III, 341.

195. Parker in Dugmore and Duggan (eds.), *Studies*, I, 29-30.

196. Tyacke in Russell (ed.), p. 130; Hugh Watt, 'William Laud and Scotland', *RSCHS*, 7 (1941), 176.

197. Peter Smart, *The vanitie and downe-fall of superstitious popish ceremonies: or, a sermon preached in the cathedrall church of Durham, July 27, 1628* (Edinburgh, 1628), sig. 4r. Banned by the privy council on 15 September 1628. *RPCs*, II, 449-450.

198. *RKS*, p. 155.

199. Calderwood, *Solution*, p. 49.

200. [David Calderwood], *An answere to M. J. Forbes of Corse, his peaceable warning* (n.p., 1638), sig. C4r; poem appended to Melville, *Black bastel*, [p. 12].

201. W. Row, *Life of Blair*, p. 41. On Cameron, Henry M. B. Reid, *The Divinity Principals in the University of Glasgow* (Glasgow: James Maclehose and Sons, 1971), pp. 170-251; Gaston Bonet-Maury, 'John Cameron, a Scottish Protestant Theologian in France 1579-1625', *SHR*, 7 (1910), 325-345; Armstrong, pp. 42-70.

202. G. D. Henderson, *Religious Life*, p. 50; McMahon, 'Scottish Episcopate', p. 256.

203. Scot, *Apologetical Narration*, p. 64; [Robert Baillie], *Ladensium autokatakrisis, the Canterburians self-conviction* ([Edinburgh], 1640), p. 11; *The answeres of some brethren of the ministerie, to the replyes of the ministers . . . of Aberdene* (Aberdeen, 1638), p. 15; *RBLJ*, I, 148-149.

204. Walter R. Foster, 'The Operation of Presbyteries in Scotland, 1600-1638', *RSCHS*, 15 (1966), 24.

205. James Cameron Lees, *The Abbey of Paisley* (Paisley, 1878), p. 290. The minister, John Crighton, was cousin to Robert Baillie. *RBLJ*, I, 10. See also G. D. Henderson, 'Arminianism in Scotland', *London Quarterly and Holborn Review*, [157] (1932), 495.

206. Lees, p. 289.

207. Calderwood, *Perth assembly*, p. 7.

208. *RBLJ*, I, 9, See also Grub, II, 371; and Batten, p. 59.

209. Samuel Rutherford, *Letters* (Edinburgh, 1891), p. 300.

210. *Ibid.*, p. 53.

211. Henry Guthry, *Memoirs of Henry Guthry, Late Bishop of Dunkel in Scotland* (London, 1702), p. 13. See the discussion of Guthry's reliability in Grub, II, 379-381.

212. Foster, *Church*, pp. 61-62.

213. *Anti-Montacutum*, p. 34.

214. Th. A. Fischer, *The Scots in Germany* (Edinburgh: Otto Schulze & Co., 1902; reprinted Edinburgh: John Donald, 1973), p. 314; McMahon, 'Scottish Episcopate', p. 57.

215. Guthry, p. 14.

216. *OL*, II, 504.

217. Scot, *Apologetical Narration*, p. 318.

218. Guthry, p. 14.

219. Trevor-Roper, *Archbishop Laud*, p. 141; Laud, *Works*, III, 321; 'A Caveat for

Scotland', in *A Book of Scotish Pasquils, 1568-1715* (Edinburgh, 1868), p. 65.

220. *The Hamilton Papers 1638-1650*, ed. S.R. Gardiner (London, 1880), p.50; Guthry, p. 14.

221. Spottiswood, *History*, I, cxxxiii.

222. [Robert Baillie], *A large supplement of the Canterburian self-conviction* ([London], 1641), sig. B4r.

223. Pattison, p. 302. See Wedderburn's letters in Alexander Wedderburn, *The Wedderburn Book* (n.p., 1898), I, 35-41.

224. Wedderburn, I, 30.

225. Baillie, *Large supplement*, sig. B4v; *Ladensium autokatakrisis*, p. 11; Robert Baillie, *The life of William* (London, 1643), pp. 11-12.

226. *Earl of Stirling's Register*, II, 855.

227. Baillie, *Large supplement*, sig. C1r-C1v.

228. *Ibid.*, pp. 17ff.

229. BL, Harley 750, ff. 63v, 64v, 72v.

230. *Ibid.*, f. 71r.

231. *Ibid.*, f. 74v.

232. *Ibid.*, f. 62v.

233. *Ibid.*, f. 70r.

234. Cowper, *Workes*, p. 1089.

235. J. H. Baxter, 'Scottish Students at Helmstedt University', *SHR*, 24 (1927), 237; Andrew L. Drummond, *The Kirk and the Continent* (Edinburgh: Saint Andrew Press, 1956), p. 54; Cameron (ed.), *Letters*, p. xxi.

236. Robert Wodrow, *Selections from Wodrow's Biographical Collections* (Aberdeen, 1890), p. 246.

237. *DCH*, VII, 542; see also pp. 571-572. In March 1634 he tried to enforce them. Wodrow, *Selections*, pp. 256-257.

238. *DCH*, VII, 596; see also pp. 604-605; and *OL*, II, 740, 742-745.

239. William Forbes, *Considerationes Modestae et Pacificae* (Oxford, 1850-1866), II, 507.

240. *Ibid.*, I, 3.

241. Grub, II, 351.

242. W. Forbes, II, 141.

243. [Gilbert Burnet], *The life of William Bedell, D.D., bishop of Kilmore in Ireland* (London, 1685), sig. A5r.

244. See Row's comments in *History*, pp. 371-372.

245. William Guild, *A compend of the controversies of religion* (Edinburgh, 1627), p. 68.

246. *Ibid.*, p. 98.

247. *Ibid.*, p. 136.

248. Lee, *Government*, p. 100.

249. W. Row, *Life of Blair*, p. 15.

250. *Ibid.*, p. 12.

251. James Gordon, I, 3.

252. At least since the introduction of the Five Articles there had been demonstrations of aristocratic favour toward presbyterian ministers. Allen B. Birchler, The Influence of the Scottish Clergy on Politics, 1616-38 (Ph. D. thesis, Nebraska, 1966), pp. 105-106.

253. *DCH*, VII, 250.

254. William Lithgow, *Scotlands welcome to her native sonne, and soveraigne lord, king Charles* (Edinburgh, [1633]), sig. C1v.

255. Balfour, II, 156.

256. Sir William Fraser, *Memorials of the Earls of Haddington* (Edinburgh, 1889), II, 148-151; William Prynne, *Hidden workes of darkenes brought to publike light* (London, 1645), p. 165; David Stevenson, *The Scottish Revolution 1637-1644: The Triumph of the Covenanters* (Newton Abbot: David and Charles, 1973), p. 38.

257. Sir William Brereton, *Travels in Holland, the United Provinces, England, Scotland, and Ireland, 1634-1635* ([London],1844), pp, 100-101; *RBLJ*, I, 6; Scot, *Apologetical Narration*, pp. 336-337; John Spalding, *The History of the Troubles and Memorable Transactions in Scotland and England, from 1624 to 1645* (Edinburgh, 1828-1829), I, 45.

258. Prynne, pp. 150-151.

259. Laud, III, 312.

260. *Ibid.*, III, 313-314.

261. *Ibid.*, III, 313; Prynne, p. 164.

262. *Earl of Stirling's Register*, I, 62. Confirmed in 1637. *RPCs*, VI, 471.

263. Stevenson, *Scottish Revolution*, p. 26.

264. Guthry, p. 12.

265. Spalding, I, 32-33.

266. Guthry, p. 14; Gilbert Burnet, *The memoires of the lives and actions of James and William dukes of Hamilton* (London, 1677), p. 30; *RBLJ*, I, 7.

267. Stevenson, *Scottish Revolution*, p. 27; Donaldson, *Scotland: James V - James VII*, p. 299. Collins, pp. 186-201, surveys the secular powers of the bishops.

268. EUL, Laing III, 69, 1, f. 1r.

269. Donaldson, *Scotland: James V - James VII*, p. 299.

270. Foster, *Church*, p. 62.

271. McMahon, 'Scottish Episcopate', p. 72; but see his earlier 'Scottish Courts of High Commission', p. 208.

272. *Canons and constitutions ecclesiasticall gathered and put in forme, for the governement of the church of Scotland* (Aberdeen, 1636), sig. A3r.

273. Prynne, p. 152.

274. There was also a plan to publish a new ordinal which would ensure that the diaconate was an order of the ministry, not a lay office as in presbyterian polity. Prynne, p. 153.

275. *Canons*, p. 43.

276. *Ibid.*, p. 20.

277. *RBLJ*, I, 439.

278. [John Maxwell], *An answer by letter to a worthy gentleman* ([Oxford], 1644), p. 26. Also published as *The burthen of Issachar* (London], 1646) and *Presbytery displayd* (London, 1663).

279. *Canons*, p. 15.

280. See Sprott; also 'A Scottish Liturgy of the reign of James VI', in *Miscellany of the Scottish History Society*, vol. X (Edinburgh, 1965), pp. 89-117.

281. *Grievances*, p. 29; *State Papers, Melros*, p. 415; Donaldson, *Making of the Scottish Prayer Book*, p. 39.

282. Prynne, p. 155.

283. Sprott, p. xlvi; Hugh Watt, p. 183.

284. *Grievances*, p. 30. Also in Balfour, II, 181-184. On Struther's views on the Five Articles, see *DCH*, VII, 461; on bishops, see VII, 347-348.

285. Rutherford, p. 60.

286. *Earl of Stirling's Register*, II, 677-680; Prynne, p. 148; *RBLJ*, I, 422.

287. Andrew Boyd, *Ad augustissimum monarcham Carolum . . . in Scotiam redeuntem, carmen panegyricum* (Edinburgh, 1633), sig. B3v.

288. Prynne, p. 149; *RBLJ*, I, 432; Laud, VI, 370.

289. *RBLJ*, I, 436. More trouble ensued in his new diocese, this time over unauthorised fasting. Prynne, p. 152.

290. *RBLJ*, I, 437.

291. *Earl of Stirling's Register*, II, 797. See also Guthry, p. 16.

292. Hugh Watt, pp. 186-187.

293. Prynne, p. 169, after the Edinburgh riot of 1637.

294. *A short relation of the state of the kirk of Scotland since the reformation of religion, to the present time* ([Edinburgh], 1638), sig. C3v. See the same opinion repeated by Hugh Watt, p. 188.

295. But any readings from the Apocrypha would have been too many. Even king James had rejected them, since he was not a papist, '& indeed some of them [Apocryphal books] are as like the ditement of the spirite of God, as an Egg is to an Oyster'. *Basilicon Doron*, I, 34. At Hampton Court in 1604 he did allow some readings 'which were cleare, and correspondent to the scriptures'. Barlow, *Summe*, p. 61. The new confession of 1616, produced officially but never published, denied the Apocrypha to be an authentic part of the Scriptures. *BUK*, III, 1134. See also P. Forbes, *Exquisite commentarie*, p. 86.

296. Donaldson, *Making of the Scottish Prayer Book*, pp. 61-70. But see Hugh Watt, p. 186.

297. Donaldson, *Making of the Scottish Prayer Book*, pp. 81-82; *The Book of Common Prayer . . . Laud's Liturgy (1637)*, ed. James Cooper (Edinburgh: William Blackwood and Sons, 1904), p. xix.

298. Charles I, *A large declaration concerning the late tumults in Scotland* (London, 1639), p. 18.

299. EUL, Laing I, 292, 1, f. 1r.

300. Spalding, I, 55; Prynne, p. 1696; Burnet, *Memoires*, p. 33; Donaldson, *Making of the Scottish Prayer Book*, pp. 82-83.

301. *RBLJ*, I, 4: Guthry, p. 17. See also Prynne, p. 169.

302. *The booke of common prayer, and administration of the sacraments. And other parts of divine service for the use of the church of Scotland* (Edinburgh, 1637), sig. A2v.

303. Laud, III, 335; Prynne, p. 155; Philip Hardwicke, *Miscellaneous State Papers* (London, 1778), II, 114: *Answeres of some brethren*, p. 26.

304. Prynne, p. 165.

305. Guthry, p. 20.

306. J. M. Henderson, 'An 'Advertisement' about the Service Book', *SHR*, 23 (1926), 204.

307. Johnston, p. 265. See also John, earl of Rothes, *A Relation of Proceedings concerning the Affairs of the Kirk of Scotland, from August 1637 to July 1638* (Edinburgh, 1830), pp. 198-200; James Gordon, I, 7-9.

308. Prynne, p. 168.

309. Johnston, p. 267. See also *Select Biographies*, I, 397 (in 1634).

310. [George Gillespie], *Reasons for which the service book, urged upon Scotland ought to be refused* ([Edinburgh], 1638), sig. A1r. On the authorship, see *RBLJ*, I, 90.

311. EUL, Laing, I, 292, 1, f. 6v.

312. W. Row, *Life of Blair*, p. 150; *RPCs*, VI, 699-716.

313. Rothes, p. 46; Prynne, p. 167.

314. Rothes, p. 47.

315. W. Row, *Life of Blair*, p. 151. See also Rothes, p. 35.

316. 'The National Petition to the Scottish Privy Council, October 18, 1637', *SHR* (1925), 241-248.

317. Rothes, p. 20.

318. *Correspondence of Sir Robert Kerr*, I, 94-96; Johnston, p. 270; *RBLJ*, I, 37.

319. Rothes, p. 40.

320. 'National Petition', p. 245; Rothes, p. 50; *RPCs*, VI, 709-710.

321. Prynne, p. 168.

322. *RPCs*, VII, 7.

323. Rothes, p. 113; Balfour, II, 263.

324. *DCH*, VII, 149.

Chapter 10

1. Gordon Donaldson, *Scotland: Church and Nation through Sixteen Centuries* (Edinburgh: Scottish Academic Press, 1960), p. 84: See also Stevenson, *Scottish Revolution*, p. 47; and McMahon, 'Scottish Episcopate', pp. 288-297.

2. Mathieson, I, 400.

3. *Grievances*, pp. 4-9; Scot, *Apologetical Narration*, pp. 330-334; Row, *History*, pp. 357-362; Balfour, II, 207-214.

4. Rothes, p. 56. See also *Hamilton Papers*, p. 11.

5. Rothes, p. 79.

6. Johnston, p. 322.

7. *Newes from Scotland* ([Amsterdam? 1638?], sig. Alv; Stevenson, *Scottish Revolution*, p. 82.

8. S. A. Burrell, 'Apocalyptic Vision', pp. 11-12.

9. *RBLJ*, I, 52. See also James Gordon, I, 43.

10. *The confession of faith of the kirk of Scotland* ([Edinburgh? 1638?]), p. 13.

11. See Strang's reasons in NLS, Wodrow Mss., Folio XXXI, no. 2. Noted in Henry M. B. Reid, pp. 280-281.

12. *RBLJ*, I, 67.

13. *RBLJ*, I, 2. See F. N. McCoy, *Robert Baillie and the Second Scots Reformation* (Berkeley: University of California Press, 1974), pp. 30-31.

14. Baillie, *Ladensium autokatakrisis*, postscript, p. 28.

15. *RBLJ*, I, 157, 177, 182.

16. Donaldson, *Scotland: Church and Nation*, p. 83.

17. Donaldson, *Scotland: James V -James VII*, p. 314.

18. [John Maxwell], *Episcopacie not abjured in his majesties realme of Scotland* ([Dublin], 1641), p. 11.

19. *RBLJ*, I, 181.

20. Walter Makey, *The Church of the Covenant 1637-1651: Revolution and Social Change in Scotland* (Edinburgh: John Donald Publishers, 1979), p. 30 states that although 'radical presbyterianism was still a conspiracy whispered in dark corners', Johnston, the ringleader, could not long be contained. See also S. A. Burrell, 'The Covenant Idea as a Revolutionary Symbol: Scotland, 1596-1637', *CH*, 27 (1958), 346.

21. Calderwood, *Re-examination*, see especially sig. A2r-A2v.

22. Johnston, p. 338; *Presbytrie Booke of Kirkcaldie*, pp. 127-128; Rothes, pp. 128-129.

23. Williamson, p. 142. See also William M. Campbell, *The Triumph of Presbyterianism* (Edinburgh: Saint Andrew Press, 1958), p. x, where he wrote that the Covenanters 'objected *in toto* to the bishops because they *were* bishops'.

24. Gillespie, *Dispute*, part III, p. 160.

25. *Confession of faith*, p. 12.

26. *RBLJ*, I, 62.

27. Johnston, pp. 320-321.

28. *Ibid.*, p. 269.

29. *Ibid.*, p. 348.

30. John Forbes, *A peaceable warning, to the subjects in Scotland* (Aberdeen, 1638), p. 4 where Forbes's letter to Huntly is dated 6 April 1638.

31. J. Forbes, *First Book of the Irenicum*, pp. 126-133.

32. J. Forbes, *Peaceable warning*, p. 17. See also James Gordon, I, 42.

33. J. Forbes, *Peaceable warning*, pp. 18-19.

34. *Generall demands concerning the late covenant: propounded by the ministers and professors of divinity of Aberdene* ([Edinburgh], 1638), pp. 11-14. On the Aberdeen controversy, see James D. Ogilvie, 'The Aberdeen Doctors and the National Covenant', *Papers of the Edinburgh Bibliographic Society*, 11 (1921), 73-86.

35. Calderwood, *Answere to John Forbes*, sig. Elr refers to the proclamation of 22 September 1638.

36. *Ibid.*, sig. C4r-C4v.

37. *Ibid.*, sig. D1r-D1v.

38. *Ibid.*, sig. D2r.

39. *Ibid.*, sig. D3r.

40. *Ibid.*, sig. D2v-D3r.

41. *DCH*, IV, 305. For the earliest possible reference, see *CSPS*, VII, 219; also in *DCH*, IV, 76. See also Williamson, pp. 68; 170, n.17. *WM*, p. 441 seems to be an allusion to the Negative Confession in 1586.

42. *Informations*, p. 6.

43. Scot, *Course*, p. 31; see also pp. 44, 48.

44. *JMAD*, p. 506; *DCH*, VI, 317-319; Melville, *Black bastel*, [p. 7]; *JMAD*, p. 629; *Briefe and plaine narration*, sig. A2v.

45. Row, *History*, p. 194.

46. *JMAD*, p. 558.

47. J. Forbes, *Certaine Records* in Scot, *Apologetical Narration*, p. 347.

48. *Ibid.*, p. 483. See also *DCH*, VI, 405, 472.

49. *Informations*, p. 16.

50. Murray, *Sermon*, pp. 44-45.

51. *WM*, pp. 569-570, 573-574.

52. *DCH*, VI, 729. See also Hume, *Patricio Simsono*, sig. Alr.

53. *DCH*, VII, 67.

54. *DCH*, VII, 141-142. See also Hume, *Patricio Simsono*, sig. A3r.

55. *DCH*, VII, 140.

56. *DCH*, VII, 142; see also p. 147.

57. Scot, *Apologetical Narration*, p. 47.

58. Calderwood, *De regimine*, pp. 12, 27.

59. Calderwood, *True history*, p. 96; *DCH*, III, 506. See also VII, 126, 628.

60. Cowper, *Dikaiologie*, p. 128.

61. John Hay, *A speach, delivered to the kings most excellent majesty, 16 May 1617* (Edinburgh, 1617), p. 7. Also in J. Adamson, *Muses welcome*, pp. 38-43.

62. Cowper, *Dikaiologie*, p. 174.

63. *Ibid.*, p. 139.

64. *Ibid.*, p. 140.

65. Lindsay, *True narration*, p. 12, second sequence.

66. Spottiswood, *Refutatio*, p. 37. See also *History*, p. 416.

67. Rothes, p. 102; see also p. 97.

68. *Reasons for a generall assemblie* ([Edinburgh], 1638), sig. A3v.

69. *Ibid.*, sig. A4r. The bishop of Ross had in 1637 claimed that the bishops were 'the representative Church of the Kingdom'. Prynne, p. 167.

70. Rothes, p. 174.

71. *Generall demands*, p. 14; see also p. 27.

72. *Ibid.*, p. 33.

73. *Answeres of some brethren*, p. 23.

74. *Ibid.*, p. 27.

75. *Duplyes of the ministers and professors of Aberdene* (Aberdeen, 1638), pp. 39-40.

76. *The protestation of the noblemen . . . immediately after the reading of the proclamation, dated September 9. 1638* ([Edinburgh], 1638), sig. C1v.

77. James, duke of Hamilton, [*A declaration on episcopal government in Scotland*] (Edinburgh, 1638).

78. Burnct, *Memoires*, pp. 86-87.

79. *Duplyes*, p. 114.

80. F. C. Eeles, 'The Teaching of the Aberdeen Doctors on Ordination as expressed in the *Irenicum* of Dr. John Forbes of Corse, 1629', in *Historical Papers*, pp. 144-155.

81. *Ibid.*, p. 148. Donald Macmillan, *The Aberdeen Doctors* (London: Hodder and Stoughton, 1909), pp. 86-92, set Forbes between the extremists on either side. G. D. Henderson, 'The Aberdeen Doctors', *The Burning Bush: Studies in Scottish Church History* (Edinburgh: Saint Andrew Press, 1957), p. 91 wrote that the Aberdeen Doctors 'did not accept any doctrine of Divine Right of Episcopacy'. Perhaps the confusion arises from the implicit assumption that belief in the *jus divinum* of episcopacy cannot coexist with tolerance and appreciation of a different polity.

82. *Historical Papers*, p. 150. Selwyn and Snow wrote that Forbes saw episcopacy as not the *esse* but as the *melius esse* of the church. Selwyn, p. 211; Snow, p. 154.

83. One Scot who wrote in behalf of episcopacy was James Maxwell. Dedicated to the 'Jacob from the North', Maxwell's *A new eight-fold probation of the church of Englands divine constitution* (London, 1617) was in large part a declaration of royal power over the church, the king being both lay and clerical in character. He also argued that England's episcopacy was to be preferred to the Genevan polity of Scottish presbyterians on biblical grounds — archbishop corresponded to archangels, hence the church of England was more 'Angelicall' (p. 32). Maxwell described his work as a refutation of the 1617 protest by fifty-three preachers in behalf of the kirk's liberties (sig. A2v), but neither the book nor its author formed an essential part of the Scottish scene. Since graduating from the University of Edinburgh in 1600, Maxwell had lived on the continent and in London (*DNB*), and the author made no secret of his strong ambition to gain appointment to the new Chelsea College (sig. B2v-B3r).

84. Row, *History*, p. 354. William Forbes had in 1623 anticipated Maxwell's definition. Grub, II, 331-332; McMahon, 'Scottish Episcopate', p. 204. Selwyn, p. 211, attributed the fall of episcopacy in Scotland to the want of a solid ecclesiology of divine right episcopacy. But see George I. R. McMahon, John Forbes of Corse His Life and Work (B. Litt. thesis, Oxford, 1961), p. 284.

85. Rothes, pp. 166, 169.

86. *Protestation of the noblemen [after 9 Sept. 1638]*, sig. C4v.

87. *Hamilton Papers*, p. 23. Not much earlier, however, St. Andrews had countenanced an assembly. *RBLJ*, I, 466. It may be that rapidly developing events caused a change of heart and an assembly now portended dissolution rather than pacification.

88. Burnet, *Memoires*, p. 91.

89. *RBLJ*, I, 151; *Fasti*, VII, 337; III, 253; on Whitford, VII, 334-335 and *DNB*; but

Keith, *Historical Catalogue*, p. 167, disagrees on Whitford's father. See Hamilton's authorisation in *The declinator and protestation of the archbishops and bishops, of the church of Scotland, and others their adherents within that kingdome* (London, 1639), p. 32.

90. James D. Ogilvie, 'A Bibliography of Glasgow Assembly, 1638', *Records of the Glasgow Bibliographic Society*, 7 (1923), 8-9.

91. *Declinator and protestation*, p. 13.

92. *Ibid.*, pp. 29-30.

93. Guthry, p. 29. See also *RBLJ*, I, 87.

94. Burnet, *Memoires*, p. 74.

95. *Hamilton Papers*, p. 24; Burnet, *Memoires*, p. 79; Birchler, 'Archbishop John Spottiswoode', p. 318.

96. Burnet, *Memoires*, p. 82; *Hamilton Papers*, p. 33.

97. Burnet, *Memoires*, p. 75.

98. *Declinatour and protestation of the some some-times pretended bishops* (Edinburgh, 1639), p. 4; *RBLJ*, I, 135; Burnet, *Memoires*, p. 98.

99. Charles I, *Large declaration*, p. 220. See also Johnston, pp. 394-395, where he mentions 'summonds against the Praelats'.

100. Lord Hailes, Sir David Dalrymple, *Memorials and Letters relating to the History of Britain in the Reign of Charles the First* (Glasgow, 1766), p. 46. See also Stevenson, *Scottish Revolution*, pp. 113-114.

101. *The protestation of the generall assemblie of the church of Scotland . . . at the mercat crosse of Glasgow, the 28, and 29. of November 1638* (Glasgow, 1638), sig. B3v.

102. Stevenson, *Scottish Revolution*, p. 121.

103. Charles I, *Large declaration*, p. 247.

104. *RKS*, p. 44.

105. *The principall acts of the solemne generall assembly of the kirk of Scotland . . . at Glasgow the xxi of November 1638* (Edinburgh, 1639), pp. 7-13. This and many other documents cited in this chapter may also be found in *RKS*.

106. Charles I, *Large declaration*, p. 217.

107. Hailes, p. 47. There were widespread suspicions about the real motives of religiously active nobles. William Guild, *To the nobilitie . . . a friendly and faythfull advice* (Aberdeen, 1639), pp. 3-4. Also in Spalding, I, 313-315. See also Spalding, I, 48; Hardwicke, II, 118; Hilary L. Rubenstein, *Captain Luckless: James, First Duke of Hamilton 1606-1649* (Edinburgh: Scottish Academic Press, 1975), p. 53.

108. Maxwell, *Episcopacie not abjured*, pp. 10-11.

109. *RBLJ*, I, 99; James Gordon, I, 121.

110. Rutherford, p. 462.

111. Charles I, *Large declaration*, pp. 218-219.

112. 'Pasquil against the bishops', in *Book of Scotish Pasquils*, pp. 20-21.

113. On the importance of Arminianism, see Tyacke in Russell (ed.), p. 142; and Michiel C. Kitshoff, Aspects of Arminianism in Scotland (M.Th. thesis, St. Andrews, 1967), p. 105.

114. [Robert Baillie], *A parallel or brief comparison of the liturgie with the masse-book* (London, 1641), p. 85.

115. *Book of Scotish Pasquils*, p. 65.

116. *RKS*, p. 163.

117. *DCH*, VII, 276.

118. *RKS*, p. 166.

119. *RKS*, p. 162.

120. *Book of Scotish Pasquils*, p. 65.

121. William Drummond of Hawthornden, 'Lines on the Bischopes, 14 April 1638', in *Poems* (Edinburgh, 1832), p. 406. Also in *Book of Scotish Pasquils*, pp. 67-69.

122. *RKS*, p. 182.

123. *RKS* p. 166. See also James Gordon, II, 101; *RBLJ*, I, 105.

124. *RBLJ*, I, 154.

125. *RKS*, p. 170.

126. *RKS*, p. 146.

127. NLS, Wodrow Mss., Folio XLII, no. 112, f. 289r.

128. *RKS*, p. 151.

129. Johnston, pp. 402-403.

130. *RKS*, p. 167.

131. *RKS*, p. 168.

132. Johnston, p. 403.

133. *RKS*, p. 168; *Principall acts*, p. 26; James Gordon, II, 104-106.

134. *RBLJ*, I, 158.

135. *RBLJ*, I, 142; Baillie, *Ladensium autokatakrisis*, postscript, p. 28.

136. *Principall acts*, pp. 45-46.

137. *Contra* Kitshoff, pp. 109-110.

138. *Principall acts*, pp. 14-19.

139. *Ibid.*, p. 14.

140. *RKS*, p. 170.

141. James Gordon, II, 131.

142. *RKS*, p. 173.

143. *RKS*, p. 172.

144. *RBLJ*, I, 164.

145. *RBLJ*, I, 372; II, 53, 93-94.

146. *Fasti*, I, 329.

147. *Fasti*, VII, 349-350; VIII, 710.

148. *RKS*, p. 185.

149. *RKS*, p. 173; see also pp. 164-165.

150. James Gordon, II, 95.

151. *RBLJ*, I, 153. See Chapter 8.

152. *The recantation and humble submission of two ancient prelates, of the kingdome of Scotland* ([Edinburgh], 1641), pp. 1-2.

153. *Fasti*, IV, 245.

154. *RKS*, p. 171; see also pp. 44, 159; and James Gordon, II, 47.

155. *Recantation*, pp. 2-3.

156. *Fasti*, VII, 353.

157. Grub, III, 88, accused Fairlie of near-inexcusable conduct in accepting consecration.

158. Joseph Hall, IX, 144; see also X, 537-539.

159. *Ibid.*, IX, 277.

160. *Ibid.*, IX, 278-279.

161. *RKS*, p. 172.

162. *Fasti*, VII, 451.

163. Spalding, I, 54, 98.

164. *Ibid.*, I, 228.

165. *APS*, V, 482.

166. *RKS*, p. 170; James Gordon, II, 102.

167. *RKS*, p. 172.

168. *RBLJ*, I, 150.
169. *RBLJ*, I, 157.
170. *Fasti*, VII, 322.
171. *Fasti*, VII, 334-335.
172. *Fasti*, VII, 355-356; Grub, III, 90.
173. Spalding, I, 138.
174. *Fasti*, VII, 330-331. *DNB* places his death in 1638 or 1639, but see Dowden, p. 399.
175. *Fasti*, VII, 353-354.
176. Spottiswood, *History*, sig. alv.
177. NLS, Wodrow Mss., Quarto LXXXIII, no. 2, pp. 2-3.
178. *Ibid.*, p. 19.
179. *Ibid.*, p. 8.
180. *Ibid.*, p. 16.
181. *Ibid.*, p. 4.
182. *Ibid.*, p. 18.
183. Maxwell, *Episcopacie not abjured*, pp. 25-26.
184. *Ibid.*, pp. 57, 59.
185. *Ibid.*, p. 43.
186. Maxwell, *An answer*, p. 1.
187. Maxwell, *Episcopacie not abjured*, pp. 29-30.
188. Maxwell, *An answer*, pp. 18-19.

Conclusion

1. T. H., *The beautie of the remarkable year of grace* (Edinburgh, 1638), sig. A4v.
2. *RKS*, p. 192.
3. Guthry, p. 30.
4. SRO, GD 188/31/7/2-4. See also NLS, Wodrow Mss., Quarto LXXXIII, no. 2, pp. 17-18.
5. 'Scotland's Encouragement', in *Ballads, and other Fugitive Poetical Pieces, chiefly Scotish; from the Collections of Sir James Balfour, Knight* (Edinburgh, 1834), p. 16.

Bibliography

I. Bibliographic Guides

Aldis, Harry G. *A List of Books Printed in Scotland before 1700*. Edinburgh: National Library of Scotland, 1970.

Allison, A. F. and V. F. Goldsmith. *Titles of English Books*. 2 vols. Hamden, Conn: Archon Books, 1976-1977.

Arber, Edward, ed. *A Transcript of the Registers of the Company of Stationers of London, 1554-1640*. 5 vols. London, 1875-1894.

Dickson, Robert and John P. Edmond. *Annals of Scottish Printing*. 2 vols. Cambridge, 1890.

Matheson, Cyril. *A Catalogue of the Publications of Scottish Historical and Kindred Clubs and Societies, 1908-1927*. Aberdeen: Milne and Hutchison, 1928.

Ogilvie, James D. 'The Aberdeen Doctors and the National Covenant'. *Papers of the Edinburgh Bibliographic Society*, 11 (1921), 73-86.

——————. 'A Bibliography of Glasgow Assembly, 1638'. *Records of the Glasgow Bibliographic Society*, 7 (1923), 1-12.

Pollard, A. W. and G. R. Redgrave. *A Short-Title Catalogue 1475-1640*. London: The Bibliographical Society, 1963. 2nd ed. of vol. II, I-Z, 1976.

Shaaber, Matthias A. *Check-list of Works of British Authors Printed abroad, in Languages other than English, to 1641*. New York: The Bibliographical Society of America, 1975.

Stevenson, David. 'Scottish Church History, 1600-1660: A Select Critical Bibliography'. *Records of the Scottish Church History Society*, XXI (1982), 209-220.

Terry, Charles Sanford. *A Catalogue of the Publications of Scottish Historical and Kindred Clubs and Societies, 1780-1908*. Glasgow: James Maclehose and Sons, 1909.

Wing, Donald. *Short-Title Catalogue 1641-1700*. 3 vols. Vol. I, 2nd ed., New York: Modern Language Association, 1972; Vol. II, 2nd ed., New York: M.L.A., 1982; Vol. III, New York: Index Society, 1951.

II. Primary Sources

    A. Manuscripts
British Library
    Additional
    Harley
    Royal
Edinburgh University Library
    Laing
Glasgow University Library
    Manuscripts General, Wodrow Biographical Collections
National Library of Scotland
    Accessions
    Wodrow

Scottish Record Office
Gifts and Deposits

B. Printed Works

Abernethy, John, *A Christian and heavenly treatise containing physicke for the soule.* London, 1630.

————. *The dignity and duty of a Christian.* London, 1620.

Acts and Proceedings of the General Assemblies of the Kirk of Scotland. 3 vols. Edinburgh, 1839-1845.

The Acts of the Parliaments of Scotland. 12 vols. Edinburgh, 1844-1875.

[Adamson, John]. *The muses welcome.* Edinburgh, 1618.

Adamson, Patrick, *Catechismus latino carmine redditus.* Edinburgh, 1581.

————. *De papistarum superstitiosis ineptiis.* Edinburgh, 1564.

————. *De sacro pastoris munere tractatus.* London, 1619.

————. *Gratiarum actio illustrissimae et potentissimae principi. Do. Elizabetae Ang. Franc. et Hyberniae Reginae, propter liberatem civili seditione Scotiam.* London, [1573].

————. *Poemata sacra.* London, 1619.

————. *The recantation of Maister Patrik Adamsone, sometimes archbishop of Saint-Andrewes in Scotlande.* [Middelburg], 1598.

Analecta Scotica: Collections Illustrative of the Civil, Ecclesiastical, and Literary History of Scotland. 2 vols. Edited by James Maidment. Edinburgh, 1834-1837.

Ancient Scottish Poems. Published from the Ms. of George Bannatyne. 1568. Edinburgh, 1770.

Andrewes, Lancelot. *A sermon preached before the kings majestie, at Hampton Court, concerning the right and power of calling assemblies, on Sunday the 28. of September, anno 1606.* London, 1606.

The answeres of some brethren of the ministerie, to the replyes of the ministers . . . of Aberdene. Aberdeen, 1638.

Anti-Montacutum. An appeale or remonstrance of the orthodox ministers of the church of England; against Richard Montague. Edinburgh, 1629.

[Baillie, Robert]. *Ladensium autokatakrisis, the Canterburians self-conviction* [Edinburgh], 1640.

[————]. *A large supplement of the Canterburian self-conviction.* [London], 1641.

————. *The Letters and Journals of Robert Baillie.* 3 vols. Edinburgh, 1841.

————. *The life of William.* London, 1643.

[————]. *A parallel or briefe comparison of the liturgie with the masse-book.* London, 1641.

Balfour, Sir James. *The Historical Works.* 4 vols. Edinburgh, 1824-1825.

Ballads, and other Fugitive Poetical Pieces, chiefly Scotish; from the Collections of Sir James Balfour, Knight. Edinburgh, 1834.

Bancroft, Richard. *A sermon preached at Paules Crosse.* London. 1589.

The Bannatyne Miscellany. 3 vols. Edinburgh, 1827-1855.

Bannatyne, Richard. *Memorials of Transactions in Scotland, 1569-1573.* Edinburgh, 1836.

Barlow, William. *One of the foure sermons preached before the kings majestie, at Hampton Court in September last. This concerning the antiquity and superioritie of bishops.* London, 1606.

————. *The summe and substance of the conference at Hampton Court. January 14, 1604.* London, 1604.

[Beza, Theodore]. *The judgement of a most reverend and learned man from beyond the sea, concerning a threefold order of bishops.* n.p., [1580?].

The Bible and Holy Scriptures. Edinburgh, 1579.

The Bible and Holy Scriptures. Geneva, 1560.

The Book of Common Order commonly called John Knox's Liturgy. Translated into Gaelic anno domini 1567 by Mr. John Carswell, Bishop of the Isles. Edited by Thomas MacLauchlan. Edinburgh, 1873.

The Book of Common Prayer . . . Laud's Liturgy (1637). Edited by James Cooper. Edinburgh: William Blackwood and Sons, 1904.

A Book of Scotish Pasquils, 1568-1715. Edinburgh, 1868.

The booke of common prayer, and administration of the sacraments. And other parts of divine service for the use of the church of Scotland. Edinburgh, 1637.

Boyd, Andrew. *Ad augustissimum monarcham Carolum . . . in Scotiam redeuntem, carmen panegyricum.* Edinburgh, 1633.

Brereton, Sir William. *Travels in Holland, the United Provinces, England, Scotland, and Ireland, 1634-1635.* [London], 1844.

A briefe and plaine narration of proceedings at an assemblie in Glasco, 8. Jun 1610, anent the innovation of the kirk-governement. [London?], 1610.

Browne, Robert. *A New Years Guift.* Edited by Champlin Burrage. London: Congregational Historical Society, 1904.

Buchanan, George. *The Aret and Science of Government among the Scots.* [*De. jure|regni apud scotos*]. Translated by Duncan H. MacNeill. [Glasgow]: William MacLellan, 1964.

Buckeridge, John. *A sermon preached at Hampton Court before the kings majestie, on Tuesday, the 23. of September, anno 1606.* London, [1606].

The Buik of the Kirk of the Canagait 1564-1567. Edited by Alma B. Calderwood. Edinburgh: Scottish Record Society, 1961.

[Burnet, Gilbert]. *The life of William Bedell, D.D., bishop of Kilmore in Ireland.* London, 1685.

————. *The memoires of the lives and actions of James and William dukes of Hamilton.* London, 1677.

[Calderwood, David]. *The altar of Damascus or the pattern of the English hierarchie, and church-policie obtruded upon the church of Scotland.* n.p., 1621.

[————]. *Altare Damascenum.* n.p., 1623.

[————]. *An answere to M. J. Forbes of Corse, his peaceable warning.* n.p., 1638.

[————]. *A defence of our arguments against kneeling.* n.p., 1620.

[————]. *De regimine ecclesiae scoticanae brevis relatio.* n.p. 1618.

[————]. *A dispute upon communicating at our confused communions.* n.p., 1624.

[————]. *An epistle of a Christian brother.* n.p., 1624.

[————]. *An exhortation of the particular kirks of Christ in Scotland to their sister kirk in Edinburgh.* n.p., 1624.

————. *The History of the Kirk of Scotland.* 8 vols. Edinburgh, 1842-1849.

[————]. *The pastor and the prelate.* n.p., 1628.

[————]. *Parasynagma Perthensis et juramentum ecclesiae scoticanae.* n.p., 1620.

[————]. *Perth assembly.* n.p., 1619.

[————]. *Quares concerning the state of the church of Scotland.* n.p., 1638.

[————]. *A re-examination of the five articles enacted at Perth, anno 1618.* n.p., 1636.

[————]. *A solution of Dr. Resolutus, his resolutions for kneeling.* n.p., 1619.

[————]. *The speach of the kirk of Scotland to her beloved children.* n.p., 1620.

————. *The true history of the church of Scotland.* [Rotterdam], 1678.

Calendar of State Papers relating to Scotland 1547-1603. 13 vols. Edinburgh: HM General Register House, 1898-1969.

Calvin, John. *Institutes of the Christian Religion.* 2 vols. Edited by J. T. McNeill.

Philadelphia: Westminster Press, 1954.

————. *Theological Treatises.* Edited by J. K. S. Reid. Philadelphia: Westminster Press, 1954.

Cameron, James K., ed. *Letters of John Johnston c.1565-1611 and Robert Howie c.1565-c.1645.* Edinburgh: Oliver and Boyd, 1963.

Canons and constitutions ecclesiasticall gathered and put in forme, for the governement of the church of Scotland. Aberdeen, 1636.

Cardwell, Edward. *A History of Conferences.* 3rd ed. Oxford, 1849.

The Catechism set forth by Archbishop Hamilton printed at Saint Andrews, 1551. Edinburgh, 1882.

Charles I. *A large declaration concerning the late tumults in Scotland.* London, 1639.

Clarendon, Lord. *History of the Rebellion and Civil Wars in England.* 6 vols. Oxford, 1888.

A Compendious Book of Godly and Spiritual Songs commonly known as the Gude and Godlie Ballatis. Reprinted from the Edition of 1567. Edited by A. F. Mitchell. Edinburgh: Scottish Text Society, 1897.

The complaynt of Scotland. [Paris, c.1550].

The Complaynt of Scotland. Edited by J. A. H. Murray. London, 1872-1873.

Confessio fidei et doctrinae. St. Andrews, 1572.

The confession of faith of the kirk of Scotland. [Edinburgh? 1638?].

Correspondence of Sir Robert Kerr, first Earl of Ancrum and his son William, third Earl of Lothian. 2 vols. Edinburgh, 1875.

Cowper, William. *The bishop of Galloway his apologie.* [London? 1613?].

————. *The bishop of Galloway his dikaiologie: contayning a defence of his apologie.* London, 1614.

————. *The life and death of the reverend father and faithfull servant of God, Mr. William Cowper, bishop of Galloway.* London, 1619.

————. *Phosphoros or a most heavenly and fruitfull sermon, preached the sixt of August. 1615.* London, 1616.

————. *Seven dayes conference, betweene a Catholicke Christian, and a Catholicke Romane.* London, 1613.

————. *Two sermons.* London, 1618.

————. *The workes.* London, 1623.

Craig, Sir Thomas. *De unione regnorum Britanniae tractatus.* Edinburgh: Scottish History Society, 1909.

Cranstoun, James, ed. *Satirical Poems of the Time of the Reformation.* 2 vols. Edinburgh, 1891-1893.

[Davidson, John]. *D. Bancrofts rashnes in rayling against the church of Scotland.* Edinburgh, 1590.

A declaration of the just causes of his majesties proceeding against those ministers, who are now lying in prison, attainted of high treason. London, 1606.

A declaration of the kings majesties intention and meaning toward the lait actis of parliament. Edinburgh, 1535.

Ane declaratioun of the just and necessar causis, moving us of the nobillitie of Scotland & uthers ye kings majesteis faithful subjectis to repair to his hienes presence. [Edinburgh], 1582.

The declinator and protestation of the archbishops and bishops, of the church of Scotland, and others their adherents within that kingdome. London, 1639.

The declinatour and protestation of the some some-times pretended bishops. Edinburgh, 1639.

Ane discourse tuiching the estait present in October anno domini, 1571. St. Andrews, 1572.

Downame, George. *Two sermons, the one commending the ministerie; the other defending the office of bishops.* London, 1608.

Drummond, William, of Hawthornden. *Poems.* Edinburgh, 1832.

Duplyes of the ministers and professors of Aberdene. Aberdeen, 1638.

The Earl of Stirling's Register of Royal Letters. 2 vols. Edited by Charles Rogers. Edinburgh, 1885.

Englands wedding garment. London, 1603.

Erastus, Thomas. *The Theses of Erastus Touching Excommunication.* Edinburgh, 1844.

Extract from the Despatches of M. Courcelles, French Ambassador at the Court of Scotland, 1586-1587. Edinburgh, 1828.

Ferguson, David. *Ane sermon preichit befoir the regent and nobilitie . . . in the kirk of Leith, 13 Januarie 1572.* St. Andrews, 1572.

————. *Tracts 1563-1572.* Edinburgh, 1860.

The first and second booke of discipline. [Amsterdam], 1621.

The First Book of Discipline. Edited by James K. Cameron. Edinburgh: Saint Andrew Press, 1972.

Foirm Na N-Urrnuidheadh. John Carswell's Gaelic Translation of the Book of Common Order. Edited by R. L. Thomson. Edinburgh: Scottish Gaelic Texts Society, 1970.

Forbes, John, of Corse. *The First Book of the Irenicum.* Edited by E. G. Selwyn. Cambridge: University Press, 1923.

————. *A peaceable warning, to the subjects in Scotland.* Aberdeen, 1638.

Forbes, Patrick. *A defence of the lawful calling of the ministers of reformed churches, against the cavillations of Romanists; An epistle to a recusant; A short discovery of the adversarie.* Middelburgh, 1614.

————. *Eubulus, or a dialogue.* Aberdeen, 1627.

————. *An exquisite commentarie upon the Revelation of St. John.* London, 1613.

Forbes, William. *Considerationes Modestae et Pacificae.* 2 vols. Oxford, 1850-1856.

The Funeral Sermons, Orations, Epitaphs, and other Pieces on the Death of the Right Rev. Patrick Forbes, Bishop of Aberdeen. Edinburgh, 1845.

Funerals of a right reverend father in God Patrick Forbes of Corse, bishop of Aberdene. Aberdeen, 1635.

Generall demands concerning the late covenant: propounded by the ministers and professors of divinity of Aberdene. [Edinburgh], 1638.

[Gillespie, George]. *A dispute against the English-popish ceremonies, obtruded upon the church of Scotland.* n.p., 1637.

[————]. *Reasons for which the service book, urged upon Scotland ought to be refused.* [Edinburgh], 1638.

Gordon, James. *History of Scots Affairs, from 1637 to 1641.* 3 vols. Aberdeen, 1841.

Gordon, John. *England and Scotlands happinesse: in being reduced to unitie of religion, under our invincible monarke king James.* London, 1604.

————. *Henotikon or a sermon of the union of Great Brittannie.* London, 1604.

————. *A panegyrique of congratulation for the concord of the realmes of Great Britaine in unitie of religion, and under one king.* London, 1603.

The grievances given in by the ministers before the parliament holden in June 1633. n.p., 1635.

Guild, William. *A compend of the controversies of religion.* Edinburgh, 1627.

————. *To the nobilitie . . . a friendly and faythfull advice.* Aberdeen, 1639.

Guthry, Henry. *Memoirs of Henry Guthry, late Bishop of Dunkel in Scotland.* London, 1702.

H., T. *The beautie of the remarkable year of grace, 1638.* Edinburgh, 1638.

Hailes, Sir David Dalrymple, Lord. *Memorials and Letters relating to the History of*

Britain in the Reign of Charles the First. Glasgow, 1766.

Hall, Joseph. *The Works.* 10 vols. Oxford, 1863.

Hamilton, James, Duke of. [*A declaration on episcopal government in Scotland*]. Edinburgh, 1638.

The Hamilton Papers 1638-1650. Edited by S. R. Gardiner. London, 1880.

Hampton, Christopher. *A sermon preached in the cittie of Glasco in Scotland, on the tenth day of June, 1610. At the holding of a generall assembly there.* London, 1611.

Hardwicke, Philip. *Miscellaneous State Papers.* 2 vols. London, 1778.

Harington, Sir John. *Nugae Antiquae.* 3 vols. London, 1799.

Hay, John. *A speach, delivered to the kings most excellent majesty, 16 May 1617.* Edinburgh, 1617.

Hay, Peter. *An advertisement to the subjects of Scotland.* Aberdeen, 1627.

Historical Manuscripts Commission. *Report on the Laing Manuscripts preserved in the University of Edinburgh.* 2 vols. London: HMSO, 1914-1925.

————. *Report on the Manuscripts of the Earl of Mar and Kellie.* London: HMSO, 1904.

Historie and Life of King James the Sext. Edinburgh, 1825.

Holinshed, Raphael. *Chronicles.* 6 vols. London, 1807-1808.

Hume, David, of Godscroft. *Patricio Symsono.* n.p., 1609.

————. *The history of the houses of Douglas and Angus.* Edinburgh, 1644.

Informations, or a protestation, and a treatise from Scotland. [Netherlands?], 1608.

James VI and I. *An apologie for the oath of allegiance . . . together, with a premonition.* London, 1609.

————. *Basilicon Doron.* 2 vols. Edited by J. Craigie. Edinburgh: Scottish Text Society, 1944-1950.

————. *His majesties speach in the Starre-Chamber, 20 June 1616.* London, [1616].

————. *His majesties speach in this last session of parliament.* London, 1605.

————. *His majesties speech to both the houses of parliament the last day of March 1607.* London, [1607].

————. *The kings majesties speach to parliament, 21 March 1609.* London, [1609].

————. *The kings majesties speech in parliament the 19. day of March 1604.* London, 1604.

————. *The Political Works of James I.* Edited by C. H. McIlwain. New York: Russell and Russell, Inc., 1965.

————. *The true lawe of free monarchies: or, the reciprock and mutuall dutie betwixt a free king, and his naturall subjectes.* Edinburgh, 1598.

————. *The workes.* London, 1616.

Johnston, Sir Archibald, of Wariston. *Diary 1632-1639.* Edinburgh: Scottish History Society, 1911.

King, John. *The fourth sermon preached at Hampton Court on Tuesday the last of Sept. 1606.* Oxford, 1606.

Knox, John. *The appellation of John Knoxe from the cruell and most injust sentence.* Geneva, 1558.

————. *The copie of an epistle sent by John Knox.* Geneva, 1559.

————. *History of the Reformation in Scotland.* 2 vols. Edited by W. C. Dickinson. London: Thomas Nelson and Sons Ltd., 1949.

————. *Works.* 6 vols. Edinburgh, 1846-1864.

Laud, William. *Works.* 7 vols. Oxford, 1847-1860.

Lauder, William. *Ane compendious and breve tractate, concernyng the office and dewtie of kyngis, spirituall pastoris, and temporall jugis.* [Edinburgh], 1566.

————. *The Extant Poetical Works.* London, 1870.

Leith, John H., ed. *Creeds of the Churches.* Revised ed. Atlanta: John Knox Press, 1973.

Letters of Queen Elizabeth and King James VI of Scotland. Edited by John Bruce. London, 1849.

Letters and State Papers during the Reign of King James the Sixth; Chiefly from the Manuscript Collections of Sir James Balfour of Denmyln. Edited by James Maidment. Edinburgh, 1838.

Lindesay, Robert, of Pitscottie. *The Historie and Cronicles of Scotland.* 3 vols. Edinburgh: Scottish Text Society, 1899-1911.

Lindsay, Sir David, of the Mount. *Works.* 4 vols. Edinburgh: Scottish Text Society, 1931-1936.

Lindsay, David, bishop of Brechin. *De potestate principis aphorismi.* Edinburgh, 1617.

————. *The reasons of a pastors resolution touching the communion.* London, 1619.

————. *A true narration of all the passages of the proceedings in the generall assembly of the church of Scotland, holden at Perth the 25. of August, anno dom. 1618.* London, 1621.

Lithgow, William. *Scotlands welcome to her native sonne, and soveraigne lord, king Charles.* Edinburgh, [1633].

The Maitland Folio Manuscript. 2 vols. Edited by W. A. Craigie. Edinburgh: Scottish Text Society, 1919-1927.

Maitland, Richard. *Poems.* Glasgow, 1830.

Maxey, Anthony. *The sermon preached before the king, at Whitehall.* London, 1605.

Maxwell, James. *A new eight-fold probation of the church of Englands divine constitution.* London, 1617.

[Maxwell, John]. *An answer by letter to a worthy gentleman.* [Oxford], 1644.

[————]. *The burthen of Issachar.* [London], 1646.

[————]. *Episcopacie not abjured in his majesties realme of Scotland.* [Dublin], 1641.

[————]. *Presbytery displayd.* London, 1663.

[————]. *Sacro-sancta regum majestas: or, the sacred and royall prerogative of Christian kings.* Oxford, 1644.

Melville, James. *The Autobiography and Diary of Mr. James Melvill.* Edinburgh, 1842.

————. *The black bastel.* [Edinburgh], 1634.

Melville, Sir James, of Halhill. *Memoirs of his own Life.* Edinburgh, 1827.

Meriton, George. *A sermon preached before the generall assembly at Glascoe in the kingdome of Scotland, the tenth day of June, 1610.* London, 1611.

Michaelson, John. *The lawfulnes of kneeling.* St. Andrews, 1620.

Miscellany of the Scottish History Society. Vol. II, Edinburgh, 1904. Vol. VIII, Edinburgh, 1951. Vol. X, Edinburgh, 1965.

Miscellany of the Spalding Club. Vol. II, Aberdeen, 1842. Vol. IV, Aberdeen, 1849.

Miscellany of the Wodrow Society. Edinburgh, 1844.

Mosse, Miles. *Scotland's welcome.* London 1603.

Moysie, David. *Memoirs of the Affairs of Scotland. 1577-1603.* Edinburgh, 1830.

[Murray, John]. *A dialogue betwixt Cosmophilus and Theophilus anent the urging of new ceremonies upon the kirke of Scotland.* n.p., 1620.

[————]. *A godly and fruitfull sermon preached at Lieth in Scotland.* n.p., 1607.

'The National Petition to the Scottish Privy Council, October 18, 1637'. *Scottish Historical Review,* 22 (1925), 241-248.

Newes from Scotland. [Amsterdam? 1638?].

The CL. Psalmes of David in meter. For the use of the kirk of Scotland. London, 1587.

Original Letters relating to the Ecclesiastical Affairs of Scotland. 2 vols. Edinburgh, 1851.

Pauck, Wilhelm, ed. *Melanchthon and Bucer.* Philadelphia: Westminster Press, 1969.

Peel, A. and L. H. Carlson, eds. *The Writings of Robert Harrison and Robert Browne.* London: George Allen and Unwin, 1953.

[Penry, John]. *A briefe discovery of the untruthes and slanders . . . contained in a sermon . . . by D. Bancroft.* [Edinburgh, 1589].

P[ont], R[obert]. *De unione Britanniae, dialogus.* Edinburgh, 1604.

The Presbytrie Booke of Kirkcaldie. Edited by William Stevenson. Kirkcaldy, 1900.

The principall acts of the solemne generall assembly of the kirk of Scotland . . . at Glasgow the xxi of November 1638. Edinburgh, 1639.

Proclamations – untitled, listed chronologically.

28 June 1638. Concerning canons, service book, free assembly. Edinburgh, 1638.

9 September 1638. Annulling the service book, etc. Edinburgh, 1638.

29 November 1638. Discharging and inhibiting the pretended assembly. Edinburgh, 1638.

8 December 1638. Against acknowledging the Glasgow assembly. Edinburgh, 1638.

The protestation of the generall assemblie of the church of Scotland . . . at the mercat crosse of Glasgow, the 28, and 29 of November 1638. Glasgow, 1638.

The protestation of the noblemen . . . immediately after the reading of the proclamation, dated September 9. 1638. [Edinburgh], 1638.

Prynne, William. *Hidden workes of darkenes brought to publike light.* London, 1645.

The questions to be resolvit at the convention of the estaits and generall assemblie, appointed to be at the burgh of Perth the last day of Februarie nixt to come. Edinburgh, 1597.

Ramsey, David. *A sermon, or litle treatise, upon the three last verses of the seaventeenth chapter of Deuteronomie.* Aberdeen, 1629.

Reasons for a generall assemblie. [Edinburgh], 1638.

The recantation and humble submission of two ancient prelates, of the kingdome of Scotland. [Edinburgh], 1641.

Records of the Kirk of Scotland. Edited by Alexander Peterkin. Edinburgh, 1838.

Register of the Ministers, Elders, and Deacons of the Christian Congregation of St. Andrews. Part first 1559-1582. Edited by David Hay Fleming. Edinburgh, 1889.

Register of the Privy Council of Scotland. First series. 14 vols. Edinburgh 1877-1898.

Register of the Privy Council of Scotland. Second series. 8 vols. Edinburgh, 1899-1908.

Register of the Privy Seal of Scotland. 7 vols. Edinburgh, 1908-1966.

Rollock, Robert. *In epistolam Pauli apostoli ad Ephesios . . . commentarius.* Edinburgh, 1590.

Rothes, John, earl of. *A Relation of Proceedings Concerning the Affairs of the Kirk of Scotland, from August 1637 to July 1638.* Edinburgh, 1830.

Row, John. *History of the Kirk of Scotland, from the Year 1558 to August 1637.* Edinburgh, 1842.

Row, William. *The Life of Mr. Robert Blair, Minister of St. Andrews.* Edinburgh, 1848.

Rushworth, John. *Historical Collections.* Second Part. London, 1680.

Rutherford, Samuel. *Letters.* Edinburgh, 1891.

Scot, Patrick. *Vox vera: or, observations from Amsterdam.* London, 1625.

Scot, William. *An Apologetical Narration of the State and Government of the Kirk of Scotland since the Reformation.* Also includes John Forbes. *Certaine Records Touching the Estate of the Church of Scotland.* Edinburgh, 1846.

[--------]. *The course of conformitie.* n.p., 1622.

Scots Confession, 1560 and Negative Confession, 1581. Edited by G. D. Henderson. Edinburgh: Church of Scotland Committee on Publications, 1937.

The Second Book of Discipline. Edited by James Kirk. Edinburgh: Saint Andrew Press, 1980.

Select Biographies. 2 vols. Edited by W. K. Tweedie. Edinburgh, 1845-1847.

Selections from the Records of the Kirk Session, Presbytery, and Synod of Aberdeen. Edited by John Stuart. Aberdeen, 1846.

Sempill, James. *Sacrilege sacredly handled.* London, 1619.

A short relation of the state of the kirk of Scotland since the reformation of religion, to the present time. [Edinburgh], 1638.

Ane shorte and generall confession. Edinburgh, 1581.

Simson, Archibald. *Heptameron.* St. Andrews, 1621.

Smart, Peter. *The vanitie and downe-fall of superstitious popish ceremonies: or, a sermon preached in the cathedrall church of Durham, July 27, 1628.* Edinburgh, 1628.

Spalding, John. *The History of the Troubles and Memorable Transactions in Scotland and England, from 1624 to 1645.* 2 vols. Edinburgh, 1828-1829.

Spelman, Henry. *De non temerandis ecclesiis. A tract of the rights and respect due unto churches.* London, 1613.

Spottiswood. James. *Concio . . . ad clerum . . . pro gradu doctoratus.* Edinburgh, 1616.

Spottiswood. John. *History of the Church of Scotland.* London, 1655.

————. *History of the Church of Scotland.* 3 vols.. Edinburgh. 1847-1851.

————. *Refutatio libelli de regimine ecclesiae scoticanae.* London, 1620.

[————]. *A true relation of the proceedings against John Ogilvie, a Jesuit.* Edinburgh, 1615.

Spottiswood Miscellany. 2 vols. Edinburgh, 1844-1845.

Sprott, G. W., ed. *Scottish Liturgies of the Reign of James VI.* Edinburgh: William Blackwood and Sons, 1901.

State Papers, and Miscellaneous Correspondence of Thomas, Earl of Melros. 2 vols. Edinburgh, 1837.

Statutes of the Scottish Church. 1225-1559. Edited by David Patrick. Edinburgh: Scottish History Society, 1907.

Struther, William. *Scotlands warning, or a treatise of fasting.* Edinburgh, 1628.

Treason pretended against the king of Scots . . . with a declaration of the kinges majesties intention to his last acts of parliament. Out of Skottish into English. London, 1585.

A trewe description of the nobill race of the Stewards. Amsterdam, 1603.

Viri clarissimi A. Melvini musae et P. Adamsoni vita et palindoia et celsae commissionis ceu delegatae potestatis regiae in causis ecclesiasticis brevis & aperta descriptio. n.p., 1620.

Winzet, Niniane. *Certane Tractatis for Reformation of Doctryne and Maneris in Scotland. 1562-1563.* Edinburgh, 1835.

III. Secondary Sources (from c.1700)

A. Books and Articles

Ainslie, James L. *The Doctrines of Ministerial Order in the Reformed Churches of the 16th and 17th Centuries.* Edinburgh: T. & T. Clark, 1940.

————. 'The Scottish Reformed Church and English Puritanism'. *Records of the Scottish Church History Society*, 8 (1944), 75-95.

Allen, J. W. *English Political Thought 1603-1644.* London: Methuen, 1938.

Armstrong, Brian G. *Calvinism and the Amyraut Heresy: Protestant Scholasticism and Humanism in Seventeenth-Century France.* Madison: University of Wisconsin Press, 1969.

Baker, Derek, ed. *Schism, Heresy and Religious Protest. Studies in Church History.* Vol. IX. Cambridge: University Press. 1972.

Batten, J. Minton. *John Dury: Advocate of Christian Reunion.* Chicago: University of Chicago Press, 1944.

Babbage, Stuart Barton. *Puritanism and Richard Bancroft.* London: SPCK, 1962.

Baxter, J. H. 'Scottish Students at Helmstedt University'. *Scottish Historical Review*, 24 (1927), 235-237.

Bindoff, S. T., *et al*, eds. *Elizabethan Government and Society*. London: Athlone Press, 1961.

Birchler, Allen B. 'Archbishop John Spottiswoode: Chancellor of Scotland, 1635-1638'. *Church History*, 39 (1970), 317-326

Bonet-Maury, Gaston. 'John Cameron, a Scottish Protestant Theologian in France 1579-1625'. *Scottish Historical Review*, 7 (1910), 325-345.

Brother Kenneth. 'Sir David Lindsay, Reformer'. *Innes Review*, 1 (1950), 79-91.

Brown, Peter Hume. *John Knox: A Biography*. 2 vols. London, 1895.

Burnet, George B. *The Holy Communion in the Reformed Church of Scotland, 1560-1960*. Edinburgh: Oliver and Boyd, 1960.

Burrage, Champlin. *The Early English Dissenters in the Light of Recent Research*. 2 vols. Cambridge: University Press, 1912.

Burrell, S. A. 'The Apocalyptic Vision of the Early Covenanters'. *Scottish Historical Review*, 43 (1964), 1-24.

--------. 'The Covenant Idea as a Revolutionary Symbol: Scotland, 1596-1637'. *Church History*, 27 (1958), 338-350.

Burton, John Hill. *The History of Scotland*. 2nd ed. 8 vols. Edinburgh, 1873.

Cameron, James K. 'The Cologne Reformation and the Church of Scotland'. *Journal of Ecclesiastical History*, 30 (1979), 39-64.

Campbell, William M. *The Triumph of Presbyterianism*. Edinburgh: Saint Andrew Press, 1958.

Chadwick, Owen. 'Richard Bancroft's Submission'. *Journal of Ecclesiastical History*, 3 (1952), 58-73.

Collinson, Patrick. *Archbishop Grindal 1519-1583*. London: Jonathan Cape, 1979.

--------. *The Elizabethan Puritan Movement*. London: Jonathan Cape. 1967.

--------. *The Religion of Protestants: The Church in English Society 1559-1625*. Oxford: Clarendon Press, 1982.

Cooper, James. 'Archbishop Spottiswood 1565-1639'. *Transactions of the Glasgow Archaeological Society*. New series, 7 (1924), 79-104.

Cowan, Edward J. 'The Angus Campbells and the Origin of the Campbell-Ogilvie Feud'. *Scottish Studies*, (1981), 25-38.

Cowan, Ian B. *The Scottish Reformation: Church and Society in Sixteenth Century Scotland*. London: Weidenfeld and Nicolson, 1982.

Cragg, Gerald R. *Freedom and Authority: A Study of English Thought in the early Seventeenth Century*. Philadelphia: Westminster Press, 1975.

Craven, J. B. *Records of the Dioceses of Argyll and the Isles 1560-1860*. Kirkwall: William Peace and Son, 1907.

Curtis, Mark H. 'Hampton Court Conference and its Aftermath'. *History*, 46 (1961), 1-16.

Davies, E. T. *Episcopacy and the Royal Supremacy in the Church of England in the XVI Century*. Oxford: Basil Blackwell, 1950.

Davies, Godfrey. 'The Character of James VI and I'. *Huntington Library Quarterly*, 5 (1941/2), 33-63.

Dictionary of National Biography. London: Oxford University Press, 1917-.

Donaldson, Gordon. 'Alexander Gordon, Bishop of Galloway (1559-1572), and his Work in the Reformed Church'. *Transactions of the Dumfriesshire and Galloway Natural History and Antiquarian Society*. 3rd series, 24 (1947), 111-128.

--------. *All the Queen's Men: Power and Politics in Mary Stewart's Scotland*. London:

Batsford Academic and Educational Ltd., 1983.

————. 'The Attitude of Whitgift and Bancroft to the Scottish Church'. *Transactions of the Royal Historical Society*. 4th series, 24 (1942), 95-115.

————. 'Bishop Adam Bothwell and the Reformation in Orkney'. *Records of the Scottish Church History Society*, 13 (1954), 85-100.

————. 'The Bishops and Priors of Whithorn'. *Transactions of the Dumfriesshire and Galloway Natural History and Antiquarian Society*. 3rd series, 27 (1950), 127-154.

————. '"The Example of Denmark" in the Scottish Reformation'. *Scottish Historical Review*, 27 (1948), 57-64.

————. 'Leighton's Predecessors'. *Journal of the Society of Friends of Dunblane Cathedral*, 12 (1975), 7-16.

————. *The Making of the Scottish Prayer Book of 1637*. Edinburgh: University Press, 1954.

————. *Scotland: Church and Nation through Sixteen Centuries*. Edinburgh: Scottish Academic Press, 1960.

————. *Scotland: James V -James VII*. Edinburgh: Oliver and Boyd, 1978.

————. 'The Scottish Episcopate at the Reformation'. *English Historical Review*, 60 (1945), 349-364.

————. *The Scottish Reformation*. Cambridge: University Press, 1960.

————. 'Sources for the Study of Scottish Ecclesiastical Organization and Personnel, 1560-1600'. *Bulletin of the Institute for Historical Research*, 19 (1942/3), 188-203.

Dowden, John. *The Bishops of Scotland*. Glasgow: James Maclehose and Sons, 1912.

Dowding, W. C. *German Theology during the Thirty Years' War: The Life and Correspondence of George Calixtus*. Oxford, 1863.

Drummond, Andrew L. *The Kirk and the Continent*. Edinburgh: Saint Andrew Press, 1956.

Dugmore, C. W. and Charles Duggan, eds. *Studies in Church History*. Vol. I. London: Nelson, 1964.

Durkan, John. 'The Beginnings of Humanism in Scotland'. *Innes Review*, 4 (1953), 5-24.

————. 'The Cultural Background in Sixteenth-Century Scotland'. *Innes Review*, 10 (1959), 382-439.

Dwyer, John, Roger A. Mason, and Alexander Murdoch, eds. *New Perspectives on the Politics and Culture of Early Modern Scotland*. Edinburgh: John Donald Publishers, [1982].

Elton, G. R. *England under the Tudors*. 2nd ed. London: Methuen, 1974.

Fischer, Th. A. *The Scots in Germany*. Edinburgh: Otto Schulze & Co., 1902. Reprinted Edinburgh: John Donald Publishers, 1973.

Fleming, David Hay. *The Reformation in Scotland: Causes, Characteristics, Consequences*. London: Hodder and Stoughton, 1910.

————. 'Scotland's Supplication and Complaint against the Book of Common Prayer (otherwise Laud's Liturgy), the Book of Canons, and the Prelates, 18th October 1637'. *Proceedings of the Society of Antiquaries of Scotland*, 60 (1927), 314-383.

Foster, Walter R. *The Church before the Covenants: The Church of Scotland 1596-1638*. Edinburgh: Scottish Academic Press, 1975.

————. 'The Operation of Presbyteries in Scotland, 1600-1638'. *Records of the Scottish Church History Society*, 15 (1966), 21-33.

Fraser, Sir William. *Memorials of the Earls of Haddington*. 2 vols. Edinburgh, 1889.

Greaves, Richard L. *Theology and Revolution in the Scottish Reformation: Studies in the Thought of John Knox*. Grand Rapids: Christian University Press, 1980.

Grub, George. *An Ecclesiastical History of Scotland*. 4 vols. Edinburgh, 1861.

Hall, Basil. *John à Lasco 1499-1560: A Pole in Reformation England*. London: Dr.Williams's Trust, 1971.

Haller, William. *The Rise of Puritanism*. New York: Harper and Brother, 1957.

Hannan, Thomas. 'The Scottish Consecrations in London in 1610'. *Church Quarterly Review*, 71 (1911), 387-413.

Harrison, Archibald W. *Arminianism*. London: Duckworth, 1937.

————. *The Beginnings of Arminianism to the Synod of Dort*. London: University of London Press, 1926.

Henderson, George David. 'Arminianism in Scotland'. *London Quarterly and Holborn Review*, [157] (1932), 493-504.

————. *The Burning Bush: Studies in Scottish Church History*. Edinburgh: Saint Andrew Press, 1957.

————. *Presbyterianism*. Aberdeen: University Press, 1954.

————. *Religious Life in Seventeenth Century Scotland*. Cambridge: University Press, 1937.

Henderson, J. M. 'An "Advertisement" about the Service Book'. *Scottish Historical Review*, 23 (1926), 198-204.

Hewat, Kirkwood. *Makers of the Scottish Church at the Reformation*. Edinburgh: Macniven & Wallace, 1920.

Historical Papers submitted to the Christian Unity Association of Scotland. Edinburgh: T. and A. Constable, 1914.

Howie, David I. 'Some Remarks on the Episcopal Ideal in Sixteenth Century Scotland'. *Scottish Tradition*, 7/8 (1977/8), 47-66.

An Introduction to Scottish Legal History. Edinburgh: Stair Society, 1958.

Keith, Robert. *An Historical Catalogue of the Scottish Bishops down to the Year 1688*. New ed. Edinburgh, 1824.

———*History of the Affairs of Church and State in Scotland. 3 vols*. Edinburgh, 1844-1850.

Kelly, J. N. D. *Jerome: His Life, Writings, and Controversies*. New York: Harper and Row, 1975.

Kirk, James. 'The Influence of Calvinism on the Scottish Reformation'. *Records of the Scottish Church History Society*, 18 (1974), 157-179.

————. "The Polities of the Best Reformed Kirks': Scottish Achievements and English Aspirations in Church Government at the Reformation'. *Scottish Historical Review*, 59 (1980), 25-53.

Lamont, William M. *Godly Rule: Politics and Religion, 1603-60*. London: Macmillan, 1969.

Lee, Maurice, Jr. 'Archbishop Spottiswood as Historian'. *Journal of British Studies*, 13 (1973/4), 138-150.

————. *Government by Pen: Scotland under James VI and I*. Urbana: University of Illinois Press, 1980.

————. 'James VI and the Revival of Episcopacy in Scotland: 1596-1600'. *Church History*, 43 (1974), 50-64.

————. *John Maitland of Thirlestane and the Foundation of the Stewart Despotism in Scotland*. Princeton: University Press, 1959.

————. 'The Scottish Reformation after 400 Years'. *Scottish Historical Review*, 44 (1965), 135-147.

Lees, James Cameron. *The Abbey of Paisley*. Paisley, 1878.

Leslie, James B. *Clogher Clergy and Parishes*. Enniskillen: privately published, 1929.

————. *Raphoe Clergy and Parishes*. Enniskillen: privately published, 1940.

Lorimer, Peter. *John Knox and the Church of England*. London, 1875.

McCoy, F. N. *Robert Baillie and the Second Scots Reformation.* Berkeley: University of California Press, 1974.

McCrie, Thomas. *Life of Andrew Melville.* Edinburgh, 1899.

MacFarlane, Leslie. 'The Primacy of the Scottish Church, 1472-1521'. *Innes Review,* 20 (1969), 111-129.

McGinn, Donald J. *The Admonition Controversy.* New Brunswick, New Jersey: Rutgers University Press, 1949.

McGrath, Patrick. *Papists and Puritans under Elizabeth I.* New York: Walker and Co., 1967.

Macgregor, Janet G. *The Scottish Presbyterian Polity: A Study of its Origins in the Sixteenth Century.* Edinburgh: Oliver and Boyd, 1926.

MacKay, P. H. R. 'The Reception given to the Five Articles of Perth'. *Records of the Scottish Church History Society,* 19 (1977), 185-201.

MacKinnon, Donald. 'John Carswell, 1520-1572: Superintendent of Argyle and the Isles'. *Records of the Scottish Church History Society,* 4 (1932), 195-207.

MacLean, Duncan. 'Catholicism in the Highlands and Isles, 1560-1680'. *Innes Review,* 3 (1952), 5-13.

MacLeod, John. *Scottish Theology in relation to Church History since the Reformation.* Edinburgh: Publications Committee of the Free Church of Scotland, 1943.

McMahon, George I. R. 'The Scottish Courts of High Commission 1610-1638'. *Records of the Scottish Church History Society,* 15 (1966), 193-209.

Macmillan, Donald. *The Aberdeen Doctors.* London: Hodder and Stoughton, 1909.

McMillan, William. *The Worship of the Scottish Reformed Church 1550-1638.* London: James Clarke, 1931.

McNeill, Peter and Ranald Nicholson, eds. *An Historical Atlas of Scotland c.400-c.1600.* St. Andrews: Conference of Scottish Medievalists, 1975.

Mahoney, Matthew. 'The Scottish Hierarchy, 1513-1565'. *Innes Review,* 10 (1959), 21-66.

Maitland, F. W. 'The Anglican Settlement and the Scottish Reformation'. *Cambridge Modern History,* II (1907), 550-598.

Makey, Walter, *The Church of the Covenant 1637-1651: Revolution and Social Change in Scotland.* Edinburgh: John Donald Publishers, 1979.

Matheson, Angus. 'Bishop Carswell'. *Transactions of the Gaelic Society of Inverness,* 42 (1965), 182-205.

Mathieson, William Law. *Politics and Religion: A Study in Scottish History from the Reformation to the Revolution.* 2 vols. Glasgow: James Maclehose and Sons, 1902.

Maxwell, William. *A History of Worship in the Church of Scotland.* London: Oxford University Press, 1955.

Meek, Donald E. and James Kirk. 'John Carswell, Superintendent of Argyll: A Reassessment'. *Records of the Scottish Church History Society,* 19 (1975), 1-22.

Moffatt, Alexander. 'The Office of Superintendent 1560-1581'. *Records of the Scottish Church History Society,* 4 (1932), 37-47.

Murison, William. *Sir David Lindsay: Poet, and Satirist of the Old Church in Scotland.* Cambridge: University Press, 1938.

Nicholson, Ranald. *Scotland: The Later Middle Ages.* Edinburgh: Oliver and Boyd, 1978.

Patry, Raoul. *Philippe du Plessis-Mornay. Un Huguenot homme d'Etat (1549-1623).* Paris: Fischbacher, 1933.

Pattison, Mark. *Isaac Casaubon 1559-1614.* 2nd ed. Oxford, 1892.

Paul, James B. *The Scots Peerage.* 9 vols. Edinburgh: David Douglas, 1904-1914.

Pearson, A. F. Scott. *Church and State: Political Aspects of Sixteenth Century Puritanism.*

Cambridge: University Press, 1928.

Rait, R. S. *The Parliaments of Scotland.* Glasgow: Maclehose, Jackson and Co., 1924.

Reid, Henry M. B. *The Divinity Principals in the University of Glasgow.* Glasgow: James Maclehose and Sons, 1917.

Reid, W. Stanford. 'French Influence on the First Scots Confession and Book of Discipline'. *Westminster Theological Journal,* 35 (1972), 1-14.

--------. 'Knox's Attitude to the English Reformation'. *Westminster Theological Journal,* 25 (1963), 1-32.

Rogers, Charles. *History of the Chapel Royal of Scotland.* Edinburgh, 1882.

Rubenstein, Hilary L. *Captain Luckless: James, First Duke of Hamilton 1606-1649.* Edinburgh: Scottish Academic Press, 1975.

Russell, Conrad, ed. *The Origins of the English Civil War.* London: Macmillan, 1975.

Schwarz, Marc L. 'James I and the Historians: Toward a Reconsideration'. *Journal of British Studies,* 13 (1974), 114-134.

Scott, Hew, ed. *Fasti Ecclesiae Scoticanae: The Succession of Ministers in the Church of Scotland from the Reformation.* New ed. 9 vols. Edinburgh: Oliver and Boyd, 1915-1961.

Selwyn, E.G. 'The First Scottish Episcopacy'. *Church Quarterly Review,* 180 (1920), 193-218.

Shaw, Duncan. *The General Assemblies of the Church of Scotland 1560-1600: Their Origins and Development.* Edinburgh: Saint Andrew Press, 1964.

--------. 'The Inauguration of Ministers in Scotland: 1560-1620'. *Records of the Scottish Church History Society,* 16 (1969), 35-62.

--------, ed. *Reformation and Revolution.* Edinburgh: Saint Andrew Press, 1967.

Shriver, Frederick. 'Hampton Court Re-visited: James I and the Puritans'. *Journal of Ecclesiastical History,* 33 (1982), 48-71.

Simpson, Martin A. 'The Hampton Court Conference, January 1604'. *Records of the Scottish Church History Society,* 21 (1981), 27-41.

Smith, Alan G. R., ed. *The Reign of James VI and I.* London: Macmillan, 1973.

Snow, W. G. Sinclair. *The Times, Life and Thought of Patrick Forbes, Bishop of Aberdeen 1618-1635.* London: SPCK, 1952.

Sommerville, J. P. 'The Royal Supremacy and Episcopacy *Jure Divino,* 1603-1640', *Journal of Ecclesiastical History,* 34 (1983), 548-558.

Sommerville, M. R. 'Richard Hooker and his Contemporaries on Episcopacy: an Elizabethan Consensus'. *Journal of Ecclesiastical History,* 35 (1984), 177-187.

Southern, Richard W. *Western Society and the Church in the Middle Ages.* Harmondsworth: Penguin Books, 1970.

Stevenson, David. 'Conventicles in the Kirk, 1619-37. The Emergence of a Radical Party'. *Records of the Scottish Church History Society,* 18 (1973), 99-114.

--------. *The Scottish Revolution 1637-1644: The Triumph of the Covenanters.* Newton Abbot: David and Charles, 1973.

Strype, John. *The Life and Acts of John Whitgift, D.D.* 3 vols. Oxford, 1822.

Sykes, Norman. *Old Priest and New Presbyter.* Cambridge: University Press, 1956.

Thompson, W. D. J. Cargill. 'A Reconsideration of Richard Bancroft's Paul's Cross Sermon of 9 February 1588/9'. *Journal of Ecclesiastical History,* 20 (1969), 253-266.

Thomson, J. A. F. 'Innocent VIII and the Scottish Church'. *Innes Review,* 19 (1968), 23-31.

Trevor-Roper, Hugh R. *Archbishop Laud 1573-1645.* 2nd ed. London: Macmillan, 1962.

Usher, Roland G. 'Bancroft and the Divine Right of Bishops'. *Theology,* 1 (1920), 28-34.

--------. *The Reconstruction of the English Church.* 2 vols. New York: D. Appleton and Company, 1910.

Walker, James. *The Theology and Theologians of Scotland chiefly of the Seventeenth and Eighteenth Centuries.* Edinburgh, 1888.

Watson, William J. 'Bishop Carswell's Liturgy'. *Transactions of the Gaelic Society of Inverness,* 30 (1924), 287-312.

Watt, D. E. R. *Fasti Ecclesiae Scoticanae Medii Aevi ad Annum 1638.* 2nd draft. Edinburgh: Scottish Record Society, 1969.

Watt, Hugh. 'William Laud and Scotland'. *Records of the Scottish Church History Society,* 7 (1941), 171-190.

Wedderburn, Alexander. *The Wedderburn Book.* 2 vols. n.p., 1898.

Williamson, Arthur H. *Scottish National Consciousness in the Age of James VI: The Apocalypse, the Union and the Shaping of Scotland's Public Culture.* Edinburgh: John Donald Publishers, 1979.

Willson, David Harris. *King James VI and I.* London: Jonathan Cape, 1959.

Wodrow, Robert. *Collections upon the Lives of the Reformers and most eminent Ministers of the Church of Scotland.* 2 vols. Glasgow, 1834-1848.

--------. *Selections from Wodrow's Biographical Collections.* Aberdeen, 1890.

Wright, Robert S., ed. *Fathers of the Kirk.* London: Oxford University Press, 1960.

B. Unpublished Theses

Birchler, Allen B. The Influence of the Scottish Clergy on Politics, 1616-38. Ph.D. thesis, Nebraska, 1966.

Collins, Jacquelin. The Scottish Episcopacy, 1596-1638. Ph.D. thesis, Illinois, 1964.

Kitshoff, Michiel C. Aspects of Arminianism in Scotland. M.Th. thesis, St. Andrews, 1967.

McMahon, George I.R. John Forbes of Corse: His Life and Work. B. Litt. thesis, Oxford, 1961.

--------. The Scottish Episcopate 1600-1638. Ph.D. thesis, Birmingham, 1972.

Index